RETURN OF THE DRAGONBORN

THE COMPLETE TRILOGY

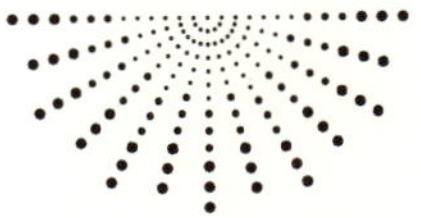

N.M. HOWELL

Written in collaboration with

H.F. STARK

Cover by

COVERS BY JUAN

DUNGEON MEDIA CORP.

To anyone who has ever been bullied, judged, persecuted, or forgotten because of who they are or where they come from.
The world is more beautiful because you are in it.

MARKED BY DRAGON'S BLOOD

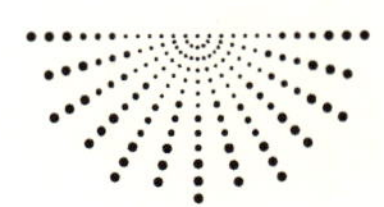

PROLOGUE

HIGHTOWYR. IT WAS ONCE THE GREATEST CITY IN THE western-most reaches of the province of Noelle, in the great land of Shaeyara, and was ruled by a powerful royal lineage. The streets of that ancient city were bursting with sorcerers and sorceresses, all dedicating their lives and resources to innovation, knowledge, and the perpetual ascension of magical might. But the city fell. And almost all of the great magical minds who survived, fled to the far side of the continent. That magnificent royal lineage became a byword and a whisper. For centuries, the city languished in ruin and darkness.

As the land lay wasted and devastated, collapsing on itself, the rest of Noelle flourished. Great cities like Taline to the north and Thabes in the True Isles, rose up from the earth and became beacons of knowledge, power, and beauty. Eventually, the few sorcerers who had remained in Hightowyr grew jealous and angry. In the five hundred years they had managed to stay alive in the ruins of the city, only that envy and hatred was powerful enough to cause them to shed their weariness. They began searching for ways to bring the people back, to encourage the greatest magical beings to return to the city and help rebuild, but the sins and the destruction of the past had not been forgotten. No one would come.

Riddled by their own failure and their endless rage, these seven men and women made a pact and a sacrifice. They each tasked their families to build a university; for these seven had been among the most brilliant of that lost time and had passed all their knowledge to their families. It was meant to be the greatest university in Noelle. No matter what happened, regardless of forces acting upon the city or time ravaging the earth, their descendants were to watch over that institution and seek, above all, to be the most prestigious and powerful.

As for the seven themselves, they vowed to use every ounce of their considerable magic to rebuild as much of the city as they could. And for one year, they did. For one year, they worked tirelessly to clear the rubble and strengthen the foundation. For one year, they touched the ground, drawing the stains of dark magic from the earth. For one year, they pulled on every bit of magic in their bodies, even the core spirit centers of their souls. But it was too much. By the end of the year, they each fell sick and, shortly after, wasted away.

True to their word, their families established the University. They created it in the gargantuan black marble husk of the ancient mint and the many annexes once used by the royal government. They began to invite new students. At first, only the poor came, as the wealthy and the truly brilliant went to the beautiful, inveterate universities across Noelle. But as the years passed and word spread of the potential of the Hightowyr

University, more people came. Hundreds. Then thousands. The University gained wealth, prestige, and professors who were known the world over. The time came when the past was too distant to have its name in the present, and so the city and the University were renamed.

Arvall City began.

Today, one thousand years after the fall of Hightowyr, Arvall City is the greatest urban center in all of Noelle. Perhaps even in all of Shaeyara. Taline is the closest rival, but that wonderful city has been plagued by terrorist attacks for thirteen years. Arvall City built itself on the ruins of Hightowyr, its infrastructure rising in tandem with the ruins in some places and covering the old stone completely in others. While Hightowyr was stone and mortar, Arvall City is made of glass and steel, its buildings rising hundreds of feet in the air and catching the sun to make it a city of light and promise and might. At the south end of the city, the buildings have been built right into the mountainside. The mountain is Brie, and even after its hard trials and the Great Erosion of the Third Cycle, it is still the tallest mountain in the world. No one knows for sure how tall it is, but its peak pierces the atmosphere, and soars even taller still.

The University sits high upon the mountainside, even higher than the buildings, and sprawls across the vast bowl that was made in the mountain in a time before memory. From the other side of the city, the University looks like some great, dark specter, menacing Arvall from its perch. Bordering the city to the east is the beginning of the String Fields, and to the west is the Spider Sea. To the north are a smattering of small towns and hamlets, one of which is Michaelson, where a powerful sorceress named Andie was riding the train, heading to Arvall City.

It was the two hundred eleventh day of the Ninth Cycle of the First Age. So it began.

CHAPTER ONE

She was flying. No, not just flying, but soaring high above the gold and rolling fields of Michaelson. Not too slow or too fast, but at that perfect speed that allowed her to feel exhilarated, while still giving her the presence of mind to see and feel and need her surroundings. Soon, she left Michaelson behind and was so high that she couldn't follow her shadow on the ground. The farther she was from home, the higher she flew until she was nearing the edge of Arvall City, and the clouds were nearing overhead.

She felt so good, so unlimited, that she thought her heart would burst as she soared in the soft, iridescent glow of the evening sun. There was no wind, no friction on her skin, and nothing whipping or rolling in the breeze. And even though she knew this was odd, she liked it: the feeling of flying and being still at the same time. It felt like she belonged.

She was only just nearing Brie when she was swallowed by darkness. Then there was no wind, no light, no sound, no sensation, or movement at all. There was only a nameless, formless pain—an anguish so vast and terrible that it wasn't just in the darkness. It was *the darkness. She couldn't tell if it was coming from some other source or from herself, but it was crushing. Maddening. But then she heard it. It was even worse than the anguish. Screaming.*

"Ma'am?"

Andie woke with a jolt, her books slipping from her lap. She turned toward the voice and saw a stewardess.

"Ma'am, are you okay? Bad dream?"

"I'm... I'm fine. Yeah, bad dream. I'm sorry, was I too loud?"

"No, not at all," the stewardess said, suddenly smiling. "You never made a sound. It's just that ... Well, the spellglass."

She pointed toward the window and Andie followed her finger. Spellglass looked like regular glass, yet anyone with magic in their blood could control its shape and density with only a thought. The spellglass had totally transformed, becoming opaque and protruding like knife points in some places, while in others, it flowed like liquid. It was like a tesseract that could *feel*, that kept collapsing on itself and rebuilding in the same instant. With just one thought, Andie calmed the spellglass. It returned to its normal state.

"Is there anything I can get for you, ma'am?"

"No, I'm fine," Andie said, embarrassed and not wanting to seem like a charity case. "I'll try to stay awake."

The stewardess smiled and walked away. Andie took a deep breath and looked out the window. Most of her life was passing her by: the mayor's fields, the coal mine, the Forest of the Orange Pines where the poorest farmers lived, and the little twin creeks snaking their wet bodies through the fields with impunity. She had lived in Michaelson her entire life, and though she had been in Arvall City almost regularly since she and her father stopped going into Taline years ago, it still felt as if she was doing something adventurous and new.

She bent forward to pick up her books, still shaken by that beautiful and terrible dream. All of them were there; everything she needed for her first semester of classes at the University. But there was one she couldn't find. It wasn't for school, and in fact, she shouldn't have even been reading it on the train. She was never supposed to take it from the house, let alone be seen with it in public. As she told herself to stay calm, she started to panic anyway. She tried not to think of what her father would say if she had lost it. He'd be furious, or worse—disappointed. Suddenly, a blonde head peeped around the seat in front of her.

"Lose something?"

"Oh, yeah." Andie forced a small smile. "I'm sorry, I didn't mean to disturb you. It's just that I lost one of my books and I thought it might have slid under your seat."

"I think you mean... this!" the girl exclaimed, flourishing the book like the end of some corny magician's routine. She clearly didn't care if anyone saw the title of the book. From Dragons to Men.

"Oh... Uh..." Andie fumbled, anxious and baffled.

"This is pretty heavy. Someone has a lot to say about... er... dragons and men. Ooh, sounds exciting! Here."

She handed the book to Andie as if it were just a

thing, maybe a leaflet from the Church of Stone and Sea. Andie took it, thanked the girl, and quickly tucked the book away into the bottom of her bag, where she planned to keep it safely hidden from prying eyes until she was locked away in her new apartment. She gave the girl another smile and then gazed out of the window, turning the spellglass into a double-paned latticework that transformed the early morning light as it streamed in the train compartment. The girl was still peeping around the chair, eyeing her curiously. Andie felt uneasy, but she didn't want to be rude so she did her best to smile back and then turned her attention back towards the window. She wasn't in the mood for talking and definitely didn't want to encourage the very thing the girl did next.

The trains in Noelle were golden, sleek, and narrow. The seats were arranged in single file, with a moderate walkway running parallel. If someone wanted to talk to a friend behind them, they'd have to press a button to swivel the chair around, which is exactly what the blonde girl did, nearly tripping a steward in the process.

"Oh, no! I'm so sorry. I'm such a cub sometimes. So," she said, turning her attention to Andie, oblivious. "I'm Tristtle."

"Andryne," Andie said as she extended her hand. Her eyes then widened and she quickly corrected, "I mean, Andie. Please." She extending her hand, hoping the girl wouldn't latch on to her real name. She cursed herself for letting it slip. She didn't even know why it had slipped from her lips, as she hadn't gone by that name since her mother had died. No one outside her family knew her by that name. The girl beamed back at her.

"Wow, super old-fashioned. Andie. So cute. Totally blue. I didn't know people still shook hands. I'm not a germaphobe or stranger-phobic, or even phobic at all, but it's really... vintage. Blue, you know? Anyway, so I'm totally on my way to see my uncle. He's a total boss. I'm going to see him *eternally* and I'm not sure why, because I don't really like him, but I'm here like flow. Between us girls, it's really his money I'm after. I'm not a bum or anything—and I'm completely not bum-phobic—but he's got money on top of money. I should probably keep things like that to myself. I'm such a cub. But he's this really big architect who designs all kinds of buildings and stuff, and now he's working on the tallest tower in Vall and he—"

"I'm sorry, where?" Andie said, not wanting the answer so much as a break for silence.

"Vall. Arvall City? They're saying this thing is going to be a monster, which is okay, I guess, even though I thought it was going to be a little baby business building —super cool, super blue..."

Andie had her mother's unfailing kindness, and so she listened to Tristtle talk and even made a genuine effort to focus on the conversation. Yet her mind wandered to Arvall City and all the things waiting for her there. Towers that touched the sky, standing closer together than dogs in the field. Strange powered vehicles floating through the city in dense, angry waves, with the mist from their crystals trailing in soft pastel clouds. Trains that ran vertical, up the sides of buildings. Red Ravens, which had been given civil liberties in Arvall City, just as they had been in Taline. And, of course, the Academy. She'd seen all these things before, but never as a student. Never as someone who belonged there.

The Academy was the department of the University that instructed students in their first year. It was the second most rigorous year of the program—the most demanding being the last year. First year students went to classes year-round, with only ten breaks of ten days each. That meant that for three hundred of the four hundred days of the year, Andie would be in class. To her, it was as daunting as it was thrilling. She longed to learn, to discover, to grow. And, more than anything, she desired greater control over her dragon magic before it got her killed.

After almost an hour, the train finally pulled into the station.

"So, promise to look me up sometime?" Tristtle asked.

"I'd love to," Andie said, thinking that Tristtle was kind of sweet in her own way.

"Super blue. And I've totally been eyeing your books the whole ride. Are you going to the University?"

"Yeah. I start at the Academy today."

Tristtle was silent for a moment; Andie didn't think anything of it until Tristtle looked like she'd stopped breathing.

"Are you... still alive?" Andie asked.

"Yes. Yes!" Tristtle said, suddenly full of life. "I just can't believe I've been sitting here with a sorceress this whole time. Hey," she said, leaning closer. "Ever used your magic at home?"

"Of course not," Andie lied. "It's illegal unless you've graduated the University."

"Of course. I'm such a cub. Anyway, I hope I see you again soon."

When she was gone, Andie breathed a sigh of relief and packed up the rest of her books, making sure *Dragons* was on the bottom. She left the train and before long was heading down Avenue 204. The whole city was laid out in a perfect grid: numerical avenues running from north to south and magical herb names running from east to west. She was seeing the city through new eyes. The air here was thinner, cooler. In fact, Arvall itself was on the mountain, only much lower than the University. Truth be told, Brie started some one hundred kilometers before the incline became noticeable. The city was vast and Andie knew the avenues went up to at least one thousand.

She shook herself and tried to focus. She was a couple days later than she'd intended to be, but what had delayed her was unavoidable. For some time, she'd been caring for her father—his illness was part physical, but, more than anything, it was the result of a broken heart and crushed spirit. The tragedy that had hit their family had fractured him and he would never recover. Andie knew that.

Now that she was starting school, she had decided to hire a healer to live with him. It didn't feel right, and it wasn't what she wanted, but it was paramount that she learn to control her magic. Just days ago, the healer had disappeared, totally unreachable.

The woman Andie eventually hired was a nonagenarian, with her hair wrapped so tight it was a wonder it didn't cut off all circulation above the neck. Her voice was oddly musical and strident at the same time. She wasn't a great fit, but in all honesty, Andie didn't really trust anyone other than herself to take care of her father.

"It's only until I finish school," she thought out loud. "And then I'll be all his again."

Even so, the guilt was crushing her as she reached

the financial district. Even necessity can't assuage guilt. Her father had wanted this even more than Andie did, and it was he who had convinced her to go. She breathed out a deep sigh as she slowly made her way down the winding street.

"You need to learn control," he'd said.

"Teach me. You used to be on the council. I know you can do it."

"That was the council in Taline, and you know how it ended. I don't want you anywhere near those people, but you need to be able to protect yourself. I can't risk someone catching us practicing here. And even if I wanted to..."

He didn't finish his sentence, but held up his hands as they trembled uncontrollably.

"Dad, I won't forgive myself for leaving you."

"Andie, this is for your life. Go. We'll find someone who can stay with me. You're my daughter. It should've been me taking care of you. Go."

He was right. She'd already been putting off the Academy for years and if she did it again, she would lose her eligibility. More than that, it was time Andie began to live, truly live. She couldn't spend her entire life hiding behind her father and wanting her mother.

She boarded SKY 6 and thought of her past, present, and future as the train sped through the seemingly endless city. She watched as they passed hundreds of other trains going up and down and turning all over the city and its buildings. Up ahead was the University, claiming most of the mountain side and looming like the powerful and dangerous place it was. She loved that she'd gotten her magic from her mother, but sometimes she wished more than anything that she didn't have dragon blood or the powerful and unpredictable magic that came with it. Dragon blood had brought her family nothing but trouble.

The train reached the base of the next and steepest incline, and Andie watched the world from almost a ninety-degree angle as the train climbed the mountain side. It was a quick ride and she was soon standing on campus, taking a few deep breaths to acclimate herself to the atmosphere.

She'd only taken a few steps when she saw it. She didn't even know they still had these signs. There weren't even enough dragon blooded people left to warrant this kind of hate. It was unbelievable, but there it was: a sign with a young girl whose hands were softly glowing purple. There was a black crossed circle over her torso and it sent a clear, terrible message. Andie didn't know which was more disturbing: the sign's existence, the girl's age, or the fact that the sign looked brand new.

Just then, a man hurrying by bowled right into her and nearly knocked her down. He didn't apologize, never even stopped walking. Anger ripped through Andie. Her magic flared and the man tripped. He hit his head on the sign as he fell. Andie rushed to him.

"Are you okay?"

"Get off me!" he said, regaining his feet and hurrying off.

It wasn't exactly the welcome she'd hoped for.

LATER THAT EVENING, Andie was back down the mountain at city level. Her first day at the Academy hadn't really been a first day at all. The only thing she'd managed to do was miss both her classes—which were actually scheduled for two hours before she even got there—and find out that she still needed an icon. Icons were the size and shape of almonds and a prerequisite for study at the University. They monitored the students, made sure they stayed out of trouble and were safe. They were magical monitoring devices made of gold, bear wicker, and a proprietary blend of spells, and were essentially just a way for the University to spy on its students. Fortunately, her father had warned her about them before hand, so she wasn't surprised when they handed her hers.

The University once used bracelets with computer chips, but those were too easy to turn off. Andie had picked up an icon on the way down and now was searching for her apartment. She knew she was in the right part of town. University Park. It was where University students went who didn't have much money. There were other communities for students on scholarship and wealthy students. University Park was built over the ruins of Hightowyr, like the rest of the city, but this was the part of the city that got the least new infrastructure and the least maintenance. There were places here where the ancient ruins were still visible. Even now, Andie was passing what was left of an arch. First, they got to live in barely habitable apartments, then they got to deal with debt for the rest of their lives. She turned and, sure enough, could still see the black marble of the University sitting on the throne of the mountainside.

Even with the map she picked up at the University registrar's office, Andie still had a hard time finding her way. She'd never been this deep in the city before. It was a wonderful city to be lost in—beautiful, storied, massive, and diverse—but it was getting late. She turned a few more corners, just because, and found a dragon post.

Or what was left of it.

The University had had them all destroyed when the hate first started, leaving only the foundations as a warning and a threat. Dragon posts were where the dragons used to land to keep watch over the area. Legend said the dragon posts were huge, nearly half a kilometer high, and made of gold and iron. Dragons would land there and, with their keen eyes, spy across the land, keeping watch on all they knew and loved.

That was before the hate began. Before the dragons and the dragonborn people were betrayed and hunted to extinction.

Andie stopped and stared at the map. It wasn't possible for her to be this lost. She knew that this section of the city wasn't well taken care of and the streets here ran in every direction possible, rendering the grid completely useless, but she'd been walking for almost an hour. Two women were passing so she hurried over to ask directions.

"Excuse me," she said. "Could you point me to the corner of Rholdan and Avenue 652?"

"It's only ten blocks that way," the taller one said. "You can get there in fifteen minutes. That's an odd-looking map. May I?"

Andie handed her the map and it was only a moment before the women began to giggle.

"I'm sorry, dear, but this map is over a hundred and twenty years old. I can't imagine how it's still in this good of shape. See here..."

Andie followed the slim finger. In the lower left hand corner she saw the date: Two Hundredth Day of the Seventh Cycle of the First Age. The University was preparing to celebrate five hundred years and they were beginning to put out some of their old memorabilia. She must've picked from the wrong pile.

"Oh," she said. "I see."

"Well, goodbye. Remember, ten blocks that way."

The women left and Andie smacked herself in the head. One hundred and twenty years?

"Great job, Andie," she said to herself. "Maybe you need a lesson in how to tell time. A Life Age equals sixteen thousand years. An Age is two thousand years. A Cycle is one hundred twenty-five years. One year is four-hundred days. Do you think you can manage to read things before you take them from now on? Sorceresses don't live for hundreds of years anymore, so maybe you'd like to spend your time more wisely."

Still beating herself up, she headed in the direction the lady had pointed and in fifteen minutes she was staring up at her apartment building: a hole in the wall that looked as dingy and run down as the ethnic restaurant it sat on top of.

Climbing the stairs didn't inspire confidence, either, since they were so creaky the sound almost seemed to come before her foot fell. She met with her landlady, a middle-aged spinster who seemed to have given up on life entirely. She never spoke a word, simply handed

Andie the keys and held up seven fingers to show her which floor to go to. She seemed incredibly ordinary, even if jaded, and Andie probably wouldn't have given Kristole another thought if she hadn't seen the mark on the back of her neck. A tattoo of a hand in flames. It stuck in Andie's mind as she climbed to the seventh floor and found her room. As she approached the door, she slowed. It was open and there were sounds inside. She paused, half wanting to go inside and half knowing she should get help. Yet, of the many things she was, a coward wasn't one of them. She crept to the door and opened it, her hand at the level of her eyes, ready for anything. She pushed the door open and saw a man in overalls. He turned at the sound of her entry.

"This ain't a robbery," he said. "I'm just fixing the window."

"Um. Okay. Can I have your name, sir?"

"I'm just the handyman. I work downstairs. Speaking of which, they're expecting you. Better go down soon as you're settled."

"Yes. Right. 'They.' And what're you doing here again?"

"Window," he said, tapping the glass with his screwdriver.

"Of course," she muttered under her breath, cautiously crossing the living room as she kept an eye on him.

She set her things down in the kitchen, what little there was of it, and looked out of the window at her surprisingly spectacular view. She could see over the four blocks directly across from her building, all the way to an incredible complex of glass towers. It was the publishing district, which handled the magical, philosophical, business, and religious text for practically all of Noelle. Andie thought it was the coolest thing she'd seen yet.

After a couple minutes of gazing out into the night, she walked over to close the curtains, or, at least, the rags that were pretending to be curtains, and checked out her apartment. It was small, but she'd expected that. Aside from the shabby curtains, nothing looked bad at all. It was incredibly clean, had good proportions, new tiles, and everything in the bathroom and kitchen worked. She was especially thankful for the gas stove. Electrical ones frequently melted. She even had an ice maker in the fridge that was noisily busy at work. The kitchen faced the living room, divided from it only by a thin partition to which the counter was attached. The bathroom was the first door to the right in the hallway and, although it was clean, there was barely enough space to turn around. A small closet was across from it. Her bedroom was at the end of the hall— actually, twice as big as she'd expected —and her mattress and frame had already been delivered.

She decided to put a couple things out, just to start making it feel like home. She placed her books on the shelves of the small stand in the living room and set her mother's picture on top of it, but only for a moment before she decided to move it to her bedroom. Her mother had been beautiful, brunette, and powerful. Andie remembered that. She wasn't much older than Andie was when she died. Andie hid her small bag with *Dragons* in it under the bed. And then it was time to go downstairs and meet the mysterious "they."

She went downstairs to the restaurant, which had an alarming number of grills, and stood in a place where she could be seen by everybody. Hopefully "they" knew what she looked like because she couldn't identify them. It was only a moment before a man came up to her, smiling. He seemed middle-age, pushing the back end of the age group, and his face was covered in stubble. Yet, he didn't seem unkempt, just sweet and tired. He extended his hand.

"Hi. I'm Marvo," he said.

"Andie," she said, shaking hands with him. "I'm sorry, I don't mean to be rude, but—"

"But how do I know you? I knew your father many years ago. As a matter of fact, we met under similar circumstances. I met him the day he first started at the Academy."

"Wow, you're Marvo? *The* Marvo? My dad used to tell me stories about you. You guys were great friends."

"Yeah, it's a shame how people grow apart. And it's a travesty what happened to your father."

"Um... thank you," she said, turning a bit.

It wasn't a subject she liked to talk about, even with her father.

"Here, let's sit down," Marvo said.

He took her to a table in the corner and motioned for a server to come over.

"We'd like some cloudcakes, please. There should still be some batter left from the batch we made this afternoon. I assume your father told you about my cloudcakes," he said, turning back to Andie.

"He's told everyone. I think they're more famous in Michaelson than Arvall City itself. So, if you were at the Academy, are you a practicing sorcerer?"

"Oh, no, I was never at the Academy. I only mentioned it because your father was going there. I'm a non-magic person, or a nomag, as we call them in the city. My family's always been nomag and always married nomags. Not that we have anything against magic. In fact, we've always been friends of sorcerers and sorceresses, but the magic life was never for us."

"We have the same term in the country. So, what do you do?"

"I cook. You're sitting in my restaurant. I bet you've probably got some questions about how your father was back then. I know I've got some about how he is now. But it's your first night in Arvall, and I don't want you to spend it having your ear talked off by an old-timer. We'll have plenty of time to talk later. Welcome to the city."

"Thank you."

Marvo stood and after a final parting smile, he turned and went back to the kitchen. Andie sat, waiting for her food, wondering why she never figured out that Marvo was a nomag or why her father never told her. She looked around the unimpressive restaurant, noting its general dinginess and almost hidden antiquity. The place was old—judging by some of the fixtures and the design of the molding, *very* old—and Andie began to see that it wasn't that Marvo's family weren't good with maintaining or cleaning, only that time was finally catching up. While she was gazing around, and beginning to sense the charm of the old place, she saw a boy coming to her with a plate of cloudcakes. He was tall, black-haired, and muscled in a sinewy kind of way; clearly used to hard work. He was handsome, surprisingly so. He was smiling, seemingly at no one, as if it just felt good to smile, to be happy and excited about life. Even from a distance, Andie could tell he had a warm spirit. He set the cloudcakes down on her table.

"These are my dad's secret recipe, and I do mean *secret*. He'll let me go over his checkbook, but he won't tell me what's in these. I'm Raesh," he said, extending his hand as his father had done.

"Andie. So why so secretive? Do these cure Maeludrax disease or something?"

"No, but if you have Maeludrax, this might be the only thing that will take your mind off it. That is, unless you have a girl you can't take your eyes off."

"Oh."

That was all she could manage. Raesh was doing just that: not taking his eyes off her. His smile was warm and sweet, and she could tell that he was probably a good person, but his bravado had shocked her. Or was he just really friendly? As beautiful as she was, Andie didn't have much experience with boys in Michaelson. The boys still tended to go after girls who were less work and less picky. As all that was going through her mind, Raesh sat down across from her at the table and the surprise only deepened.

"So, go ahead," he said. "Try them."

Andie gave herself a little shake to move past the surprise, and then picked up her fork. The cloudcakes were at least a foot wide, each thick enough to be three regular cloudcakes, and there were four of them. There was no way she could eat them all. But they looked and smelled incredible. Raesh reached to hand her the syrup, or so she thought, until he began to pour it for her. She watched his hand roam slowly back and forth above the plate, his face totally at ease, as if nothing about pouring a stranger's syrup was unusual. Andie couldn't keep back the smirk that rose to her lips. This guy was bold.

"There. Waiting for you," he said.

Andie pushed the fork into the cloudcakes and it sank right through. She cut out a bite and ate. It was beyond words. Perfect.

"That's fantastic," she said. "The syrup, too. What is this?"

"I have no idea. The syrup is a secret, too. He comes in an hour earlier than everyone else and bars us from the kitchen until he's done making the batter. He mixes a giant barrel of the syrup on the weekends. Can you believe he carries all of his spices and the recipes in a briefcase, which he locks in a safe or keeps by his side?"

"That's some secret, but I have to say it's worth it. These are the best cloudcakes I've ever had. By far. And I've eaten a lot of cloudcakes. Perfect meal for a first night."

"So, you like cloudcakes? Add that to the list. I know your name, I know you're a first-year sorceress, and I know your eyes are incredible. Not a bad start I've made for myself."

"No one's going to accuse you of being shy," Andie said, grinning.

"I could be subtle, but then who'd be here to make you smile?"

Andie just grinned and nodded. She couldn't help it, he was magnetic.

"But, seriously, I hope you enjoyed your first day. I know the city's not the kindest place, especially not *this* city, so I hope it was on its best behavior."

"Well... no. But I guess it could've been worse. At least I finally made it here in one piece."

"Ah, got lost in University Park, huh? Don't feel bad, the streets in this part of the city can do some weird things. Trust me, you'll be weaving your way around like a native in no time. You must be excited to start at the Academy."

"Yeah. I think. It's a complicated thing with me."

"That only makes me want to know more, but I can take a hint. I've always wanted that. Magic. I guess it's just not for some people. My cousin got it though. She's in her second year."

"I thought your dad said your family was nomag?"

"Most of us are. My dad's side of the family is completely non-magic. No one ever married anyone with magic until he married my mother. Couldn't help himself, I guess. And even on my mother's side it's hit and miss. That side is like a lot of other families these days. You just never know who's gonna get magic and who won't since the bloodlines are so diluted and mixed. But my cousin on my mother's side was a hit. So, I know what's up. Just wish I hadn't been a miss. I guess moms aren't as quick to pass their genes down."

He was quiet for a few moments after that. Andie watched him and she could see the sadness there, but also the immense warmth. Even though he wasn't living the life he wanted, he was still living life. It was admirable. But what he'd said about mothers had struck home. She needed to move.

"I'll be right back," she said. "Which way is the restroom?"

"Right in that corner back there."

She moved quickly through the tables and through the swinging doors that led to the hallway where the men's restroom was on one side and the women's on the other. Inside the restroom, she locked the door and turned to the mirror. There they were, eyes and nose and mouth and cheeks and hair and the barely noticeable soft dusting of freckles. All passed right down from her mother as reminders. Andie could see in all the old pictures how much they looked alike. Looking in the mirror was like looking at the face of the woman who was getting harder to remember with each passing day. Andie turned from the mirror. She took off her jacket and rolled up her sleeve.

On the underside of her forearm, a pattern was emerging, slowly but surely, more and more palpable with every week. The pattern was in tiny heptagon shapes and now a few hundred were visible there. The skin still felt the same, though she suspected that would change, too, with time. The pattern had begun to turn iridescent, not quite shining, but mesmerizingly colorful. And it was as terrifying as it was beautiful.

She quickly pulled her sleeve down to cover the evidence that could easily have her killed. She held her hand firmly over her sleeve, wondering just what she was thinking, risking her life by moving to the most dangerous place in the world for her kind.

Raesh was wrong. Mothers could pass on genes just fine.

CHAPTER TWO

RAESH FOLLOWED HER UP THE STAIRS, BRINGING UP A plate of extra food that he and his father insisted she have. It was unnecessary, of course, because she'd eaten so much of the cloudcakes in an effort to finish them that she didn't think she'd be hungry until this time the next night. He was still trying to change her mind.

"My dad meant what he said. You don't need to pay to live here. The room is yours. Take advantage of the hospitality."

"That's incredibly kind of both of you, but I can't do that. I insist on having a job around here, it doesn't matter what."

"Your dad sent you here because he knew my dad would be able to help you."

"You're probably right," she said, stopping and turning to face him. "But my dad should've told me who he was sending me to, that way I could have insisted Marvo give me a job before I even came in to settle down. Besides, the landlady didn't seem like she'd be okay with anyone freeloading."

"Fine, but if you change your mind, the offer stands."

They reached the apartment and Andie unlocked the door. The repairman was gone, but he'd left some things in the corner, which meant he'd probably be back. Andie took the food from Raesh and placed it inside the fridge. She walked over to the window, back to that great view, and sat on the windowsill. Raesh came over.

"I don't remember inviting you in," she said, smirking.

"Well, I know you needed help bringing in the heavy plate. Plus, I'm not a vampire."

"Oh, can you even imagine living with vampires?"

"Absolutely not, I bet it was terrifying. I'm so glad they got wiped out. I don't know which was worse: the mind controlling or the flying."

"I vote mind control."

"Yeah, but you know what? I'd have fun with that one."

Andie laughed, glad of having made at least one friend. Nothing could ever truly take her mind off her father or the task ahead of her, and she definitely couldn't be distracted from the danger, but Raesh was just the person she needed to meet on the first night. He was kind, friendly, welcoming, and in a way, he reminded her of home. There was something about him that was patient, deliberate. She knew he liked her and he wasn't shy at showing it, but he wasn't pushing himself on her. He was sweet.

"You know, even after the vampires, our parents' generation faced terrible times," he said, his smile fading into a grave expression. "They were all brave. They had to be."

"You mean the terrorist attacks in Taline?"

"And the other thing. The Quelling."

For a moment, Andie stopped breathing.

Not this. Any subject in the world but this. Something in her chest constricted, tightened beyond belief at the thought of what she'd lost and what her father had suffered. Even after eighteen years, it still hurt. There were a lot of things about her family before the Quelling that she had forgotten, but she could never forget the night itself. Never.

"I… I don't even know how to ask this," Raesh began. "I don't even know if I should, but looking at you now, I think I have to. I've heard stories about your father my entire life. Are the rumors true? Was it really a spell that went wrong?"

"I really don't want to talk about that, Raesh," she snapped.

Raesh looked away, embarrassed or ashamed, she didn't know which. She instantly regretted what she'd said and how she'd said it. After all, there was no way he could've understood the emotional pain that she had to endure ever since the accident. Even she could barely understand it, and it was her own pain.

"Look. I'm sorry. I'm just really tired. All the trains I've been on today, I guess. Can we please just continue this conversation later?"

"Ah, the old 'later' ploy, right? How original." He laughed. She laughed, too. Neither of them meant it.

Raesh turned and headed to the door, and Andie watched and wished there was something she could say to make up for the mood she'd ruined. He really had been great to her, and after the dizzying reception she'd gotten when first arriving in the city, she really needed

Raesh's comforting presence that night. He turned back at the door.

"We don't need to continue this," he said. "I can see on your face how much it hurts. We can talk about whatever you want. We don't ever need to discuss this again."

He turned to leave and was almost out of the door when she stopped him.

"Raesh. Thank you for sharing with me earlier. About your family and how much you want magic. That was really nice."

He smiled that warm smile of his and left. Andie sighed and leaned back against the wall. She was alone again with her thoughts. Always alone with her thoughts.

ANDIE SAT in bed and prepared to lay down as she watched the reflection of the setting sun bounce off the shining glass walls of the building across the street. She'd gotten everything ready for the next day, and there was nothing left except to be anxious and to implant her icon. She wasn't in a hurry to have the university monitor every move and magical use, but there was no way around it. If she was going to commit to her studies at the University, she had to conform to their rules.

"Here goes my freedom," she said to herself.

She held the icon in the palm of her hand and took a deep, shuddering breath.

"I, Andie Rogers, of sound mind and spirit, do take the oath of the Academy and accept my duties, responsibilities, and limitations as a student of this great body."

As the final syllable passed her lips, the icon rolled over in her hand and vanished under her skin in a soft flash of golden light. At first, she didn't feel anything, even after turning her hand over and making a few fists, but then the cold set in. Then the heat. Together, the impossible sensation of hot and cold flowed through her veins and to her heart, and from there, it was sent through her entire body. She opened her mouth in a silent scream as a violent convulsion made its way from head to toe. The feeling only lasted a moment, though, and it faded with every beat of her heart until she felt perfectly like herself again. She laid back in bed and kicked herself under the covers.

Sleep didn't come easy, but that was unsurprising, and tonight she had even more on her mind. She tried to suppress the memories of what happened to her mother and her father's accident. She tried to trust Mirth, the healer who was staying with her father back home. Of course, there was also her new life in the city to consider. This city that didn't seem as welcoming or as promising as she had hoped. She'd given up trying to see the silver lining in Arvall City after she'd picked up the rest of her books earlier. Thinking of the books made her remember.

She rolled over and reached under the bed to retrieve the bag she'd hidden there earlier. She opened it and then uncovered the secret compartment in the bottom of it. She dropped the bag and opened the book on her lap. It was dusty. *From Dragons to Men.* A history of dragon-blooded people and their magic. She wanted so badly to flip through it with relish, as she did almost every night, but she had enough on her mind. She closed it and locked it away in the cabinet of the nightstand, and slid the key into her pocket.

She laid down again, trying to block out the blackness of her thoughts. But she couldn't suppress them and she knew there was only one way that she would be able to get to sleep. She let it all in, all the worry and pain and memories, and once they rooted themselves deep in her mind, she accepted that everything was her fault. After that, the guilt crushed her into sleep.

She dreamed again. She'd been dreaming the same dream for years and only the way she saw it changed.

It always began the same.

She stared out in front of her, through an odd and exciting haze. Somewhere in the haze, there is a mirror that isn't clear. She can't tell if it was because of the haze or if the mirror itself was somehow... wrong. All she knew was that the mirror was really a window—a sight into some other world or other life—and that she must see through somehow. She has to know what's there to see.

And then a sound. Slight, soft, hardly a sound at all, almost as if it were only made of the most delicate of sounds for certain ears to hear. It was the smallest of echoes.

Over the years, the haze lightened and lifted until finally it subsided. Eventually, she could see a field and a woman standing in the middle of it. Beautiful, majestic, and covered in blood, the woman reached out, maybe to Andie, maybe to the universe, and then fire fell from the sky in terrifying waves of light and flames and brilliant destruction.

The sound cleared as well and revealed itself to be the woman's voice. Louder and louder it grew. She was screaming. The woman in the field who was drenched in blood, who seemed to be destroying the earth, was screaming for help.

Andie woke violently, sweating and breathing as if she'd just finished a race. She was shivering, from fear or sweat it didn't matter. The iridescent pattern on her left arm burned as it always did after the dream. She was thankful that she only had the trace in one spot on her body. For now.

Something compelled her to move, to run, to escape the bed and the room and the apartment. A dark energy that shrouded her mind and made her desperate to clear her head. She jumped out of bed and pulled on her favorite pair of jeans and a faded t-shirt that she had left piled on the floor in her late-night exhaustion, and hurried through her room and into the hallway, slipping on a pair of flats and grabbing a crumpled sweatshirt on her way out. She stopped for a quick breath, a moment to clear her mind and realize that the dream was over. That she was safe.

She didn't know what made her run from her room. It could've been fear, but she was never one to show herself to be a coward. It had to be something more, and maybe she'd never know until she understood the dream itself. She turned and headed down the stairs. Maybe Marvo was up and could make her some coffee at the restaurant. At the bottom of the stairs she halted, shocked by the sight.

The restaurant was completely full; people were everywhere, eating, drinking, or waiting for their order. There weren't even any open chairs. She wondered what they were all doing there so early in the morning, until she looked to the front of the place, where the giant panes of glass that made the storefront showed that it was late morning. The sun was already halfway across the sky. Then she heard laughter. She turned and saw Raesh, posted in the corner with a steaming cup, taking a break or slacking off. He was watching her.

"I was just getting ready to come up and wake you. You're gonna be late."

Andie's eyes widened with the realization that she had slept through the night. Without so much of a glance at her watch, she ran out the door into the warm late-morning light and raced down the cobbled street towards the direction of the University.

Her arm burned and with a mad panic, she realized the iridescent glow on her arm was visible. She desperately pulled on her sweatshirt and tugged down the sleeves to cover the evidence, panting from the exertion of her sudden and unexpected sprint. She couldn't let anyone see.

She contemplated turning back to get her backpack when she realized she had left it behind, but her legs propelled her ever forward down the long and winding roads of Arvall City, towards the great walls of the University. She ran her hands down her jeans as she walked, and was relieved when she found her class schedule and University map folded in her back pocket. At least she would be able to find her way to class. She held it tightly in her hand as she trudged onward.

She couldn't be late and risk expulsion. Not now. Not when she needed answers the most.

CHAPTER THREE

ANDIE COULDN'T MISS ANOTHER DAY. IF SHE MISSED even one class today, she would blow her shot at learning to control her powers and discover her abilities forever. Nineteen is the oldest age the Academy accepted without a special letter of recommendation, which she had no way of getting, and the first eleven days are the most a student can miss before they forfeit the year. The Academy opens its door on the two hundredth day of each year, and today was the two hundredth and twelfth day. Crunch time.

She raced through the streets toward SKY 6. Without meaning to, her powers manifested in her haste and before she realized it, her magic was pushing people aside and creating a clear path for her. She stopped and checked the icon; it was glowing faintly, warning her against using her magic, but as long as she kept it to small things - and nothing too frequent - she would be okay. Realizing she would never make it in time at this pace, she tried hailing a cab, but not a single one stopped.

All at once, she felt everything: her tardiness, her new life, her anxiety, her hurry, the sights, the sounds, the hard and steady breath of Arvall City, and she felt overwhelmed with the energy and activity.

"So, this is what it's like?" she wondered out loud.

As if in rude answer, someone snatched her folded map from her hand and waved it before her eyes. "What's this, now?" a husky voice taunted her. "An antique, is it? Looks valuable."

Andie glowered at the man. "Not valuable, but I do rather need it. Hand it back."

The man smiled a toothy grin. "Nah, looks of value to me." And with a final wink he turned on his heels and ran back the way Andie had just come.

Her mind was still floating in wonder, but luckily her body reacted on instinct. She turned and was chasing him down the street, across the intersection, around two corners, and finally into an alley. She needed that damn map to get to the University, and she wasn't going to let some petty thief ruin her chances of getting there.

On and on they ran, rounding corners and racing down alleyways. The thief had been tiring steadily, but growing up in a rural area had bred Andie for this moment. She caught him and threw her weight on him. They both came crashing down, but Andie hit her head on the stone of the alley floor. For a moment, she was dazed and the world swam before her eyes while the thief scrambled to his feet and grabbed her map again.

When he saw that Andie had hit her head, he took a moment to catch his breath. He looked down at her and laughed. At least, until he saw the cut on her head begin to heal. He gasped, dropped the map, and took off running as if the great dragon Gordric himself were chasing him. He knew what everyone knew. Healing is a sign of dragon magic. Andie saw the fear on his face and suddenly only that look mattered to her.

"No, wait!" she screamed.

But he was already gone. She cursed herself—her lack of control and her dragon blood—and hoped he would be frightened enough to keep his mouth shut. She stood up and folded the now crumpled map, which was fortunately still in one piece. Why someone would want to steal a piece of paper, she had no idea. She slid it in her back pocket and looked around to regather her bearings.

Now, she had even less time. She turned and started off at a jog, and then she remembered. The icon. She stopped mid-stride and checked her palm. Nothing. It was glowing again, warning her, but no alarm was sounded, no searing pain. It was unbelievable. She couldn't be that lucky. She waited and waited and waited, but nothing happened.

"They must not be able to detect dragon blood," she mused out loud. "That's the only explanation."

After a few more moments of nothing, she started walking again. She decided to simply see how it acted on her way to the Academy. She kept her head low and ran.

Somewhere along her route, after getting lost in the baffling streets of University Park, Andie caught a cab. It dropped her at the train station and she only just managed to board before the doors closed. While she rode the train up the mountain, almost completely vertical, she fixed herself.

All the trains were charmed so that the relative gravity inside the cars didn't change. Everyone could walk around just as they would on level ground. The train seemed to reach the top faster than it had the day before, but she knew it was only her nerves. Once off the train, she was running again, almost leaping to catch the class that started in two minutes. She began to slow as she got closer to the front doors and then she looked up and took a good look at that magnificent black marble.

"You going to come in or just stare at the damn thing?" asked a voice beside her.

Andie turned to face a beautiful girl. She had a familiar smile. It took Andie a moment to realize that it was familiar because it reminded her of Raesh.

"Are you Carmen?" Andie asked. "Raesh's cousin?"

"Guilty," she said, looking coy as if she knew something she might or might not share. "And you're the prodigy girl with the dad who spelled himself into an almost vegetative state." She shook her head as if watching a kitten try to climb something it couldn't understand was too tall.

Andie's jaw dropped a little at Carmen's complete tactlessness.

"Don't feel bad, sweetie. This is the city. We've all got sad stories here."

"Do you all say what you're thinking without any concern for people's feelings?"

"You're upset. And you have a right to be. Look, I'm sorry, I didn't mean any disrespect to you or your father. I barely have the semblance of a filter. The truth is, that no one in Vall is going to play by your country rules of hospitality and patience. It just won't fly here. But, for my part, I apologize."

"Thanks," Andie said, not quite sure how else to respond to the girl.

Carmen looked Andie over from head to toe,

scanning with intense concentration as if she were x-raying her skeleton. Then she looked Andie right in her eyes and smiled that beautiful, warm, familiar smile. Andie could tell that even if she was uncouth, she was genuine.

"I really should get going," Andie said. "My class is starting practically as we speak."

"Morning classes? Black the stars, girl."

"What?"

"Black the stars. It means something like 'I can't believe it.'"

"Ah. Well, I'll have to catch up on the language, I guess," Andie laughed. "I'll see you around?"

"Yes, you will. I'll be looking out for you. Which is a big deal because it's not something I would normally do, even for a girl my cousin has a crush on." She winked.

"He doesn't have a crush on me," Andie said, suddenly defensive. She looked down at her feet as she felt her face redden, knowing full well that it was true.

"Not sure why you said that or which one of us you think is stupid enough to believe it, but he most certainly does and you know it, don't you?" Carmen asked with a grin. "Just let him down easy."

With that she pushed Andie through the front doors.

CHAPTER FOUR

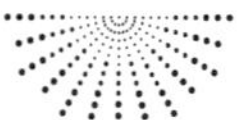

IT WAS UNREAL. THERE WASN'T A SINGLE DREAM OR mental picture or sprawling fantasy that could capture what Andie saw when she crossed the threshold. She never expected it to be that beautiful. The ceilings, walls, and floors were made of the same black marble as the outside. The doors and fixtures were all made of solid gold. The light—if it could be called that—almost looked like an ethereal glow bleeding from the very marble itself. It was magical. Transformative. It lit the halls and the rooms like no regular light could.

While outside the marble was still the way it should be. Inside, the floors and ceiling seemed to be moving. It was incredible. Once they reached the end of the entrance hallway, the ceiling disappeared into an endless black void. They had passed into the heart of the mountain. Flying over their heads were hundreds, maybe thousands of tiny yellow creatures, zipping back and forth as if they were on a mission.

"Mountain Faeries," Carmen said. "Think of them as

little messengers. They handle all correspondence inside the University."

"Fitting, I guess. They never lie, right?"

"Correct. Pretentious little self-righteous snitches if you ask me. That endlessness above us is where you go if you use too much magic outside of school. I'm not sure what happens up there, but I hope I never find out."

They walked on and Andie began to notice just how many students there were. Thousands upon thousands. They were everywhere. Some had skin in hues and tones she'd never seen before, and some she figured were from the north, were so pale they were almost transparent. They were speaking all kinds of different languages, some of which she'd come into contact with before, but most of which she couldn't even begin to decipher.

"How many students are there?" she asked.

"Five, six hundred thousand. Who knows? More just keep coming. That's SKY 1, the faculty train. It runs up to their rent-free homes a little higher up the mountain."

She pointed to a train of silver and gold that was just pulling off from the tiny station in the middle of a vast interior park.

"Down that way is distress training. Farther on is dangerous species, which is the adjacent wing to extinct species."

"Like dragons," Andie muttered.

"Like dragons," Carmen agreed, squinting at Andie from the corner of her eye. "That way is for students who have graduated from the Academy on to the next levels. That hallway to the far left... well, I don't know what that is, but I'd steer clear. So, how do you feel?"

"It's nothing like what I could've imagined. I've

heard stories from my father, even seen pictures, but this is different. Huge. I mean really, really huge. I never made it past the front office yesterday. I feel... kind of insignificant."

"Great. You're already fitting in, then. Although, tomorrow, lose the I'm-a-cute-country-girl aura. You'll never get any worthwhile guys with that act," she said, having another long look at Andie. "Speaking of, if you're thinking about staying around here after dark to make out with a warlock hottie, think again. This place locks down when the moon comes up, and the security is insane."

"Insane?"

"Yeah. I mean animated soldiers of steel and immobilizing mist among others. You ever hear of matrices?"

Of course she had. How could she ever forget those terrible things?

"Yeah. I've heard of them," she said, looking away.

"Well, that's me," Carmen said.

"What is?"

"Oh, you can't hear it? I forgot what it was like to be new here."

Carmen reached over to touch Andie's forehead and traced a small circle. A shot ran through Andie's head and then the sweetest, most alluring song Andie had ever heard rushed through her mind and senses.

"Hear that?" Carmen asked. "That's the siren's call. It'll take you where you need to go. What's yours anyway?"

"I don't know. I didn't even know I had one."

"Yeah. We can listen to each other's, but everyone

has their own individual call. I thought it was supposed to be something beautiful, but mine sounds almost like some sort of horn. I guess I got the short stick. See ya, haybale."

Carmen bounded away and Andie was left to fend for herself. She kept listening to the song, but it didn't sound like a horn. It must be her own call. She turned a couple times, trying to find which direction the song was coming from. When she caught it, she just followed it. It was the easiest, most satisfying thing in the world.

The siren's call led her on a winding path into the Academy and around its many corners. It felt right and yet she couldn't understand it; it felt good, even, but she couldn't imagine anything capable of making so sweet a sound. It was like music and laughter and a waterfall all together. It was the single most beautiful sound she'd ever heard. It seemed extravagant to have a specific call for each student, especially when considering that there were six hundred thousand of them.

Andie turned right and found herself walking into a classroom. She was smiling softly, lost in the beauty of the call, and so, for a moment, she didn't notice where she was. After she'd been standing there some moments, she began to look around as her mind focused. It wasn't History of Magic in Noelle. There were potions, bubbling pots, strange and cloying smells, assorted pieces of animals, and hundreds of vials. It was a potions class and she was in the wrong place. She apologized profusely and had to duck several times to avoid the giant, rotating ball of viscous liquid the professor was floating in front of the class.

Back in the hallway, she heard the call again. On and

on she went, eventually being led out into a garden on the mountainside. There again, Andie was happily surprised. There were thousands upon thousands of gorgeous, luminous blooms in the garden. Every imaginable flower in every imaginable variety. They were sprouting, hanging, twisting, draping, creeping, and even floating. They were in every color Andie had ever heard of and many more she didn't even know were possible. Some even changed color. Buzzing among the blooms and falling petals were skops. Similar to faeries, but tended flowers and only lived for about twelve days. Andie came upon a row of vibrant green bushes that must have continued at least half a kilometer long. They were brimming with pearlescent flowers that were rising and falling over and over again. As Andie drew closer, she saw that they were actually dying and blooming again in an endless cycle that lasted only a matter of moments.

Shaking herself out of the daze of beauty, Andie began to run. Her class had definitely started by then, and she had no idea if she was even anywhere close to the classroom. There would be plenty of time to explore the Academy later, if she wasn't expelled first.

She ran as hard as she could, weaving through and under the flowers that were everywhere. Her foot caught on something and she fell, slamming chest first into the ground. Her breath fled her. She coughed, having breathed in some dust, and turned.

There was a pair of legs sticking out from under a tangle of roots and peach-colored blooms. The legs bend down onto their knees and they scooted backward out of the roots. A torso then appeared. Then a head. Soon the complete figure was standing over Andie. A perfect, tall figure who smiled down at her with a smile that could melt even the coldest of hearts. He reached out a hand to help her up.

"Were you looking for me?"

CHAPTER FIVE

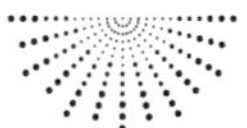

ANDIE WAS SO STUNNED BY HIS LOOKS AND HIS mesmerizing eyes that, at first, she couldn't speak, couldn't even understand that he was trying to help her to her feet. Seeing she wasn't focusing, he bent down and grabbed her by her shoulders. Firmly but gently, he lifted her to her feet and only then did Andie fall back into reality.

She stared dumbly into his eyes, then shook her head and pulled herself from her trance. What was she, some pathetic love-struck teenager? "Gross," she said at the thought.

"I'm sorry?"

She blinked and stared, then felt her face burn a horrible shade or red. "Oh, nothing. Sorry."

"I'm Tarven, a student advisor," he said. "You must be my new recruit. I've been looking for you."

"Um, I don't know. I'm not even sure where I am."

"This is the Academy. You are a sorceress, aren't you?"

"Yes. I mean, I don't know where in the Academy I am. What side of the mountain are we on?"

"West. This is the garden of Victory, the designated garden of the University and the city. I look after it sometimes. I'm really into hortological magic."

"Plant magic," Andie said. "Cool."

"Yeah, I think so. I don't really know how I got into it, though. I was born and raised in Arvall City where everything's stone or glass or iron. Don't get me wrong, I've traveled all over Noelle with my family, but always in urban centers. You'd think I'd want to have little to do with actual nature, but it turned out to be something I was really passionate about."

"I've never met anyone who could do plant magic before," she said, averting her gaze to anywhere but his eyes. "How does it work, exactly?"

"Hortological magic is all about understanding the life of the plant. The breath of its stem, the depth of its bloom, the fragility of its petal. It's about wanting to see the plant grow, not wanting to control it, even though through this kind of magic you *can* control the plant."

"Like the ones I saw coming in, dying and blooming?"

"Exactly. I've studied magic my whole life and never came across anything as noble and undervalued as plants."

"We share similar sentiments in Michaelson. We still depend on crops out there. Are you the only one with that kind of magic here?"

"Well, there's bound to be at least a couple more in a student body of hundreds of thousands. Speaking of, tell me about yourself. I've heard of Michaelson. It's one of the little farming towns north of here, right?"

"Yeah. Well, I'm nineteen and this is my first day at the Academy. I'm here because I need to learn control."

She had no idea why she told him that.

"I'm highly sensitive to other people's pain," she continued. "I believe people don't care enough about their own history, and I want to be a researcher when I graduate."

"That's great. But I think you're late."

"Oh, no!"

She'd completely forgotten about getting to class. It was so nice talking to him, so nice having a normal conversation with a normal and attractive person who didn't know about her family history. Not that being attractive had anything to do with it. But it was nice speaking to someone, anyone, who didn't know or ask about her father.

Class was probably already half over. She smiled and thanked Tarven, and began jogging off. But she didn't know which way to go anymore. The siren's call had ended. She turned and turned, trying to pick up the trail again.

All of a sudden, she felt a wave of magic rush through her. She checked her icon for a warning, but there was nothing. When she looked up again, the entire garden was on fire.

"Did I do that?" she asked, horrified.

"No," Tarven said. "I did."

"Why?"

"It's kind of my job. This is your first test. If you don't pass it, I'm afraid you'll have to go. Sink or swim here, Andie. Put it out or get out. Consider it a fire drill." A sly grin spread across his face, and she didn't know whether she should laugh or be angry. Confusion was what she ended up settling on.

She was taken aback. She had no idea how to control her magic aside from a handful of small spells and charms. She'd spent her entire life forcing herself to hold back, suppress her natural ability. Now this guy wanted her to master her skills without warning? Impossible. The reason she was there was to learn control, focus, and expansion, and yet, it seemed her journey was over before it began. The fire blazed brighter and hotter by the second. All it would take was one wrong move to accidentally tap into her dragon magic and ruin everything she'd been trying to hide since she was born.

"You have to help me," she said, turning to Tarven and pleading. "Please. I don't have this kind of control over myself yet. It's the whole reason I'm here."

"I'm sorry, but I'm not allowed. This is your test, Andie. *Yours*. I could feel your power the moment you walked in. It's one of the gifts of studying hortological magic. You can do this. And I'd love if you could stop the fire before it destroys the rose hip. I was going to use that for a pretty amazing spell later on."

She walked away a few paces and closed her eyes, trying to focus. She tried to calm herself, the way her mother used to teach her to do when she was a little girl and would get scared or frustrated. And then it dawned on her. Dragons are drawn to fire. It calms them, makes them feel safe, can even heal them in certain situations. She had dragon blood running in her veins. She stretched her hands out to her sides and then it began to fill her. The peace of the flames. She began to feel more powerful, more brave as the flames grew around her. It was almost as if the flames were calling to her. She needed a balance. She needed to embrace the flames and their power without succumbing to the dragon magic.

For the first time, she noticed the other people in the garden. Not many, but enough to make a small crowd. They were pushing together into a little group, trying to avoid the flames and also trying to watch Andie to see what she would do. She wondered if they were forbidden from helping, too.

They were staring at her wide-eyed, no doubt wondering why she felt so at ease so close to flames. She didn't even feel the heat. But she couldn't reveal that to Tarven. She tried to focus, knowing that if she failed this first task, not only would she be kicked out of the Academy, she would also hurt her father.

What was worse, if she pushed her own magic back down far enough so that the flames burned her as proof that she wasn't immune, she would hurt herself in front of Tarven and who knows what her body would do to naturally heal itself. That was not something he or anyone here could see. The panic began to rise again, but she listened to the flames and remained calm. She took a moment to close her eyes and think.

"Water," she whispered. "Water is in the plants."

She reached out toward the plants on either side of her and flexed her fingers. She focused on the sorcerer's magic inside of her, and did everything in her power to push away her dragon blood instinct. Every stem and bloom stood straight up. She made fists of her hands and all the plants leaned over toward her, releasing every ounce of moisture they had and turned brown, then black in the process. When all the water had been collected in floating pools above her, she used her powers to magnify it and then made it rain inside the garden. Within moments, the fire had been extinguished.

"Very impressive," Tarven said, smiling at her. "And look, you saved the rose hip."

For a moment, Andie couldn't focus. She was reeling a bit from the loss of the flames. All their comfort, promise, and power had fled with them. Her hands stayed in the air beside her for a moment.

"Andie. Andie, are you okay?" Tarven asked, laying a hand on her shoulder.

She snapped back into the moment, the garden, the circumstance.

She stood still, silent for a long while, and then reeled. "What kind of twisted games are you playing here?" she shouted, rounding on Tarven and locking eyes with him. "You could have burned me to death. I could've died! I'm a first-year Academy student who hasn't even taken one class. I don't even have control of my magic, yet. What if I'd lost control? Do you have any idea what could have happened?" She thought of all the weird, pathetic excuses that a first-year student could possibly use, and spewed them out at him as angrily as she could manage. She hoped it was enough to cover up any evidence of her dragon blood magic that might have seeped out during the exercise.

Andie's heart pounded in her chest as her mind raced with the thought of what would have happened had she actually lost control and hurt herself. Her dragon magic would have healed her, of course, and had she been at home or somewhere isolated, it wouldn't have been a problem. But in front of another person, especially in the University, that was the most dangerous thing she could possibly think of happening. She swallowed and cleared her throat, all the while glaring at Tarven in front of her.

She hoped he had bought her distress as being caused by fear of being hurt, rather than what she was truly hiding.

Tarven held up his hands to calm her, but he took a few steps back. He claimed to be able to sense her power. He surely must've known to treat her carefully in that moment.

"Okay, easy now. I'm not allowed to interfere as long as the situation is controllable and it looks like you still have a chance to complete the task. Rest assured, no one was going to burn alive today and I would've been right here if something had gone wrong with your magic. Also, your icon measures your distress levels and if it had gotten too high, the entire school board would have teleported in. There was never any real danger, Andie. I promise."

Andie rubbed her eyes with the palms of her hands as she inhaled a deep breath and exhaled slowly. She hadn't even been to her first class yet, and she had nearly revealed herself. What was she doing here? She was in way over her head. "You just pushed it too far, okay?"

"It wasn't like—"

"Just… Don't do anything like that to me again. Please. I wasn't ready."

"I'm sorry, Andie. It was just a test. From the moment you walked in, I knew you would have been able to handle it just fine."

Andie felt stupid and angry, not so much with him as with herself. She would need to prepare herself for surprises like this. She couldn't afford to slip up. Her life depended on this. "Well, you were wrong."

She cursed herself for sounding like such a snarky brat, but better that he thinks of her as a whiney first-year than as someone with dragon blood. The first, she could deal with, although the situation wasn't exactly ideal. The second, would end up getting her killed.

Tarven was silent then. He kept opening his mouth to respond, but something told Andie that he hadn't even fully considered the circumstances, which was even worse because he went along with the plan without thinking for himself. Andie shook her head.

"Well, I'll say one thing for my first day at the Academy," she said. "At least, it hasn't been dull." She managed a half laugh at that, and Tarven nearly smiled in return. His smile quickly turned to a frown when her expression turned back to one of utter seriousness.

"Well, goodbye then." With that, she turned to leave, mumbling a few awkward parting words about going to the library to prepare for her next class.

CHAPTER SIX

ANDIE TOOK THE LONG WAY AROUND, RELISHING IN THE cool fresh air that calmed her as she walked. She shook her head at how stupid and ill prepared she had been. Next time, she would be more confident. She would need to learn how to handle surprises and stressful situations without the risk of drawing on her dragon blood magic. She didn't have a choice. When she reached the end of the path, she turned and headed back towards the building.

She'd barely made it back inside when she realized she had no idea where to find her class. This place was massive and going on an exploratory walk would waste time she didn't have. She squeezed her eyes shut in concentration and rubbed her temples with her fingers, doing her best to think of a plan. She couldn't be late. Her eyes flashed open when an idea struck her. She held up her palm and used the opposite hand to press down on the light where the icon was. She closed her eyes and thought of the library. Sure enough, within seconds she could hear the siren's call. She opened her eyes and began to walk.

It took a while to find it, what with dodging the Mountain Faeries, weaving through the seemingly endless crowds, and listening in on other student's siren's call out of curiosity. When she finally found it, there was no mistaking it. The doors had to be at least fifty feet tall, made of what looked like Bleak Oak—wood as black as the night sky—inlaid with gold. The gold had been laid in fractal patterns of exploding curves, and, as Andie neared the doors, she could see the patterns were moving. She couldn't help smiling as she pushed open the door, which, even with its great size, was as easy to open as a regular-sized door.

She couldn't believe it. She was finally there. Leabherlann. The largest and best of the world's repositories. There was no library, no archive, no collection anywhere on the face of the earth that could rival that one. Leabherlann wasn't even half as old as most of the other libraries, yet, it was the greatest. Unparalleled. Andie had been desperate to get there. Inside were rows upon rows of gold and granite desks lined up straight down the center of the room and going back so far that Andie couldn't see the end. Above them were many, many more floors, all with the same incredibly long rows. At first, she thought the other floors were floating, but then she remembered that those were the famous invisible floors of the library.

To the right and left of the desks were the collections themselves. Stone cases that were so tall it was believed they rose hundreds of feet up into the mountain. It had been said that there was no subject, no personage, no branch of magic or its study that could not be found within those great walls. If it wasn't there, it probably didn't exist. Andie took several minutes to absorb the majesty of the place and then she headed for the main desk, a grandiose gold and silver dais whose powerful and beautiful turning gears were as much for function as embellishment. The entire thing was placed in a sunken area in the center of the space.

"Hi," she said, to which she received no answer. "I'm here to do some research."

The woman behind the desk looked at Andie as if what she'd said was the dumbest phrase ever uttered. Andie realized that hundreds of thousands of students came here to do research every single day.

"Oh, sorry," she said. "I want to know where to find the collections. I'd like to read on the dra-"

She stopped herself, knowing it was better to keep her subject to herself.

"I'd like to read on extinct bloodlines."

"Show me your icon access," the woman said, monotone and uninterested.

"My what?"

"I-con ac-cess," she said as condescendingly as possible.

"She's new, doesn't have it yet. I have clearance to let her use mine for the time being."

Andie turned to the sound of the voice and saw Carmen grinning. She walked up to the desk and turned her palm toward the woman, who, reluctantly, swiped her own palm in front of Carmen's.

"Go on," the woman said, returning her attention to whatever was below the silver barrier that Andie couldn't see. Carmen took her by the arm and led her off.

"Good old Murakami," she said. "Never smiled or

said a nice thing a day in her life. But she's pureblooded Raeynese."

"You're kidding. The Raeynese Empire was destroyed soon after Hightowyr. I didn't think there were any left."

"Very few, and they've been reduced to intermarriage, with terrifying results."

"Don't you have class right now?" Andie asked.

"Don't you?"

Carmen led her to the elevator and it carried them up to the hundred and first floor. They got out and Andie had to catch her breath. She had thought they were falling, but it was just the invisible floor. She looked down between her feet at the many levels and students beneath her.

"Cool," she said.

Carmen took her back a few cases and pointed her to a particular case.

"This is it?" Andie asked, a bit disillusioned.

"Sure. If by 'this' you mean the entire floor. You can start wherever you want."

And just like that she turned to leave.

"Carmen, wait. Thank you for helping me get in and for bringing me up here. How did you get me in, anyway?"

"I do some work as amanuensis for my bloodlines professor. He's always having me pull a book on some long dead ethnicity or culture. Gives me special access."

"Nice."

She was about to leave again when she turned back. She watched Andie for a moment.

"Be careful who sees you reading up here, Andie. An interest in bloodlines isn't really something people will understand. Even my professor is sort of a pariah. Don't talk about this with anyone."

And she left.

Andie was a bit shaken by Carmen's warning, but she went on anyway. She searched and searched, but even after half an hour she hadn't been able to find a single book on dragons, dragon blood, or the dragonborn. She went back and forth, from case to case to case, and even triple checked the floor's catalogue. There wasn't a single book on anything having to do with dragons. It was like the University was purposely keeping secrets, which was probably the truth. Eventually, tired of searching and thoroughly disappointed, she resigned herself to reading something for class.

Not too long after that, Carmen came back. She brought a friend with her. Yara. Yara was a rather plain girl, but her personality was as magnetic as Carmen's and she was as bookish as Andie wanted to be. Carmen kept looking at Andie when she thought no one was watching, and Andie got the impression that Carmen had come back because she was genuinely worried. Yara kept them both engaged with her stories and endless knowledge of all sorts of things.

"Yara, how do you know so much about Goulstnach?" Andie asked.

"Are you kidding? Those things freak me out. The sadder they get, the bigger they get and it's notoriously difficult to comfort them. Once they reached their limit, they explode and send poisonous pieces of their spine in every direction. Are you telling me that doesn't freak you out?"

"Well, they do now. I'm never going up the mountain."

"Good girl. Also, I couldn't help but notice the book you're reading. I'm pretty sure there's an older version of that that has a professor's note in it. Could be helpful." Yara winked.

"Thanks, Yara."

Just then, Andie heard her siren's call. It was time for her next class.

"I hear my call. It was great talking with you. I hope I can catch up with you again soon."

"You, too," Yara said. "And good luck with the rest of your day."

"Thanks. Thank you, too, Carmen."

"My pleasure. See you later, haybale."

Andie got in the elevator and took it back down to the ground floor. When she stepped out, she couldn't tell which direction the call was coming from. She'd heard there were at least a hundred different entrances to Leabherlann, and so she figured the call must be leading her to another one. But the farther she walked, the more unsure she became. Sometimes she thought she was following the voice, other times it seemed to be coming from behind or to the side of her. Eventually, she found herself down another floor in the archives. The air was thick with dust, the lighting ample but odd, and there didn't seem to be anyone else around. She started reading every plaque, searching for any way out.

Soon, she came across things like *Most Educated and Illustrious Serpents* and *Poisons that Attack only the Soul* and even *Great Magical Shifts of the Third and Fourth Cycle*s. She had inadvertently come upon the special and rare collections, and she was fascinated. There were all kinds of unimaginable subjects. Things she'd heard of only in legend. All that made her wonder if she should even be down there.

At the end of an inordinately long path, a bridge of sorts, she came upon another door, Bleak Oak with a gold inlay just like the much larger one upstairs. She was standing in front of it, debating whether or not to knock when she heard voices. She dropped everything in her hands. It was the same voices that had been haunting her dreams.

"What are you doing?"

The sound of a voice behind her nearly made Andie jump through the ceiling. It took her a moment to get her heart out of her throat. She turned around to see Tarven. With her head full of the siren's call and the voices, she hadn't heard him approach.

"Are you seriously dead-set on freaking me out every time you see me?" she snapped. "Honestly, I'm starting to think your sole purpose here is to make me lose my cool. And why do I keep seeing the same people everywhere?"

"Heh, sorry. Calm down. I wasn't up to anything nefarious. I just saw you over here. Students aren't allowed to be here."

Andie took a moment to breathe and to return her heart rate to normal. She stared at him, wide-eyed.

"I figured that. I just got lost."

"Well, follow me. I'll get you back." He smiled at her and picked up a book that had fallen nearest to him.

Andie bent down to pick up her books and snatched the book out of Tarven's hands as she eyed him suspiciously. "I'll take that, thanks."

Tarven shrugged and led her back the way she'd come and then locked the door behind them.

CHAPTER SEVEN

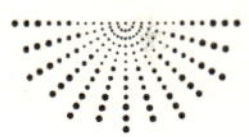

THE REST OF THE DAY PASSED WITHOUT INCIDENT. ANDIE enjoyed the rest of her classes—or, at least, as much as she could, considering she was convinced that the same voices from her nightmares were circulating the underground archives at the University—and met some really interesting fellow students.

She made it home that afternoon and settled in for a couple hours of studying, during which time she mostly worried and didn't study. After two hours, the only information she'd managed to absorb was the first sentence of the first paragraph of one of her critical texts. She'd have to finish later, though. She'd promised to have dinner with Raesh and Carmen downstairs.

When she went down, she was a bit early, which gave her some time to talk with Marvo about his family and hers. He told her some stories about her parents and the times they'd had so many years before. He remembered her mom as beautiful, kind, and one of the most generous people he'd ever met. As much as it hurt, she always loved hearing stories about her mother.

Somewhere along sharing his memories, Andie stopped him. Thinking about everything she'd lost wouldn't do. Especially, not every single day. She'd come to the city and to school with the intention of making sure the past didn't repeat itself and building a new kind of life for herself and her father. She had to learn to let go at some point. Besides, Raesh and Carmen would be there soon and she didn't want to be depressed when they showed up. Marvo kissed her cheek and left, looking a bit embarrassed, but understanding.

Carmen came first. She'd been just a couple of neighborhoods over, hanging out with some friends. She had no idea where Raesh was.

"So, what's the deal? You gonna wire my cousin or what?"

"I don't know what that means, but I think the answer's going to be no."

"Wire. It means hook up with."

"What? No. I barely even know him. I'm not gonna sleep with him."

"Whoa, whoa, easy, haybale. I meant date, not sleep with. Thanks for that image, though. Bleh."

"Anyway, what about you? Who do you... wire with?"

"My professor."

Andie paused, completely taken aback.

"Your professor? Are you serious?"

"Possibly."

Carmen grinned. Andie couldn't help herself and she smiled, too.

"Tell you what," Carmen said. "Be nice to me and I'll show you how to turn off your icon."

Andie paused. "Wait, what? We can do that?"

"Well, obviously, we're not supposed to, and we can get into serious trouble if they find out, but how are they supposed to manage each and every one of their hundreds of thousands of icons? Not to mention, thousands of students graduate or transfer all the time and thousands more come in. The trick is not to turn it off completely. We'll just kind of dampen it."

"That is so cool."

The bell over the door rang and in walked Raesh, as handsome and magnetic and awkward as ever. He waved to his dad and came to sit with them.

"What's up, my two favorite ladies?"

"There's a secret door in the underground archives that's holding voices from my nightmares."

Raesh's mouth hung slightly open to complete the look of utter bewilderment on his face. And for the first time since Andie had met her, Carmen was at a complete and total loss for words. Both she and her cousin simply stared at Andie dumbfounded.

"I'm sorry. I guess I could've said hi first. It's just that I've been holding it in all day and didn't have anyone to tell, so I figured I could tell you two here at dinner. Then, I was waiting on you to show up, Raesh, and when you came in my wall just kind of crumbled and I spat it out. I'm really sorry. It's just that even though you're both so different from me, you both seem like you can be trusted."

Carmen's look changed some, becoming more of a look of warmth, but with deeper concern than confusion. But she still couldn't speak.

"Okay," Raesh finally said. "How can we help?"

"Really?"

"You said we look trustworthy, right? Trust us," Carmen said.

"Thank you," Andie said. She tried to formulate her thoughts enough to explain what was going on to them without sounding like a complete crazy person. "Okay, so. I've been having these dreams. Dreams unlike anything I've ever felt before. I used to call them weird, but they're more than that. They're like something from another life. Totally terrifying. And I mean real, paralyzing fear. In the dreams, there are these voices. These otherworldly voices. I don't know what they're saying or what they want, but when I was down in the archives today, I heard those same voices making the same whispers. They were behind some door down there. I didn't see who was making the voices or anything, but I know what I heard."

Andie took a breath and let it out slowly as the weight of what she had been hiding lifted from her shoulders. She then added, "don't bother mentioning that the archives are a restricted area. I know that already."

Raesh and Carmen shared a look and then watched Andie. She waited for one of them to speak.

"So, what do you think?" she pressed when no one spoke.

"Honestly? I don't want to make light of your problems, but I think maybe you're reaching," Carmen said. "And just hear me out. I think you've got a lot going on back home and in your past, and you also just moved to Arvall—which we all know is not kind on the nerves—and started your first year at the Academy. Not to mention, the school board's little entrance exam. I don't deny that you might've heard something down there, but I don't think it was voices from your dreams. I think you've been expecting too much of yourself."

Andie sighed. Of course, they didn't believe her.

"Andie, I'm more worried about you getting in trouble," Raesh said. "First, you missed almost two weeks of school, then you're looking up books you shouldn't be, then you're walking around a restricted area. I think you're pushing your luck. And I agree with Carmen. I think you're just under tremendous strain."

"So, neither of you believe me?"

"It's not that we think you're crazy or anything, it's just that you're asking us to believe something pretty big," Carmen said.

"If you hear it again, or if you find something, let us know," Raesh said. "And above all, watch yourself."

At that exact moment, Marvo happened to be walking by. When he heard Raesh cautioning Andie, he stopped dead.

"What does he mean 'watch yourself?'" Marvo asked.

Even though she barely knew him, Andie suddenly felt like she'd disappointed him. He was beginning to feel like the extension of her dad in Arvall City. She couldn't even meet his eyes.

"Andie, if you're into something you shouldn't be, you need to step away. I'm not your dad, and I'm not trying to be, but you're beautiful and bright and you've already had so much happen in your life. You're here to go to the Academy, learn, and go back home to be with your father. Anything outside of that is a distraction. I don't want to meddle in your life, and I know you're an intelligent and capable young woman, but I'm asking you now, to stay within the lines. Your father made me promise to watch over you. I know you don't want to upset your father."

"You're right," she said, feeling even worse. "I'll be sure to watch myself."

Marvo didn't move. He just kept watching Andie, probably waiting to see if something would show in her face to indicate that she was being less than truthful. Yet, when Andie finally met his gaze, he seemed convinced. He smiled the same warm smile his son had inherited and walked away.

Inside herself, Andie wondered if she was truly going to watch herself or if she had been lying to everyone, including herself.

Or maybe she truly was just crazy and overwhelmed, and she had imagined the whole thing. Somehow, she doubted that.

AS NIGHT CREPT NEARER, Andie decided to lay down early. She'd been trying to study practically all day, but her mind simply wouldn't focus. She couldn't stop thinking of those voices ringing through the dark of the archives. Talking to Raesh and Carmen had assuaged her some, but she couldn't tell if it was the two of them that helped her or the fact that she talked to other human beings. On the other hand, the conversation had actually made things somewhat worse. They'd rattled her so much that now she was unsure of what she'd heard. It was an institution of magic, after all, and it was centuries old. Those voices—were they even *voices*, or just noises in the walls? —could have been anything. They might even have been real people. She'd never opened the door. What gave her the right to draw conjectures?

Of course, none of that worry went away just because she wanted to sleep. For a long time, she lay there, anxious, confused, and yet still incredibly hopeful. She really wanted to start over, to let go. She was still holding onto hope that she would find some books in the University that would tell her something about her past and her blood. She wanted to know more about herself, her powers, and who she was supposed to be. Maybe then, she could decipher her dreams. And whether those had been voices or not in the archives, she wanted to know more about them, too.

She unlocked the cabinet next to the bed to retrieve *Dragons*. She flipped through the book, skimming the mix of legend and fact, tracing the incredible sketches of dragons with her fingers and feeling a void in her life where the totality of the history of her bloodline should've been. There was something in the back of the book, too. A sort of makeshift family album that her dad had put together for her just before she left. She flipped through those pages, too, stopping once and again to read some of the words her mother had written on a picture or in a letter. She looked through the pictures, seeing herself as she truly was in all her dragon blood glory; colored hair and eyes and all. It was the dragon side she'd been forced to keep locked away inside. She almost didn't recognize herself anymore.

Sometime later, she finally fell into an uneasy sleep.

CHAPTER EIGHT

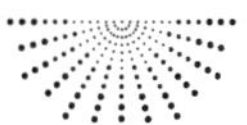

TIME PASSED. HOURS BECAME DAYS AND DAYS BECAME weeks. Andie settled into a rhythm and things began to go well. There was school, Raesh, Carmen, Marvo, breakfast and dinner at the restaurant, and a lot of good days. The time passed quietly. Andie finally got to a place where she could focus on her studies and do good work. She never missed class, never turned in an assignment late, and had gotten excellent marks in every class. She was slowly meeting more and more new people, and even knew quite a few well enough to call them friends, but Raesh and Carmen were her best friends. They were simply right for her.

Things with her dad at home were pretty good, too. He hadn't gotten any worse and had even improved some, and they'd been in contact much more. The only part of her life that still wasn't right was the voices she'd heard. For the most part, she'd been able to move on from the things she couldn't change, but there was something about those voices that just wouldn't let go of her no matter what she did. She'd gone back to

Leabherlann many times, and even tried to get back into the archive. She never found anything, though.

She'd nearly given up, then something happened in her History of Modern Magic class.

"Good morning, ingrates," the professor sneered. "I want you all to know how thrilled I am to be here with you, again, for another wonderful day of unrewarding and futile attempts to give your minds shape and your lives purpose. Look at you, already burnt-out and you aren't even old enough to have been really chewed up and digested by the filthy, malicious, maggot-ridden world that wants you dead or dying. Cheers."

The professor for that class was cynical, to say the least. He also often smelled of booze. He was a self-proclaimed nihilist and he clearly hated his job. It was anyone's guess why he continued to come to work. He was so uninterested in his students that he had never even allowed them to know his name. He cared nothing for order or work in general. He alternated between long periods of no classroom work or homework at all to consecutive days of grueling, soul-crushing work. He was undeniably brilliant, but arguably the most unpleasant, offensive, pessimistic, and angry person in Arvall City. Of all Noelle, even. Maybe even of Shaeyara, itself.

"So, I'm sure you've been wondering about this giant blank space in your syllabi. That is, if you haven't been rendered completely worthless by your inability to comprehend the nature of this course and your age group's general bewilderment. We've now come to the point in our class, excuse me, *my* class where it's time to learn about dragons, dragonborn, dragon blood, dragon magic... so on. All things dragon. Yay."

Andie couldn't believe it. She sat bolt upright in her chair and almost screamed from sheer excitement. She'd spent weeks scraping everywhere for even a hint of dragons and now it looked as if everything she ever wanted to know was about to be delivered to her without the least effort.

"Oh, by the way, the school board and the city council and the major governor and the chancellor and every other person whose designation makes them feel important doesn't want you to learn this. Screw them."

Andie was ecstatic. This was one of the reasons she'd most wanted to come to school. She didn't think she could sit still, she was so excited. She readied her pen and notepad.

"Let's start with a basic summary even you degenerates can't fail to grasp. Dragons were gigantic, ferocious, man-eating beasts who plagued the world for thousands upon thousands of years. During their time, there was no such thing as peace. No such thing as safe. They took countless lives for no reason at all. They were a curse and demonic presence on the earth, and the best thing they ever did for us was die off from inbreeding."

Andie's excitement faded. She'd been so overzealous that she'd actually written down everything up to "safe." She couldn't understand what he meant. She thought he had to be playing a sick joke or twisting the truth.

"The worst thing they ever did was manage to get their blood into human bodies, creating the most obscene and dangerous abominations in history. I'm talking about an entire race of people who were angry and evil. As a matter of fact, they weren't even people. You societal rejects aren't too much better, but who am I to judge..."

This wasn't right. She just kept thinking to herself that this wasn't right.

She knew her people, her heritage, had been persecuted and hunted throughout history. She knew that her having dragon blood magic was enough to get her killed. But she had been sure, so sure deep in her heart, that there must have been some great mistake in history. How could an entire race be evil? She didn't feel evil. She knew her mother wasn't evil. She was sure there was more to it than what the world has been led to believe. There must be.

"Luckily for you human stains, the world was purged. The dragons and their foul human spawn were all eradicated. The dragons were killed by some mysterious method that has been lost to history, but we know how the dragonborn died. Hanging. Drowning. Evisceration. Decapitation. Several unsightly and shockingly grotesque spells. The culling wasn't gentle, and we know for a fact..."

Andie didn't want to believe it, any of it. The professor went on and on about the dragons and the dragonborn and all the atrocities they committed. For a while, Andie was totally set against his philippic, but the more she listened, the more she began to wonder. What did she really know about the dragons and their keepers? All she knew was the very little contained in *Dragons* and the stories that her dad had told her. But he'd admitted time and time again over the years that he'd never known anyone with dragon blood other than her mother, who knew next to nothing about their long heritage.

Was it possible they had been completely unaware of the truth? After all, the entire world had banded together to annihilate the dragons and all of the dragonborn people.

There had been no international effort like that in all of recorded history. There must have been a truly great evil about for every living soul on the planet to want them gone. Andie thought long and hard about what she knew of dragons, which was essentially nothing except that they were massive, powerful, and extremely dangerous. Then the worst possible thought came into her mind. Could her parents have outright lied? Maybe the dragons and the dragonborn truly were evil.

After class, feeling completely heartsick and nauseous all at the same time, Andie returned to the University's vast collection of books to make one final, fleeting attempt to find some more information. Even though she remembered how the professor had said everyone was against this subject being taught, she held hope that there was at least one volume somewhere in there. Of course, without Carmen there to provide access, she couldn't even take the elevator to the bloodlines floor. Fortunately, she ran into Yara.

"Hey, Andie. Wow, you look like total crap."

"Oh, yeah. Thanks," Andie half smiled and rubbed her neck awkwardly. "It's just that I've really been trying to find something in here and I'm not having any luck. I'm just going to give up."

"Maybe I can help," Yara said, smiling ear to ear. "What are you looking for?"

"Honestly? Something on dragons or the dragonborn."

Yara caught her breath and inadvertently took a step back. For a moment, she just stared.

"Carmen told me you might be interested in

something like that," she said. "Please just tell me it's for an assignment or something."

Andie nodded quickly. "Of course, what else would it be for?"

Yara eyed her suspiciously but then nodded. "Okay. Look, I don't know much, but I do know they keep some books in the back. Some stuff they really don't want any students to see. Down deep in archives, hidden. You might find some interesting things there. There are old, damaged books there, but they also hide things there. Every now and again, a student sneaks down to find a 'dirty' book. I'm not sure what they mean by dirty. Anyway, I just saw a professor come out. Maybe the door is still open. Try giving it a good push."

"Thank you, Yara. I'm kind of going out of my mind here."

"Don't mention it."

Yara walked away slowly, as if afraid of something she'd done, while Andie hurried off to find the entrance to the archives. She walked so quickly she almost ran. She didn't even slow down when the heads began to turn, but she did remember that she was wearing the icon and she wasn't sure what kind of surveillance the thing provided. The last thing she needed was the school board sending someone to check on her. Yet, she couldn't stop herself from moving toward the archives.

She finally reached the door and, just as Yara had said, it gave when Andie pushed it. She looked around the space to make sure no one was there and just managed to see two professors talking in excited whispers behind the first bookcase. She crouched low behind an abandoned desk and waited for them to leave.

She realized how heavily she was sweating and how quickly her heart was racing.

"Calm down, Andie," she whispered to herself. She took a deep breath to calm herself and calm her breathing. The last thing she needed was to be found there. Or, even worse, to be questioned about why she was so agitated.

Within a few moments, the professors were on their way out and Andie was alone. She crept into the room and closed the door behind her. The archives, though intimidating and poorly lit, were as breathtaking as they had been on her first visit. Even in her heightened excitement, she had to take a moment to appreciate the place.

Now that she wasn't being distracted by trying to follow the siren's call, she could focus more precisely on what was in the room. The main path through the archives was a raised wooden bridge of sorts, with stairs leading up or down to the sections the path ran beside. She'd almost completely ignored the collections to the left of the bridge the last time she was there. There were haphazard piles of books that must have been at least forty feet tall, and careless stacks of paper thrown about on the tables and the floor, as if someone kept meaning to organize, but seemed to forget each time a new stack came in. It didn't look to Andie like anyone had organized those archives in decades. Without even knowing where to begin, Andie walked about halfway across the massive bridge, took a set of stairs to the lower floor, and began rummaging through the shelves.

She must've been there over an hour, searching and taking down, and guessing. She'd had no luck, not even a hint of what she'd wanted to know. She couldn't help wondering if she'd have had better luck by calling Carmen. She needed someone else down there to help her look, but if some professor walked through, she didn't want Carmen getting in trouble over something so stupid.

It was quite a while before she found something that she thought might prove worthwhile. A large, dusty tome with an embossed dragon on the cover. Her heart nearly skipped a beat as she ran her fingers over the textured cover. Behind it were three more books with similar markings on the front. She couldn't help but laugh out loud to herself, easing the tension she had felt build in the pit of her stomach since she arrived in the archives. But just as she was flipping through the opening pages and getting excited, the bells rang to signal that the University would soon be closing for the night.

She looked about to make sure no one could see her, and then she hid the dusty old books in her backpack and headed for the door.

CHAPTER NINE

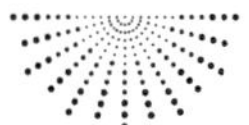

SHE GOT HOME LATER THAN USUAL THAT NIGHT, BUT SHE was ecstatic to have finally found books on dragons. She came in and threw off her things in a tornado of eagerness and self-congratulation. Just as she was settling in her chair with dinner and preparing to eat while she read, her phone buzzed.

"It's me," he said. "You busy?"

Andie stared at the screen at the unfamiliar number. "Who?"

"Tarven. Who else?"

Andie rolled her eyes. "Seriously, you're calling me at home? How did you even get my number?"

He ignored her questions.

"Are you ever going to forgive me for the fire? It's been weeks now. I only did what they told me to do. I don't know what to say to you, Andie. I was there, I would've helped if necessary. I promise."

Andie thought for a moment. He was right. It had been weeks and she knew he'd only done what he'd been told to do. She'd been threatened with expulsion if she failed. She was sure he had been threatened with something similar. That still didn't explain why he was calling her now.

"So, you busy?" he asked.

"Well, I sort of... actually... it depends. What do you need?"

"Nothing, really. Just need to see a pretty face and have fun with a super smart girl. You up for drinks?"

Andie rolled her eyes. "I don't really know about that. I'm busy with homework, and have so much to catch up on."

"Swamped with school work already? The year has barely started." Tarven's laugh was magnetic, but she forced herself not to smile. She wasn't going to be swooned that easily, especially by a guy who almost caused her to out herself.

"Not really, just… Oh, why not. I could use the distraction. It'll be low key, right?" She knew she had to stay in and study. Her mind was dead-set on pouring through her new books. Her words betrayed her.

"As low key as anything I do."

"Fair enough. When and where?"

"Plaza One. Quarter to midnight."

"Whoa, that's kind of-"

Tarven had already hung up.

"-late," she finished.

She knew she shouldn't, that she had so much more important work to do, but, for some reason, hearing his voice made her feel like she had to go. She slipped into some different clothes, grabbed her purse, checked to make sure the icon was still turned off, and headed out the door.

She met Tarven and his friends at the Plaza One bar

and they all started chatting. As with what usually happens in large groups, they eventually broke down into smaller groups, or even pairs, with separate conversations. Andie drank, but sparingly, whereas Tarven drank without restraint and without showing anything more than the most benevolent symptoms of his intoxication.

"So, where exactly are you from, Andie Rogers?" Tarven asked.

"Michaelson," she said. "But you knew that already."

Tarven grinned at her. "Where in Michaelson, I mean."

"Oh. At the southern shore of Gordric's Pain."

"Ah, so you're of the Gordric's Pain Rogers? That's good stock, I hear."

Andie laughed and rolled her eyes at him as she took another moderate sip of whipper's beer, a special brew only sold in Arvall City. All Andie, or anybody else for that matter, knew about the beer was that its process was quick, and its recipe called for, among other things, watermelon rinds and extract of orchid. It took her a while to get used to the sweet taste. Marvo would serve it at the restaurant on weekends, and it had quickly grown to be one of her favorite drinks.

"So, who is Andie Rogers, other than a girl who hates fire?"

"I'm a first-year student at the Academy and I like history." She smirked as it was his turn to roll his eyes. Andie couldn't help but smile as she mentally admitted to herself that she did deserve some time to unwind. Plus, a little flirting never hurt anyone. It had been ages since she even had time to think about anything other than her father, and she set her mind to doing everything she could to enjoy her night.

"Interesting. Historical events or timeless wars?"

"Hmm... wars."

Tarven raised his eyebrow. "Interesting. Now we're getting somewhere. What makes a girl so worried about her peers' safety so interested in war?"

"Nothing so grand as what you're imagining, I'm sure. I just find the destruction and beauty of war fascinating."

"Beauty?"

"Yes. Nothing unites people like a war. The bigger, the longer, the worse the war, the closer the survivors will be. War brings love and hope and significance to the surface. And sure, it's bloody, cruel, and most of the time it's fought over nothing, but, when it's over, the world needs to heal itself and sometimes, given the right circumstances, that can be—"

"Beautiful," Tarven finished, watching her like he'd never seen her before. "Okay, I think I'm beginning to understand you. But, just to play devil's advocate, the aftermath of war isn't always so welcoming."

"I know that better than most," she said.

Tarven watched her. She hadn't meant to say it out loud. After that, she put her drink down. Letting hints of her personal vicissitudes slip out was evidence she'd had enough.

"I just think war is one of those things that defines an age. Every age. You know?"

"I get you," he said. "Speaking of age, you're nineteen, right? The Academy starts accepting students at the age of sixteen. Why'd you wait so late?"

"Obligations," she said, somewhat more ominously than she'd meant.

"Can I ask what kind?"

Andie was silent. She wasn't trying to ignore him, she just honestly didn't know how to respond. Other than the one slip, she'd been exceptionally careful not to reveal anything personal all night. Still, Tarven was beginning to seem like he could be trusted. After all, he hadn't told anyone he found her in the archives.

"I don't mean to pry, and you don't have to answer if you're not comfortable, but did your obligations have to do with your father?"

She turned to look at him, right in his eyes. There was no malice there.

"How do you know about my father?"

"This is the University, Andie. People talk. Rumors spread. There's hardly anything about anybody that most of the students and faculty don't know."

He eyed her as he spoke and she felt her heart rate pick up slightly. Was he suggesting that he knew more about her than he initially led on? She narrowed her eyes at him and clenched her teeth.

"He had an accident," she said, bringing the conversation back around to her father. She wouldn't give him the opportunity to ask more questions about her. Not if it meant the risk of her outing herself. "He overwhelmed himself with too much magic. He hasn't been the same since. Honestly, I don't know how it happened. My mother died when I was young and my father hasn't really been the same ever since."

She stopped there. She cursed herself. Tarven did seem trustworthy, but she still hadn't really made up her mind whether or not she should share with him, and, even then, what pieces of the truth he could be trusted with.

"How did your mom die?"

He asked it gently, sympathetically, but she couldn't help thinking that she may have said too much already.

"She... I... we never really... it was... someone came... and... she was on the ground... I saw her... I... we..."

She was scrambling and even her breathing was beginning to quicken. What was she doing here, with this boy, telling him her darkest secrets? How could she trust him when she knew he'd do anything the school board told him? Maybe someone, somewhere, had seen her, followed her, knew what books she was trying to find. He watched her, and although he seemed caring at first, the more she scrambled to respond to the question the more suspicious his expression became.

"It wasn't anything, really," she finally said. "Just... sickness. Sorry, the memory of her is really upsetting, you know?"

Tarven didn't look the least bit convinced. She was lying through her teeth and he knew it.

"What about you?" she asked, putting on what her dad had said was her most attractive smile. "Your parents?"

Tarven was getting ready to respond, still looking suspicious, when Andie saw Raesh and his friends come in. Her hand came up before she'd even made the decision and she hoped desperately that they would see her. Raesh spotted her almost instantly. As he and his friends started toward her, she almost collapsed under the sheer relief. But as Raesh and his friends drew near, they seemed to see something they either didn't like or, based on some unspoken principle, couldn't tolerate. They walked right by Andie, merely nodding at her, and sat at the other end of the bar.

"You know those guys?" Tarven asked, a look of disgust passing his eyes.

"I thought I did," Andie said, actually offended.

"Don't take it the wrong way. It had nothing to do with you. Them and us... We just don't mix. My friends and I don't hang out with lowlifes."

Andie was taken aback, but in the interest of preserving what seemed to have become a fragile peace in the bar, she just nodded.

"Oh. I see," she said, grabbing her purse. "It's been a fun night, Tarven. Thanks for inviting me. I guess I should get back to my place and study."

"You sure?" he asked, though it seemed more out of politeness than genuine desire for her to stay.

"Yeah. See you in school."

She left, trying not to run at top speed. On her way home, all she could think about was how hurt Raesh had looked to see her with Tarven.

CHAPTER TEN

ANDIE WOKE UP COVERED IN SWEAT. THE BED WAS floating in midair and the walls were totally engulfed in purple flames. With a fluid swipe of her hand she extinguished the flames and the bed came back down gently. She'd had a nightmare. The same nightmare she'd been having for years, only a little clearer. It had been the same voices, same people calling for help, but that time the images had improved some. She'd seen a face, the first face she'd ever seen in that show of horrors. Even now that she was awake, the voices still echoed in her head, softer than shrieks and harder than whispers, the caustic noise of terror.

She felt different. She looked at the hair falling over her shoulder. It was purple. She could guess that her eyes had probably changed, too, to their natural, vivid byzantium. Her heart raced as she looked around the room to make sure no one could see. Pressing her hand against her chest, she let out a slow, deep breath to calm her nerves. She had locked the door, there was no chance that anyone had seen. Her heart rate slowed somewhat.

She used her magic to hide herself again, muttering an incantation to help keep a lid on her magic. She ran her hands through her hair and inspected it closely as she twirled the long locks between her fingers. A dark brunette. Classic, simple, unassuming. She let out a sigh of relief.

The magic flames had left no marks on the wall, though the room was as hot as an oven. The heat, of course, felt good. Fire was nourishment to a true dragonborn like Andie. At that moment, she was beyond grateful for Carmen showing her how to manipulate her icon, otherwise her life would have been over. The thought of it made her think of her mother and she looked over at her picture on the nightstand.

"What should I do?" she asked. Andie was so conflicted. Determined to find out more about her persecuted ancestors and war-ravaged heritage, she didn't know what to believe anymore. She stared longingly at her mother's photo and then fell back into the bed with an aggravated sigh.

Try as she might, Andie couldn't get back to sleep. After an hour of simply laying there, she got up and decided to go through the books she'd found in the archive. It was probably best to get them back soon before anyone could notice they were not only gone, but stolen. The books were ancient, full of dust that was nearly black, and the binding was barely managing to hold on to the pages. Those books were probably almost as old as Arvall itself. It wasn't until she was there in bed that she realized most of the books were in a different language.

She spoke three languages, but she didn't recognize that one. She'd picked them up because their titles or opening pages all made some mention of dragons, which was apparently the same word in that language as it was in her own, but the lighting had been so bad and she had been in such a hurry that she hadn't even noticed the strange characters of the alphabets. She couldn't make any sense of them. More still, she noticed that some of the books actually changed languages whenever she closed their covers; she'd be looking at one foreign language, close the book, open it again, and be looking at another. One book wouldn't open at all.

"What could be so bad that they'd go through this much trouble? Why not just throw the books away altogether?" Her questions echoed in her silent room, unanswered.

She knew that unless she could find a translator and a way to break the spells, she'd never discover the secrets of those texts. She'd become a thief for nothing. But she still had one option left. She could go back to Leabherlann, back to that doorway in the archives where she heard the voices. She was courting trouble to go back, and not only trouble, but expulsion, too. Still, she had to. If she couldn't know about dragons, she would at least know what was behind that door. She would learn what the voices were and where they came from.

Outside, the sun was finally rising. It wasn't long before Andie was dressed, fed, and on her way back to the University. The city streets seemed to admonish her for her boldness, warn her of the potential danger, but she couldn't stop. She was tired of being denied the answers to her past and her present. Tired of being denied the truth.

Because it was still early morning, the streets were clear, which gave her the solitude and quiet to clear her head in the fresh air. She checked her phone and saw messages from Raesh. She ignored them, not knowing if she owed him an explanation or not.

Either way, she had no time for his jealousy that morning.

CHAPTER ELEVEN

It took her most of the morning to arrive. She walked as far as she could before taking the train, and the only explanation she could give herself as to why she'd walked so far without need was that she knew she was beginning to push her luck. She'd turned down her icon and gotten fairly good at sneaking around, but she knew someone would catch her if she wasn't careful. Soon enough, she found herself on campus. She'd entered the doors and hardly walked the hall when she ran into Tarven.

"Andie. What are you doing here so early?"

The unexpected encounter left her flustered. She took a moment to collect her thoughts before she spoke. "Just… wanted to get an early start."

"Early start for what? Classes don't begin for another few hours." His eyebrow was raised in a quizzical arch as he watched her try and explain herself.

"Not that I need to explain my every whereabouts to you, Tarven, but I just wanted to finish my homework and do some studying for midterms. It's only a matter of weeks now." She crossed her arms and looked up at him, determination set on her face.

She was amazed at herself, the ease with which she'd lied and the poise she'd had while doing it. She'd been rehearsing a cover story all the way up the mountain.

"Very true," he said, suddenly breaking into a smile. "However, I think maybe your time would be better spent this morning if you skipped."

"I'm sorry, what?"

"Skip your studying and your homework. Come hang out with me for a bit. I don't want to be too on the nose, but you don't really seem to have a ton of friends. I only mention that to say that every time I see you, you're either in Leabherlann or studying in some corner. I'm sure you'll do fine on midterms. What do you say?"

She didn't want to admit it, but she was getting butterflies. She actually wanted to hang out with Tarven, talk to him, laugh with him, not to mention she hadn't missed what he said about Leabherlann. Clearly, he was watching her closer than she thought. The last thing she needed was him getting suspicious and then going back to the school board. Even if they couldn't prove she'd been in the archives, she'd be in all kinds of trouble once they found out her icon had been muted for weeks. She knew what she had to do, for now.

"Um... sure," she said. "I'd love to."

She was being sincere. It turned out not to be that much of a sacrifice after all, though it was still against her better judgement. For a moment, she *did* wonder. Why was a guy like Tarven interested in a girl like her?

She shook her head as she followed him, forcing all

thoughts of her interest in Tarven from her mind. She had more important things to worry about than some stupid boy.

"Okay," he said. "I just need to pick up some things for my own studying and then we can go."

He led her through the halls and into the Academy. They went to the west-most wing and into the section of the Academy that housed the main offices for plant studies and hortological magic.

"So," Andie began, having decided to probe the waters. "You remember finding me down in the archives?"

"Staring at a door? Yep."

"Well, I was just wondering... what's actually down there? I mean, I read a couple of the plaques, but I was still kind of confused."

"It's nothing. Just another storage room. There's nothing down there except old books that aren't any good to anyone."

"How old?"

"What?"

"How old are those books? If they go back far enough they might have some interesting stuff in them. For my history class, I mean."

"Huh," he said, nonchalant. "Nah, nothing like that. Just old dusty books that need to be thrown out, is all. Nothing that hasn't already been replaced with new. You'll find the same books in the actual library."

They continued walking and Andie contemplated what he said. She knew it to be false, but she pretended to go along with it.

"Yeah, you're probably right."

"When I found you down there, you said something about voices, like there were other people down there, but that was impossible. The archive has a register for all visitors and there were no names on it that day."

"You remember the exact page from the register from that specific day weeks ago?"

"Yeah."

His voice had changed. He was on to her, just like she was on to him. She didn't know if he wanted her to stop prodding for her own sake or for his. He sighed a little and spoke gently again.

"You didn't hear anything, Andie. It was just your imagination."

He seemed so genuine that for a moment she wondered if she truly had imagined it all. Like Raesh and Carmen had said, she was under a lot of pressure that day and the archives did have a weird vibe to them. Could she be crazy? Maybe what her professor had been saying about the dragonborn was right: maybe there *was* something wrong with their blood.

That thought hurt her, though, that she was like them and they may have been a demented and terrible race. If it were true, it meant she had inherited a broken mind and her entire life was futile. Maybe she really was losing it.

When they reached the offices, Andie waited in one of the empty ones while Tarven got his things. While she was leaning against the wall, she noticed a cabinet with names. Out of simple curiosity, she leaned over to take a closer look and nearly fell over when she noticed her own name. She reached out to take the file and saw that her father's name was behind hers. Now totally obsessed, she snatched both folders from the cabinet and opened them.

"What the hell?" Her voice came out a whisper, but it echoed in the room all around her. Andie looked around the room to make sure no one had heard, and turned her attention back to the folders.

Inside was information about her father's accident, that mysterious and terrible thing that had crippled him and changed the course of their lives forever. As she read on and looked at the various photos of the aftermath, she began to notice that it wasn't adding up. What was in that folder didn't match what she'd been told while growing up. It didn't match anything she'd ever heard about what happened. If what was in the file was true, then it hadn't been an accident at all, and the University had a hand in it. There were pictures of men in suits and the designation under them read "Searchers."

It had been many years since she'd seen one, but she could never forget them. After all, they were the only ones in the entire region allowed to carry guns—the machines that fed off of their holder's magic. Guns were the most dangerous and feared things since dragons; not only were they powered by the holder's magic, they were also fueled by that person's rage and hate. What happened when the trigger was pulled depended on the power and evil of the shooter.

The file also had several names, some of whom Andie knew were prominent politicians and high ranking officials. There were also several mentions of Taline, Arvall's rival to the north, but in all the information, she still couldn't figure out what happened.

At that point, she heard Tarven coming and nearly

dropped the folders. She put all the papers and pictures back in order and only just managed to slip them back into their places in the cabinet when he appeared in the doorway.

"Come on, let's get lunch," he said. "There's no telling what you'll get up to if you're left alone."

CHAPTER TWELVE

DAYS PASSED. ANDIE HAD GROWN MORE ANXIOUS AND more frustrated. In all the days since she'd made up her mind to sneak into Leabherlann, she hadn't been able to discover anything. A group of professors were visiting the University for research and they had been in the archives from before the school opened to after it closed, giving her no opportunity to go back there. She'd had even less luck with getting back to the offices where the files were, because there was no good reason for her to even be in that wing. Her patience was wearing thin and her mind was wearing out.

That day she was hanging out with Raesh in the restaurant. It had been a while since they'd really had a chance to talk and he'd been different with her ever since he saw her with Tarven. Andie didn't like that he felt he had a right to judge, but in his defense, she had been spending a lot of time with Tarven lately.

"I'm glad you could find the time," Raesh said.

As jealous as she knew he was, there was no hint of

anger or contempt in his voice. He was honestly glad to see her.

"Me, too. I feel like things have been kind of weird with us lately. Which sucks because I miss hanging out with you and Carmen."

"Well, my cousin's a firecracker. Good luck getting her to stay anywhere. As for me… well, I'm sorry I've been avoiding you. I was being a world-class jerk, but I'm ready to make up for it if you can forgive me."

"There's nothing to forgive," Andie said, smiling. "Wait, does this mean you're going to be your usual overwhelmingly annoying and flirty self again?" She winked at him as she said it, obviously poking fun at him. Perhaps even flirting a little bit, herself.

"Undoubtedly."

They smiled and just like that the past few days were erased. Whatever he might feel about her or the company she kept, Raesh was proving to be a great friend.

"So, what have you been up to?" Andie asked.

"Helping out around the restaurant, going to the movies with Carmen, working out. The usual. And reading some really cool books, too."

"You read an unhealthy number of books. And they're huge. Regular people don't read that much."

"Regular people aren't smarter than most of their teachers. Magic is your power, books are mine. If you describe to me what it's like to cast a spell, I bet it'll be pretty close to what it's like to find a truly great book."

"That's really cool, Raesh. I never knew you were this passionate. You ever think of writing one?"

"I did. Two of them actually."

"You're kidding," she said, sitting up straight in disbelief. "Where are they?"

"Collecting dust in the attic. Maybe I'll get them published someday."

"You're kind of amazing right now. And here I thought you were just an incorrigible flirt."

"Only when I'm near a girl who's worth it."

He gave her that same warm look that had won her over the first night.

"Have I told you how stunning you look in yellow?"

"Easy, boy."

"Sorry. You're just kind of perfect," he said, without flair, as if it were the simplest truth of all.

"Thank you, Raesh," she said, resisting the urge to touch his hand. She could feel a blush creep up in her cheeks, and she turned away so that he couldn't see. The last thing she needed was Raesh thinking that she was interested. "Now, for the real reason we came. Help with my magic."

"Right. I'm ready. I closed down the restaurant a bit early so we'd have the place to ourselves."

They stood and walked to the middle of the room. Andie held up her palm and manipulated the icon the way Carmen had taught her. The golden light in the center of her palm dimmed. With a wave of her hand she pushed all the tables and chairs away from them. Raesh grabbed the student grimoire and began reading off the difficult spells Andie had marked for practice. She practiced them quickly and with a growing skill she was becoming proud of. She still needed some work on the fluidity of her movements, though. Her professor said she lacked the grace that came with total confidence, but she had improved at a steady rate and her dragon magic hadn't slipped in once since the morning she woke with the walls on fire.

She almost got Raesh once, while practicing an immobility charm. Luckily it was on his left leg and they both had a good laugh when he tumbled over. They were having fun and Andie was even flirting with him a little.

"You're kind of gorgeous when you go full sorceress," Raesh said.

"You're kind of hot when you fall flat on your face."

"Does that mean you like the view of me from behind?"

"Neither view is so bad."

After they'd finished, they sat down again. Andie was feeling more confident now that she and Raesh were back on good terms, and she wanted to tell him about the files she found in the offices. She waited until he wasn't distracted and explained everything that had happened, up until Tarven had come back into the room. When she finished telling him everything she'd seen and read, he needed a moment to process.

"Andie, my first instinct is to ask you how you were feeling that day. I mean, are you sure you saw what you think you saw? If you say that it's there, then I want to believe you, but that's a huge accusation. Are you sure you didn't misread it?"

"I remember it as clear as day. It was a file on me and one on my father. I didn't have time to look in mine, but I went through most of his. I know what I saw. And I was feeling fine that day. I was a little frustrated, sure, but I'm always a little frustrated. It doesn't mean I'm crazy."

"Of course not. I would never suggest that. But if what you say is true, then this is big. Maybe too big for us. I'm trying to make sense of it. The University having something to do with your father's accident? I can't even imagine what it would mean for-"

The bell on the door rang and Andie turned around to see Tarven.

"Oh, I completely forgot." She waved to him as he approached and she could hear Raesh huff behind her. But when she turned around he was at least trying to smile. He was a good friend.

"Hey," Tarven said to Andie, ignoring Raesh completely. "You ready to go?"

"Sure," she said, feeling uncomfortable to be literally and figuratively between them.

She stood and began to gather her things. She was having so much fun with Raesh, but she'd already made plans with Tarven and, somehow, she just felt she couldn't give up the opportunity.

"Alright, I'm all set," she said. "I don't think you've met my friend Raesh. He's really great."

She emphasized the "great" and winked at Raesh. His smile then could have lit the night. Tarven mumbled something which might have been a greeting or a curse and then he turned to leave. Andie gave Raesh a hug and left, trying not to notice the disappointment on his face.

AFTER SPENDING some time just hanging out together and chatting, they arrived at the University's Victory garden. Tarven was working on a special project that he wanted Andie's help with. They were working diligently, laughing and joking as they went along, when somehow the conversation managed to turn around to Andie's dad again. She became vague with her answers, even a bit defensive at one point, but the butterflies inside her kept her from getting outright angry with Tarven. Maybe he was just a curious guy. Maybe he just wanted to know her better.

"So, your dad must really miss you," he said.

"Yeah. I miss him, too. We were always together before I came here. It's like losing a piece of myself. But, luckily, I'm a little ahead in my work and I think I'll be able to go home for a visit soon. Anything you want me to ask him, since you seem so keen on knowing everything about him?" She asked playfully, trying to lighten the mood and let him know she wasn't upset. He seemed to understand.

"Ask him how he raised such an amazing young woman," he said, smiling at her so beautifully that she had to catch her breath. "And ask him about his time on the council. That must have been spectacular."

The last statement made Andie pause. She'd never told Tarven her dad was on Taline's council. She'd never told anyone.

"What did you say?" she asked. "How did you know my dad was on the council?"

"Huh? Oh, you told me, remember?"

"No," she said, dropping her tools and turning to face him. "I didn't. That's not something I would talk about with anybody, ever. How did you know?"

"You must have told me," he maintained, failing to meet her eyes. "Or it must have slipped out. Come on, we have to get this finished before-"

"Tarven, why aren't you looking at me? How did you know my dad was on the council? Who told you? What else do you know?"

"Look, Andie," he said, finally putting his tools

down, but still not facing her. "You got drunk that night at the bar, okay? You were spilling all of your secrets and this thing about your dad was one of them. I don't 'know' anything, alright? Only what you told me."

She just watched him for a moment. He couldn't look at her. It told her everything she needed to know.

"I'm feeling sick," she said, taking off her apron and tossing it aside.

She left without another word.

CHAPTER THIRTEEN

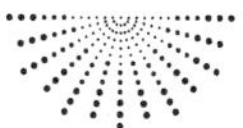

A COUPLE DAYS LATER, ANDIE HAD CALMED SOME. She'd talked things over with Marvo and decided that Tarven couldn't possibly be a spy. Marvo wouldn't let Andie know everything he knew about the University and the things it had set in motion over time, but he said as far as he knew they didn't operate like that anymore.

Andie spent some time away from Tarven, but somehow worked herself up to trusting him again, or at least wanting to trust him. If she was being honest with herself, she knew that she should stay away from him and that something wasn't right; she knew in her bones that Tarven knew more than he was letting on and that he was either up to something or knew someone who was, but she really liked him. And she believed that deep down he truly was the honest guy she thought she knew. She couldn't blame him for wanting to know more about her and her family. She was just as curious about him.

That day, she was sitting behind Carmen and Yara. When Andie registered for classes, she had decided to enroll in one class that was several stages ahead of a first-year course load. Luckily, Theory of Temporal Incantations had no prerequisites. So far, Andie had fallen somewhat behind, but the subject matter was finally starting to come together for her. Carmen and Yara were talking excitedly between themselves about the upcoming One Thousandth Winter Festival—it was actually the one thousandth and first festival, but the festival had been suspended the previous year due to concerns about an ancient curse that was supposed to manifest in the year 1,000. Of course, nothing happened, but it made for a good story. They chattered away while Professor Harrock proselytized about space-time meditation and inter-dimensional spell casting.

As it happened, Tarven had recently become Professor Harrock's teaching assistant and, at the moment, he was sitting in a corner, behind and to the left of the professor, distracting Andie with a staring contest. His eyes were almost talking, taunting, teasing her with their depth and attraction. They'd been at this game for nearly the entire class. He'd win, then she'd win, then he'd win again. They were having so much fun that they'd completely let reality and time slip away. That was especially dangerous for Andie, because she'd become so comfortable there, watching him, that she let her dragon magic slip out of her control.

She was so immersed in the moment that she was being consumed by the thought of Tarven. His eyes. His lips. The way he laughed and the way he turned in the sunlight. Her concealment spell had already begun fading before she noticed. By pure luck, she happened to look down at her arm and see that the hairs there were turning a light, but radiant purple. She sat up as straight as a beam and closed her eyes to focus on repressing the magic. After that, she turned her attention away from Tarven, sending him one last smile.

She tried to pay attention to Professor Harrock, but she had missed too much of the lecture and she had no idea what the "paradigm shift of the temporal grimoire anomaly" was. Carmen and Yara were still chatting away, so Andie leaned forward to talk with them.

"So, I've been eavesdropping and I'm kind of interested in this Winter Festival business," she said. "Want to fill me in?"

"OH, so you mean you're done ogling Tarven?"

Carmen never beat around the bush; she spoke her mind unflinchingly. Andie knew she was only kidding with her, but still there was something almost bitter about it, something strangely cold. Andie had been suspecting for a while now that Carmen resented her a little for not dating Raesh. Or maybe Carmen wanted Tarven. That was most likely the reason.

"Well, yeah," Andie said. "Sorry, couldn't help it."

"Don't apologize to me," Yara said. "That is one fantastic looking specimen. I'm kind of jealous actually."

"The world is full of great guys and I know you'll find one someday," Andie said. "Now, tell me about the festival."

"Well, it was supposed to have been held last year, but they thought a bunch of people were going to die and evil was going to rise, so on and so forth. Long story short, it's the festival's thousandth year and they're saying it's going to be the biggest celebration Noelle's ever seen. They want to make the millennial an occasion that will never be forgotten."

"Usually, they expect tens of thousands to come," Carmen said. "But this year they're expecting millions. It's going to be the most spectacular thing of our lives. Can you imagine even being alive for this? Hundreds of years from now they'll still be talking about this."

"Sounds exciting," Andie said.

"Have you never heard of the Winter Festival?"

"Sure. My dad always told me it was a really big deal in Arvall, but we never came because he said that people came in from all over Noelle and it could be potentially dangerous."

"Andie, take it from me," Carmen said, leaning in. "There is nothing like the Winter Festival anywhere in this region or even this hemisphere. It's primarily for the University and its students, but over the centuries the whole city began to take part. You have no idea what you're in for. Ball gowns, dancing, food, music, exhibitions of creatures brought from distant lands, magic you can't even imagine..."

Carmen trailed off as she noticed that Andie was once again flirting with Tarven. In her defense, Andie hadn't even noticed that she'd stopped listening.

"Andie. Andie!"

Andie snapped back into her body, her eyes landing on Carmen.

"Oh, I'm so sorry, Carmen, I didn't even know what was going on. That was rude of me."

"Are you going to go to the festival with him?"

Andie couldn't tell how Carmen meant the question: was it an accusation or a hint into her disappointment? Both? Andie became flustered and could feel her cheeks begin to burn as they reddened. Suddenly she was nervous.

"I don't see why not," she said. "If he wants to ask me."

She honestly didn't know if he did.

ANDIE CAUGHT SKY 6 on her way home after class.

She suddenly had a lot to think about, namely how her relationship—if she could even call it that—with Tarven was going to affect her relationship with her host family. Marvo, Raesh, and Carmen had been nothing but good to her and had helped her through some incredibly tough times. They were still helping her with the transition from Michaelson to Arvall City, and from taking care of her father to taking care of herself. She didn't want to seem uncaring and she didn't want them to think of her as someone who had toyed with Raesh's feelings. Though she was beginning to suspect that she had, inadvertently. What would happen if they thought she'd chosen Tarven over them? She didn't know what she would do without them.

Andie had tried to get Tarven to socialize with them, but he simply wouldn't deign to talk to Marvo and Raesh. He had no problems talking to Carmen, though, since she had magic in her blood, but he had no patience and no respect for nomags. Raesh had made an honest attempt to compromise and meet Tarven halfway, but it hadn't worked. Tarven's elitist priorities were ingrained in him. It was his greatest flaw that Andie resented, but she forced herself to see past it, through to the good in him.

Marvo was doing his very best to pretend that Tarven didn't bother him and he didn't mind having him around.

Carmen seemed too torn to make up her mind either way; she'd gotten by this far by simply avoiding the topic. But Raesh had been a complete sweetheart and a terrific friend. He seemed to understand that Andie, for whatever reason, had chosen Tarven and that he, Raesh, now had to do what any good friend should and be happy for her. And he was. Certainly, he didn't pretend to like Tarven and he'd stopped trying to greet him, but he stayed courteous through it all.

SKY 6 sped down the mountain as if furious with the world. Outside the window, the rain came in torrents. Sometime during the Fifth Cycle of the First Age the sky had changed. Some say it was because of the massive and horrific war that had spread over the earth, others say it was because of the sky being stained by the blood of the Cloud Mages as their species went extinct by the millions. Some say it was simply time. But since then, the lighting had turned green and more violent than at any other time in the history of the earth.

Arvall City was protected by powerful charms and incantations, but there were whole regions in Noelle that had been rendered uninhabitable because the lightning struck the earth with such ferocity and frequency. At the Hot Salts of Mithraldia, the lightning struck the earth some seven thousand times per hour when it rained. Now when a storm came, the world beneath flashed in green bursts of swift and violent light, like some great deity in the sky above had gone mad. Even the rain had changed over time, and if you looked closely you could see the hint of green in the drops. The spellglass had been transformed into a striated pattern with raised wavelike ridges in order to help the rain roll off easier. Andie watched the drops leaving the window almost as soon as they landed. Her mind drifted and she started thinking of her past.

THAT NIGHT they'd come to Michaelson to check for dragonborn descendants. There had been an attack in Taline earlier that day and the council of the city had contacted the University and asked for the Searchers. The Searchers were essentially just mercenaries, but no one questioned the University. By the time her parents finally got home from Taline, the Searchers were already pounding on the door and Andie was alone. Her mom and dad fought off the first wave of men valiantly; Andie could still remember their strength and power, the beautiful and mesmerizing way they used their magic to defend her. A beautiful and terrifying blend of dragon and sorcerer. Her family had run outside to escape, but they were caught in matrices, magical traps set up to stop magical beings from teleporting. The Searchers took her mom away and Andie never saw her again. They nearly killed her dad. They tried to erase their memory of her mother, but Andie's concealed dragon blood magic had protected their minds.

SOMETIMES, Andie wished her magic hadn't seeped out, hadn't protected all those memories of her mother. She could have grown up so much happier, so much more whole if she didn't always carry with her the terrible memories of that night. It definitely would have saved her father unimaginable pain and grief. So many things could have been different.

When she finally made it to the restaurant, she'd

managed to clear her head while walking through the city streets. She was ready to get to her daily tasks. Marvo and Raesh never stopped insisting that she didn't need to earn her keep, but she wouldn't hear of it. Besides, she knew they'd grown to like her company. She came in and said hi to them both, immediately getting to work. Raesh was cleaning tables and Andie worked on the floors, but she kept getting distracted. Raesh was joking with her about the way she mopped and she was trying her best to focus on what he was saying, but she couldn't stop thinking about the Winter Festival and what it would mean to be asked to it by Tarven.

"You know, mopping is supposed to have a sort of rhythm," he teased.

Andie made no reply, having not heard him because of her deep reverie.

"Well," Raesh continued, not to be daunted. "If you can't move a mop, you probably can't move your feet either. In my experience, a girl who can't find a rhythm in her daily life certainly isn't going to pick it up overnight for a dance."

"Yeah, probably will," Andie said. She had no idea what she was replying to or even what she was saying.

She'd been mopping the same small circle for nearly five minutes, and while she was clueless, Raesh had noticed. He had also guessed, correctly, that it was probably Tarven she was thinking about. But if she'd been paying attention, she would've seen the intense resolve on Raesh's face. He'd started and now he had to finish.

"And to think, I was going to ask you to the Winter

Festival," he said, finishing with a brave smile when he must have been terrified.

"Do you think Tarven will ask me to the Winter Festival? Should I ask him?"

She hadn't heard a single word he'd said.

"You know, why don't you call it a day," he said, his face looking crushed and angry. "I can manage the rest of this."

"Raesh, I'm not going to let you clean all of this on your own. Let me-"

"I said go, Andie!"

As soon as he said it his expression changed. He seemed surprised and even ashamed at himself for yelling. Still, with a last lingering look he turned his back on Andie and went into the kitchen. Andie was oblivious, having missed the entire conversation only to catch the ending rage. She leaned the mop against the wall and went up to her room, totally confused.

CHAPTER FOURTEEN

ANDIE WAS HARDLY IN HER BED FIVE MINUTES BEFORE she decided to go to Leabherlann. She made up her mind to study and engage in yet another futile search for texts on the dragonborn or anything relating to dragons at all.

When she reached the great library, Carmen was there. She was flirting—incredibly shamelessly—with Fohrn, the young green-eyed assistant who was filling in while Murakami was out sick. Fohrn was sweet and although he wasn't stupid, he was rather soft and could be persuaded to allow almost anything for the promise of friendship or romantic attention. He was the worst possible person for the job. Andie sat at a quiet table a few rows ahead of Carmen and waited, knowing Carmen would either see her or get tired of Fohrn and leave, having to pass Andie to do it. It didn't take long. Carmen seemed engrossed in whatever Fohrn was talking about, but she happened to look Andie's way and caught her eye. She excused herself and came over to Andie's table.

"So, I heard Tarven might be asking you to the dance," she said.

Andie opened her mouth to reply, but then closed it. Things with Tarven were constantly up and down, but lately they'd been relatively good. The only problem was Raesh, who, first, had feelings that couldn't be ignored, second, was a really good friend and had made every effort to be happy for Andie and get to know Tarven, and third, was Carmen's cousin. When Carmen asked Andie why she was so upset, Andie told her all of this and about what had happened at the restaurant.

"He was just so angry," Andie finished.

"Andie," Carmen began, touching her hand. "I know you care about Raesh and I know he's your best friend, but I don't think you really appreciate how he feels."

"Carmen, I know Raesh likes me, bu—"

"Raesh loves you. He's in love with you, Andie. All that flirting and nonchalance he puts on is just an act, and it's not even a good one anymore. You're a gifted sorceress, brilliant even, and you have a way and a rapport with magic that I can't begin to fathom, but you're not so good at small details. You don't notice things. Like how Raesh shifted his entire weekly schedule just so he could be with you when you work. Or how he follows you in the mornings to make sure you make it to the train safely. You don't even know that most of the time he's the one who cooks your food, not Uncle Marvo. Did you know that when we first met I didn't even like you?"

"What? Why not?"

"It doesn't matter. What matters is that it was Raesh who made me promise to stick with you. He wanted me to teach you, protect you. He's what brought us together. He's been working in the background of your life since you first got into Arvall."

And without any delay or deliberation, Andie began to understand. Truly understand. She was starting to see Raesh for the first time and it was no wonder he'd been so mad. How could she have been so blind for so long? His reaction had been so intense because his feelings were. And, strangest of all, Andie wasn't sorry he felt that way.

"That being said, nothing excuses his temper," Carmen said, regaining her composure. "Knowing Raesh, he'll be waiting for you to come back so he can apologize. It might do you some good to apologize, too."

Andie mumbled something, but didn't put up much resistance to the idea. They both knew Carmen was right. Raesh would eventually have to accept the way things were, but other than acknowledging Raesh's feelings in her own mind, Andie hadn't done much in the way of protecting him. She sat with Carmen for as long as she could stand, until the guilt became too much and she had to go.

She got up, claiming she was going to look for some books, but really, she just wanted to message Raesh from somewhere private. Even though Carmen wouldn't have been able to know what Andie was sending, it still felt weird to have someone else's eyes on her while she dealt with Raesh. "Dealt with" because there was simply no other way to put it without verbose circumvention. She found a quiet, empty corner and sat on the oak and lamb armchair, her back against the warm, smooth surface.

Raesh... It's been weird with us lately. Not my intention. Still a chance for us?

"Great," she mumbled to herself. "Now I've become those people who can't even be bothered to make full sentences. City life does not suit me."

A chance? he responded.

She knocked her head against the high back of the armchair. She'd used the wrong language. She'd led him on again. She took a breath and tried again, wondering when she'd finally break the cycle, finally allow Raesh to have just a modicum of respect.

To be real friends. She wrote. *REAL friends. I know me being with Tarven is hard for you. I'm sorry. Can you believe that?*

It seemed a terrifyingly long wait until he responded and Andie had nearly given up hope that he would.

Sure. To both. I'm trying as hard as I can to just be happy for you Andie. TOUGH. But you're worth having in my life. One way or another. If friends is the only option, I'll take it.

Me, too. Best friends. Want to come hang out at magic school?

Try to stop me. An hour good?

Great. See you soon.

Feeling perhaps a thousand times better, Andie got up and was off again to look for more books. Without even wasting time on the thought of checking the public areas, Andie headed straight for the archives on the lower levels. She skipped right down into the hallway leading to the archives, brimming with the excitement of mending her friendship with Raesh, when she saw Tarven and Professor Harrock standing in the entrance to the archives at the end of the hall. She hid in a small indentation of the wall that was barely as wide as she was.

Tarven and the professor were arguing in rough whispers, checking over their shoulders, and very nearly trembling with the force of whatever emotion was animating them. Andie tried her best to listen to them, but they were just far enough from her to be inaudible. She thought she might hear something about added security, maybe something about concealment spells, but just when their conversation was rising to a decipherable level, her phone buzzed. Knowing they'd be turning around to track the sound, Andie took off.

CHAPTER FIFTEEN

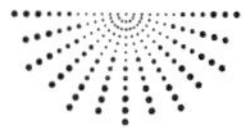

LATER THAT EVENING, RAESH MET ANDIE ON CAMPUS. They opted for a walk in front of the University's façade, the long side of the building facing the direction of Arvall.

"So, how's school been going?" Raesh asked, genuinely eager to mend ties. "I know you said your professor in your history class was a... what was it... dragon hating muckmouth?"

"I don't think I said 'muckmouth.'"

"You did. There's no way I'd make that up."

"Well, at least you know which class is my least favorite. I don't even know why the board is so upset with him. Everything he's saying falls right in line with Arvall's treatment of dragon and dragonborn history. All of Noelle's treatment. He literally hasn't said a single kind thing or mentioned even one useful contribution dragons made during their time. I can't believe they were all so bad. No race is perfect, but... I just won't believe it."

"Don't slap me, but do you think, even in the

smallest, darkest parts of yourself, that he might be right? That the whole world might be right?"

Andie hesitated, not wanting to admit the truth, but knowing her friendship with Raesh couldn't be built on things kept back from each other.

"Sometimes. But if that's true then... it would just be too horrible, wouldn't it? An entire race persecuted and killed because of the belief that they are evil. If there's even the slightest chance that we are wrong. That they weren't these awful, evil things, then their entire race's massacre has been covered by a lie. Does that not make you wonder?"

"I guess so. But Andie, it's in the past. There are no more dragons and probably no more dragonborn people in the world anymore. It's not really relevant, which is probably why the University is angry with your professor."

"Ugh. Enough about muckmouth..."

Raesh laughed. Andie tried to keep a straight face.

"... it's a shame you can't come in the University. Nomags aren't allowed inside, but I'd love to show you around."

Raesh stopped walking. He was looking down at his feet and even when Andie stopped and walked back to him, he still couldn't meet her eyes. Andie poked him playfully at first, but when he still wouldn't answer after several moments, she became worried. She grabbed him and shook him hard.

"Raesh!"

His eyes leapt up. He seemed surprised to find her holding him and himself holding her, too. His breathing seemed to be off.

"Andie, I haven't told you everything."

"What do you mean?"

"I mean I told you I was a nomag. And I was *born* a nomag, but something happened. When I was twelve, my mother died. On the day of her death she gave me something, a parting gift so that I could protect myself from the world."

"A gift?" Andie echoed, confused. "Like a protection spell or an idol?"

"Andie, have you ever heard of the Kyrian Bloom?"

"No."

"Queen Kyri was queen of Hightowyr many ages ago. Her reign was full of war, famine, misfortune, and ruin. The city nearly vanished under her watch. She was a good queen, wise and fair, but the times simply didn't favor her. Peace wasn't her destiny. Convinced that her life had brought only harm to the people she loved so much, Queen Kyri set in motion the circumstances of her own death. No one knows who helped her or who even saw it. So much has been lost to history. But the queen had a child. A daughter whom she loved undeniably. The daughter was born human, since the queen had married a human man, and the queen was scared for her. Queen Kyri created a spell, some say the most difficult and brilliant spell of all, that would allow her daughter to have magic. The spell needed so much spirit and power that the queen knew she could not survive it, but for her daughter, she did it anyway. She cast the spell, allowing the princess to have magic taken straight from the queen's blood. It worked. The queen died, but her daughter possessed her magic."

"Raesh, I think maybe you read too much," Andie laughed. "What does that have to do with you?"

"My mother did the same thing to me."

"Raesh, are you saying that-"

"I have magic. I'm a magical nomag, so to speak. A pearl-blood."

"What?" Andie asked, taking a few steps back. "I don't think I understand, Raesh. A magical nomag? Impossible. And what's a pearl-blood?"

"Have you ever seen a pearl? The way the colors on the surface of it are beautiful, but come in and out as you turn the pearl, dancing or skipping like a creek? Pearl-bloods can harness magic, but it's incredibly temperamental and even unstable. It's unreliable. Dangerous. It might lift a stone or it might lift a village, it's never consistent enough to tell, as we don't have the natural-born ability to control it."

Andie took a minute to let this in, a minute more to truly bask in the revelation. Could she have heard this right? Then she smiled.

"Raesh, you're a sorcerer," she said, throwing her arms around him. "This is incredible."

"Yeah," Raesh said hesitantly, warming to the excitement by watching Andie. "Yeah, I guess it is."

"It's amazing."

"Well, actually," Raesh paused. "Not a sorcerer. Not really. I wasn't born into the magic, so it's not really something I can go around flaunting, you know? It's not exactly viewed as favorable, if you know what I mean. The University would never let me in knowingly. They don't consider us to be true magic wielders."

Andie shook her head. "Incredible. I didn't even know such a thing existed. Magical nomags. I wouldn't believe it if I didn't already know you were incapable of lying…"

A red blush crept up on Raesh's cheeks as he ran his

hand through his hair. "Yeah. Incredible, I guess is the word."

"You're a jerk for lying to me, though," she said, punching him in the arm. "I've kind of been feeling sorry for you, for no reason at all, it turns out. I can't believe you didn't tell me, I can't believe Carmen didn't tell me!"

"She doesn't know. Nobody knows, not even my dad. Pearl magic is unpredictable Andie. I don't deny that my mother gave me a gift, but this is a hard thing."

"No one else knows? How have you managed to keep this a secret this whole time, Raesh?"

Raesh shrugged. "Self-preservation, I guess."

Okay. I get that. But how did she do it?"

"Well, she was dying anyway. She just wanted to keep watching over me. The Kyrian Bloom only works on a person who has no magic but direct magical ancestry through the mother or father."

"That's incredible, Raesh. It must be hard."

"There are worse things, I suppose."

"Yeah. Well, you say it's too bad I can't go to the University, but now you can see it's pretty complicated. But maybe I should show you."

He grabbed her hand and rushed toward the front doors. They entered the University and went down the long entrance hall. When they reached the heart of the mountain, Raesh took Andie down the hallway to the far left, the one Carmen had shown her, but avoided. Above them, the Mountain Faeries were moving slower, finishing their deliveries for the day and drifting up and off into the mountain in small droves. On and on Raesh went, pulling Andie along behind him, until they were suddenly in a very old part of the University. Judging by the size and shape of the buildings there, it was the old faculty dormitories from the school's first opening. It didn't seem as if it had been updated in centuries. No one seemed to even be cleaning it.

"Raesh," Andie gasped, when he finally stopped, "How do you know the University so well? I thought you'd never been here before?"

"That was lie number two. Sorry. I actually went here, a few years back. It wasn't for long, though."

"What? You were a student here. I don't…"

"Shh," Raesh interrupted her. "Keep your voice down."

"No one's here, Raesh. Your secret's safe with me." Andie put her arm around him and gave him a squeeze. "Why'd you leave? Were you afraid of what your magic could do? *Would* do?"

"That was definitely one of the reasons."

"What were the others?"

Raesh started to answer and then stopped. He just stood there, quietly looking at his shoes like he'd done outside. Then he grabbed her hand and was off again, this time leading her through the maze of abandoned buildings, around and across and through, back and seemingly down, down, down into the depths of the University. Andie found herself among gargantuan, stunning ruins, brittle and broken structures in every direction as far as her eye could see, like some great field of fallen things. They stumbled across the foundations of ancient buildings, hurried under arches that by then must have been friends of time, jumped over piles of jagged and glittering stones. Andie realized what it was. Hightowyr.

The world down there was ancient, fallen, and

forgotten. Dying, yet alive. A startling and mystifying contrast to the modern majesty of the skyscrapers of Arvall.

Out of nowhere, voices rang in around them and Raesh ducked down, pulling Andie with him. They were lucky because where they were, they were hidden on three sides with the open side facing away from the voices. Andie was nervous, knowing they probably weren't allowed back there. She took a chance and peeked around the top of the pile of rubble. She could see Tarven and some of his friends she met before. They were laughing and walking around as if they owned the world. They cast spells at each other as they went, having fun. Andie exhaled in relief.

"It's just Tarven," she said to Raesh. "Come on. We can come out."

But as she tried to rise, Raesh pulled her down again. She turned to him, shocked and a little angry.

"Be quiet," Raesh said.

Andie wanted to argue, but the look on Raesh's face frightened her a little, as if he knew something—*truly* knew something. She sat back down next to him, wondering if it was simple jealousy that was making Raesh act this way. She rolled her eyes in frustration, but when she looked at Raesh again, he had gone completely pale. Immediately, she went from irritated to concerned. Yet it wasn't long before Tarven and his friends were leaving and Raesh began to relax, regaining his color. When she was sure they were all gone, she helped Raesh to his feet and waited for an explanation. When it became clear that she wasn't going to get one, she started in.

"Raesh, what happened? What was wrong?"

"Nothing. I'm fine."

"Yeah, you're fine now. What about a couple of minutes ago?"

"I don't want to... you wouldn't understand."

"Raesh, you've told me a lot tonight and I appreciate it, I truly do. But you've given me even more questions and no answers. Now I've known you to not like Tarven, be critical of him, even jealous, but never scared."

"I wasn't scared."

"Raesh, I've never seen you like that before. Just be honest with me. I tell you everything, why can't you open up?" That last bit made her pause a moment, but she shook away her worry about not actually being truly honest with him. She was as honest as she could be, without outing her true heritage. If anyone understood Raesh's explanation of self-preservation, it was Andie.

"Some things are too much, Andie."

He watched her, probably trying to figure out what questions she would ask next and how he could deflect them. He seemed much calmer and now it was Andie who was going pale. It had shaken her to her bones to see Raesh like that. Raesh, who was always so strong and so true. Raesh, who was honest, direct, and fearless.

What had happened between him and Tarven? He hadn't seemed afraid the last time he saw Tarven, and Andie couldn't think of anything about where they were that could be to blame. Was it Tarven's friends? It couldn't have been, because Raesh had seen them that night at the bar. Had something happened in the time since? Andie instinctively held her head at her temples, unnerved. Raesh simply watched and waited like a dog outside of a window, like he knew Andie could come to the right conclusion by herself.

Some moments passed. Andie decided not to press the issue. Honestly, she was afraid to know.

CHAPTER SIXTEEN

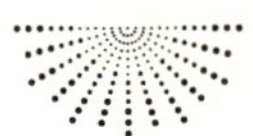

Raesh turned and continued leading Andie down through the ruins, only this time he didn't bother taking her hand. Something had just changed between them and even if neither of them could admit it out loud, they both knew it inside. Farther and farther they went, the mystical light above them beginning to dim some. Soon they came to a gargantuan tunnel entrance, and, though there did seem to be some light inside, it was significantly darker than where they were coming from.

Andie still couldn't believe that she'd had no idea this place even existed. All these months she had been going to this school and exploring with both Carmen and Tarven, and she had never even come close to these spaces. She wondered how Raesh could possibly know all this. He clearly knew more about the University than she did. And what was even more obvious—and what was doubtless to blame for this growing rift between them—was that he was hiding something and whatever it was must have been enormous.

Once inside the tunnel, Andie realized that it was

actually a corridor, a grand corridor fashioned in the style of the earliest of ancient architecture. The corridor must have been at least as old as Hightowyr. It was dusty, dark, and the air wasn't quite clear; Andie had a sneaking suspicion that it was probably damp down there. They went a bit farther before Raesh stopped and turned to her. He smiled, seemingly not sure if it would work so soon after the episode, but Andie found herself smiling in return. It wasn't that she wanted to, but it was as if some impulse in her relationship to him had overridden her new mistrust of him.

"Look around you," Raesh said.

Andie turned and looked up at the walls of the corridor. She could see now that the walls weren't blank, and, in fact, there were colors there. The colors were incredibly old, to be sure—flaking, faded, with whole sections missing where the stone had fallen out of the foundation—but still there. She peered hard through the dimness, but couldn't make out whatever it was the walls were depicting. She raised her hand.

"*Solas*," she whispered, waving her fingers as she did so.

Instantly, the light around them was amplified and the corridor went from bleak outline to golden lit majesty. Andie could see now that the colors were massive murals. Hundreds upon hundreds of murals running the long, long length of the walls and the ceiling. Now that the light had improved, Andie could see that there was not just one corridor, but many. They were standing next to the entrance to another corridor, as grand and abandoned as that one. She could see multiple other entrances down the corridor. There must have been miles of them down there.

"I know I should have shown this to you before," Raesh said, looking everywhere except at Andie. "But I just didn't know how. And I hoped that maybe you'd find the information you were after in some other place. Some other way. This was just so... gruesome. I didn't want this to be the only source you had for your questions and your research. You deserve better, Andie."

Just as she was beginning to wonder what Raesh was talking about, she finally began to fully comprehend what it was she was seeing. The murals were beautiful, masterfully crafted, but they were violent and, in some instances, even grotesque. They depicted blood, carnage, murder, magic, and mayhem. It was the dragons and the dragonborn. It was their slaughter.

Their blood was the intermittent flash of burgundy among the characters, their heads the oblong shapes at the foot of certain helmeted figures. And the so-called pure sorcerers and sorceresses were present as well, clothed in gold and surrounded by iridescent rays of power as they towered over the fragile, dying bodies of the dragonborn. It was meant to show the glory and might of "pure" magic, but all Andie could see was unadulterated hate and a totally one-sided history. In some sections, the dragonborn were placed in vertical lines, with small branches of people shooting out in wider and wider reaches as the lines went down; it was trying to convey the systematic extermination of the descendants of the dragonborn. Genocide. There are men being impaled. One woman with blue hair and eyes tied to a post and burned alive. Children being thrown into snake pits. Andie was so shocked that she was almost choking on her terror. She'd had no idea just how involved in the purge the University had been.

"Some time ago, I don't exactly know when, the council of Arvall intervened to keep the politics against the dragonborn more neutral," Raesh began. "Or at least, that was what they told everyone. There have been rumors and whispers that they still conduct raids, even today. Whenever they hear of a dragonborn or think there may be an incidence of dragon magic, they swarm. They say that the only reason they've never been caught is because the Searchers are taught a special variant of the obliviating spell. Whole communities wiped clean of any knowledge the University was ever there or ever murdered and erased a loved one, a neighbor, a friend."

Raesh paused and looked over at Andie, likely waiting for a reaction, but she was still taking in all of the horrible stories on the wall, all the destruction. The ruined lives. Tears began falling from her eyes. Raesh continued.

"I don't know. Maybe the rumors are just rumors. Maybe the University stopped all that a long time ago. Maybe I'm paranoid. All I know is that I couldn't stand to be associated with this University or with anyone or anything that could do something so terrible. Unstable magic or not, I had to get out, Andie. I felt like I couldn't breathe in this place, like I was the one who'd done all those things and hurt all those people. I don't even remember what I was doing down here when I found these," he said, indicating the murals. "But when I saw these walls, these crimes against everything good... it was my last day as a student here. They butchered an entire race."

"Two races," Andie said, barely above a whisper. "The dragons and the dragonborn."

She turned to Raesh, tears running down her cheeks as fresh as the new hurt breaking open inside her.

"I had no idea you were such an... that you felt so strongly about it," she said.

"How could I not? I can never forget these corridors. This pain that they smeared across the walls as some sort of celebration."

Andie then became conflicted. Here was a boy who'd become her best friend, who cared for her in so many ways on so many levels. He had been there for her every day, had made her laugh, had helped her practice her magic, had introduced her to Carmen, her other best friend. He'd brought her down here and shown her a whole new world. He'd even shared his darkest secret with her. And she wanted to do the same. She had longed for so many years to tell someone about herself, about who she was and what she could do. But Raesh was also proving how many secrets he'd kept. He'd kept his magic a secret. He'd kept these corridors from her when he knew how much she struggled to find even a hint of truth. He'd refused to tell her what had happened between him and Tarven and was probably doing so out of sheer jealousy. Yes, he'd shared a lot with her that day, but it had ultimately served to prove that she didn't really know who he was. She couldn't share anything with him, not yet, no matter how desperately she wanted to.

Not only that, but sharing her secret could put her life in danger. And her father's. Carmen. Marvo. Anyone she'd ever known and cared about. She couldn't do it. She'd have to keep waiting for that freedom, that paradise of a life when she wouldn't have to constantly emit magic just to hide her appearance every single hour of every single day. That time hadn't come yet.

Finally, she simply said, “Show me more.”

Raesh took her another five or ten minutes down the corridor and then they turned right onto a different one. This corridor was much more modern and of all the spaces they’d seen, this one had unquestionably had the most upkeep. In fact, it was so recent that it showed a beautiful and sprawling glass city. Arvall. The mural couldn’t possibly be too old and perhaps the entire area wasn’t as old and abandoned as she’d thought. The mural went on to show a large group of dragonborn descendants. Their faces were blurred and smudged, obviously done by the artist to ensure that even as abstract representations in an underground mural they would have no autonomy, no grace in defeat. The color of their hair varied, as did the color of the smudges of their eyes. They were being publicly executed, like the vilest criminals. She didn’t want to know, but she couldn’t help asking.

“How long ago was this?”

She knew her mother had been taken eighteen years ago. This mural looked recent enough to have been done around that time.

“The University only *agreed*—which I use skeptically—to stop the persecution about ten years ago. But the whole city knows it was only because they believed they’d already killed the last of the dragonborn.”

“I have to leave,” Andie said.

Andie turned to leave and before she knew it she was running. She was running as hard and as fast as she’d ever run in her life. She ran desperately, angrily. All those murals had brought back her mother’s disappearance in vivid and excruciating detail. It wasn’t as if Andie could ever forget, but seeing all that senseless murder and chaos, all that wanton bloodshed, had made that night appear before Andie's eyes as if it were happening again. Her parents fighting off the strangers. The guns. The matrices. The fear and confusion. The Searchers. Her mother being dragged away. Her father lying face down in the grass. The Searchers erasing her mother from every picture in the house. The screams. They'd never known for certain that it had been the University; the raids had always been merely rumors, unproven and unfounded. But now she knew. It was the University who'd kidnapped and probably killed her mother. This place she was in, that she came to every day, was responsible for the fact that Andie could never see or hold her mother again.

She found herself heading for Leabherlann, desperate to learn something, anything. There must be something in there. She swatted at low-flying Faeries as she raced through the halls.

Why did they kill all the descendants? What could the race possibly have done? Why were her people killed?

Raesh had yelled something at her as she began to run. It hadn't stuck at first and only then, with the distance between them and her blood pounding in her ears and her mind crystal clear from rage and pain, could she comprehend what he'd said.

"Stay out. This is a dangerous place."

CHAPTER SEVENTEEN

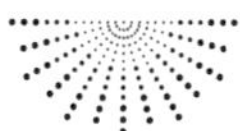

By the time she reached Leabherlann, Andie realized it was very late. Still, she couldn't go home then, not without at least checking a few rows for information. Some book somewhere inside that place had to have at least a partial history or tangential information about the persecution of the dragonborn descendants. All the professor ever taught in his tirades was that the dragons were tyrants and the dragonborn were evil, dark. That's all anybody ever said about them, and even that was rare because nobody really talked about them or what happened. Ever.

All she'd ever known of them was that they "must be destroyed." It had been drilled into her by everyone except her father. He'd always told her stories of warmth and compassion. He'd painted the dragons and dragonborn as kind, loyal, good. And while her mother was alive, she'd only ever given Andie love and safety. Her mother was pure dragonborn, could trace her ancestry all the way back to Gordric, one of the greatest dragons that ever roamed Noelle, and she had never, even for a moment, been cruel to Andie. Andie had grown up hearing one thing about the dragonborn, but her personal experience had been very different. And Andie certainly didn't feel evil herself. She needed to know more.

She slowed to a walk as she neared the giant doors of Leabherlann. At five steps, she glanced around her, making sure no one saw her coming. At four steps, she emitted a magenta wave of magic, concealing herself from sight. At three steps, she cast a charm to eradicate all sound—her breathing, footfalls, even her ponytail swinging against her back. At two steps, she sped up her central nervous system so that if she did find a book, she'd be able to read and comprehend it in a matter of moments. At the final step, she cast one last incantation.

"*Spiorad.*"

She passed straight through the wood of the door like a soundless ghost. Inside, she moved like nothing, like time itself, through and around the few students trying to get in their last-minute studying. Soundless, swift, and unseen. She moved straight for the archives, that old enemy that refused to share its secrets-if it even had any-hope that tonight of all nights would be different. As she approached the entrance, she found herself in the exact spot where she'd heard the voices before.

The feel of the place was different, thicker. There was something magical about the space now and it made Andie uneasy. She lifted her hand and let it rest in the air for several moments, just feeling the energy and the weight of the atmosphere. Then her eyes snapped open. Security spells. Her first instinct was to wonder if after all this time, someone had finally started paying attention, finally started noticing the goings-on of the dank and dusty archives.

She could try to enter anyway; after all, she recognized that she was an incredibly powerful sorceress. She'd excelled in her studies so far and she'd been studying spells for years. Her only problem had been control. However, she decided against it because if she tried to enter and overestimated her ability, there would be no going back. Her life and her father's would be over in an instant.

One good thing came out of that now barred entrance. Andie knew, without a doubt, that there was something important in the archives. Something worth hiding. Something maybe even worth killing for. She couldn't be sure if those precautions had been taken against her specifically, but she knew that there was something back there and that, come sorrow or destruction, she would find it.

She journeyed up and over to the restricted section of the main area of Leabherlann, flipping through the old books just as something to do. Book after book after book, just as she had done a hundred times or more over the last few months. And, of course, she found nothing. Absolutely nothing. She threw the book into a corner and held her head, uncertain if she would explode from the sheer weight of her frustration. But then an idea came to her, one she should have had months ago.

She whipped around to make sure she was alone. Once certain of that, she closed her eyes and opened her palms toward the ceiling; she released herself, her magic, the dragon essence inside of her and it seeped out into Leabherlann like a million waves of violet light. The magic passed through shelves, slipped between books, moved to levels above and below her. She hadn't meant for it to go so far, but only a dragonborn would have been able to see it anyway. And it felt good. Unbelievably good. It wasn't often that she had an opportunity to release that side of herself, to truly give in to everything that she was and, even then, she wasn't realizing the full potential of her might.

Still, the magic felt like life surging in her bones and power running through her blood. Soon, the seepage began to pool in a corner not far from where she was standing. She turned to follow it, her eyes still closed, simply moving her feet to the direction from which the magic called. When she reached the corner, she opened her eyes.

The magic had worked flawlessly. In her Soul Matter and Para-Corporeal Explorations class, they'd covered variants of astral projection stemming from the earliest Cycles of the new Age. Needless to say, Andie had excelled in that section of study. She'd sent out part of her spirit to search for books on her kind, the dragonborn, and it had worked.

She stood there—half relishing long-awaited success and half cursing herself for not thinking of it sooner—looking down on a small heap of aged and dusty books. They looked practically discarded and had been thrown there quite some time ago, with no apparent concern for how they landed. She grabbed all of them and placed them in her bag; she didn't even check their titles, as her instinct told her they'd be of some use. Her magic may have been beyond her control, but it was never wrong.

She made it back to the main level of the Leabherlann and found the most secluded table in sight. She laid the books out in front of her. Seven dusty and average looking volumes, probably as old as Leabherlann itself. She began flipping through the pages hungrily, madly, her increased central nervous response allowing her to consume the words on the page at a superhuman rate. But it wasn't just reading that she could do better; the spell had improved all her senses and just then she heard him. Tarven. Judging from the sound, she figured he was just entering the library, whispering excitedly with someone, roughly three hundred yards from where she was sitting. She stopped reading and started listening.

"What are we supposed to do now?" Tarven asked.

"There is no 'we,' not yet. Not until you've proven yourself."

"What have you asked me to do that I haven't done? I've been to hell and back for you people and still you all treat me like some kind of child or outsider."

"I'm sorry, are those labels not applicable to you?"

"I understand that there's a plan in place and I even understand how small my role in it is. All I'm asking is for the potential to grow in the organization. Give me a chance to give you the proof you need. I won't fail you."

"It would seem you already have. Do you understand what's happening? Do you have any idea how close certain people are to our secrets? You've taken your eye from the target and it's nearly cost us the fruition of a plan that's been in play since before you were born, boy. At this very moment, amendments are being made because you left this organization open to assault. And you think you've earned a place at the table? You want to be involved in the conversations of big, scary men when you can't even clean your own mess. Hear me now, Tarven Stirmliir, you have failed on such a monumental scale that it's a wonder I haven't been ordered to permanently remove you from the equation. But be certain of this: should you continue to fail, should you fall short of our expectations, we will rain down a wrath upon you that will burn even your ancestors in their graves. You now walk the thinnest of lines and, speaking for the entire organization, I sincerely hope you fall. I savor the thought of your demise."

Andie heard them stop moving. Even at over a hundred yards, she could hear Tarven's heartbeat increasing. She could hear his skin tightening as he made fists of his hands. She grew tense. What was Tarven involved in? Who was the other voice? What kind of trouble was Tarven in? How great was the danger? Would she lose him? Could she help him? Whoever Tarven was with started walking again. Tarven waited a moment and then he started walking, too.

"As it is," the mysterious man continued, "You're uniquely placed to solve the problem you've allowed to develop. This will be your last chance. Will you rise to the occasion or will you fall too deep to recover?"

"We won't need to have this conversation again," Tarven said.

"That's not what I asked you."

"Yes. I'll rise."

Andie grabbed the books and then hid under the table. She cursed herself for waiting so long; even though most of the lights had been turned off already, she shouldn't have waited so long to conceal herself. It was stupid and arrogant, and she'd very nearly been caught. She continued listening as Tarven and the mysterious figure passed where she'd been sitting. The way she was hiding under the table prevented her from getting a look at the man's face, but his voice sounded familiar. Maybe. The two of them continued forward without a word and then went down to the archives. Andie stopped being able to hear them and she guessed it was due to whatever magical charms had been placed on the entrance to protect it.

She spread her books out on the table again, now worried about Tarven and the people he seemed to be in bed with. And for the first time since she'd taken off running, she thought back on Raesh in the ruins. It had not been a truly successful day. Yet, all she could do at that point was try to read through the material she'd found for the truth about her ancestry.

She made it pretty far before the day caught up with her and she was unable to keep her eyes open or her head up.

CHAPTER EIGHTEEN

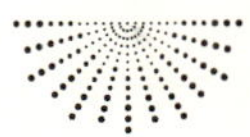

The spell has already been cast and as she stands there, high upon the mountain top with her people covering the cliffs and precipices around her, she knows there is no turning back. She and her people are standing still, stoic against the wind and the beating wings of their impending doom. She does not know how high they are; too high to see the ground and yet surely it must be somewhere below them. Grass. Land. Safety. Up here on the mountain they have no space to run, no place to hide, no safety or shelter to hope for. All they can do is wait for the purple storm of the incantation to wash over them, kill them where they stand.

They can see it in the distance—purple, as wide as the horizon and as tall as the space between earth and sky. The spell. They don't know who cast it, or maybe they do and it just doesn't matter because they know that there is nothing in their power they can do to stop it. On and on it rolls, closer by the second, as loud as the cries of a million dying souls. It is like fire and ice and wind and silence and roar and death and beauty and all the seasons of the year. It is stunning, in its own deadly way. They are all there, on that impossibly large mountain, staring at the thing they know is coming to kill them.

Silently, yet collectively, they wonder who could be so powerful. Who could have the might and the sheer hatred to cast such a spell? Such an irreversible and destructive spell? There are many millions of them there upon the mountain, gazing out across the vast expanse of nothing before them as the violet storm of the future rolls in to raze them. As it nears them, it begins to change color and where the space between the earth and sky had once been purple, it is now a dark, ominous gray. It is a gray that must've come straight from the grave, straight from all the worst of failure and suffering. Nobody will say it. Nobody will even dare to think it. But they all know, they all feel it somewhere within themselves and somewhere in the spaces between them. If the spell reaches them, their entire race will be wiped out.

The people—every soul upon the mountain—begin to panic. Before, there was silence, a kind of peace about them as if they had some time in the past decided on grace in defeat. But now, they are louder than the storm of the spell itself, screaming, crying, wanting to flee or even dive off the mountainside. They know they're all going to die.

Saeryn, who is the only one to have remained quiet amidst the pandemonium, looks at the storm in full, not flinching or even blinking. She has decided. If this is her last day, her final hour, she will not spend it in tears. She will not give over to fear or break herself with suffering. There is no fate that could find her that could steal her poise, her strength. "It is only death" she thinks to herself.

She takes a deep breath and prepares to make a final effort to save her people. She will try to call for help. She stretches out her arms to both sides of herself, reaching for the magic, all of it, all the power and spirit of her doomed race. She knows that if she can pull enough magic to herself, she can send a distress signal of sorts, though it is hard work with her people so afraid, so disoriented. Their magic is fueled in part by their emotion, which makes it stronger, but it is also fueled by their concentration, and that seems to be a difficult task for them right now. And who could be calm watching their own death approach?

She senses her bones and her blood filling with magic, brimming with the ability of her entire race. She lifts her head and opens her mouth, allowing a light brighter than anything on earth to fly up and out into the sky and beyond. A plea for mercy, aid, and protection. If no one answers...

"Help!" she screams, releasing the sound as a further emission of light racing toward the cosmos.

"Perhaps it is too late" she thinks as she looks out across her people, terrified and screaming themselves hoarse. She quiets her spirit, calms her mind. "I will not lose my peace today" she thinks, "Even if I lose my life." There is something strong about her then, some new and brilliant felicity charging through her bones. The behemoth spell looms nearer.

"If there is a single willing force in all creation, help us now."

ANDIE WOKE to find a hand on her shoulder. Someone

had shaken her awake. The first thing she saw was the library floor, much closer than it should have been. She must've fallen asleep and slipped from her chair. She wondered why the fall didn't wake her. She'd known she was tired, but not enough to fall asleep and knock her head on the floor without even stirring. Just as she was thinking of falling, her head and hip began to ache. She touched her throbbing temple but the hand came away without blood. Her hip felt like it had a bent nail in it. She rubbed her head and tried to regain her sense of self, her presence of mind. It wasn't until she tried to calm herself that she noticed she was panting and terrified. The dream she'd had was half remembered; it was like her mind had been invaded by a heavy and unrelenting fog.

"Bad dream?"

Andie turned her eyes up. The hand belonged to Yara, who was smiling down at Andie in the way people smile when they want to comfort someone. Behind Yara was Professor Harrock and a group of students and staff all staring down at her. She hadn't even realized that many people were still in the library. So many eyes looking at her, wondering about her condition and probably her sanity.

"Why are all these people here?" Andie asked Yara, trying her best not to sound rude.

"I don't think they really had a choice," Yara said, looking at Andie even harder. "We all came running when we heard you."

"What? What are you talking about?"

"You called for help, Andie. You screamed for it. I heard you seventeen floors up. It made my blood run cold the way you screamed. It's like you thought you were dying. Was it just a dream? Do you need help?"

Andie was confused. How could she have been screaming? And now she saw the true expression on every face: they thought she was some kind of helpless thing, some child who had no other recourse to action than to scream for help. They gawked at her like some kind of specimen in a jar.

"I'm sorry. I don't know what happened," Andie said, shaking her head as if to illustrate her bafflement. "I don't remember any dream."

"But you're not hurt?" Yara asked.

"No. No, I don't think so."

"Well, in that case," Yara said, her expression suddenly turning amused, "I think we can send all the would-be heroes away. Alright everyone, calamity evaded. Go home, go back, go away."

The crowd dispersed, though not without some parting glances at Andie. Yara turned back and reached her hands out to Andie. She helped pull her to her feet and then hugged her.

"Sorry," she said. "You just looked like you needed it. But if nothing else, you've given me one heck of an anecdote for the holidays."

"Thanks for getting rid of everyone. I hope I didn't scare you too bad."

"No worries. It's good for me to practice my heart attacks and nervous breakdowns. That way they won't take me by surprise in thirty years."

Andie was laughing before she could stop herself. Yara was always good for that. She realized her books were scattered all over the floor and she and Yara bent down to pick them up. It was a moment before she remembered that she was reading restricted books; perhaps Yara could be trusted, but some of the spectators had yet to leave and some had even come back for a last hopeful look. She gathered the books as quickly as possible.

Thankfully, Yara didn't seem to have paid attention. However, the librarian hadn't left yet and she was peering down at Andie's bag incredibly hard as if she knew something or had intentions of finding out. Murakami had made it back to work. Andie met her eyes and tried to stare her down, but Murakami wasn't so easily fought off and it was Andie who looked away first.

"Andie, your arm!" Yara said, her expression one of total shock.

Andie looked down to find the hairs on her arm had changed color to a light purple. Even her veins under her skin, though difficult to see, had returned to their natural purple state. Andie quickly jerked her sleeves down to cover the evidence and could only pray that her eyes and hair hadn't changed, too. There'd be no explanation for that. Yara continued to stare at her as if she'd never seen her before and Andie continued to stare back in utter fear. Could Yara be trusted? After all, didn't everyone hate the dragonborn? Andie looked around at the bystanders still hanging around. None of them had Yara's expression, but that didn't mean they hadn't seen. For all Andie knew, they were staring at her purple hair and byzantium eyes at that very moment.

"You, girl," Murakami said, slowly and with a dense suspicion in her voice. "You need medical attention."

"No. No, no, I'm fine."

"I see you, girl," Murakami said, advancing.

"Something is not right. You are... not as you should be. You need to see someone."

"I- I- I'm fine."

"Medical attention, girl."

Without waiting to finish the exchange, Andie turned to run. It was all she could think to do.

CHAPTER NINETEEN

Andie felt as if she were losing her mind. She'd somehow made it out of the University and had run all the way off campus before her legs gave out. Fortunately, there was no one else at the train station, only a few staff members. She could hardly breathe, and it wasn't just from the desperate sprint she'd made without stopping. It was the fear.

The world around her was an undulating blur, the buildings and signs and trees melting into a giant, unsteady mirage driven by her pounding heart. Her mind was hardly a mind at all, torn in too many directions and trying to regain control over a body that clearly couldn't resist the panic welling inside. Her eyes were either swimming or darting back and forth, trying to focus on something, anything. Her hands were trembling as if they'd been set to vibrate and her stomach was doing something very odd.

She felt not merely empty, but as if something had been drained from her chest, her blood, her very spirit. The fear was overwhelming, blinding. She'd been afraid before; in the nineteen years of her life she'd been scared many times, but only once before had she ever been scared like this. The night her mother was taken.

That was the last time Andie had to truly fear what she was, who she was by blood. The night the Searchers came and took her mother, Andie was terrified that they would take her, too, because she was a dragonborn. Dragon magic flowed in her veins. She was an outcast, a pariah, unwanted. That was the last time the world had ever come close to discovering the truth. And she would not have been able to deny it; how could she run from her own ancestry, her genetics?

Being in Leabherlann—not knowing how much of her magic had failed or for how long, with so many eyes watching her, and the look on Yara's face—was like being six years old again, kneeling in the grass while her house burned and her mother was taken from her. The world was peeking behind the curtain again, searching for her.

On top of that, she'd had a momentous afternoon. Learning Raesh had magic, learning he had so many other secrets, learning the true extent of the slaughter, the confirmation of the University's iniquity, Tarven's life-threatening danger, finally finding books, the poorly remembered dream that somehow still managed to haunt her, her magic failing. It had simply been too much.

When SKY 6 finally arrived, she shakily climbed aboard. Something about the staged gravity calmed her stomach, but not her mind. She'd never seen Yara look like that before, not even when she first woke up screaming on the floor. Or had she? Her mind was so clouded, so baffled by circumstance that she was beginning to forget what she remembered. Maybe Yara hadn't been looking at her at all or maybe it wasn't Andie's hair she'd seen. But what could it have been? Murakami didn't seem phased, but the words that came out of her mouth had shaken Andie to her core. What had happened? Had anybody seen what she was reading? What had she been screaming while she dreamed? What did she dream?

As her eyes struggled, she turned to gaze out of the window. She finally began to focus on the sight of the mountain, enormous and jagged, sliding away into the night as the train slithered down its side. She'd never realized what incredible speed the train had. If she listened closely, she could hear the low whistle of the wind being cut. The view calmed her some. Some of the weight was lifted from her shoulders as she watched the city of Arvall rise toward her with all its lights and glass monsters. From a perpendicular angle the city looked like a beautiful, convoluted starry night, planets and galaxy crashing together in a tumult of light, innovation, and time.

When the train reached the city, Andie thought of taking a cab home, but decided to walk. She was flustered and scared, and she needed to clear her head. She'd calmed some on the train, but she'd been so full of emotion that settling down merely a little wasn't enough. At last she decided that if someone had seen her true appearance and reported it, she'd just have to deal with it. There was nothing she could do about it now. Instead, she turned her attention to the dream. She seemed to remember a high point. A cliff, maybe. And a large cloud or mist. There seemed to be a woman. A woman with a mission. Andie worked hard to put the pieces together because she was starting to suspect that her dreams were something more. She wanted to figure out what they meant and what puzzle they fit together to make.

Nearing the apartment, she suddenly realized that she might not have the chance to be alone if she went inside. Raesh had no doubt told Carmen all about the day and of course Marvo would want to sit and chat. Andie just didn't have the stomach for company just then. Even more, for all she knew Yara had called Carmen about the episode in the library and everyone inside was waiting to comfort Andie the moment she came home. Raesh would be waiting.

Not ready to see anyone she knew, especially those who cared about her, she ducked into a tavern on the way home, hoping for privacy and a place to read. She'd passed the place every day on her way home from the Academy and it seemed perpetually empty or scarce—perfect for her needs. It looked rather ominous at first glance. No windows, black paint, crossed axes on a thick, heavy door.

The tavern was dimly lit and sunken into the lower level of what seemed a fairly old building. The outside was painted with salt paint and it was hard to tell what it was made of, but from the inside she could see it was stone. She was confident no one would find her there, in a small, bleak tavern located in the narrowest bend of a winding road. On the rare occasions she was out with friends, they always stopped at bright and open bars with nice views and dance floors. No one would be looking for her there.

She walked in, careful to avoid what looked like an unnaturally large glob of spit, and was met with the smell of grindleward—a nasty and addictive herb that was bought and sold on the black market. Grindleward usually meant you were probably among the worst possible crowd. There were also Glycerinnds, mountain pirates that also indicated horrible company.

"'Ave a drink teeny lass, if 'at be what you're a wantin'."

Andie turned to face the voice and found that she was being spoken to from behind the bar. The man could only be described as a wrinkled sack, with eyes as blue and as sad as Gordric's Pain, the famous fjord.

"Yes. Thank you," she said.

Before she could say what she wanted, the barman pulled down a glass the size of her head and filled it with beer as red as blood. She hesitantly accepted and then moved to an empty table near the fire. She pulled out her books, sipped her ridiculously large beer, which turned out to be delicious, and set to work reading again. All the spells she'd cast had worn off while she was sleeping, but now she had time to read at her own pace.

Not long after she'd settled in, the barman came over with a plate of food. It looked as if it could feed her entire Extinct Beasts of the Northern Lands class.

"Ask me, ye look right close to faintin' or tearin' asunder. I'll 've no expirin' of such a base thang as 'unger in this 'ere tav'rn."

"I'm actually... Thank you very much," she said, deciding against a further lecture.

But he wasn't listening. His eyes were going over the books she had so carelessly spread over the table. Her hands leapt up, but she put them back in her lap; it was too late to cover them then.

"Curious about the dragonborn, are ye?"

"It's... It's just research. For school."

"Then why be ye sweatin' 'n shakin' like a demon's got ahold of ye?"

She stared at him, totally lost as to what to say. Finally, he nodded and began to move away. Then he turned back.

"Ye best take care who sees ye wi' those," he said, his warmth replaced by a chilling gravity. "It ain't never been safe to look into such things. 'specially not in the last thousand years. This 'ere is a city what sees everythin'. Ye can't be so naïve as to think ye can get away wi' it."

He turned and left, but what he'd said had given her pause. Of course, he was right and she was being stupid. She'd never even been in this place before, had no idea who might frequent the establishment. But who was the barman? What did he know of the dragonborn? What she'd learned from the books so far was harrowing. It turned out that the seven books were journals; she'd only made it through three so far, but they were the journals of the families of the seven men and women who began Arvall's birth and commissioned the University. They told of the hatred and bloodlust the families held for the dragons and for the dragonborn. There were very few dragons left in Noelle by their time, but they hated them unrelentingly. The journals told the tale of how the families set about spreading that hatred across Noelle and once they succeeded, they assembled an army of sorcerers and sorceresses that numbered in the hundreds of thousands; all across Noelle the dragons were hunted and slaughtered, their vital organs sold for crates of gold and other various parts of their bodies preserved for use in powerful spells. From its earliest beginnings, the University had been a poisonous institution.

As the final dragons were murdered senselessly, the seven leading families of the newly established Arvall city used their influence to turn the evil against the dragonborn. They feared retaliation for the slaughter of the dragons, which the dragonborn had fought to protect, and they also feared that the blood of the dragonborn might hold the secrets to bringing the dragons back. The second slaughter was even worse than the first. It took at least a hundred strong sorcerers to kill a dragon, but only one stealthy man to kill a dragonborn. They were decimated in every way imaginable. The journals told of the streets literally running with blood. And with every death, the University grew in power and stature, its black marble hiding horrors galore.

Andie continued reading the journals, feeling sick more often than not. The barman visited her often, asking if she wanted more food, more beer, or more logs in the fire. He was kind, but she wasn't in the mood for company. Then he came and stood for a moment until she was forced to look up at him.

"Ye be in the University, and by the looks of ye, first year at the 'cademy. Tell me, ole Harrock still strutin' about wi' his theories of magic across time?"

Andie's face expressed her shock. He chuckled.

"Don't look so worried, dearie. I taught 'ere once. In another lifetime. They still holdin' 'at wretched winter ball?"

She couldn't help herself. She laughed.

"It *is* a pretty ridiculous tradition. All that dancing and formality," she said, trying to quiet the voice inside of her still wondering if Tarven was going to ask her.

In the hours that followed, Andie read avariciously, asking the barman questions whenever something didn't make sense. He formally introduced himself as Lymir. He was extremely knowledgeable about the dragonborn, about history in general, but he was always careful to speak softly, even after all the guests had left. It was nearly midnight when she finally came across what she was looking for. She turned the page of the fourth journal and gasped.

It showed an ancient portal, somewhere deep in the recesses of the University.

CHAPTER TWENTY

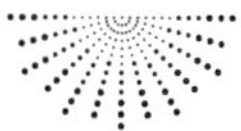

For a moment, she was breathless. For months, she had been searching for information on perhaps a hundred different things and of the few subjects she actually thought she had a chance of locating, the portal was nowhere near the top. This was a hope beyond hope. Instinctively, her head leapt up and she looked around her, lest someone should be looking over her shoulder or peering over from the counter. The bar was totally empty and Lymir had gone in the back to do whatever closing tasks he needed done. She was alone. She gazed back down into the pages in front of her, still not fully believing she'd found it. She felt like smiling, but not much of her body was moving at the time.

"What a day," she managed out loud.

Her search for the portal had been a complicated one; originally, it wasn't even part of her mission. Roughly a month before, she'd still been wholly obsessed with all things dragon—including the dragonborn, dragon magic, the great slaughter, the spread of anti-dragon sentiment across Noelle, and even Amanna Deireadh, the mythical end of days event when the remnants of the dragonborn discovered the means to restore the dragons and wreak hellish revenge.

She'd tried everything: sneaking into restricted sections, asking professors, attempting to get into the archives, and even antique bookstores, which is where her father found *From Dragons to Men*. She'd had absolutely no luck and that was including the use of virtually every ounce of her considerable magical prowess. Then one day, during her failed research she remembered something. It was some legend she faintly recalled from childhood: a portal. Since then she'd been trying to find information on that as well, but she could barely even remember the legend.

When she finally returned to the present and her seat in the bar, it seemed several minutes had passed, but she couldn't be sure. She turned back to the page and began reading. The journal described a series of portals, most lost to history, that magically connected realms through time. The founding families had used the one portal they could find and control. It was how they'd acquired so much knowledge when they'd been cut off from the rest of civilization for all those years.

The writer of the journal, Jacobi of House Clio, wrote of how they'd studied the entire history of Shaeyara from its birth. They'd gone back as far as three Life Ages of the Earth and seen a world of pure darkness and void, a time when life was fleeting and hard and perilous. It mentioned that they'd made one—and only one—voyage to the future, but it did not say what they saw there, only that it affected them greatly and caused them to vow to never look forward again.

Jacobi wrote that the portal eventually proved

dangerous when some members found they could use the portal as more than simply a looking glass. Their better senses prevailed and the unanimous decision was the portal should be magically sealed and remain so for all time. Apparently, many battles had been fought in a bloody war for the power of the portal; that war soon destroyed the portal.

At the bottom of the page, several blank lines after Jacobi finishes telling of the war, she wrote a single statement.

It is believed by all that the portal of Scáthán Ama was destroyed in that great and wasteful war of avarice, and perhaps it is so—but I believe this doorway may still exist.

As if he knew she was thinking about him, Lymir emerged from the back of the room and traveled around the bar, coming out to stand just near the table. He was still wiping one of his giant beer glasses and smiling like he was rather self-satisfied. She held up Jacobi's drawing of the portal.

"Lymir, do you know anything about this portal? Have you ever heard of it before?"

"'At be the portal of Scáthán Ama," he said, the color draining from his face. "A most wicked thing 'at is. All the legends be of grand times 'n gold 'n terrific adventures through history 'n space, but 'at ain't the whole story. Not by a half."

Lymir looked genuinely perturbed. Andie almost regretted asking as she watched the drawing's effect on Lymir. He obviously knew something, had maybe even experienced something. She had a moment of hesitation, but she had to know.

"Lymir, please," she said.

"When I be much younger, younger than you now, girl, I was a student at the University. In them days we knew what was underneath the mountain. They even let students go down to look at it. We'd write out our lessons in the shadow of the thing. Wasn't supposed to be no hanging 'round under it, but there was never anyone 'round to enforce 'at rule. We'd spend whole afternoons down 'ere wi' it. Then one day, three of the boys what was down 'ere wi' us decided to go up to touch it. Understand, 'at was somethin' we never dared afore. Soon as they laid their fingers on it, the bloody thing lit up like a star breakin' free and took the three boys. 'N it sucked all the air from the room, too. What of us was left almost suffocated to death.

"It turned out 'at it had happened afore. The bloody University had covered it up. Didn't want anyone deciding to skip this school because 'ere was a deadly... thing in the basement. A bunch of boys and girls had been sucked up over the years. Magic seal or no, the blasted thing couldn't be touched. Of course, the parents put up such a fuss 'at the University 'ad to either close down or put the thing somewhere else."

"I see they're still open," Andie said.

"And how."

For a moment, he simply stared down at the drawing, clearly reliving the sight of seeing those boys sucked up.

"Aye, it was sealed up. But don't believe everything you read. I don't trust them at that school. You seem like a curious girl, dearie," he said, looking down at Andie as if she were some fragile thing he'd been charged to protect. “You be careful not to mettle. People ‘ave been hurt for far less things than what you’re lookin’ into. Don’t pry.”

He said the last part with a point and wave of his finger that was so emphatic she inadvertently promised out loud. Though from the look on his face, they both knew she couldn’t be expected to keep her word.

After Lymir had returned to cleaning up, casting the occasional glare of suspicion, Andie read a little while longer and managed to finish her cranium-sized beer. Her dragon blood gave her a naturally high tolerance level, but that didn’t stop her eyes from beginning to roll in their sockets.

She stared into the fire, trying to focus. She began to remember bits and pieces of her dream, possibly from the alcohol. There was screaming. And the woman at the precipice was calling for help. She thought she could feel her magic growing stronger in her veins, which she quickly chalked up to the gargantuan beer. It suddenly occurred to her that the portal might have something to do with her dreams. It didn’t make sense, of course, but she couldn’t shake the feeling. It might have something to do with the room in the back of the archives, too. Her dreams had intensified ever since she heard the voices through the door.

Then she just knew. It was the portal that was behind the door.

Some minutes after her epiphany, Andie was finally ready to go home. She began packing up the journals and picking over the plate Lymir had brought her, as there was still over half of the enormous helping left. Just as she was slinging her bag over her shoulder and getting ready to say goodbye to Lymir, the door opened. It was

Tarven. It was hard to tell who was more surprised to see him: her or Lymir.

"What are you doing here?" she asked, trying not to think of the conversation she'd overheard in Leabherlann.

"I saw you come in and I just wanted to know if it was okay if I joined you for a drink."

"Tarven, I've been in here for hours. Have you been standing outside this whole time?"

"Well, practically," he said.

She got the distinct impression he was lying, which bothered her. If he hadn't followed her, then how had he found her there? But he smiled that impossible smile of his and she was won over. He moved to sit down, but then he caught Lymir's eye. She had no way to describe the look they shared, it seemed one of ominous recognition.

"Why don't we grab a drink somewhere else?"

Andie looked over at Lymir, who pretended not to notice and kept wiping glasses.

"Okay. Sure," Andie said, suspicious in spite of herself.

On the way out, she looked back at Lymir and that time he was ready for her. He moved one of his worn fingers slowly to his mouth, a silent plea for Andie to keep her secrets to herself.

CHAPTER TWENTY-ONE

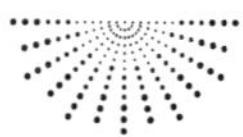

As they were leaving the tavern, Andie was considering Tarven. Not only was he caught up in something that sounded beyond dangerous, he was clearly not very good at whatever his job was supposed to be carrying out. His position, his very existence, was on the line. Then of course there was the business with Raesh and whatever Tarven or his friends, or Tarven *and* his friends, had done to frighten him so deeply to his core.

These things in connection with the many things Tarven knew that he wasn't supposed to know was beginning to wear on Andie, and not merely wear on her, but wear her down. How could she trust him knowing everything she knew? He'd had a full day with her and hadn't even known it.

"You know, it's later than I thought," she said. "A lot later. I'm actually pretty tired."

To give authenticity to the charade, Andie looked at her phone to check the time. Her eyes bulged. It was almost four in the morning. As if they were merely waiting for an acknowledgement of the time and their limit, her eyes got so heavy she bent her head.

"Oh," Tarven said, clearly searching for something persuasive to say. "You... come on, you're in the Academy now. Live a little."

"How original," she responded.

She was as unimpressed as she sounded, though she meant to sound more joking. She tried to make up for it.

"I mean, what are we going to do at this time of the night anyway? And, just out of curiosity, how did you find me?"

"I told you, I saw you go into that tavern."

"No, you didn't."

Tarven stopped in his tracks. He stood there, looking at the ground, and breathing irregularly. She'd caught him lying again and he knew it.

"There's no way you followed me from the University," Andie continued. "So, unless you just happened to be in the neighborhood and happened to walk into that tavern and happened to see me and decided to lie, you must've had some device or something that helped you find me. So, how did you do it?"

She'd decided to get the truth out of him and was doing it before she'd even really thought about. She hoped going on instinct could work twice in one day, but she was also conscious of the two-way street of suspicion. The last thing she needed was to arouse his suspicion by over-saturating him with her own, especially considering the mystery and danger surrounding whoever it was he was working for. That fear grew in her mind as she waited for Tarven to respond.

Finally, he said, almost sheepishly, "Let me walk you home."

Torn amongst fear, uncertainty, suspicion, and the growing desire for self-preservation born out of the ubiquitous cautions to mind her business, Andie caved. "Coward," she thought to herself.

They walked on, quietly at first, but then they began to chat about trivial things. Somewhere between Avenue 664 and Maith Root, Tarven showed surprising dexterity and slipped his hand in hers almost without her knowing. Contrary to her better judgement, she allowed herself to forget about the secrets surrounding him—well, not forget, exactly.

There was no way she could forget the cloud of deceit Tarven moved in, but she couldn't help how much she liked him. There were times, like that very moment, when he was near perfect. Sweet, charming, handsome, and all-consuming. She definitely had mixed feelings, but she was aware now of something much stronger than that beneath. She didn't know if he had a way with women or a way with her, but it was a fantastic way. Sometimes it seemed surreal that he should be giving her so much attention, that he should be so interested in her. He could have anyone in the entire school—she was pretty sure he was aware of this—and maybe even all of Arvall.

"So, what happened to you in the library?" he asked. "That was some screaming fit."

She had to think for a moment. She couldn't say that she'd seen him in Leabherlann, as she had hid when he passed her. But she also knew that he was supposed to have work that time of the evening. He should have been in a completely different wing of the University. Or maybe he'd been lying all along. Or maybe someone just called him with the news. Who knew?

"I just had a bad dream," she said. "A really, really bad dream. And on top of that, I've been feeling a little overworked lately. Just a bad combination."

"Want to talk about it?"

The honest concern in his voice only further warmed her to him.

"Not really. Maybe some other time. I think the best thing to do might be to drop a class to lighten the stress."

"But you were doing so well."

"Yeah, but it's been really tough. The Academy's been a lot harder than I expected. What about you? How's your hortological work in the gardens? All about understanding the life of the plant, right?"

"And I am struggling to understand and to not strangle the life from said plants."

She laughed and he smiled at her. That smile.

"Actually, I could use some more of your help out there."

"Funny you should ask. I'm actually eager to get back there and practice my magic. With you."

Half an hour and a tremendous amount of flirting later, they arrived at Marvo's restaurant. As if on Cue, Raesh appeared in the window and of all the things in the street for him to look at his eyes went straight to her and Tarven. Noting this, Andie tried to wrap things up with Tarven quickly.

"Okay, so I'll-"

Before she could finish, Tarven pulled her into a kiss. Her immediate instinct was to resist, for Raesh's sake, but, much to her own personal chagrin, she mildly swooned in his arms. Her hesitation and inhibitions swept away, she kissed him back with everything she had. She would try to describe it in words to herself later, but there were none. It was perfect.

"Come to the Winter Festival with me," he said.

The look in his eyes was the one Andie imagined in the eyes of every man risking his pride for something, someone, he truly wants. He seemed so beyond genuine, as though he not just wanted her there, he needed her there.

"Yes. Of course, I'll go with you."

Simultaneously, she was convincing herself that she had been insane to doubt him. Certainly, there were things about him that didn't make sense to her, but how could she cast doubt on him just because she didn't understand? After all, she was the one who was blatantly lying to everyone, every day. Right then she decided that he was kind, trustworthy.

Tarven turned and left.

Raesh was still standing in the window. Slack-jawed. Devastated.

Somehow, he seemed like a child there; it was like he was lost or thought he was lost. Maybe he was frozen there, stuck in his disbelief, or even paused by his own volition until his mind and his heart caught up to each other. Andie couldn't face him and yet couldn't quite turn away, leaving herself turned half away from him, looking back at his hurt expression almost over her shoulder. Neither of them was moving, like some agreement of shame and despair. She kept thinking to herself "That didn't happen. That didn't happen. That didn't happen." Yet the taste and the feel of Tarven's lips were still on her mouth.

Unconsciously, her hand rose to her mouth and felt

the skin there and it was almost like she was trying to confirm or deny it. Raesh still hadn't moved an inch and even when Marvo came up behind him, smiling and chattering away, he remained still as a statue. When Marvo found his son was unresponsive, he turned over his shoulder and called.

He still hadn't seen Andie in the street. As if the situation weren't bad enough, Carmen came hurrying over to check on her cousin. But she'd hardly made it to the window when she saw Andie outside, not ten yards from the glass. She simply pointed outside. Marvo turned his head and found Andie. His mouth threw questions at her, but she couldn't answer. She really couldn't. And then Carmen was anxiously pointing at something behind Andie.

The next thing Andie knew, she was on the ground. A car was speeding down Rholdan, its exhaust blowing vermillion as its crystals died from age and probably ill-keeping. Andie gazed around her and found no one. She realized she must have jumped aside by some survival instinct. When she looked back at the restaurant, she had just enough time to see Raesh storming away into the back, Carmen following close behind and obviously trying to get him to calm down. Marvo was hurrying out of the front of the store to come check on Andie, but she held her hand up to stop him.

"It's not right," she thought to herself. "He shouldn't have to come and check on me, not when his son needs him more. I can't believe that happened. I can't believe I let it. He'll never forgive me."

And of that last part she was almost certain. Raesh had a good heart, a pure heart, but everyone had their limits. And what would it mean for Carmen? Would she decide to take her cousin's side? Were there really sides? Was it coming to that? And if Carmen left, she was sure to take Yara and anybody else she'd introduced Andie to. Even Fohrn in the library. And Marvo. But she couldn't lose Marvo, too.

She picked herself up and walked right by Marvo, answering his multitude of questions with a curt guarantee of her wellbeing, never stopping her forward motion. And she never stopped moving until she reached her bed and then she collapsed into a breathing ball of shame and regret.

The moment was made even harder because she was so happy to have finally been invited to the festival by Tarven. So much joy and remorse, all at once. She thought of her dad, far away in Michaelson, who she knew was probably thinking of her, too. He would know what to say, and if he didn't he would hold her, kiss her cheek, and tell her something sweet beyond comprehension. She'd never wanted so much to be back home.

She waved her hand above her and cast a silence charm, blocking out everything in the world. The day had been impossibly long and she just wanted it to be over. She wanted to skip ahead to a time when things were okay again. She closed her eyes and tried to rest. It was nearly five o'clock. She had to get up and get ready in two hours.

CHAPTER TWENTY-TWO

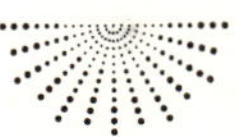

TWO WEEKS PASSED AND EVERY RELATIONSHIP IN Andie's life changed.

She hadn't spoken to Raesh since that night. She saw him constantly, of course, in the restaurant and around the building. She even saw him at most of her hangout spots because he was the one who had shown them to her in the first place. She continued to help Marvo out, but she did less and less and he stopped asking her to do some of the things she'd been doing for months.

Raesh seemed fundamentally different during those weeks; he still went out with his friends and still worked the same schedule at the restaurant, but even when he smiled there was something beneath it. Something that was maybe sad and maybe furious, but something that was, without a doubt, not Raesh. Yet he wasn't cold toward her. He certainly didn't put himself in a position to talk to her and he avoided her as often as possible, but when circumstance dictated he needed to interact with her he was as civil as imaginable. And that hurt her even more.

Whatever Raesh had or hadn't told Marvo, nothing much seemed to have changed. Marvo did what he could to keep them working in different areas or different schedules—after all, he wasn't an idiot—but outside of that he didn't treat Andie any differently. He spoke to her more often, if anything, and gentler, as if he'd thought it over and decided that she needed him more than his own son. More likely, however, was that Marvo and Raesh had had at least some minor conversations about Raesh's feelings for Andie and Marvo had decided to play mediator. He was a good man.

Carmen was more difficult; since that night her signals had been all over the place and Andie couldn't quite pin down what Carmen wanted or expected, how she truly felt. Andie never knew what side of Carmen she was going to get: it might be the same, playful Carmen Andie had grown close to, or it might be the sullen Carmen who seemed to prefer brooding and judgmental looks, or it might be an outright frustrated and dismissive Carmen, or it might be any one of ten other Carmens who presented themselves without reason or pattern.

It was clear that she was Andie's friend and equally as clear that she was Raesh's cousin. Andie accepted that Carmen had been placed in an impossible predicament and simply took her moods as they came, doing her best to let Carmen know that she understood the stunning difficulty of it all.

Andie's circle outside of Raesh, Marvo, and Carmen was small, but everyone else that she knew seemed to have taken sides. It was either Andie or Raesh. Most people chose Raesh, understandably. But Andie got to keep Yara and most of the students she'd met at the Academy, so things weren't so bad.

IT WAS the morning of the Winter Festival and Andie was in Victory among the twisting, draping, floating plants. She was helping Tarven with an experimental cross-pollination of fuil glas and anáil fuar; it was for the mirror room, for the festival. There was a total of twelve mirror rooms in the University, but for the one thousandth festival they were using the Grand Mirror Hall of Terpsichore, designed and named in honor of one of the seven founding families. The mirror rooms were made by ancient magic and their texture, dimensions, and design could be changed at will, like spellglass, but only by the board members. The mirror rooms could also appear as one thing to all or as an individual fantasy to each dance couple. There was nothing like the mirror rooms in all of Noelle. Andie and Tarven had been hard at work; after all, no one wanted to be the person responsible for ruining a thousand-year-old celebration.

Andie's magic had grown steadily stronger since she'd started at the Academy and a strange surge in power had come to her over the last two weeks. The dragonborn was most feared because their magic was so heavily influenced by their mood—a frightened dragonborn could struggle to take on one adversary, but a dragonborn filled with rage could stand against an army.

The University understood this and worked diligently to instill fear in the dragonborn before slaughtering them; just another reason why the massacre was so catastrophically horrible. But, Andie had been happy the last two weeks. Incredibly happy. Tarven seemed to have undergone a change. He was more open with her and he didn't always seem as if he were hiding something. They were growing closer every day.

"You know, you're showing a lot of promise out here," he said. "Maybe you could work at the University one day."

"Yeah. Yeah, that's actually exactly what I want to do," she teased. "Stare at roots all day and wonder if the stem will be half a centimeter longer in two weeks or three."

"Don't forget the joy of working with the Seile."

"Oh, how could I forget. Best part of my day."

They both laughed. Tarven knew Andie enjoyed working in the gardens as merely a hobby, but he teased her often. Seile was a classification for plants that could shoot poison or psychotropic saliva as projectile crystals. Once they hit their target, the crystals would sink under the skin and disperse. Strong or knowledgeable sorcerers could use magic to delay the effects until they received medical attention. Humans almost always died.

Andie had taken careful note of Tarven's change over the past fortnight. His whole demeanor had changed and now she felt comfortable with him. She could say that she trusted him with no qualms. It was as if he'd finally decided to put her first and transcend whatever other dark dealings he had. She was no fool, and she remembered everything that had happened, but who was she to judge when she had so many secrets of her own? And it was just that thinking that lead her to want to change herself. She was tired of lying and hiding, and if anyone was there for her to talk to and share with it was Tarven. She'd decided to tell him the truth. Still, true to her cautious nature, she wanted to start with something small, or as small as she could get with the life and death secrets she kept.

"Tarven," she said, cautiously, like a fish testing waters. "Have you ever heard of a portal?"

"Sure. You know, big, lots of light, bridges across time and space, totally nonexistent."

"No, I mean here, in the University. A portal that no one talks about."

Tarven stopped and turned to her. There was a moment.

"You mean the portal that no one talks about because there's no such thing as a portal in the University."

He broke into a smile and it was obvious that he'd been joking with her. She smirked, briefly. She couldn't tell if he was joking because he was covering or because he honestly didn't know. There was a chance he had no idea what she was talking about. He was so knowledgeable that Andie always assumed he knew everything, but he was a student himself, after all. Even with his mysterious connections there was no way he could know everything about everything. Still, Andie being Andie, she pushed anyway.

"No, Tarven. I'm talking about something real. I'm talking about the portal of Scáthán Ama."

Instantly, he stiffened. It was like some kind of coagulant had been poured in his veins. He tried to shrug it off, but she'd already seen it.

"It's a myth," he said, flat. "That thing no longer exists. It's been sealed for centuries and even before that it had been moved. No one knows where it is. And that's assuming it's real and the whole story isn't some hoax, which many experts say it is."

This went totally against everything Lymir had told Andie at the tavern. One of them wasn't telling the truth. The difference was that Lymir had absolutely no reason to lie to Andie. Tarven did.

"Tarven, I think you're lying," she said. "Actually, I'm pretty sure of it."

"What do you know, anyway?" he snapped. "Every time I turn around, you've got some new theory or question about things that don't even concern you! You have no idea how horrible it was when the portal was here. The fear. The disappearances. The least you could do is show some respect for the people who died getting sucked through that thing. What about the thousands and thousands who died in the wars? Do you have any sensitivity at all for those people? Their families? Their suffering? Can you even fathom the catastrophe?"

"I'm sorry," she said. "I won't ever bring it up again."

Tarven walked a small, frustrated circle. Breathing hard and holding his head. Andie regretted not showing more concern for all those who suffered at the hands of the portal.

"I understand if you don't want to go to the festival with me anymore," she said.

Tarven exhaled a long breath and then turned to her, took her in his arms and held her for a minute, silently forgiving her. Then he let her go and kissed her cheek. Then her lips. They returned to normal.

"Of course, I do," he said. "I wouldn't miss it for the world. I'm sorry I snapped, Andie. I've just always been... sympathetic to large groups of people suffering or dying when it's not their fault. That portal changed things for so many people. For all of Shaeyara. It just gets to me. But you didn't deserve that and there is no possible excuse."

"Even though you just tried to give me one?" she asked.

He looked at her and she broke into a smile. He smiled, too. She was happy.

"Well, as much fun as I'm having out here with you and the twenty-foot roses, I have to go to class," Andie said.

"So, I'll see you tonight?"

"You most certainly will. Have fun with your plants. And, seriously, the roses freak me out."

She kissed him once more and then turned to leave. Before she did, she noticed a small plant reaching toward Tarven. It was incredibly attractive and the whole thing was no bigger than the palm of her hand; it had a long, thin stem and only four petals in its bloom. The petals and bloom were the color of bronze, but the stem was as black as the night sky over an old field. Its petals were waving languidly, though there was no breeze, and it seemed to be trying extraordinarily hard to reach Tarven. Andie leaned toward it and discovered it was making tiny, barely audible sounds, almost like it was breathing.

"What's this one?" she asked, pointing. "It's so cute."

"That little guy is Decepticatus."

"It almost looks like it's trying to touch you. What does it do?"

"Believe it or not, I have no idea."

"Shocking," she said.

She waved again and walked away. She couldn't see it, but Tarven was watching her the whole time.

CHAPTER TWENTY-THREE

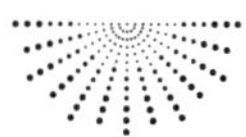

NOT FOOLED AT ALL BY TARVEN'S FAILED COVER-UP—and even less by his pathetic attempt to accuse her—Andie skipped class to try to investigate the portal room. She knew in her heart, beyond all doubt, that it was still in the University. And she knew where it was.

She made her way to Leabherlann, though with some difficulty. The entire University was alive with the preparations for the event. The school was also hosting some eleven thousand dignitaries, heads of state, relevant celebrities, and scholars, all of whom were being housed in a specially erected condominium placed in the mountainside above the University. The halls were bustling with people decorating or cleaning or giving tours to foreigners and important people. She was also seeing several strange creatures from the lands beyond Abhainn. They'd traveled a long way. Andie had to push her way through dense crowds.

She reached Leabherlann and even there she had to search for a quiet, secluded corner. She opened her bag and retrieved the enhancement items she'd bought the week before—she'd found them in a peculiar antique shop that Lymir had recommended. She turned each of them over, trying to decide what she would need going in and what she could save until later. Finally, she decided to put everything back except the craiceann, a gossamer magical veil in the androgynous shape of a human face.

Andie checked her surroundings once more and then lifted the craiceann to her face. She held it there. The light fabric began to cling to her face, and not merely cling but attach itself. It sealed itself to her skin around the edge of her hairline and then quickly began stretching, flowing down her neck, back, and chest, always clinging tight. At first it was as cold as ice, but as it finished covering her entirely, it began to warm to her body temperature. She took out a compact and checked her reflection. The craiceann had altered her appearance completely; it had even changed the shape and height of her body. She didn't look anything like herself.

She felt more confident with it on; at least now if something happened and she weakened or was distracted, her appearance wouldn't betray her. She was still careful around Yara. Nothing between them had been the same since that night in the library. Yara had been treating her differently and Andie couldn't tell if it was because Yara had seen her true self or because she'd found her screaming. The craiceann would ensure that didn't happen with anyone else.

Andie packed up her things and walked back to the center of Leabherlann to head in the direction of the archives. She passed some people she knew and decided to test the device.

"Hi, there," she said.

They looked up at her, right in the face, and didn't recognize her.

"Hi," Sheila said. "Have we met before?"

Andie grinned and left, now one hundred percent sure she was safe. "I should have tried this years ago," she thought.

Suddenly, incredible pain stabbed in her hand. She very nearly screamed out loud. Before she could recover from the shock of the first stab, another came. This time it lingered for a bit and she went down on one knee. The pain kept coming intermittently and she looked at her hand, turning it over furiously to try to find what was causing the pain. It nearly made her cry.

Then she saw it. The faint red glow in the center of her palm. The icon. In all the months she'd had it, it had always been a dim, pretty golden glow. Never once had it shone red. The longer she watched it the brighter it became and the more intense the pain became. Whatever magic the craiceann was using on her body, it was interfering with the icon, which was growing hot in the flesh of her hand. Ducking into an unoccupied aisle, Andie held her arm at the wrist, squeezing as hard as she could in an effort to close off the pain—the sensation was starting to shoot down her arm.

Once she was alone again, safely away from the eyes that had begun to watch her whimper in pain, Andie began an incantation. She had to stop the pain and she also had to try to stop the reaction of the icon, which would definitely send signals to the University, if it hadn't already. She recited the incantation for the pain; it dulled considerably, but her hand continued burning. It was clearly not going away completely as long as the craiceann and icon were acting on her body at the same time.

She cast another spell, one she'd learned from one of the founding family journals. It was designed to interrupt the ability of magical artifacts to emit magic at all. She said it quickly, not sure if she remembered the words or if it was too late. Just as the thought crossed her mind, she heard the doors of Leabherlann bang open. She ran to the end of the aisle, breathlessly scared.

"Andie Rogers!" a woman called.

Andie was rooted to the spot, no more able to move than she was able to change the course of events that had led her here.

"Andie Rogers!" the woman called again.

Andie thought the woman sounded genuinely concerned, which perhaps meant that the signal hadn't told them what was happening, only that something wasn't right. As the woman moved around a group of onlookers, Andie could see that she was small, but focused. The woman moved in an almost unnaturally straight line, coming straight down the center of Leabherlann in Andie's direction. And still Andie was frozen, terrified, wondering what she was supposed to do and how she could have been so stupid, so arrogant as to think she could fool an institution that had hundreds of years' worth of hunting and those it wanted destroyed. The woman—who had three men with her—kept coming, her short stride quick and her footfalls surprisingly heavy on the black marble.

Andie was seemingly paused, half leaning out from behind the bookcase, just watching the woman bear down on her. Her entire history was playing itself behind her eyes. Tarven. Raesh. Marvo and Carmen. Arvall.

Michaelson. Her father, who she hadn't called in far too long. She skipped going home to see him last week in order to be in the gardens with Tarven and there were no words to express how much she regretted that then, as the end of her world bore down on her. At last, after what seemed a thousand years and also a single second, the woman came to a stop in front of Andie. The look her eyes gave was one Andie would never forget.

"Excuse me," the woman said, in a voice that was as lyrical as it was authoritative, "Andie Rogers?"

Andie's mouth opened for speech, but no words would come. It was all over.

"Have you seen her?"

Andie simply stared. It was impossible.

"What?" Andie asked, totally confused.

"Have you seen Andie Rogers? Do you know her?"

Andie almost laughed out loud. The spell had worked, and the icon was no longer sending whatever magical signal it had sent out before. It had managed to send no more than her name and the fact that she was in Leabherlann. And the craiceann was doing its work as well; the woman was staring right in Andie's face and didn't know. Andie tried to bury the smirk.

"No ma'am, I don't know anyone by that name," she said, realizing her voice had also changed.

"Hm. Have you seen anyone in distress? Anyone who looked like they were hurt or needed help?"

"No. I'm sorry, I've just been looking for texts for my exams."

The woman nodded and moved on. Andie allowed herself mere moments to celebrate before moving on. If the pain in her arm were to flare again, it might not be something she could stop up so quickly. She hurried along, keeping a good distance between herself and the searching woman, and turned off into the archives.

At the entrance to the hallway, she paused. The craiceann was supposed to alter her appearance and hide her magic from virtually all defenses—at least the simple ones the University was likely to be using in a library—but she was still nervous. However, she had to admit that the magical device had already saved her life once and she had no reason to doubt it now. She took a single step across the threshold and found herself safely in the hallway.

She raced along the way, dashing past the peculiar and enticing volumes of history and study as she headed for the back room. All she could think of was the portal and the secrets it held. The secrets it could reveal. She reached the end of the path and turned the corner to find the door, just as she remembered it, just as she had seen it all those months ago. Without warning her head was filled; she'd almost forgotten how the voices overwhelmed her, how they weighed on her spirit and tore at her mind.

She kept walking, but the closer she got, the louder and wilder the voices became. She kept putting one foot in front of the other until she couldn't anymore. She moved her leg forward, but collapsed in a heap under the barrage of screams. She held her head, desperate to hold the screams in or perhaps keep them out, but they were so loud, so many. The voices were crying out for help. They were suffering. The voices in her head were more painful than the icon had been, and even her hand was growing hot again. She didn't know what to do.

She crawled the remaining feet to the door and placed her hands on it. It was warm from the sheer volume of magic on the other side. She suddenly pulled her hands away, bewildered. Sorcerer's magic, though powerful, is cold. It must feel normal to those without dragon blood, but to a dragonborn only dragon magic is warm. The magic on the other side of the door is warm. She put her hands back on the door and held them there. Soon enough she felt it: the dragon magic igniting in her blood. It swam through her, burning in her chest and stomach. The dragon magic in her grew stronger and stronger, and if it wasn't for the craiceann, she probably would have reverted to her natural appearance. She needed to break into that room. Instinct moved her. She closed her eyes.

"Who are you?" she asked. "What do you want?"

There was no answer.

She reached up to try the handle, but was thrown several feet back by the defensive magic. She knew then, that to get into the room she would need help. Just then she heard someone coming. She panicked. It took all of her strength to regain her feet, but as soon as she did, she ran.

As her feet moved, her mind planned. She would find help. She would get into that room. Not only to stop the voices and the dreams, but also to save something. Maybe her own life.

CHAPTER TWENTY-FOUR

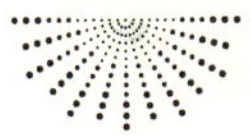

By that evening, Andie had discarded the craiceann and her icon had returned to its normal state. The searing pain vanished completely about an hour after Andie removed her disguise and she'd heard no more from the woman who was searching for her, though she knew she would have to face her sooner or later. She would need to remove the blocking spells Carmen had shown her; being searched for was suspicious enough.

She was at Carmen's apartment—Carmen lived in the Publishing District, twenty blocks away from Marvo's restaurant—getting ready for the first night of the festival. The first night is traditionally the night of dancing at the Founder's Ball, with the rest of the week, or month in this case, being designated for a plethora of other means of celebration. Yara was also there, strangely her old self. Andie assumed Yara had come to some decision within herself and as much as Andie wanted to know what it was, she decided not to press her luck.

Carmen was in a stellar mood and Andie was

incredibly grateful that that side of Carmen was the one that manifested that night. Carmen was laughing, teasing, fantasizing as if there were nothing more between them. Andie had a burning desire to ask how Raesh was; she knew that the night would be a hard one for him. It was hard for her, too. She couldn't pretend that Raesh wasn't important to her, even if she couldn't care for him the way he cared for her. But she buried all of that at the base of her mind, reveling in having Carmen and Yara as her friends again.

"I need to congratulate you again on this dress," Yara said, holding Andie's dress against her own body and spinning to bring out the true luminousness of the dress. "I can't believe your sense of style is this good."

"It's not," Carmen interjected. "I picked that. Should've worn it myself."

"And I hate both of you," Andie said with a smile, snatching the dress from Yara.

Carmen had taken Andie to the store, took one look at her figure, and chosen her dress in under five minutes. The dress was ankle-length, the color of a bronze sun. It flattered Andie in every way a dress should and complemented her hair. She thought to herself that it would probably look good with her natural hair color and her byzantium eyes, too, but that wasn't an option. Not yet.

"Let me be the first to say it," Yara said.

"First to say what?" Andie asked.

"How lucky you are. I'm not going to go weak in the knees when I say this, but Tarven is gorgeous."

"I second that," Carmen said, beginning to apply her foundation.

"I don't want to cross any lines here, but that boy

takes up half of my many, many fantasies. And of all the girls in the Academy, the University, and even Arvall, he chose you."

"You probably don't know this," Carmen began, "But most of the girls at the University are wishing they were you tonight. That or wishing they could rip your heart out, but either way is a pretty good omen, I'd say."

"I feel lucky," Andie said. "I almost feel like I'm in a dream. And if I am, I hope I won't wake up, not this week and hopefully not at all. I'm happy, really happy, for the first time in a long time and I have Tarven to thank for that. I nearly gave up waiting for him to ask."

"Trust me, the rest of us saw it coming," Yara said. "I may or may not have secretly tried to poison you, but, you know, bygones and all that."

The girls laughed and chatted excitedly about the night. Andie was anxious to see whether or not the attendees would like the cross-pollinated species she and Tarven had put up. Yara and Carmen were beside themselves about the full night of dancing.

"I'm surprised you two are so excited for this," Andie said. "I know it's the thousandth year, but haven't you been to this festival two or three times already?"

"Yes. And no," Yara said.

"We usually sneak off with our dates about a third of the way through," Carmen added. "It's really kind of stuffy with all the professors and faculty there. All these years and we've never actually danced at one of these things. We come, listen to the introductions and brief, mandatory history, drink the ale, watch the faculty members take the floor, and then we disappear into the night."

"Every time."

"What could be more interesting than the Winter Festival?" Andie asked, incredulous.

"Nothing," Yara said. "Absolutely nothing. Which is why we'll be staying this year."

"Probably," Carmen added with a sly smile.

Carmen and Yara continued talking, but Andie became silent. An idea had dawned in her mind and it only took a few short moments for her to begin to fixate on it. If all the professors, faculty, and students were celebrating in the mirror rooms and down in the city of Arvall itself, it would mean that Leabherlann would be empty. Totally empty. In fact, she'd already read the announcement saying that the library would be closed that evening due to the celebration.

As she stood there with her bronze dress draped over her arms, she knew without a doubt that she might never have that kind of opportunity again. Of course, the spells would still be in place, but there would be no eyes around. She'd have an entire night of uninterrupted time to get into the archives, open the door, and discover what the portal could tell her about herself and the world. And she had two potential accomplices standing right in front of her.

"I want you two to help me break into a place," she said.

"Sure," Carmen said immediately. "And right after, we'll assassinate in Taline."

"And resurrect the dragons and bring on Amanna Deireadh," Yara added joyously.

They laughed, playfully shoving Andie and returning to getting dressed.

"I'm serious," Andie said, as solemn as the grave. "I want to break into somewhere inside the University that's been sealed shut with powerful magic. If we're suspected, we get expelled. If we're caught, we probably get worse. I've tried to do it myself half a dozen times, but I need help. Two powerful sorceresses who I trust more than anyone else in the world could help me do this. If they had a mind to."

Carmen and Yara stared at Andie for a long time. When they were satisfied she was serious, they turned to each to share something only they understood—a sort of timid curiosity perhaps—and then looked away. A few tense moments passed while Andie stood waiting, her hands anxiously made into fists and her temples beginning to sweat. Had she made a mistake?

"I'm in," Carmen said, suddenly looking up from her feet. "If you need my help, of course I'm in. I'd do anything for you."

"Yeah. Count me in, too," Yara said. "You won't be off having illegal adventures without me. You're strong and brilliant, so whatever you're after must be critical. I'm there."

"Thank you," Andie said.

She wanted to say more, but couldn't. She was overwhelmed by her own gratitude. She looked up to see them smiling at her.

"What?" she asked.

"Nothing," Yara said, coyly. "It's just nice to see you break from the sweet, doe-eyed girl habit."

"Agreed," said Carmen, devilishly. "Mischievous looks good on you."

They all smiled and held hands. Andie knew then, beyond a shadow of a doubt, that no matter what differences of unvoiced things lay between them, these girls were her friends. Her best friends.

“I’m getting too excited,” Carmen said. “Sneaking around, getting past hooded monitors. It’s more fun than I thought I’d be having tonight.”

“We usually do this stuff pretty often to hook up with boys, or drink, or whatever else we decide to get into. But breaking into the University. Priceless.”

“Well, I’m glad you’re so eager,” Andie said, beginning to enjoy herself now. “But I should warn you, it could be dangerous. There’s already powerful magic in place and there’s bound to be more of it since everyone will be out celebrating.”

“Oh. Oh, well excuse me,” Carmen said.

“Good heavens!” said Yara. “Danger? Like real danger?”

“Perhaps we’ve been too hasty accepting, darling.”

“Yes, yes, quite so, how right you are.”

“We should back out now, if at all possible. Wouldn’t want to be implicated.”

“Oh, no, no, no, no, no. That simply wouldn’t do.”

“Thank goodness we’ve come to our senses, Yara.”

“Yes, Carmen, quite fortunate, indeed. We were very nearly made criminals.”

“The shame...”

“The sheer horror...”

“Terribly nasty business...”

“Unthinkable consequences...”

“Everlasting dishonor!”

“The infamous rogues of history!”

“Forever cast out and away!”

“Totally and irrevocably unwanted!”

“Okay, okay, I get it,” Andie said, laughing heartily. “I just thought you should know. No need to be so dramatic. I didn’t know you all cared this much.”

"We're your friends, haybale," Carmen said, leaning over to hug her.

The girls continued to chat about their plans while they finished getting dressed. Carmen handled everyone's makeup and Yara handled their hair. They asked Andie all sorts of questions about their new mission, but she was playing it close to the chest until they made it to the portal. She trusted them, but she didn't want to freak them out either. She hoped dearly that there wouldn't be anyone watching the portal, but the more she thought about it, the less likely it seemed.

The University was smart; they already knew that someone had been sneaking into the archives and trying to break into that room, and they would have foreseen that tonight, of all nights, would be the perfect opportunity for that person to try again-with an almost guaranteed chance of success. In addition, this *was* the portal of Scáthán Ama, the last extant portal in Noelle and perhaps the last one in the entire land of Shaeyara. Not only that, but the portal wasn't even supposed to still exist or be in the University. They couldn't afford to have that secret exposed.

Andie tried to stay calm. For better or worse, she was going to get into that room.

CHAPTER TWENTY-FIVE

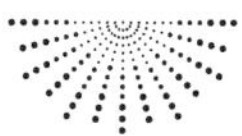

After another half hour, all three girls were ready. The trio was stunning: Andie in bronze, Carmen in red, and Yara in white. They mooned over each other for a few moments and then prepared to leave.

"You two go ahead," Andie said. "I need to do a couple things before the dance. I'll meet you there."

"Oh," Yara said, raising her eyebrows and turning from Andie to Carmen. "She needs to *do a couple things*."

"I'm sure," Carmen said. "Like Tarven. And Tarven. And a little more Tarven."

"Let's be on our way then."

The two girls moved to the door, leaving Andie blushing in the middle of the room. Yara left and Carmen was right behind her, but turned back around at the door.

"It's okay for you to have fun tonight, Andie," she said. "Everyone knows how much you care for Raesh. Even he knows it. It's a tough situation, but nobody thinks you meant to hurt him. I don't know if you two can ever be friends again, but he'll heal. In time. But tonight is about you and Tarven. Just be happy."

"Thank you, Carmen," Andie said. "I really needed to hear that. I was hoping someone would say that and I wanted it to be you. Thank you."

Carmen winked at her and disappeared. Andie waited a few minutes, until she was sure they'd had time to leave the building and make their way down the street, then she left. She hurried out of the elevator as the doors opened and in a matter of moments she was walking swiftly and determinedly toward her goal. It only took about fifteen minutes for her to reach it. Lymir's tavern.

She hadn't seen him for a while, having spent almost all of her time with Tarven, but after the conversations they'd had that night, she was sure he'd remember her. She needed to ask him a question; he was probably the only man in all of Arvall who she could trust with this and who might actually be able to answer it. The closer she got to the tavern the more careful she became, moving in shadows and searching every passing face, discreetly but carefully, to ensure her stealth. Luckily, almost everyone was in downtown, midtown, or the west side between the sea and mountain. The celebration had virtually taken over the city. Andie couldn't imagine how many millions of uncia it had cost.

She arrived at the tavern and entered to find it nearly empty, as usual. Lymir was standing behind the bar and as she neared him, he seemed dumbfounded and more than a little surprised.

"Surely, ye be the girl who was in here askin' all the hard questions a fortnight ago. But the lightin split me if ye aren't not a hundred times more beautiful even now.

Hearts'll be breakin' by the thousands just at the sight of ye."

Andie blushed, so hard her face began to sting.

"Thank you, Lymir."

"Don't thank me for tellin' things how they be. 'At dress suits you, girl. Its color and yours be bosom buddies."

Andie thanked him again, although for some reason she got the feeling that by "color" he hadn't meant brown hair and green eyes. But there was no way he could know that. Still, the man was truly a mystery.

"I'm sorry Lymir, I don't want to be rude or to rush you, but--"

"But time be of the essence. Ye need not explain to an old man. What's botherin' ye?"

"I know you've seen people get sucked up into the portal and leave this realm. But have you ever heard of anyone come through the portal *into* our world?"

Andie waited for his reply. Lymir seemed to be thinking hard, but Andie quickly gave up waiting; if someone had come through the portal into this realm there was no way it would be something anyone would forget. It wasn't exactly a common occurrence.

"I can't really remember, but to give ye an answer I'd say no. Not liable to be a thing even an old man would forget. Hard to tell, though. The stories 'ave been so many and so muddled, 'at they sort of blend together over time. All the same, just 'cause I never seen it doesn't mean it never happened. I'm just one man. And I'd bet my life it were more than possible. Why ye be askin' that?"

"No reason," she said, not even convincing herself.

"Girl," Lymir said, leaning toward her over the bar,

"What did I tell ye the last time ye came to me wi' questions and stories? Ye're playin a dangerous game wi' powerful folk, and trust me when I say they wouldn't lose a night's sleep after watchin' ye burn for 'at curiosity. There were a time when the lust for knowledge, secret or no, were counted as a skill to be proud of. But those days are far behind."

Andie only half heeded his warning. Her mind was on the voices behind the door and their connection to the portal. Whose voices were they? Were they hurt? Where were they; here, there, some strange realm between? If she could get to the portal and open it, what could she do to help them? Could she help them?

"Thanks, Lymir," she said, turning. "I'll come back to see you when I can. I promise it won't be another two weeks."

"Now just ye hold on a moment. Rushin' like the hessian was after ye..."

Andie turned back.

"I've got somethin' for ye. Just a minute."

Lymir disappeared into the back room, leaving Andie to wait. She walked back and sat at the bar. A rotund sorcerer with the mark on his cheek turned to her and grinned. He was missing half of his teeth and the remaining half were as gray as a cold morning. He slid his hand along the bar until it was almost touching Andie.

"You look like a good time," he said in a rich tenor.

"I probably am," she replied nonchalantly.

"Tonight's the festival. What do you say to a nice long romp with ole Trisoldan? There's things I could show a pretty little thing like you."

"Come closer," she said. "Whisper some of those things in my ear."

"Oh, I'll do more than whisper."

He only managed to lean over about six inches before Andie flicked her wrist. Trisoldan was thrown thirty- five feet across the length of the entire tavern. He collided with the back wall and went halfway through it before he came to a violent stop, stuck in the wall like a barbaric and grotesque decoration. Lymir walked back out to the bar, seemingly nonplussed.

"Well," he said, "I always knew someone would give it to 'im. Never thought a wee thing like ye would be the one. Nice work, girl."

"Sorry about the wall."

"Don't bother ye head 'bout it. I had a mind to remodel anyway. Time to class the place up a bit."

Andie smiled. She noticed he had something in his hand; it was small and glimmering. He held out his open palm to her and she saw that it was a bracelet.

"'At's white gold there. Can hardly find the stuff no more."

The bracelet was beautiful, slim, made of interwoven links shaped like leaves. No, not leaves. Scales. Like a dragon's scales. There was a small charm on the bracelet, also made of white gold, but in the shape of a sphere and on one side was an intricate stamp in the form of a dragon's head. It was incredibly subtle and would probably go unnoticed by most. There seemed to be something inside the charm and whatever it was glowed dimly. Glowing purple.

"What is it?" she asked, mesmerized as she lifted it from his hand.

"It's clear to me 'at ye've no intentions of being

careful or takin' my advice. It's like ye've become hellbent on annihilation, 'erefore, ye're goin' to wear this and I'll have no arg'ments 'bout it. It's just an old family heirloom, probably offer as much protection as a popsicle, but it'd make me feel better to know ye had it. What say ye? Will ye indulge an old man?"

"Of course I'll wear it," she said, putting it on right then and there. "You sure it's just an heirloom? You seem pretty adamant to have me wear it."

She was partly nervous to ask. Lymir was an incredibly perceptive man, for all his self-deprecating jokes about being old and dull. And he had already given several hints, though certainly minor, that he knew more about her and her mission than he was letting on. Andie had come to trust him almost instantly, but that didn't change the fact that she'd only ever met the man twice and she had asked him some of the most dangerous questions possible. He was, after all, the owner of a rather sketchy and bleak tavern that served the very dregs of society in a less than reputable part of the city. Andie hadn't been nearly as careful as she should have been. And to top it all off, he'd given her a purple glowing charm with the stamp of a dragon's head on it.

"Of course, it's just mere superstition," Lymir insisted. "Like I said, probably goin' to be nothin' to ye at all, but wear it all the same, eh? Set me old mind at ease a bit."

"I won't take it off. I promise."

She smiled at him, a genuine smile of thanks and then got up to leave. She was still confused and suspicious, but she knew whatever the bracelet actually meant to him he was only trying to look out for her. He was no fool. After all the questions she'd been asking it wasn't that much of a leap to think she was off gallivanting through dangerous and secret places she had no business being. It was what she had been doing and what she was on her way to do at that very moment.

As she headed for SKY 6, Andie noticed that the bracelet felt weird. No, not weird, good. She held up her wrist to check it. The purple glow made her wonder. Could it be dragon magic? Whatever was inside of it was very dim, almost extinguished. She couldn't tell exactly what it was, but she knew it was magic. That much was clear.

CHAPTER TWENTY-SIX

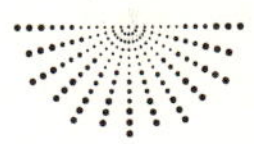

As always, Andie was able to relax on SKY 6. The train was traveling somewhat slower that night and whether it was to show off the views of Arvall City and Brie Mountain or the amenities of the train itself, Andie didn't know. Every seat on the train was taken, filled with the sleek silver tuxedos or luminous, pearlescent ball gowns of people who looked far too wealthy to be sitting in coach. Andie felt strangely at ease among them; they were rich and thrilled, and she knew that they would leave her to herself.

She was becoming nervous about her mission. She knew she could trust Yara and Carmen, and she knew that when the moment came for her to reveal to them exactly what they had signed up for, they would follow her into danger. She also knew that despite Lymir's claims to ignorance and superstition he was a wise man, and the charm bracelet he'd given her was somehow meant to protect her. The other thing she knew was that she had an even wider network of people looking out for her. There was Marvo who—human or not—would give his dying breath to help her. There was also Tarven, the boy who'd changed her life. Despite all his secrets there was no doubt in her mind that he would come to her if push came to shove. Even her father back in Michaelson would risk everything just to be able to protect her for a single moment. And Raesh. Warm, sweet, loyal Raesh, who would never let so small a thing as jealousy keep him from her.

Andie's concern now was moving more toward what would happen to that network of friends. She wasn't without her own sense of self-preservation, but she'd long since come to terms with the realization that she was probably going to die. Lymir was right: she was playing the game, but without knowing the rules or who the other players were. And the University had hundreds of years of murder under its belt. Every day she walked into that black marble structure, she knew it might be the last. But that was for herself. If anything were to happen to the people she cherished—the people who believed in her enough to follow her—she hoped that she would die first because she would never be able to forgive herself.

SKY 6 reached the University and the passengers began to unload, more than a few of them were already reeling from wine and whatever else they'd been ingesting on the way up. As soon as the mountain altitude hit some of them, they collapsed into heaving piles. Andie skirted the chaos and went inside. It was a struggle to navigate the halls as almost all of the University's six hundred thousand students were in attendance. There were also the faculty, visitors, and important figures from around the world. Andie fought hard for every step, with perhaps a hundred "Excuse me's" and "Sorry's." Things petered out some when she finally reached the end of the hall and was under the endless void. The ethereal glow of the marble was even more magnificent than usual and even after her many months there, Andie still didn't know where the light came from.

To reach the Grand Mirror Hall of Terpsichore, Andie had to venture down a new hallway. There was no hope of getting lost though, for the closer she got to the ballroom, the more the smell of the mixed fuil glas and anáil fuar filled her body. She knew immediately it had been a success. How could it not be? There were simply no words for the smell and as she turned the corner and entered the room she was nearly bowled over by the sight. The entire upper halves of the walls were covered with the mixed species, which Tarven had named anáil saol. The new species was cerulean and forest, brilliant in the University's glow and strong in the greatest way. Andie couldn't help but feel a swell of pride.

She felt prouder still when she noticed that several eyes were watching her make her entrance and more were turning by the second. She walked slowly, trying to affect some grace if it were possible, smiling that beautiful smile that had won so many hearts in her favor. People were whispering as she passed by and from their expressions, Andie knew they were impressed. She kept talking to herself to stay calm. "Don't fall." "Head high." "Remember to thank Carmen for this dress." "Find Tarven." People began to smile and nod at her. She nodded back, queenly for a girl not used to the spotlight. For once in her life, she had some true conception of her beauty.

As she was thinking his name, she saw his face. Tarven was standing in the middle of the room, his arm already up and waiting for her as if he'd known where she was all along. He'd decided to skip tradition and wear a dark blue tuxedo with a black shirt and tie. He did, however, opt for one of the traditional hairstyles. He looked exceptionally handsome. Perfect. She walked up to him and took his arm.

'Hi," she said. "I feel like all of Arvall's watching me. I guess with so many foreign dignitaries all the world is watching."

"Well, you're the most beautiful woman breathing. And now the whole world knows it."

It was the perfect thing to say.

Tarven led her up the stone steps onto the main level of the mirror room where the dancing would be. Andie looked around and saw that the board had formed the room to look like one of the great ballrooms of Hightowyr. Three rooms, in fact. Now that Andie had reached the main level, she could see that the room had been thought into an additional grand ballroom on either side. Tarven held her hand and they walked over to a fountain that had to be at least fifty feet tall. Andie was surprised to see people holding their cups beneath the stream.

"Am I seeing things or are those rich people drinking the water from the fountain?" Andie asked.

"It's not water, silly. Of course, we call it fountain water, but it's actually a kind of wine made from the recipe of the Terpsichore founding family. It's only made during the time of the Winter Festival."

"And they couldn't think of a better name than 'fountain water?'"

"Its proper name is *comhlacht bunaitheach*, but I suppose that was a bit of a mouthful."

The voice belonged to a young-looking man dressed in the traditional silver tux and holding a champagne flute of the fountain water. He had a smile that made one trust him instantly, but wasn't arrogant or pompous in the least.

"Where are your manners, Tarven?" he asked, grinning. "Introduce me to this beautiful lady who seems to have gotten drunk and accidentally fallen into your company."

Andie smiled and blushed for the third time that night.

"This is my date, Andie Rogers. And this, Andie, is one of my professors, Marcus Iceubes, professor of folklore."

"I resent that," Marcus said, shaking Andie's hand.

"Well, you are."

"True, but that makes me sound so boring and narrow. I want to be exciting."

"Well, you did introduce yourself with a historical anecdote."

"Hm. Fair."

"It's a pleasure to meet you," Andie said, taken with him immediately.

"Not quite. You have to try this very, very old wine first."

He turned to pick something up. It was a glass figure shaped like a funny sphere. Andie looked closer and saw that it was a palm-sized miniature of earth with a snowflake perched on top. Marcus handed it to Andie, shaking his head as if embarrassed on behalf of whoever had crafted it.

"You never know what they're going to do with the

spellglass from year to year," he said. "How about a champagne flute?"

He looked at the spellglass and it formed itself into a frosted champagne flute to match his own.

"Thanks, but I think a brandy glass will do," Andie said. "You know, country girl and all."

Instantly, the spellglass shrunk and widened to become a brandy glass. Andie thought for a moment then decided to manifest a panorama of a snowstorm along the sides.

"Oh, I see we have a show off among us," Marcus said. "Welcome home."

He led her and Tarven to the fountain and Andie held the glass under the stream. Marcus handed her a napkin and she wiped the side. She took one sip of it and from the look on her face, they knew she'd never tasted anything so delicious. She downed the glass and reached for more.

"Oh, I like you," Marcus said.

TARVEN LED Andie around the crowd and introduced her to some faculty members and professors, as was customary for anyone working at the University who brought a date. Andie also met the provost, an old woman with kind eyes and the air of someone who never intended to die. She spent the greater part of the evening with Tarven. Marcus popped in occasionally and kept them from the boredom that was the introductory phase of the celebration. Still, Andie couldn't stop herself from getting anxious. It was getting later and later, and she was no longer sure she would have a chance to get away.

Every time she tried to excuse herself, someone started a conversation with her. She was flattered by all their attentions, but she had somewhere to be. If it wasn't other people, it was Tarven. He really was trying to be a terrific date—and he was succeeding—but he never let her get more than a few feet away.

Finally, she managed to get Tarven deep into conversation with three young men who'd tried to talk to her. She was slowly slipping away when Carmen and Yara found her.

"Come on," Yara said. "Girl time."

"Definitely," Carmen added, in that accept-this-as-your-circumstance way of hers. "We'll have her back soon enough for you to dance her off her feet."

"Or whatever you were planning on doing to her," Yara mumbled devilishly.

"But I've not had my chance yet."

It was Professor Harrock. Andie nearly sighed in despair, but he was actually one of her favorite instructors. He held out his hand, like the shiest, but most determined gentleman on earth, and she accepted.

"After this one," she said to the girls.

They walked out to the middle of the dance floor. Andie wanted desperately to be investigating the secrets of the archives, but she knew she could last one more dance. She gave Professor Harrock a genuine smile and tried not to laugh when Marcus put on a face of exaggerated sympathy across the room. Andie prepared herself for another sweet, but mundane dance. But she was greatly shocked when he pulled her in close, all the way against him and whispered in her ear.

"So, you think your magic protects you?"

"What?"

"You think no one can see who you are or know what you're doing. You think you've outsmarted an institution that has enslaved or destroyed every enemy to cross its path in the last five hundred years. You think you're powerful. Special."

Andie tried to pull away, but Professor Harrock was strong, much stronger than he looked. Much stronger than he should have been. She tried to release magic into his arm from her hand, but it didn't seem to have an effect.

"You've been putting that pretty little nose where it doesn't belong. You think we're oblivious because you meddled with your icon, but we know everything you've been up to since you first sunk it into your palm."

"That's impossible."

"Is it? Who do you think allowed that so-called spell to reach the students? We wanted you all to think that we weren't watching you and like dumb sheep every last one of you believed yourself free."

"You're a villain. I don't know what's going on here, but I'll-"

"You'll mind your tongue or I'll rip it out and send it home to your cripple of a father. You've been warned. The dragons and everything they spawned is off limits, and by off limits I mean on pain of death. I do not fear death and thus I deal it willingly. You're beautiful and brilliant, maybe even stronger than we think, but we will lay waste to you and every inch of the nineteen years of your life. Everything. Everyone. Even Tarven."

"You won't touch him."

"Touch him? Stupid girl. We've already done more than that. Look at him."

Andie started to turn her head and then stopped. She didn't want to give him the satisfaction.

"Look at him or I'll burn your friends in their beds tonight."

Andie tried to think of a way out, an escape, but couldn't. She wouldn't risk her friend's lives for her own pride. She turned and looked for Tarven. He was already watching her. As soon as he caught her eye, he tried to smile and look excited, but she'd already seen the truth on his face. He knew what Professor Harrock was doing. He was a part of it.

"See, we took him and made him ours. That's what we do. We corrupt for the sake of purification. One more thing. Stay away from the portal. We'll know if you go near it again."

Professor Harrock let go of her and stepped away. He bowed, smiling, and then left. Andie made her way back to Tarven, not because she wanted to see him, but because she didn't yet know where else to move to.

"Are you okay?" Tarven asked, in full cover-up mode. "Come here. What was Professor Harrock talking about?"

"Nothing," she said. "It was just about some research I was doing. He says it won't be... suitable for my final essay. Excuse me, I need some air."

She left. She couldn't look at him anymore and it took every ounce of her strength not to vaporize him where he stood.

CHAPTER TWENTY-SEVEN

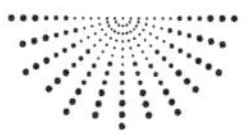

On her way out, Andie found herself walking between Carmen and Yara. She didn't know if she'd found them or they found her, but she felt a surge of strength the moment she knew they were beside her. They never stopped walking, just left the grand mirror room side by side, three young women with a secret purpose.

Andie moved differently then. With purpose. She'd heard everything Professor Harrock had said and she was afraid—she *knew* she was afraid—but she couldn't stop. She had to open the door, touch that portal, save those voices. Consequences or no. Yara and Carmen moved silently beside her, giving her a kind of fortitude as they weaved through the crowded halls in the direction of Leabherlann. Andie couldn't lie to herself: She was playing fast and loose with their lives. She'd been told, explicitly, only moments ago, that if she continued to look into these things she would be condemning everyone in her life. Truth be told, she hadn't yet decided what to do and she knew she had until they reached the archives to decide. It was coming to the point where she would have to decide between saving the voices in the portal and saving the living bodies around her.

They reached Leabherlann and Andie taught Yara and Carmen the spell that allowed them to pass through the door. Once inside, Andie made straight for the archives without a word. How would she tell them their lives were in danger? How would she tell them the University had been watching them ever since they put the icon in? How would she handle their fear? She began to move quicker and with more focus, perhaps driven somewhat crazed by the sheer weight of the moment that waited ahead. Leabherlann was totally empty, not a soul apart from the three of them, and their footsteps echoed like sharp yelps in the great darkness. As they neared the archive, Andie could hear Carmen's footsteps slowing, lightening, the fire going out of the girl as she realized where they were heading. Yara seemed less apprehensive, but Andie could hear the change in her footsteps, as well. At last they descended the short staircase to the lower level and stood facing the entrance to the hallway, beyond which lay the archives and the door that hid the portal, Andie turned to face them.

"If you go into this room with me your lives will be in danger," she said. "After that, the chances of things returning to normal for you are pretty slim."

"As in our lives are completely screwed if we take one more step," Yara said.

"Exactly."

Yara took a step back and collapsed against the wall. Carmen stood bewildered and mute, gazing around her as if she didn't know which way to turn.

"There's more." Andie said. "They're monitoring us,

right now. They have been since we put the icons in. The dampening spell never worked. They only wanted us to think it did. They've known everything we've done since we inserted it. I'm still not sure exactly who we're up against or what is going on here, but Professor Harrock is in on it. He just threatened me on the dance floor. He basically said that anyone I care about will be killed if I continue. I don't know if I'm going in yet or not, but you two need to turn back."

"Turn back?" Carmen asked.

"Now. For all I know they're already planning our deaths and I won't have the two of you on my conscious. You've been too good to me."

"Who do you think you are?" asked Carmen, staring at Andie with utter fury. "Do you think the world revolves around you? That you can just... just take what you want when you want without consequences? Do you think you get to make all the decisions for the rest of us? Beg for our help one minute and turn us away the next? Do you think we didn't understand what you wanted? Do you think we're stupid, or blind, or foolish? You don't control us."

"You never will," Yara said. "You asked us to come with you because you trusted us and you needed us. I cast an augmentation spell on myself earlier tonight. Like I do every year. I make it so that I can hear a conversation a hundred yards away because I like to know what the foreigners think of Arvall. I heard virtually every word of Harrock's poison. I heard what he told you to do, the things he threatened he'd do, and yet here I am. I told Carmen and yet there she is."

"We're your friends, Andie," Carmen said, standing straighter then than Andie could remember. "Danger or no. Don't insult us by trying to push us away when you so clearly need us with you."

Andie simply nodded. She was so happy she could have collapsed against them there.

"Besides," Carmen added, "If they've really been watching us since we first got our icons, I expect they've already gotten quite an eyeful from me."

"They'll be long dead before they finish sorting out my perversions and crimes," Yara said with a smile.

The three girls shared a smile. Andie turned and faced the hallway. There was no point in hiding now. She raised her hand and with her mind began to disassemble the magic of the hallway. She'd grown strong and the handful of defensive spells were no good. It had been a long while since she'd doubted her own sanity, but she had a wavering moment then. There was just something about her circumstance that night that felt at odds with what it should be. She didn't have time to worry about that then, though. The three girls moved swiftly down the hallway and walked as a unit through the archives. Yara and Carmen gazed up and across at all the strange and ancient volumes. Andie had seen it all before.

They neared the door and this time not only were the voices louder, more painful, but Andie could feel the magic of the door before they were even close to it. They'd done something to enhance the magic and whatever it was had intensified the voices as well. But as Andie struggled to stay on her feet and focus her mind, Carmen and Yara seemed completely unbothered. She could tell by the orientation of their bodies that they felt the magic, but they couldn't hear the voices. Then Andie remembered: Tarven couldn't hear them either. Maybe only the dragonborn could hear them.

"Andie, what's wrong?" Carmen asked.

"The voices. They're too loud. I can't... I can't..."

"Just tell us what to do."

"You have to get that door open."

Carmen and Yara approached the door, wary. Andie sank to her knees, unable to think or move. Carmen and Yara seemed to be arguing over something. They both tried a spell on the door and when nothing worked, they began to alternate, giving the door everything they had. With every failure, the voices grew in Andie's head; her bones began to ache and blood was coming from her ears.

"You have to open it!" she screamed, desperate.

Yara was holding her head, wracking her brain for something while Carmen tried spells, charms, incantations, and even hexes. Suddenly Yara's eyes leapt open and she grabbed Carmen. Yara said something to her and then they both kneeled down in front of Andie. They grabbed her under her arms and drug her over to the door. Carmen took Andie's bloody hands from her ears and placed them on the door, then she and Yara both placed their hands on the door. They began to chant as Andie began to swoon. Louder and louder the girls became, and lower and lower the voices went. Soon the whispers that had once been screams were fading into nothing as the magic flowed out of the door and into the three girls. The sorcerer's magic felt odd against Andie's flesh, but anything was better than the voices.

"Andie, you're bleeding," Yara said. "Maybe we should go."

"No," Andie said, louder than she meant to. "I'll be fine. There are worse injuries. I didn't come all this way and go through all that to leave without having some of my questions answered."

She wasn't lying; her dragon blood had begun to heal her instantly. In a matter of moments she would be fine.

With her friends' help, Andie rose to her feet and stepped forward to the door. Carefully, with the gravity of everything she'd suffered on her shoulders, Andie pushed the door open. It was like nothing she could have imagined. The room is massive, obviously spelled to seem smaller from the outside. It was made entirely of blue stone, which was said to have magical properties, but Andie had never seen it before. The room was so huge it seemed that it must have been bigger than the archives, bigger than Leabherlann itself. In the center of the space was an enormous circular pool bordered by yet another kind of stone; on the stone were carved symbols that Andie couldn't decipher. There was a mist, heavier and more nerve-wracking than any natural mist, hanging about.

The voices suddenly came back again, but now only as whispers. As the three young sorceresses neared the pool, Andie could hear a multitude of fleeting cries rising from the pool. Andie hurried forward, despite herself.

"I don't believe it," Carmen said.

"This is impossible," said Yara. "This shouldn't even be here. It shouldn't even exist. It's just a legend."

"Hello!" Andie said, leaning over the pool. "Hello! Can you hear me? Tell me how to help you! I'm here to save you!"

"Andie, I meant what I said, I'd follow you anywhere, but maybe we should take a minute to think this through," Yara cautioned. "If this portal is real, then maybe the legends are, too."

"You mean the terrifying stories?" said Carmen. "The ones where a few kids mysteriously go missing every few years, never to be heard from again? Or the ones where entire nations waged war just to look at this thing? Nothing good can come of that thing."

But Andie was beyond them. Leaning far over the pool and peering inside, she could see them. The people. *Her* people. The dragonborn were there, with their colorful hair, iridescent eyes, and dragon scale armor. There, too, were dragons—great magnificent beasts larger and more beautiful than imagination, stunning beyond description. One of the people looked up, straight up and into Andie's eyes.

"Help us," he called weakly.

It was in that moment that Andie knew her dreams were real. All of them.

"Carmen, Yara, they're in danger. We have to help them."

"Who?" they asked simultaneously.

Andie beckoned them over to the pool. At first, they didn't seem to see anything, but when she saw their eyes go wide she knew they finally saw.

"I see them!" Yara said.

"Yeah," said Carmen. "And I can hear them, too!"

"Good," Andie said. "Because this is the only opportunity we'll ever get to save them."

CHAPTER TWENTY-EIGHT

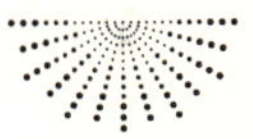

Carmen and Yara took a moment, clearly still not fully believing. Maybe they couldn't believe it was real or maybe they couldn't believe it was happening to them, but Andie couldn't afford to give them the time they needed to process. And neither could her people.

"Carmen, Yara, I need you to guard this room," she said. "We know they're watching us and we know they mean to stop us. I need you now. All my people need you."

The two girls looked at each other and then at Andie.

"We'll do everything we can," Carmen said.

She and Yara hurried back over to the door and stood guard. They began to slowly wave their hands in front of themselves, the fingers beginning to glow as they closed the door and cast enchantments across it. Andie turned back to the pool and leaned over it as far as she could without falling in. As Carmen and Yara chanted into the hallway behind her, Andie called into the pool below. It seemed as if they could hardly hear her and only intermittently, as if she were some radio signal that couldn't come through clearly. She could see them turn their faces up every now and then, responding to some clip of her voice that had fought its way through. She couldn't hear them either, try as she might, and she nearly fell in twice trying to put her face close enough to the pool to make sense of the rising murmurs. Then she got an idea. She remembered how she'd released her dragon essence in Leabherlann. Astral projection had allowed her spirit to be free in order to accomplish tasks her mind could not; it wouldn't be necessary to go full spirit, just enough to get a certain degree of distance between body and spirit. She released the smallest part of herself, enough to connect with the visions in the pool, but not so much that she lost the effective use of her corporeal body. She existed then in two states simultaneously.

"Help us, please!" one woman cried.

"Time is running out!" said another.

Andie's projection allowed her to see beyond the women to the mountain. Covering every inch of the peak that she could see were her people, frightened, breathless, unable to move for lack of anywhere to run to. Husbands were cradling their wives, who were in turn cradling their children. Suddenly their numbers and suffering were laid out before Andie in a vast panorama of misfortune. And then she saw it: the spell rolling across the land that was so massive it took up all the space between land and sky. On and on it came, relentless, inevitable, a storm of violent magic unlike anything ever seen on earth and as purple as the deepest heart of lavender. It was so close, unbelievably close, and it was destroying everything it touched. If the dragonborn couldn't escape, their entire race would be finished. And what would that mean for their descendants?

Then Andie saw her, looking up from the portal and speaking to her. The woman seemed calmer than the rest, as if she had decided on a course of peace. She was standing on the forward-most precipice of the mountain and she was so beautiful the word must have been created for her. She gazed up at Andie like a mother gazing at her child and, amazingly, despite the destruction and fear surrounding her, the woman was smiling. Andie knew the smile was for her, to calm her down so she could focus and help them. She focused on the woman.

"Tell me what to do," Andie said. "I'll do anything."

"What is your name?" the woman asked.

"Andie."

"It is my honor, Andie. I am called Saeryn. All you need to do is focus on the dragon magic inside of you."

"How did you know-"

"Only a dragonborn could have heard my calls. And only a dragonborn can save us. Just focus on the magic that is already inside of you, deep within, in the very paoum of your soul. Let those deeper parts of yourself guide you. Your spirit and instincts already know what to do."

Andie felt the anxiety and fear like a thousand tons of cold pressure on her chest. She turned to look at Carmen and Yara—now done casting enchantments and patiently standing guard. They had no idea she was one of the dragonborn. She loved them and trusted them, but she'd never asked them how they felt about dragons and the race they created. What if they feared her? What if they couldn't accept her? What if they tried to kill her?

"I can't," she said. "It's too dangerous."

"Be brave, Andie. Fear alone is the great danger. Only you can pull us through and when you do we will protect you. There will be nothing on Earth that can harm you. Our moments here in our own time are diminishing. We cannot stay here a minute longer, you must bring us through to your time."

Necessity had taken her choice from her and now all Andie had left was her duty to her people. She closed her eyes and dropped the veil of her disguise. She returned to the brilliant, luminous truth of her heritage and she was more beautiful than can be described. But just as she dropped the veil, there was a massive explosion on the other side of the door. The blast jolted all three girls and Andie's projection snapped back home as Carmen and Yara stumbled against the pillars.

"What was that?" Yara screamed.

"Andie, I think we're going to have to-"

But as Carmen turned and saw Andie she stopped short. Yara saw her, too. There was a long silence while Andie grew tense, watching her friends watch her and waiting for some reaction, any indication at all of how they truly felt. And then, like a light in the darkness, Yara laughed.

"I knew it!" she said. "I'd been suspecting for months, but I knew it! All your questions and research and mystery. All those items you tried to find and your secrecy about your mother and your family. I knew it, I knew you were dragonborn."

"Is that okay?" Andie asked.

"Are you kidding? It's awesome. You're my friend, Andie, I'll take you as you are."

They smiled at each other. Andie turned to Carmen, who was still staring slack-jawed.

"And you?" Andie asked.

"Why didn't you tell me?"

"I was scared and I didn't know if you would be afraid. Or, kill me, if we're speaking truthfully."

Carmen simply stared. Just then another explosion shook the entire room and several of the huge chandeliers fell from the ceiling. They were running out of time and in more ways than one. Carmen ran over to Andie and hugged her. The embrace said so much that nothing else was necessary.

"You and I are going to talk about this later," Carmen said. "But right now, we need to do what we came here for."

"What's on the other side of that door?" Andie asked.

Another explosion boomed through the hall and this one caused cracks to spread through the entire wall. Whatever or whoever was outside would be inside soon enough. Carmen and Yara waved their hands again and sealed the cracks in the wall, but they knew time was short. Now they could hear shouting on the other side of the door. Andie recast her partial projection. It allowed her to see through the door as if nothing were there: on the other side were several professors, hooded monitors —the University's security—and Tarven. So, finally, he'd chosen a side. Fortunately, there were no Searchers or guns, which would have meant a sure and painful death. At least now maybe they had a chance, however slight. Andie couldn't help herself: she wished Raesh were there.

"Andie, you must hurry."

It was Saeryn calling from the pool. Carmen and

Yara, understanding, hurried back to the wall and pushed with all of their magic to protect it, yet there was no way the two of them could stand long against the power on the other side of the wall. Andie ran back to the pool and took a deep breath. She turned her spirit inside, into her blood. She'd held herself back for so long that to release her full ability again would take real effort. She searched and reached deep down into the magic she hadn't disturbed since she was a child. Since her mother was taken. It was obvious the magic was there, but perhaps it had been dormant too long. No. There it was, curled and slumbering like the great beasts from which it came. She reached for it, almost had it in her grasp, when an explosion ripped the room asunder. Carmen and Yara were thrown back several feet and Andie was blasted into one of the pillars. The explosion was so powerful that it split the room in two across the ceiling. Only the strength of the mountain and the pillars interspersed throughout the room kept it all from collapsing.

Through the rip where the door used to be came Professor Harrock, Tarven, and all the others. Their faces were full of rage.

CHAPTER TWENTY-NINE

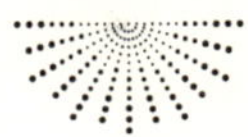

ANDIE GOT UP, SLOWER THAN SHE MEANT TO, BUT IT FELT as if some of her ribs might be broken. The dragon magic was kicking in to help heal her, but before she could say a word or even get all the way back on her feet, one of the apoplectic professors threw a lightning bolt at her. It came faster than sound and more blinding than a flash of the sun. It hit Andie before she even knew it had been cast and knocked her even further back. This time she didn't try to get up.

"Tarven," she called from where she lay, "Help us."

"There's no help for you now, Andie," he said. "Just lie there. Maybe this can be over quickly."

Andie tried to raise herself up, just to her knees, but even the dragon magic couldn't heal those wounds so fast.

"Why?" she asked. "What could possibly make you so evil?"

"Why does it matter? I've been with them for years, before I ever even met you. There was never even a chance for you. I studied you and memorized your history before you set foot in Arvall City. We knew who you were when you applied to the University. Do you really think the University doesn't keep a record of the people they've killed? When they took your mother, they marked your family for surveillance. You and your father were never alone in Michaelson. I bet you think what happened to him was an accident."

Andie almost stopped breathing.

"That's impossible. It *was* an accident."

"It was made to look like one. They were never going to let you go. The only reason you lived this long is because they were curious about their own security. They only let you live to test the weaknesses of their own system. Your entire life was an experiment."

"And a very successful one," said a new voice.

Andie recognized it instantly. It was the voice she'd heard talking with Tarven that night in Leabherlann. And now she knew why his voice sounded familiar. It was Myamar Mharú, chancellor of western Noelle. Andie had only ever seen him once before; he gave a speech at the University around the beginning of the year. Still, Andie could hardly focus on him or anything else. She was heartbroken to know that Tarven had betrayed her so absolutely. She'd always known something was off, always had her suspicions. She even caught him in the middle of one or two blatant lies, but she'd never suspected that his deception ran this deep, that his disdain for her and everything she was could be so huge. But she had to focus. Tarven had made his decision and now she had to make hers. She had people to save, and now that included Carmen and Yara. Tarven stepped forward. He reached inside his tuxedo jacket and removed a small bronze and black plant in a tiny pot. Decepticatus.

"Remember this little guy?" Tarven taunted. "I'm surprised you didn't guess from the name, but they feed on human lies. The day you saw him leaning toward me was because I was lying to you. Idiot. Now, let's see what you have to say. Do you know where any other dragonborn are?"

"No," Andie said through gritted teeth.

The plant leaned toward her.

"Is your father fully disabled?"

"Yes."

"Have you found any books in Leabherlann with information you shouldn't have?"

Andie paused for a moment, trying to make herself believe her words.

"No."

The little bronze plant leaned further toward Andie and waved its limbs.

"Lie number two," Tarven said. "Do you have the means of opening this portal?"

"No."

The plant leaned over even more and waved a little harder.

"Lie number three. Are there any dragons that are still alive?"

"No."

The plant leaned even more and Andie was ashamed.

"Hm."

The power of the dragons that ran through her blood had healed her enough to stand and without thinking she pushed herself to her feet with magic. No one was expecting it. Andie raised her hands and slammed them down against the floor; a wave of energy rippled out across it, cracking the stones and flinging the men as it went. She waved her hands and erected a shield before her. Her spells could go out, but theirs couldn't get in. Before anyone had time to think, spells were flying back and forth everywhere in a kind of crazed firework show. Stone exploded into dust in the air as wildly aimed spells missed their mark and collided with the walls and pillars. Andie moved like water, casting counter charms faster than ever before. She ducked and slid to safety as one of the professors held his throat and breathed fire. Andie gripped him with magic and fused his body with a stone pillar. He struggled, but couldn't pull away. He wouldn't be bothering her for a while. She hadn't even fully understood how she did what she did to him. Tarven was across the room, behind Professor Harrock, pretending to be fierce, but really just hiding. He never was very good at casting.

"What's wrong with you people?" Andie screamed, taking shelter behind a pillar while she regrouped. "If you don't let me get to that portal, an entire race of people will die! Don't you understand that? All my people will be dead!"

"It's really for the best," came Professor Harrock's condescending voice. "The dragonborn are a threat and a plague. If you honestly think we would risk allowing them to be free in our time, then you haven't been paying attention. They *will* die tonight. And only time will tell if you die before or after that portal is a pile of ash. If your race goes extinct in history…Well, let's just say it doesn't bode well for those of you still around today.

There's no escape, no resistance, no hope. You can only-"

Andie heard Professor Harrock give a grunt and then she heard a heavy thump. She peaked around the pillar and saw him on his knees. He seemed to have fallen there and he was clutching his chest. When his hands dropped, Andie could see that his chest had been shot through and a hole was left straight in the middle, next to his heart. He fell forward head first, unconscious or dead, Andie couldn't tell. Andie froze in a daze and held her hand to her mouth in shock, holding in a scream, as she stared at his body lying still on the floor. She was quickly brought back to reality as she heard crashes and bangs around her, spells flying this way and that. What was this coming to? She looked around as she cast spells, trying to see where the attack had come from. She saw Yara still lying unconscious near the door, but Carmen had her hand up and extended in Harrock's direction, as if just finished casting a spell. One of the other professors tried to bring a pillar down on her, but Carmen shielded herself and the part of the pillar that touched her vanished into particles.

"Carmen, over here!" Andie shouted.

Carmen got to her feet, trying to defend herself from the barrage of spells.

"What about Yara?" she asked.

Andie strengthened her shield and then stepped out into the floor. She flicked her wrist and Yara's body snapped over into her arms. She returned to her shelter and moments later Carmen joined her. Carmen worked on trying to revive Yara while Andie cast retaliation spells. She caught one professor right in the face and the woman fell instantly, taken by the purple flames.

"Your kind are destroyers," Mharú's voice said. "You cannot be allowed to survive."

"We're destroyers?" she responded, incredulous. "You're the ones who've been hunting us for centuries. You're the ones who slaughtered the dragons. It was you and all the people like you who made sure that the reign of terror lasted all these centuries without any hope or quarter for my people. Don't talk to me about destroyers!"

"We are the rightful rulers of this land! The dragonborn had their chance and they were too weak to withstand! They were insects compared to us!"

"Is that why you were so scared? Why you're still terrified that one day they could come back? What did the dragonborn ever do to you? To anybody? What was it about them and the dragons that just seemed so dangerous and so insurmountable that you people had to slaughter them continuously without remorse?"

"They existed."

And that was enough. Andie had had enough.

Andie was growing more and more furious: with the sorcerers, with the plight of her people, with the threats and the hatred and the fact that Carmen still couldn't wake Yara. Andie stood and released a wave of magic that ran hot and rapid through the room. She erected a second shield, but this one stretched from floor to ceiling and ensured a safe path to the portal. The professors continued to cast at the shield, but to no effect. Andie ran to the portal and prepared to project.

"Carmen, don't worry about Yara just now. You can cast spells from behind the shield. Give me as much time as you can."

Carmen nodded and gently laid Yara down. She rose

and took a stance behind the shield, beginning to cast with a stunning ferocity. Andie projected again, this time drawing on the core of her magic, and found a multitude of spells suddenly appearing in her mind. Without questioning it, she began to recite them over the portal with her eyes closed. She followed Saeryn's words and simply trusted the history and power in her own blood. Soon she could hear Saeryn below, chanting along with her. Then all the people began to join in. It felt good to give in, to be one with her people, but the spell was powerful. So powerful. Andie wasn't used to this: channeling so much magic, doing a spell with others, pulling on the very root of her dragon magic. It began to overwhelm her almost immediately and the more she pushed herself, the harder it became.

Behind her, Carmen was fighting with everything inside her. The shield was beginning to fail as Andie lost strength and cracks and holes began to appear in the soft light of the barrier. Carmen continued to cast, fierce and unstoppable as ever. Andie was feeling weak now, weak enough to want to lay down, but she kept pushing and reaching and reciting. Her head began to droop and her sense began to go, but she kept reciting. She began to bleed again and the dragon magic within her stopped healing, but she kept reciting. She fell to her knees, but she kept reciting.

"Please," she thought. "Just let me have the strength to do this one thing." But she continued to weaken. Against her own wishes, she began to lose hope. She could barely hold herself up and the shield was almost down. Maybe this was it. Maybe this was the end of everything.

But just as she was growing faithless, there was a

blast near the door. Andie had just enough strength to turn her face in that direction. A group of people in black came rushing in, tight, quick, and casting spells as if they were born to it. And at the head of the group were Raesh and Marvo.

CHAPTER THIRTY

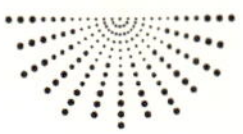

RAESH CAST A SPELL AT THE NEAREST PROFESSOR AND when it left his body on its trajectory it looked like a bolt of light with a hundred whipping tails, twisting furiously as it shot across the room and sent the professor soaring so far up and away in the cavernous room that Andie lost track of him. Raesh had said his magic was unpredictable and now she saw what he meant. He cast again and again and again, making his way across the room to Carmen. The others with him were casting rapidly as well, and the professors were finally starting to understand there was a chance the tide could turn against them.

Marvo was the only one not casting and that was because he had a gun; not the unpredictable, blood fueled weapons of modern-age Noelle, but one of the Old-World weapons. Every time he shot it, the barrel flashed and boomed. Unlike the spells that were flying wild, the gun was deadly accurate and Marvo knew how to use it. The professors had to erect shields of their own to protect themselves from him.

Tarven, whether out of his extreme cowardice or

premeditated feint, launched an attack on the newcomers from behind. They hadn't seen him when they came into the room and he was taking full advantage of it. He took down two of the newcomers with a few snaps of his wrists and then he reached in his coat and pulled out the new plant species he and Andie had bred together. He waved his hand in front of the blooms and extracted the liquid from the plant. He threw it into the faces of three of the newcomers and they began to choke and shrivel. Soon their faces were smoking and they dropped to the floor, bodies limp before they even touched the ground. Andie couldn't believe it. There was a mirror room full of people dancing under thousands of those flowers.

"You'll pay for this," she said in his direction, weakly.

"Not before I see you dead," he said back to her.

Tarven disappeared behind a pillar and Marvo fired off a couple rounds while making his way to Andie.

"What are you doing here?" she asked.

"Well, what a fine way to say thank you," he said, digging for something in his pocket. "Let's just call it a rescue mission. Unless of course you don't need us?"

"But how did you know? How did you find us?"

"Andie, I promised your father I would watch over you. He never told me you were dragonborn, but I'm no fool. I knew your mother was and I always suspected she passed on the gene. I've kept a closer watch on you since you've been in Arvall than I ever have on anyone else, even Raesh. You're important to me. But to answer your question, when you split up from Carmen earlier tonight she called Raesh and told him she thought you were up to something dangerous. This isn't the first time she's called us about you, but like every other time we got ready just in case. When she didn't call us back to say it was a false alarm, we came. Of course, with the festival going on, it was the perfect cover to get into the University and it didn't take a genius to figure out where you'd be."

He stood up to take a few more shots and then kneeled down again. He found something in his pocket and gave it to Andie.

"Here. Drink this and don't waste time asking me what it is."

Without hesitation, Andie turned the vial up and drank every drop of the liquid. She couldn't describe the effect other than to say that it put a fire in her. It didn't heal her, but it dampened the pain so that she could hardly feel it.

"I have to be honest," Marvo said, still shooting, "You've looked better. Can you finish what you started?"

"I don't have a choice," she said.

Andie pushed her fists against the ground and gained her feet. She leaned over the portal again and projected.

"Can you hold them off?" she asked Marvo.

"I was born for it," he said, cocking the gun and moving with a dexterity she wouldn't have thought he had.

Andie went back to chanting as the spells and gunshots flew around her. Marvo and the newcomers were strong and more than able to hold their own against the professors. Andie's shield had fallen, but Carmen had erected a new one. Andie felt a hand on her shoulder and realized that Carmen was standing behind her, one hand on Andie and another hand casting angrily. Andie felt stronger just having her there.

Across the room, Raesh was unleashing his magic

like a madman. His magic was unpredictable and by the look on his face you could tell he didn't always cast the spell he meant to, but he was a terrible force in that room. He guarded Yara's body fiercely. Marvo couldn't shoot the professors now that they had shields, but his incredible aim kept them from getting too close or going anywhere he didn't want them to. The newcomers, whoever they were, were expert sorcerers and sorceresses. They were relentless, unafraid, powerful. The professors were as arrogant and destructive as ever, but they grew desperate. They tried to bring down the pillars and even some spots of the wall to kill their opponents. They fought with no decency and no shame.

Andie felt numb, weak, cold, but she didn't stop chanting this time. Saeryn and her people below were doing their part and it was Andie's duty to do hers. Everyone around her was fighting with all they had. She couldn't do any less. Suddenly someone was kneeling beside her.

"Andie."

It was Raesh. Andie couldn't stop chanting, but she felt a wave of relief wash over her. She was happy he was there beside her.

"Andie, what were you thinking? How could you come in here with just Carmen and Yara, without even knowing what you're doing, without even having other people who know where you are? You could've been killed! You could've gotten them killed!"

"We could still be killed, Raesh!" Carmen interrupted. "Leave her alone, she can't stop! She has to finish the spell or everybody in that portal dies! Come cast while I hold up the shield! I'll fill you in!"

Raesh huffed in frustration, but didn't say anything

else. He kissed Andie on the cheek and went to help Carmen. He didn't see it, but she smiled.

Andie pushed harder, chanted louder. The fight was now being carried across the entire side of the room. The newcomers must have numbered at least forty and more professors had come running in shortly after Raesh and Marvo arrived. The air was dangerously alive with vivid spells and shrapnel and whatever was coming out of Marvo's gun. In some places the fighters had gotten so close that it turned into a fist brawl, like the old ages. The black marble was cratered and reduced to ash and blown across the room and the air was thick with magic and dust, the sound was unimaginable. It was so loud. So unbelievably loud.

Somehow a professor got around Carmen's shield. He must have run around the outer edge to come up behind. By the time anyone saw him it was too late. He cast a viscous light into Carmen and she collapsed into a heap, the shield falling with her. He was quicker than the rest and blocked the incoming retaliation, but he opened himself up to do one more thing. He held both his hands out and sent a red beam right into Andie's side. She couldn't defend herself or stop chanting; all she could do was try to stay on her knees, despite the unbearable pain of the beam burning her side. They tried and tried to break his shield, but they couldn't and he kept fueling the beam. Finally, a spell hit his shield and decayed the light in a matter of moments, following which he took a blast from Marvo's gun and a spell from Raesh at the same time. He was torn in half.

It was Yara. She'd woken up. She came running over to Andie. She casted as she went, sending the decaying spell at several other professor's shields and leaving them vulnerable. She dropped to Andie's side.

"Someone get a shield back up!" she yelled. "Andie, how bad is it? Let me see."

Yara tugged the fabric loose from Andie's dress. Andie never let her focus fail, even to look at the wound, but she could feel the blood rolling down her side.

"I can heal this," Yara said. "Just keep doing what you're doing, Andie. You're so brave."

Yara put her hands against Andie's side and pressed in. Andie winced but didn't move. Yara began to whisper an incantation and Andie began to feel better within a matter of moments—though the wound felt large and it would likely take actual medicine to fully heal it. But Andie kept her mind on the portal; she and they continued the spell.

CHAPTER THIRTY-ONE

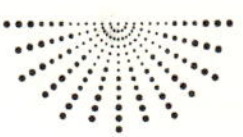

ANDIE COULDN'T TELL WHICH WAS MORE HAUNTING: THE screaming in the room or the screaming coming from the portal. The men and women on the mountain were reciting the incantation, but the children couldn't conquer their fear. The screams of children were terrible.

Finally, something began to happen. A tiny, gossamer connection began to manifest between herself and her people. Andie focused on it, focused every ounce of will and strength and magic on it, and tried to pull on it with the dragon essence inside of her. Now she understood what the spell was for: it was to reestablish the blood connection between herself and her people. She'd denied herself the benefit of her heritage for too long and had drifted, spiritually, from everything that made the dragonborn who they were. Even her 'natural' appearance had dimmed over the years because she hadn't allowed herself to live as she was.

Andie seized the connection, something like a supernatural thread, and began to try to reel her people back. She couldn't tell if she was summoning them or drawing them in or something else, but she knew she couldn't let go. Suddenly the pain spiked in her side and she lost focus for a split-second. The connection slipped some, but she held it. She began the incremental process again. She couldn't afford to fail now.

Her friends were fighting admirably and in fact they were proving stronger than their foes, but more professors kept coming. Andie knew that at this rate they would soon be overrun and there was only one way out of that room. But if she could get the dragonborn out, if she could set them free, they just might live to see another day.

"Andie!" Marvo shouted from somewhere behind her. "I don't know what you're doing or how much strength you have left, but your father wanted you to know something. He told me I couldn't tell you until you were ready and that I would know when that was. I think it's now. He wanted you to let go. To let go of everything: the past, what happened to your mother, your fear, your instinct to hide. He wanted you to be everything you were born to be, not what the world demanded from you. He said you couldn't be his protector or your mother's mourner or an outcast in a world that hated its own history. Let go. Embrace the power in your blood."

Her father. It had been so long since she'd seen him, but as Marvo spoke those words she could hear his voice, feel his arms. Even now, miles and circumstances apart, he was still guiding her. Still loving her. She rose to her feet, forgetting all her cares of the world and the times and the dangers of the night. In that moment, she knew only one thing: the dragon inside of her. As she tapped into that power and it exploded within her. Her hair grew and the color of it and her eyes intensified to what it was always supposed to be. Her skin took on a pearlescent sheen and the faint outlines of scales, barely noticeable, appeared on her arms. Her wounds healed in mere moments and she lifted off the ground. The thread was solid now and she reeled it in, faster and faster. She saw the end of it approach and shouted the final words of the spell, opening the portal to world.

The dragonborn poured from the portal, so many and so quickly it was impossible to count. Women, children, men, warriors, all were returning to the earth. The professors crowded together and probably would have run for the door if they were not so frightened. The newcomers smiled at the return of the dragonborn, but even they moved back. And then the real magic came. Dragons began to burst through the portal, almost too large to fit through the pool. They were incredible, colorful, powerful. Their riders were already on their backs as they circled the room.

For several brief but eternal moments, the room was frozen; newcomers, professors, monitors, Marvo, Raesh, Yara, and even Andie was frozen as they watch the dragonborn leap from the portal. Those few moments when no one moved was like a magic all its own, soundless, inert, and historic. The expressions of dragonborn were matched only by the sheer gravity of their presence. An entire race had been brought forward in time. They had very nearly been extinguished forever and yet there they stood, alive and happy and powerful. The bloodlines had become so diluted and so uncertain that it was doubtful there were many dragonborn left in the world. For all Andie knew she was the only one. But now she was surrounded by her people and by her friends, too. Andie had so many questions, so much joy, so many things to say, but she knew there would be time later. That's what the return of the dragonborn meant: time.

Suddenly, a huge wave of professors and monitors flooded the room, all of them shocked and disheartened to see the dragonborn alive again. But they weren't alone; following the monitors were the Searchers and their guns. It was clear that this was meant to be more than an attack; they were prepared to wage a small-scale war in that room and who knew how many more would come. They were right in the heart of the University. Soon enough, the shock wore off and from somewhere in the room she heard Chancellor Myamar Mharú shout over everyone's heads.

"Kill them! Kill them all!"

"Not so fast, Mharú," said Saeryn.

"You dare speak to me? Like I was your equal?"

"You know him?" Andie asked.

"No. At least not directly," Saeryn said, gliding forward with the grace of a thousand queens and fierceness of that entire room of dragon warriors. "But the Mharú family has always hated us and they've always had those horse faces. Easily recognizable, a feature they never lost when they came over from the Old World. Of course, the name used to be Melpomene. One of the so-called great founding families."

"We are great! And we'll be even greater once we throw your corpses back into the portal. It seems you came back only to die. Fools. You could've died relatively easily by staying in there, but you came out here to our waiting hands, for a death so exacting and so brutal that even the secret histories will not be able to bear the telling of it. Such courage and stupidity you show, facing us. I sincerely hope you've said your goodbyes because I'm coming now to rip your tongue out."

"You threaten us?" Saeryn asked, perfectly calmly. "You want to test yourself against dragonborn?"

"We defeated you before."

"No, your ancestors did. Sorcerers and sorceresses much more powerful and terrifying than you. And they only succeeded because they spent decades instilling fear into the dragonborn. Decades of propaganda circulated by brilliant, if wicked, wizards who were themselves hundreds of years old. But you don't have decades. You have only minutes. If we couldn't be killed then, all those centuries ago, what makes you think you can kill us now? You're a pale approximation of the men who defeated us. Don't you know who we are? What we can do? What power we hold?"

Myamar Mharú became visibly frightened. It seemed to finally dawn on him who he was looking at and how foolish he sounded. He glanced up to see the dragons clinging to the pillars above, warriors armed with swords and no doubt trained in the most arduous and potent magic. He looked over all the dragonborn and turned pale. He didn't back down, obviously too scared of what would happen if he showed weakness, but every eye that could see him saw his fear.

"Look around you," Saeryn said, this time addressing all the professors, monitors, and Searchers. "We are not some common street nuisance. We are born of dragons. Look at our numbers, our armor, our ferocity. You would stand against us? Against all of us? And for what, so you can fulfill some age-old vendetta that even your father's father's father cannot recall? Is your hatred so strong that it has blinded you? Are you so willing to die?"

Their enemies began to look regretful, some even squeamish. Saeryn looked like a queen: beautiful, proud, and pure, as poised as the great dragons themselves.

"This one girl could dispatch you," Saeryn said, indicating Andie. "And you would pit yourselves against all our people? Think again. This may be your time, your place. But we are ancients, born of a time long past with more magic than you can know. I breathe in your diluted air and can tell that after these long centuries, even your sorcerer's magic has likewise diluted. The sorcerers nearly won in our time, nearly succeeded in eradicating us for good. We have hated and raged and feared, but now we are saved and we are strong. So now, descendants of sorcerers long past, our sworn enemy who forced us from our lands and nearly stripped us of our people, we offer you not friendship—for we could never forget those crimes of yore—but peace. Shaeyara is a vast land and there must be a place where our people can live without harm. Will you accept this offer?"

Everyone was silent. Andie watched the professors and their servants. Everyone on her side seemed to be waiting for what surely seemed inevitable: who in their right minds would challenge so many angry ancient warriors who have magic so much stronger than any we have had in our world for centuries? Dragon warriors were the fiercest fighters of ancient times and not only that, but there were dragons as well. Andie counted at least twenty and a single one would have been more than enough. Andie's allies all looked hopeful, some even lowered their hands and moved out of their stance, certain the fighting would end there. But Andie knew better; she'd lived among these people. She'd read their histories, attended their University, remembered the legends and the murals she'd seen in the secret corridors beneath them. She'd watched them drag her mother away. These people had lived in hate so long, that it had overcome them, made them numb to any other sentiment. They would never accept the dragonborn into the world again and despite their obvious apprehension, not a single one of them had lowered their hand. Not one Searcher had put away their weapon. Saeryn turned to her.

"Andryne, would you care to say anything?"

Andie paused at being called that name, but quickly held her ground and gazed fiercely out at those around her. "That won't do any good," Andie said, her feet finally on the ground again. "Look at them. All they know is destruction."

"Then what do you propose?" Saeryn asked, her hands already turning into glowing fists as she anticipated the response, the only possible answer.

Andie moved forward until she was standing between Saeryn and Carmen. Yara, Raesh, and Marvo walked up to join the line as well. They had no misconceptions. Andie surveyed the enemy: Mharú cowering silently, Tarven hidden out of sight, professors and monitors and Searchers frightened, but determined. Andie faced Saeryn.

"Redemption. War."

CHAPTER THIRTY-TWO

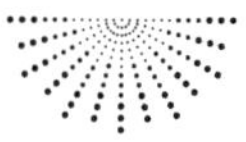

It began in a kind of slow haze. The dragons moved first, at the bequest of their riders, and began to soar lowly, threateningly over the enemy. The dragon warriors on the ground began to glow, unsheathing their swords as if the ancient times were not behind them but right before—a world where iron and rock still ruled the earth. The children were herded out of harm's way, but even they seemed to have some minor training in defense. The dragonborn moved like one body—men, women, old, young—driving themselves into highly coordinated ranks, impenetrable. Raesh, Marvo, and the newcomers backed up and were absorbed into the dragonborn formation. Andie, Carmen, and Yara joined the front lines. The Searchers had advanced training and formed a rather intricate phalanx designed primarily for attack. The monitors, too, engaged in a sort of crude flanking technique. The professors, who were powerful magicians but also first and foremost scholars, tried forming up, but the result was pitiable. The dragons began to move in more ferocious patterns, roaring and spitting fire at the walls; they were limited in what they could do because they were so large and had to share the space in a small corner of the room, but they were far from being set at a disadvantage.

The first spell was cast by a monitor, frightened into attack by a dragon gliding low overhead. His spell rebounded off the dragon's scales without hurting it at all. And it began.

The entire University group attacked as if they'd all been counting down the moment in their heads. The dragonborn seemed most surprised by the Searchers' guns, but even that could not intimidate them. The dragonborn shields came up like a cosmic blast of light; the enemy was still ten feet away and still they were sent back by the expulsion of wind. The dragon riders were the first to retaliate. Down they dived, spreading fire and hexes like the thickest rain, and the dragons snapped up the enemy in their great jaws and ravaged them. Some riders dismounted, dropping sword first from thirty feet in the air.

As University security, the monitors had been given two weapons. The first of these was the white fire, which could be shaped and controlled much the same as spellglass. It was a fearsome weapon and had had success against the newcomers, but the dragonborn didn't even flinch. There was no fire on earth, magical or otherwise, that could hurt them.

When the monitors saw this, they tried to use their second weapon. It was called deighilt, a very old weapon made of light and wind. The weapon was designed to tear, separate, and divide the body; it touched a person's skin and began to divide the body, first at the joints, then the waist, and finally the head. If you survived long enough to be breathing when it got to your head, you would've suffered an unimaginably painful death. It was the size of a large marble and they had pouches that contained perhaps a hundred of them. They began throwing them.

But none were so terrible and decisive as the dragonborn. They moved and fought with the honor and viciousness of another time. They struck with flashing swords and cast room-shaking spells at the same time. Their agility, strength, and instincts were flawless. They were the most lethal force Andie had ever seen. Legend told of the skill and might of the dragonborn, in war and peace times, but this was greater than all of that. They were unstoppable. Not only were they skilled on foot and on dragons, but some of the warriors could leap ten or even twenty feet in a single bound. Saeryn herself—ever calm, ever focused—was like a nightmare or a terror in the dark, lethal and swift as a storm. Even the newcomers gave the dragonborn a wide berth.

The Searchers were the most skilled on the enemy side, by far. They could cast and shoot in rapid succession, and were highly skilled in evasion. Andie saw immediately that the cruelty of their guns had not been exaggerated: the most frightening and bloody spells shot amplified from their barrels and many newcomers fell. The professors, hardly in control of themselves now that they were full of fear, advanced behind the Searchers, casting and ducking like the cowards they were.

Raesh's devastating magic was something to behold. He cast wildly and without hesitation, furious, exacting, and strong. His father fought beside him, shooting with an aim that was a wonder all its own. Carmen and Yara fought side-by-side, more clever and more precisely than even they could believe. They erected a joint shield and cast in tandem, Yara decaying the enemy shields and Carmen whipping them with lightening and smoke. The newcomers quickly learned to fight within the dragonborn formation and the side of the allies was advancing steadily.

Andie fought like a deity. After having tapped into the magic of her blood, she became a limitless force. Her feet left the ground again and she threw spells across the enemy without mercy or restraint. She lifted them, crushed them, made ash and void of them. Following Saeryn's lead, she unleashed the purple fire of the dragons on the hooded monitors, blasting them off their feet and igniting the deighilt, which burst in their pouches and did monstrous work. Neither Andie, nor her people, relished the taking of lives, but this fight was not for individual morals or untenable peace. It was not for virtue or for honor or even for pride. It was for survival. They had to wage war and to win decisively, else-wise they would be wiped out. For good.

The fight was one-sided from the beginning and even the Searchers couldn't make way against the dragonborn. This ancient race moved with a lethal and methodological confidence. But Andie's heart broke when she heard it. His scream. She turned and saw Raesh colliding with a pillar, his chest cut from shoulder to pelvis and deep enough to see bone. She flew over to him, cascading unquenchable fire on the professor who'd cast the spell. She kneeled down beside him and took him up.

"Raesh! Raesh!"

He was unresponsive and now that she was closer,

Andie could see that the wound was much worse than she'd thought. She kept shaking him and calling his name, but he wouldn't wake up. She pressed her hand on the wound and began to heal it, though it would need closer attention by someone more trained than herself. She set him up against the pillar where he would be safe and called Marvo over.

"What's wrong?" he said.

"He's been hit and it's bad. It's really bad. I can do some superficial healing now, but he needs real medical attention. I don't know enough about healing spells."

"Listen, you can't worry about that now. This is good, you did fine. Go help your people end this. We've almost got them beat and I can watch Raesh until this is over. Go be dragonborn."

Marvo gave her an encouraging smile and Andie nodded back. She looked down at Raesh again: he'd been so brave, so fierce, so unimaginable. He'd hidden his magic for so long and then he'd gone there that night and fought with the strength of ten sorcerers. He was incredible. She kissed his cheek and shifted him over to his father. She rose and headed back to the fight.

Floating above her enemies, with her shield encompassing her completely, Andie was a force that could not be reckoned with. She was not as strong or as practiced as the rest of her people, but she was a mean opposition. She rained the fire of her ancestors down on the professors relentlessly and when they erected shields above themselves, she burned right through them.

The dragonborn were making short work of their foes and even though more forces from the University had streamed in, the fight was nearly over. At that point it had become a mere formality for the professors and

Searchers to resist; they could not have stood against the dragons or the dragonborn, and certainly not the two together. Their screams were pitiable to hear and there was a grotesque carnage where men and women once stood, but they had been offered the chance of peace and denied it.

Spells, hexes, swords, fire, deighilts, bullets, and dragons filled the air. There were screams and grunts and the dull sound of bodies collapsing on the black marble. Pillars were lifted, split, or vaporized. There was carnage and destruction like the worst nightmare. The next wave of professors and monitors ran in, saw the havoc, and immediately retreated. That was the moment everyone knew which way the battle would turn. There was a certain feel in the air as the tide turned, as centuries of bloodshed, fear, and persecution met its end. The world sat then in a new condition where might was no longer the way of the executors.

Then a dragonborn warrior was struck in the chest with something small and dark; as it hit her, it grew and tangled itself around her. It bound her arms, her neck, her head, and grew so thick she could not be seen beneath it. It was some sort of magical plant. The rider couldn't manage to stay on her dragon and she fell—it must have been close to forty feet. She fell head first and just before she hit the ground, the vines rolled back to expose her skull.

Andie would never forget the gut-wrenching sound it made as the rider hit. The dragon reared its head in the air; it had dived to catch her but hadn't moved fast enough. It gesticulated and roared in the air, turning and coughing smoke in terrifying display of ancient fury. It opened its great jaws and Andie saw the bright glow of the flames rising from its chest. She looked to see the dragon's target. It was Tarven. He was standing stock still in his fright, a tiny ball of vines in his hand like the one that had bound the rider. The dragon's fire rose quickly. For some reason—perhaps for the good times, however false they were, or perhaps because her heart was so much purer than even she knew—Andie couldn't stop herself for reaching for him.

"Tarven, look out!"

Her scream seemed to jolt him out of his horrified stupor and he dove out of the room. Saeryn moved swift as the wind and cast a shield over all the newcomers and dragonborn, a great and luminous shield that was the strongest Andie had ever seen. The dragon's attack was unlike the small bursts it and the other dragons had used so far; this was a blast born of true hurt.

The fire filled the front of the room and then spread as far as the sides. It leapt high into the air and flooded over the shield like a flickering manifestation of death itself. Even through the shield they could feel the heat. Hundreds of cracks broke the marble as it was superheated by the flames and most of the professors and Searchers lost their lives when their shields were burned away. The only reason the rest managed to survive was because they escaped the room just in time.

Andie watched in horror at the scene of burning, death, and destruction that lay in front of her. This isn't what she had wanted. This isn't what she had wanted at all.

CHAPTER THIRTY-THREE

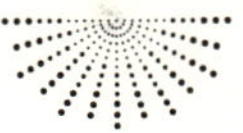

BY THE TIME THE FIRE SETTLED DOWN, THE PROFESSORS and their bevy had escaped. Andie could hear them shouting as they ran out through the hallway and into Leabherlann. They were crazed, frightened. They were screaming at the top of their lungs, telling everyone near that the dragonborn had returned.

Saeryn exhaled in a way that Andie had not known before and not just Saeryn, but each of the dragonborn, warriors and folk alike. Even the dragons snapped shut their jaws and lay down on the floor. Strangely, without reason or logic, Andie felt it, too. The relief, the sheer ecstasy pouring into them from the undercurrents of the last centuries. Peace. Breath, life. Possibility.

Safety.

Andie also experienced the emotion of her friends and the newcomers: utter shock. For centuries, the legends of the dragonborn had been in circulation—mostly as bywords or cautionary tales to scare children and delight evening parties—but never had they understood even a piece of the majesty and power that the forgotten race possessed. Before them stood warriors, priests, artists, tradesmen, and children from another time, herded from all around Shaeyara and captured at their weakest. But now they had returned more fearsome and shining than ever before. Andie and her friends were shocked to see the immensity of the dragons, the sheen of the armor, the scope and color of the spells, and the incalculable will of these fine and glorious people. Saeryn walked to Andie and took her hands.

"I was not born a warrior," she began. "I was made one through many years of hard training and persistence. I had no natural talent or appetite for war or the strength it required, but it was necessary. You, however, are a born warrior. Perhaps a scholar and priestess as well. I cannot say what single gift I see, but there is potential in you which I have not seen since that time from which I came. Thank you, on behalf of my people and their families. And on behalf of our dragons. But I also thank you for myself, for it was no mean feat to retrieve us from such peril. I owe you the very air I breathe."

And much to Andie's surprise, Saeryn kneeled before her, still holding both of her hands.

"You don't need to do that," she said, nervous, flattered, and embarrassed. "I'm no queen."

"Of course not. I am."

Andie drained of color; it seemed unreal, unfair that a queen knelt to her. But before she could absorb the shock of Saeryn's gesture, the rest of her people began to kneel as well. Elderly, children, warriors, everyone bent the knee to the nervous girl who'd finally accepted herself and her place in time. The entire dragonborn race kneeled before Andie Rogers.

"It is the custom of these people to show respect to

its guardians," Saeryn said. "Make no mistake, that is what you are now. I'm afraid this pales in comparison to the rites we would normally perform, but we have not the time just now. One day we will be able to repay you."

Saeryn rose and lifted her hand toward the ceiling. An enormous suction swept the room and seemed to gather all the air at once. It formed a flat, whistling vortex against the ceiling and as Saeryn flicked her fingers upward, the vortex shot up through the ceiling. Higher and higher it went, ripping and tearing marble, stone, earth, plants, and snow until it broke into the air hundreds of feet above. The hole led out somewhere on the mountainside far above. The dragon riders mounted the beautiful beasts and saluted Andie and her friends as they roared off into the giant hole on their journey to the sky. The adult dragonborn gathered the children and the elderly and ascended in crackling beams of purple light, some magic Andie had never known. She looked at Saeryn, confused.

"What's happening?"

"Andie, we must go where it's safe," Saeryn said, the space around her beginning to glow.

"But how will I find you? What will we do here? You can't leave me here. You can't leave me here alone!"

"Trust your blood and you may find us whenever you need us. Fight for who you are. Never live in shame. Together, we will prove to the world that we have every right to breathe and know peace as the rest of the lands. We are unique from sorcerers, but we need not be seen as dangerous. Merely different. We will meet again, soon, guardian. For now, we seek asylum."

And as the final word left her lips, Saeryn vanished. And with her the dragonborn were gone, again. Andie hadn't even realized that she was crying. She only wished her mother had lived to see that night.

"Everyone, to me now," Marvo called. "It's time to tell them who we are."

Marvo walked over to Andie to put his arm around her. He held her for a moment.

"Are you going to be okay?" he asked.

"Now that I know my people are alive... yeah, I'll be fine," she said, smiling.

"Good."

The newcomers gathered around Andie, Carmen, and Yara. Andie gazed around the faces and saw people she recognized: Murakami from Leabherlann, one of the working ladies from the mess hall, even the lady she'd met in the street her first night in Arvall.

"I see you found your way home after all," she said.

Andie saw professors she'd seen in the hall, a student or two, and the landlady from the restaurant—the middle-aged spinster who hadn't said a word. Kristole.

"I see you recognize a few of our faces," Marvo said. "I'm sure you remember Kristole, but what about her tattoo?"

Kristole turned around to show Andie the tattoo on the back of her neck. A hand in flames.

"Andie, cast a revealing spell on my neck," Marvo said, turning.

She waved her hand and suddenly the same hand in flame appeared on the back of Marvo's neck. She looked at it in awe. The other newcomers turned and Andie revealed the hand on all of their necks.

"Andie," Marvo said, "We're part of a secret society of allies to the dragonborn. We don't have a name, though we have from time to time been known as the

Council. We're made up of outcasts; some of us are purely human, like myself, but almost all of us have sorcerer's magic, but chose to refine it by natural means rather than be brainwashed by the University. I know you've never heard of us and that's because we've stayed hidden for centuries, passing our secrets on to our children so they could be ready to fight when the time came. This is a big day for both you and us. Our ancestors fought for your people. I'm sorry that they lost, but I'm overjoyed that we succeeded. For a very long time the University led the persecution of the dragonborn and their descendants, but we've been working on that, too. From the shadows, we've gained influence and spread a desire for peace. There's a quiet, but growing push against the University and every hateful policy it seeks to uphold. Your father was at the forefront of that."

For once, Andie wasn't shocked. She knew what kind of man her father was and how much good he was capable of.

"The University found out," Marvo continued. "That's why they caused your father's accident. To corrupt his memory and take him away from the vanguard. But don't be afraid. We're going to help you and your people reunite and stand for the justice that never should have been denied you. And I can promise you one thing," he said, taking her shoulders. "You are free to be everything you always were."

Marvo hugged her and Andie looked over his shoulder to see all the encouraging and smiling faces of the newcomers. "So, this is finally it," she said quietly to herself as she pulled away from Marvo's kind embrace. "The life and the friends and the future I always wanted." Marvo let her go and Andie hurried over to

Raesh. He was still unconscious, but the wound hadn't opened again. If they could get him to a doctor soon, he would be just fine.

"Stay with him while we check to make sure it's safe to leave," Marvo said, cocking his gun. "This place is full of dragon-hating sorcerers who just heard this battle echoing through the halls."

Andie nodded and took Raesh up into her arms again. Marvo and about half of the newcomers took off into the hallway and then up into Leabherlann. The rest of the newcomers combed the room looking for survivors and tending to their wounds. Carmen and Yara dropped down next to Andie. Carmen took one look at Raesh and started crying, holding her hand to his face.

"He'll be fine, Carmen, I promise," Andie said. "We just need to get him to a healer. I've done all I can for now, but a healer will fix him completely."

"He should never have been here," Carmen said through her tears. "This is all the University's fault. They'll answer for the things they've done."

"And we'll be the ones to ensure that," Yara said, reaching out to comfort Carmen and reaching the other hand out to Andie. "We won't leave you, Andie. I promise. Through fire and storm and battle, we'll stand by you."

"And I'll need you," Andie said, softly stroking Raesh's hair. "All my people will need you. The University has no idea the hell it just brought down on itself. I think that with the right words and a little patience we can reason with the rest of Noelle. Hell, we'll reach even the farthest edges of Shaeyara. I'll go to them, just as I am, and show them that we're not dangerous or evil, and that all we want is the peace they stole for themselves. But the University must pay. We'll show them no mercy, give them no advantage. The land has had too many cycles of hate and prejudice. Now we've turned the tide."

Andie held Yara's hand, Yara held Carmen's, and Carmen touched Raesh as Andie held him. A bond was struck then and there, a pact of loyalty harder than steel. Andie looked up.

"There'll be no corner in this world where they can hide."

FUELED BY DRAGON'S FIRE

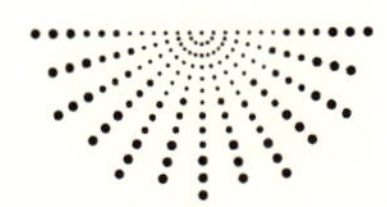

PROLOGUE

THE DRAGONS HAVE RETURNED.

It began as a rumor. A rumor like any of the hundred others that had been spread countless times over the centuries. But not once had they proved to be anything other than fabricated stories. Lies propagated by governments and institutions to incite fear and chaos throughout the great land of Shaeyara. Such a rumor had spread so frequently that this time no one seemed to care.

No one even blinked.

It had already been some time since the University in Arvall was ruined and shut down, but still, no one fully understood what took place there that night. No sense could be made from that wreckage. All the world knew was that the University had finally been toppled from its pedestal. The inhabitants of Arvall, one of the greatest cities of all of Noelle, all believed the professors to have gone crazy. As, after all, no one living had ever seen a dragon. Those creatures and their masters had not walked the earth in centuries, and it was insane, impossible even, that they had returned. No one believed it.

Not until they saw for themselves.

The dragons and their riders were first seen in the skies over Abhainn. Even from a thousand feet below, the dragons seemed like enormous manifestations of nightmares. People ran screaming, gathering their children and searching for shelter. No one had ever seen such creatures, such magnificent and terrible beasts that could cut the sky with speed like a thousand celestial knives. They had all heard the stories. Dragons were vicious beasts, capable of slaughtering villages in minutes with their fire. Dragons were evil beasts.

Or so the people were led to believe.

From the moment the first dragon was seen in the skies, rumors spread like wildfire through a brown field, to even the farthest reaches of Noelle. Even to the mine cities in the north where hardly any news ever came or went. Rage and panic began to move through the people. Several attempts were made to find the dragonborn, but it was impossible to track them. The dragons were too fast, and when they sensed they were watched, they could soar so high the eye could not follow them through the clouds.

When the tales began spreading from all corners of the land, however, people began to believe. What everyone once knew to be outlandish stories had finally come alive. The rumors spread by those who survived that horrible night at the University were finally believed. Not only did this mean the dragons had returned, but it also confirmed the deaths of all eight-hundred innocent people who had lost their lives in the mirror hall of the University on the night of their return.

The dragons killed them, people claimed. The evil dragonborn warriors brutally attacked the University that night, a great and angry race who had no business existing in modern time.

Fear grew among the people of Noelle, and the University was only spoken of in whispers for fear of drawing the dragons near. Although many were glad to finally see the University deposed as the leading influencer of Noelle, the people who died were most of the over one-thousand diplomats who had traveled to Arvall to enjoy the Winter Festival. The abrupt and terrible end of so many world leaders left Noelle in utter, devastating confusion as hundreds of politicians across the country clambered over each other to fill the power vacuum. Each claimed to be the one strong enough to lead the people to victory against the evil dragonborn and their dragons. The world waged war.

The threat of the dragons and their riders loomed over the land, increasing with each day that passed without the dragons being found. And so, all the world lived in fear.

But there was at least one who knew the truth.

CHAPTER ONE

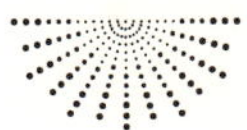

Andie stared down into the endless depths of the chasm that spread across the largest cavern they'd come across yet. Her toes clung dangerously over the edge, and the cool, damp air sent goosebumps up her arms as a strange breeze made its way up from the abyss, the wind a haunting song in her ear. "There's no way out," she whispered.

Their party had traveled through nearly every tunnel and corridor in their search for a way out, but they just kept going in circles. Every path eventually led back to that same cavern with the chasm they could never hope to cross. She was tired, hungry, and had grown thin and pale in the near constant darkness they had been living in for the past few months. Worse still, she had ceased to feel the connection to her people and their magic.

She feared for herself and her friends, but she worried more for the dragonborn out there in a modern world that wanted them slaughtered. A world that must be completely foreign and unwelcoming to them, and so far from home. She knew that with her and her friends trapped underground, nothing but evil rumors would spread throughout Noelle. Whether the University had shut down after their bloody battle or not, she knew in her heart they wouldn't stop until her people were found. Until her people were destroyed.

"Ow."

Carmen's voice pulled her out of her reverie. She had broken her ankle weeks before, and without their magic, they hadn't been able to mend it. Andie went over to her and kneeled beside her and began to rewrap the torn shirt tied around Carmen's ankle. It needed to be tighter. Even after all the time that had passed, her ankle still hadn't healed. Andie thought it was finally better some weeks ago, but when they found the bone was mending at the wrong angle, Marvo had to rebreak it. That certainly hadn't been their best night.

All of Andie's injuries had healed because of her dragonblood, but Carmen couldn't heal herself without a spell, which would bring the Searchers right to them. Since the night of the battle in the archives, the University had been monitoring the icons that remained implanted in Andie, Carmen, and Yara's hands. If any of the girls so much as cast a simple levitation spell, the University would know exactly where to find them. That was not an option. Not after all the trouble they had taken to hide themselves where no one would think to look for them.

"I'm so sorry, Carmen," Andie said as she yanked the wrapping as tight as she could. "I never meant to get you in this mess. I never meant to get any of you in—"

"I'm old enough to make my own decisions," Carmen snapped, ever defiant. "I did what I needed to do to protect my friend, and I would do it again. We'll get out of here, Andie, and we'll win. We'll win."

"Yeah." Andie wasn't so sure. Their party grew weak, and their chances of survival decreased with every passing moment.

"You know, this isn't the first time I've had to look out for one of my friends." Carmen unsteadily pushed herself to her feet and began collecting whatever small sticks and withered vegetation she could get her hands on to make a fire. "Raesh doesn't talk about it, but something happened when we were younger. I don't know if he ever got over it. Did he ever tell you?"

Andie took the sticks from Carmen's arms and began making a small fire away from the edge of the cavern. It took her numerous tries with the limited supplies they had collected, but eventually, the flame took and cast a much-needed warmth over their shaking bodies. Carmen curled on her side next to the fire, and Andie joined her, eager to hear what she had to say.

"When we were eight our parents took us to Taline. We were going to stay in a hotel there for a little while. It was back when they still had the Glass Games. You probably don't remember it, but there was loveglass everywhere in the most beautiful and brilliant shapes. The athletes were so talented; I remember one of them offered to take me on a short run and my parents said yes. He took me all the way up to the thirteenth floor of a building, then we swirled and flipped and drifted back down. It was incredible. Raesh was scared to be in the city then. I guess all the people and the size of the buildings scared him. I held his hand as we walked through the city."

Andie did remember. She held her hands out in front

of the small fire for warmth as she listened intently to Carmen's story. She had never heard this story before. Obviously, it was one Raesh didn't want her to hear, or else he would have told it to her himself. Nevertheless, she listened quietly as Carmen reminisced, staring dazed out into the dark corners of the cavern.

"Anyway, we'd been in Taline for a couple of nights already, and then one day we were around midtown, just looking for new collar robes for my father. I looked up, and I saw this pair of Red Ravens flying in circles above us. They say it's a sign of great fortune to have the ravens dance over you, to be chosen by them." A flash of a smile crossed Carmen's lips in the flickering firelight, but the smile was quickly replaced with a haunted expression. "I was so excited. I grabbed Raesh and pointed to the sky. But when I looked up again, the ravens had changed color and were flying away. I never knew until then that they turn black when they're scared. But I looked down Owl's Line, the main boulevard of the city, and there was this huge purple wave crashing toward us. By the time we knew what it was, the explosion had already reached us. Every one of us was knocked off our feet. I can't even describe what it was like. Hot, powerful, relentless energy. I've never seen anything like it. I can still hear the screams."

Andie nodded solemnly along to Carmen's recount. She knew it well. "The first terrorist attack in Taline. They've been plagued by them ever since."

"When the blast wall passed us, I couldn't find my parents or Raesh's. The air was so thick with dust. My eyes were burning, and my ears were ringing. A few moments passed, and I realized I could hear Raesh. He was screaming. He'd gotten thrown through the glass window of a nearby store, and his legs were buried in debris. But the building was collapsing; the debris was already falling off of it as the building collapsed in on itself. But I couldn't leave him there." A single tear trickled down Carmen's cheek. Andie pretended to look away as she wiped the evidence away with a torn sleeve.

"What happened?" Andie asked.

"I ran inside, ducking through the people rushing out. I helped him dig himself out, and then I half carried him out. I barely got him out in time before the entire building had collapsed right where he had been trapped. Our parents found us, took us up, and ran. I almost lost everyone I loved that day."

"You saved Raesh," Andie said, her eyes tearing lightly. "That's an incredible story. Is that why you're so… so…"

"Headstrong?"

"I was going to say protective."

Carmine laughed. "Yeah, that works, too. It's strange. That day helped make me who I am, but what I remember most isn't the explosion or the chaos. It's all those people running out of that building and ignoring that little boy stuck in the debris, screaming for someone, anyone to help him. To save him. I could never understand how people could be so cruel and so selfish."

"Fear and the unknown can make a person do anything, but more often than not it just shows you who you really are." These words held more meaning to Andie than Carmen could ever know. "But you didn't run. You saved him. You're a hero."

"No. I'm just someone who won't leave a friend behind. Where were you that day?"

"I was at home," Andie said, trying to hold onto her

emotion. She turned away from Carmen and looked back to the chasm behind them. "I never saw the explosion."

"You're lucky."

Andie nodded. "I..." she began, but she couldn't bring herself to say the words. The memories of that day have haunted her since she was a child. It was the day her mother had been taken away from her. The day her mother had been killed.

Andie managed to hold herself together with the exception of a few tears that refused to obey her. She turned back to Carmen and offered the most genuine smile she could. Carmen reached out to wipe Andie's cheek with her own sleeve and took hold of her shaking hand. She gave Andie a moment to breathe, to calm. They had gotten to know each other enough over the past few years that Carmen knew there was more going on behind Andie's eyes than she let on.

"Andie, I'm so sorry. I didn't mean to bring up anything painful for you."

Andie shook her head, and a hoarse laugh sounded from her throat. "No, no. It's fine. I'm fine."

"I only mentioned the story so that you know beyond the shadow of a doubt that I will never abandon you. Whether it's a falling building or racist professors. I'll be here."

Carmen took Andie's other hand and gave it a light squeeze. Andie could tell from her hands just how weak her friend had gotten. Carmen yawned, and Andie pulled her pack over for her to use as a pillow while she rested. Andie offered a final smile and got up to go back to the precipice, leaving Carmen to rest. There was something about staring into that cold and endless void that took Andie's mind off all the problems waiting above ground.

She glanced back momentarily to Carmen, who had already fallen asleep next to the dying fire.

After what seemed like an endless amount of time trapped in her own thoughts, Raesh walked up beside her and stood silently. He did that often, always knowing when to speak and when to be silent, almost as if he were reading her mind. He knew her that well. Right then Andie was hoping that he knew what she needed, which was to hear his voice, even if it was only bad news. She had grown to love that voice over the past few months, not that she would ever admit that to him. Not after she had brushed him off for so long while she was at the University. It was just one of the many things she regretted.

"Eight months," he finally said to her. "That's how long we've been stuck down here, roving back and forth through these tunnels, looking for a path that isn't here."

"What else can we do?" Andie asked, still staring out into the black. "It's almost a hundred percent guarantee at this point that there's only one way out of this place, and it's probably guarded with hundreds of professors. Without the dragonborn here to back us up, we'll never make it out alive."

"We have the dragonborn," he said. "We've got you."

Andie stood silent for a long moment. "I'm not enough."

Raesh turned to her, slowly, deliberately. For a moment, he just stared at her, as if he couldn't believe the words that had just come out of her mouth. "I don't ever want to hear you say that again. You're all we'll ever need."

She shared a look with him then that escaped her ability to define. With the immensity of the pressure and the reality of their situation, there hadn't been much time for romance, but she felt it whether he was near her or not. And she knew he felt it, too. It just wasn't the right time to act on it.

"Raesh," she began. "It's just that now…we can't really…I know what I've put you through with Tarven and the Archives and…the timing—"

"Isn't right," he said, nodding. "I know. Maybe someday."

He smiled at her and then left. She felt incredibly grateful. She turned around, looking for Marvo, and couldn't help but smile at Carmen snoring softly on the ground, curled up next to the burnt-out fire. Yara was also asleep, sprawled out near the dregs of the food reserves. They hadn't been able to scavenge in a while, and their reserves has gotten dangerously low. Andie's stomach grumbled just thinking about food.

She wrapped her arms tight around her waist, hoping no one had heard.

CHAPTER TWO

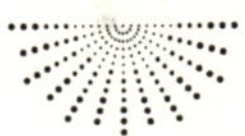

Marvo's fighters were scattered over the tunnel, sleeping, staring, eating, or finding some small way to pass the time, which was all they'd really had since the group came into the tunnels. Marvo was walking toward her, picking his way through the seated bodies and trying to dole out smiles as he went. He reached her undaunted, even though only one person had smiled back at him.

"It's getting harder to keep everyone motivated, Andie," he said. "A lot of them have already given up, and every day we lose a few more to this depression. We're dying down here. I think it's pretty clear now that the only way out is the way we came."

Andie stared at him with wide eyes, but in her heart, she knew what he said was true. "If we go back the way we came, they'll slaughter us for sure."

Marvo nodded. "I agree, but if we're just going to die down here anyway, it's a risk we need to take. If we'd known this eight months ago, we'd have had no problem fighting our way out, but we're weak now."

"I know. Even with my own healing abilities, I'm

finding myself growing weaker by the day. But if we try to face what's up there, I don't think we'll win."

"We'd have to approach it cleverly. We do have the element of surprise. They don't even know we're down here."

"We hope they don't. But even if we surprise them, we don't know what we'd be walking into. There could be no one up there, or there could be hundreds. We chose to come here to the tunnels under the University because we thought it was the last place they'd look for us, but that whole plan was contingent on them not knowing we're down here. If they've figured it out, they could just be waiting."

"We sent up scouts," Marvo said, his hands on his hips. "They just got back an hour ago."

"What?" Andie asked, excited and anxious at once. "Any good news? What did they see?"

"Nothing, but they only went as far as the cafeteria to scavenge some more food. They didn't see anyone at all, and they didn't hear anything, but that's not conclusive."

"It could be a ruse," she said, deep in thought. "Make the scouts think everything is okay so that we all go up."

"Possibly. But we can't continue like this. We need to get above ground. We might have won the first battle, but you know that this is far from over. The University has been in power for hundreds of years, and there is no way they're going to just give that up. If by some chance they go down, they'll do their best to bring the whole world with them." Marvo ran his hands through his hair as he spoke, his eyes narrowed in intense desperation.

"I agree."

"You know as well as I do that the lies about your people and their dragons have probably already spread coast to coast. Chancellor Mharú looked like a man on a mission, and he's had eight months to get his poison into Noelle. Factor in the droves of professors who are just as angry and hateful as he is, and you can imagine what that many powerful sorcerers can do."

Andie turned away from him, contemplating. Her mind was racing for a solution, anything that would help her escape having to risk the lives of everyone again. There had been so much death that night. She couldn't handle anymore. She wished she could find the connection to her people. She knew they would know what to do or even be able to rescue them. But the dragonborn had their own problems, and she and the rest of her party underground were alone.

"Maybe I can make it to the other side of the cavern," she said. "I think I could still be strong enough. We don't know what's on the other side. It could be our salvation."

"Andie, you're not listening," Marvo said, gently but firmly taking her by the shoulders. "We have to get out of here. And there is only one way to do that. You know it."

Andie looked at him, wanting to disagree, to fight him on it, to save her friends. But she knew he wanted to spare them as much as she did. And she knew he was right about what they had to do. She could see his heart breaking in his eyes. And then it hit her, solidly and without any illusions. The war for the heart of Noelle had only just begun.

"Okay," she said with a deep breath. "We'll all come together, finish the rations, and then leave as soon as everyone's rested."

Marvo nodded in response and then turned to go. He took a few slow steps away and then turned back to

Andie, his expression softened into one of compassion. "Hope is not lost, Andie. We still have a chance at survival."

Marvo's words filled Andie with a flicker of hope, but she dared not hold onto it for risk of setting herself up for disappointment. She knew their chances of survival were slim to none, but she supposed she could offer him what little faith she had left. When Andie finally nodded in agreement, Marvo turned again and left her to her own thoughts.

Andie spent a few more moments at the precipice before she came down to be with her friends. Scenarios of their escape ran rampant through her mind, none of which featured a desirable outcome. Still, she trusted Marvo's instincts. If he truly believed they had a chance, she would do everything in her power to make sure it happened. Andie closed her eyes and let out a deep breath she had been holding, the cool breeze that blew up from the depths of the chasm offered her a moment of peace. Finally, she opened her eyes and turned to gaze out at those who remained of their party.

Raesh was over with Kristole, talking something over vehemently. Carmen had begun stirring, possibly from a bad dream or the pain in her ankle. Yara was waking up, and she smiled when she and Andie made eye contact. Yara beckoned her over, and Andie went to join her friend. She and Yara had grown close over the past eight months. They had been friends at the University too, for sure. But something changed when they embarked on their journey underground. The two had grown closer than sisters, and Andie always relished the moments they shared together, no matter how brief.

Yara offered Andie one of the last pieces of stale

bread from their stores, but Andie refused as she sat down next to her friend. Yara shrugged and nibbled on the bread, and from the expression on her face, Andie imagined it hadn't kept all that well in the damp cavern. The two chatted quietly between themselves for some time, about nothing and everything all at once. They strengthened each other while Andie told Yara about the new plan. Yara seemed as uneasy about it as Andie was, but she knew what needed to be done. Perhaps that was why Andie had grown so close to her. She was always the first to act when anything was needed, and she supported Andie in all her decisions. She was the rock that grounded her.

Not too long later, Marvo made the announcement to everyone. There wasn't much of a reaction from the fighters. Like Marvo had said, they seemed to have given up completely. Raesh did what he could to rally them, but they mostly just sat down to eat and then drifted off at their own paces. Hardly anyone seemed to even listen or care. They were defeated, and Andie's flicker of faith began to go out as she looked on at the faces of the men and women around her.

"I know what this looks like," Marvo said loudly when it became clear his troops weren't responding to his announcement. "It must seem like suicide. Like we fought all those people and sat through all those nights of planning just to die here, in the dark. But that's exactly what we're trying to avoid. We can't stay here anymore, not if we ever want to see our families again. There is no way out of here, no back way, no secret passage, no magical tunnel waiting to be revealed."

Marvo's fighters began to stir. Andie listened from a distance with a small smile on her face. She was the reason they were all down there, and it was her duty to lead them to safety. But these were Marvo's men, and she knew only he could be the one to truly convince them of their strength.

"The only way out is back where we came in, and we all know what is waiting there," Marvo continued. "But I'm not scared. How can I be? We beat them once, and we'll do it again if necessary. Fortunately, it's unlikely that they even know we're down here. I wish I had something better to say, but the time for grand speeches hasn't come yet. All you need to know is that I'm going up there and I'm leaving, no matter what I find."

Andie walked over to join the fighters, the Council, looking up at Marvo and thinking that what he was doing was brilliant. He knew as well as she did that the fighters were tapped, borderline hopeless, and trying to rally them in any traditional sense was futile. But everybody loved Marvo, and the easier, better option was to inspire them not to believe in themselves but to believe in him. Give a soldier orders and someone to look up to and their path becomes clear.

"I think they believe him," Yara said as she joined Andie among the now livelier-looking crowd.

"I hope so," Andie replied, threading her arm through Yara's extended elbow. "Whoever we find up there isn't going to be happy to see us. If we can't muster the courage to take them on, then we'll die in this tunnel. In the dark."

"Personally, I'm more concerned about what comes after that. Not only do we have to make it through the city and find somewhere safe, but we have to fight the lie. By now everyone up there thinks that your people are dangerous, evil. They must be so afraid, and you know what people are capable of when they're afraid. What kind of horrors are waiting for us up there? What kind of world are we going up to?"

"I don't know, but I suspect they won't be welcoming us back with open arms anytime soon. I just hope my people have managed to escape. I can't imagine how much this world has changed since their time. Everything must be so different to them now, and they have no one to trust. I just want to see them again."

"You will. Soon," Yara said, leaning her head against Andie's. She then gave her friend a brief hug and left to go help Carmen recover their packs and get ready for their journey back up to the surface.

Within an hour, everyone had rolled up what few things they had and was ready to go. Raesh seemed hopeful, or at least was trying his best to look so. Marvo now looked sullener than he had before, and Andie knew the toll all of this was taking on him. Just as she worried for the dragonborn, she knew Marvo worried for his fighters. They had risked so much in coming there to her aid. There were no speeches or last looks at the dark, cold place that had been their makeshift home, just a high signal from Marvo and then the moving of feet. Andie was the only one to look behind her and stare off into the deep dark of the cavern one final time.

The journey was slow, measured. Everyone was thinking the same thoughts and feeling the same fears, but it was eerily quiet as they walked. Carmen and Yara walked a few paces ahead of Andie, who walked side by side with Raesh, though even they were quiet. Andie nodded to both Kristole and Murakami, who had held up well even though they were the two oldest members of the group. Andie looked around her, took a serious look at the state they were in for the first time in a while.

They were thin, haggard, the men unshaved and the women's hair pulled back in loose, rough ponytails. All of the fighters wore black, but their clothes were horrendously dirty, frayed, and threadbare. Everybody walked slightly bent as if the invisible weight of the world was pulling their shoulders down. And although she couldn't see it with her eyes, she knew that they were all hungry and worn out inside. The battle at the University had been one fight, and living underground had been another. And, as much as it hurt Andie to think it, these fights were only just the beginning.

They may have won some battles, but they were still far off from winning the war.

CHAPTER THREE

IT ONLY TOOK A FEW HOURS BEFORE THEY NEARED THE surface. A muted, warm light flooded in from before them, and Andie could sense everyone's spirits rise immediately. Raesh had been sent ahead to scope out their exit, and Andie stood strong before the rest of the party, soaking in what little sunlight she could. Even the faint glow on her skin revitalized her, and she felt stronger than she had in months.

"It looks clear," Raesh said when he returned. "I didn't see or hear anything, but I don't like this at all. It doesn't feel right."

"I agree, son, but we don't have a choice. There's no way we can go back." Marvo paced back and forth as we all stood ready, waiting for his orders. Andie had stepped back and allowed Marvo to take over command. There was no one better than he to lead the group to victory, but she remained ready to step forward when the time came. Marvo turned back to face everyone and gave his commands. "Raesh, you stay up here at the front with me. I may need you and your pearlblood magic to blast through some things."

"Or some people," Raesh grinned. He looked like he was actually having fun, and Andie couldn't help but laugh. Raesh winked at her when he caught her staring, and a slight blush crept up her cheeks. She feigned a cough and turned the other way. It was definitely not time for flirting.

"Andie, I want you and Yara to bring up the rear. We don't need anything surprising us from behind. Carmen, you stay in the middle and try to be as light on that ankle as you can. Everybody stay in tight and stay ready. We're only going to get one shot at this."

"What do you think this is?" Yara asked.

The group looked around at one another, waiting for someone to answer. Andie rubbed her neck and let out a loud sign. "A trap," she finally said.

Silence swept through the tunnel at her words, but soon after everyone fell into position as Marvo directed. The fighters formed into a loose phalanx and Andie and Yara kept their heads up, looking for anything and everything. Andie had great instincts, and everything inside was telling her they had walked into something strange. It was simply too easy.

In a matter of moments, everyone had cleared the edge of the tunnel, and they were above ground for the first time in months. But the farther they moved, the less sure Andie was. She tried to convince herself that their plan had worked, that the University had never known they were down there—after all, that was the point of their plan in the first place.

"Yara, how do you feel?"

"Like I'm going to be sick. My stomach is in knots."

"Good. Something isn't right. Don't do anything sudden, but get yourself ready. If they're going to attack it's going to be soo—"

Just as the words were leaving her mouth, a spell came from somewhere in the grand hallway and shattered the wall above the entrance to the tunnel. The debris fell in over the entrance and blocked it completely. Suddenly, people began to appear out of nowhere. Professors, Searchers, and some new adversary wearing all silver. Where before there had only been space and passageways, there were now dozens of enemies. They had apparently been using an invisibility spell. Andie looked in every direction, panic forming at the pit of her stomach. They were surrounded.

Time slowed for Andie. Suddenly she was thinking about all the questions she'd never have the chance to ask about her people. For all she knew they were dead already, and if they weren't, then it wouldn't be long before there was all out war. A thousand regrets passed through her mind as she gazed out at their enemies. They looked strong, fearless. She and her supporters were no match for these hateful people.

One of the silver-clad people moved forward, and Andie took a small step back. But as it came closer, Andie realized that it wasn't, in fact, a person dressed in silver at all. It looked to actually be *made* of silver. It wasn't human. It moved sedately, almost like a specter, yet it radiated danger and death. Andie could feel its magic radiating off it, an electric sting over her pale skin.

It moved to within a few feet of her and became still. Too still, as if all life had left it. Its mouth opened so wide that the rest of its face slid to the back of its head.

Andie stood, paralyzed, staring into the blackness of the thing's mouth.

Its voice was metallic and void of all emotion. She had never met anything so inhuman in her life. "I am one of the twelve Sentinels. Forged in the furnaces of the Old World and reawakened now to restore peace."

The words were monotone, yet oddly hypnotic, no doubt spelled to mess with the mind of anyone who heard it. The thing that was hardest to comprehend was that as it spoke, its lips didn't move. It didn't even have lips. The sound simply came up from the center of it through its mouth. It was terribly unnerving.

"You and your fellow anarchists have been deemed enemies of the state, and it is only by your capture or execution that the land of Noelle may return to peace. You should choose your next step wisely." The mouth closed and the sentinel moved back to its post.

Andie tried to look to Marvo for a plan, but she couldn't see him. It didn't matter. She knew they didn't have time to compare notes and draw up a plan, but she did have her dragon magic. There was no point in hiding anymore since they were staring right at her. Quicker than the enemy could react, Andie raised her hands and pushed her magic out through space. She harnessed all the power she could muster, drawing on the energy she felt from the sunlight. Two great walls of lavender magic raced out to either side of her, crushing everything in their paths and destroying the walls of that room and the next three as well.

As the bodies flew and the dust and debris began to cloud the air, the Council began their attack. They erected shields to block the incoming hexes and created gaps through which they could cast in retaliation. The professors and Searchers hid behind the stone of the passageways and ducked the onslaught of magic. Raesh and Yara, despite how tired they must have been, cast furiously. Even Carmen pulled her strength together to fight.

They were making excellent progress, slowly continuing to inch forward as the spells flew all around. Andie, however, was barely able to stand. She hadn't quite noticed just how weak she was. Never realized how much the dragonborn needed warmth and sunlight. She had so much to learn about her people. The cold, damp, dark of the tunnels had been the worst possible place for her. The environment had sapped her even more than the constant hunger. The massive spell she had just done had taken a tremendous amount of what little strength she had left; it would have been nothing to her on a regular day, but now she felt weak, lightheaded. Yara sensed that something was wrong and caught Andie under her arm to support her.

"Hey, what's wrong?" she asked. "Andie, what's wrong?"

"Don't worry about me. Keep fighting."

"When your all-powerful best friend, who happens to be a member of one of the oldest and strongest races on earth, starts turning pale, something is wrong."

"I need the sun. I need warmth. I didn't know how depleted I was. I just need to get outside."

"And I'll get you there, I promise. Just stay on your feet."

Yara took on a new ferocity then, supporting Andie with one arm and casting with the other. Marvo was nearby, fighting like a wild man. He'd run out of ammo the night of the Winter Festival, and now he was getting in close for combat, and despite his age, he was too much for the professors who only knew how to fight with magic. The group was almost around the corner of the hall; all they needed to do was fight through a dozen professors.

Just when they were nearly through, though, three of the Sentinels dashed in front of them, no longer sedated and unbelievably quick. They stood there, silent and still, and waited for the group to come to them. The fighters began casting at the Sentinels, but the beings moved too quickly. One of the Sentinels reached forward, and its arm stretched ten feet and pierced right through Kristole. Andie screamed as she tried to call on her strength to help, but the older woman was dead before she hit the ground.

The other Sentinels changed their shape, made themselves bigger and began to knock the fighters aside with incredible force. With every hit, she could hear bones breaking. The Sentinels were merciless. Raesh turned to one that was moving in to attack him and tried to defend, but the Sentinel was too quick. It knocked him back several feet and then raced to hit him before he stood. Raesh rolled out of the way and came back to his feet. He cast a spell, missed, and was hit so hard he shook dust from the walls. Yara was about to release Andie to go help when Raesh unleashed his frenzied, unbridled magic and ripped right through the Sentinel in a brilliant blaze of yellow light. As the Sentinel flew back, Raesh looked to Andie with the widest grin on his face she had ever seen.

Andie looked all around her and saw the carnage that had fallen on them. She knew there were only a few moments left before the end. She gathered every ounce of strength she had left and pushed Yara aside. One of the Sentinels had liquefied itself and then completely submerged one of the fighters. It was impossible to tell exactly what had happened. As it turned to Andie, she raised her hands in front of her.

"Everybody down!" she yelled.

The fighters ducked, and Andie sent out the hottest, brightest flame she could muster. The two remaining Sentinels were blown back and incinerated in the air before they could even fall back to the floor. She had saved her friends. The enemies withdrew, but she felt herself falling backward, leaving, disappearing.

Then darkness.

"GET HER UP, we have to move!"

The sound of running feet. So many running feet.

"Lookout, there's more of the— "

"Hold her, come on, faster, faster— "

Speed. Gravity. The world sliding by at a sheer angle and the green-tinted rain pounding across space.

"There's too many of them!"

"Everybody run for the front! Don't get left be— "

Crashing. Something huge and fast and dangerous crashing. The world is tilting, turning, tumbling.

"Is he dead? Turn him ov— "

The soft falls of the thick rain. Feet hitting water. Yelling.

"Yara! Raesh!"

"Coming up from behind!"

A ship.

. . .

WHEN ANDIE WOKE, she didn't know what time or even what day it was. She looked around and didn't know where she was. The only things she recognized were Raesh sitting in a chair across from her and Yara in the bed next to her. The room was small, brightly painted, and simply furnished. It didn't take her long to realize that the room was lolling gently from side to side. They were on a ship. She was more confused than ever. The only things that brought her comfort were her friends and the sunlight streaming in through the open window, though the window was small. She turned over and lay her hand on Yara's shoulder. Yara woke with a start.

"Andie! Are you okay? How do you feel?" Yara pushed herself up on the bed and looked down at Andie with concern in her eyes.

"Better. A lot better," Andie said. She stretched out her arms and realized what she said was true. She felt totally fine. "Whose ship are we on?"

"The Council's," Yara said through a yawn. "Turns out they're a lot bigger than we thought they were. They've got factions all over west Noelle. They were waiting for us at a port on the coast of Arvall."

Andie sat bolt upright. "What? Why didn't Marvo tell us he had a plan? Where is he?"

"He was injured in the escape, but they say he'll pull through. Andie, I have to tell you something."

Yara took Andie's hand and looked in her eyes. Andie knew that whatever was coming was going to hurt.

"The enemy knew we were coming."

CHAPTER FOUR

ANDIE STARED AT YARA FOR A LONG MOMENT BEFORE she spoke. "What do you mean, they knew we were coming? No one knew we were down there."

Yara shook her head and rubbed her eyes with the palms of her hands. "They knew we were coming, Andie."

"But how?"

Yara simply stared at her until comprehension dawned on Andie's face. "You mean someone betrayed us? How?"

"I don't know, but I suspect it's why Marvo didn't tell any of us about the ship," Yara said. "He'd been trying to smoke them out weeks before the battle in the Archives, but nothing ever happened, and he thought maybe he'd misjudged. But he started to get suspicious again after we hid in the tunnels. Someone had been throwing away our rations from the scavenging trips. And even if the University had known we were down there, there was no way they could have known exactly when we'd come up. Somebody told them to be ready to ambush us."

"Well, who is it?" Andie asked, disbelieving. "Who betrayed us?" The idea that one of their own was a traitor made her feel sick to her stomach. After everything they had been through together, she couldn't imagine any of them turning their back to the cause.

"We don't know. We lost some people in the escape, but whoever it is must be on the ship with us. The University wouldn't hurt them and risk losing an informant if we got away."

"Did you see anyone in the fight who wasn't being targeted?"

"No. Did you?"

"No. I have to find Marvo. We need to find this person now."

"Wait," Yara said, pointing to Raesh. "Let him rest. Let's talk outside."

The girls got up and quietly moved around Raesh until they were outside. They walked down several hallways, and they exited up onto the lower deck. Andie's body was still healing, and the moment the direct sunlight touched her, she began to fill with energy, power. It felt amazing.

"I don't know if I can believe it," Andie finally said as they leaned against the wooden deck rails. She stared out into the open ocean, curious where they were headed but not wanting to change the subject before she found out the truth about their traitor. The sea breeze sprayed salt water over her skin as she stood there in silence, contemplating what Yara had told her. Andie squeezed her eyes shut as she thought, relishing in the warmth of the sun and the refreshing sea air.

"Andie, I know how you feel," said Yara, looking out over the sea. "We have to keep this to ourselves for now, though."

"Are you kidding me? No way. I have to find out who did this to us. How many people did you say we lost?"

Yara shook her head. "I didn't. Right now, it doesn't matter."

Andie turned to her friend, her eyes flashing with anger. "Of course, it matters. Every single person here matters. I have to know who would betray us like this."

"Please, Andie. Promise me you'll stay quiet. Just for now."

"Are you insane? I'm not letting us go another minute with a traitor amongst us. Whoever it is could be using a hundred different methods of invisible communication to talk to the University. We have to do something now."

"Andie, there's no way to tell who it is. If they've been in the Council this long, they're obviously good at pretending."

"It must have been someone doing scavenging missions."

"Andie, we were all doing scavenging missions. And almost all of us have done at least one solo mission. Look, Marvo took a huge risk in telling me. The only people we know it can't be are you, me, and Marvo."

"And Carmen and Raesh."

"We hope Carmen and Raesh."

Andie couldn't even respond. She just stared at Yara, dumbfounded.

"Don't look at me like that, Andie. You know Marvo wants to trust his own family, but this thing is too big to leave to chance or love. We have to be one hundred percent sure before we even think of giving anyone the benefit of the doubt."

"Let's just find Marvo."

Andie didn't say a word as Yara lead her through the halls. It wasn't until they reached the rooms that Andie began to greet and check on the fighters. Carmen was sleeping, having finally gotten her ankle properly seen to. The ship was much bigger than Andie had anticipated, and there were fighters stationed everywhere. Andie couldn't help giving them all a cold stare when they weren't looking; any one of them could have been the spy. When they reached Marvo's room, he was sitting up in bed, a bandage covering most of the right side of his face and several smaller bandages in various places across his arms. Andie had to take a breath when she saw him. Yara went to sit in the corner.

"Easy, Andie," he said. "I'm perfectly fine, aside from some minor scrapes. There's a lot of them, but nothing too serious. I'll heal…"

Andie took an angry step forward and opened her mouth to scold him for not trusting his own family, but Marvo held up his hands and spoke before she got a word out.

"… And before you berate me for not trusting Raesh and Carmen, just trust that I've thought it out and that it's even harder for me than it is for you. Now have a seat, we've got some catching up to do."

Andie stared at him incredulously for a long moment, then finally let out a loud sigh and pulled a chair up to his bedside. She took Marvo's hand and waited for him to start, holding her own words in until she fully understood what he had to say.

"First, we've been branded enemies of the state. Not just Arvall City, but all of Noelle. There are wanted posters of our faces up for thousands of leagues, and who knows whatever else around the entire rest of Shaeyara outside the boundaries of Noelle. You don't even want to know how much the reward for our heads is. If we're caught, that's it. We'll be executed the same day. We've got to be more than careful in the coming weeks."

The news didn't surprise Andie. She had figured as much was happening from the first day they entered the caverns below ground eight months before. "What else?"

"We still don't have any word on your people. There were some sightings in north central Noelle, but that was months ago. But no news is good news because it means—"

"They haven't been captured yet," Andie finished.

Marvo nodded. "Exactly. It seems they've evaded capture so far. We've barely even heard whispers of their potential whereabouts."

"They're probably headed somewhere with mountains. That's where they'd be most comfortable. I haven't tried reaching out to Saeryn in a while, but maybe I could—"

"Trust me, Andie, for now, let them hide. We'll find them when the time is right. We've been lucky so far. I had my people waiting at the docks the night of the battle, thinking we'd come straight out. But when we decided to stay inside, they stayed at the dock and waited."

"Who are these friends of yours?"

"Just more people on our side, Andie. But never mind about that. The University is going to reopen, and it's going to be more dangerous than ever. They're planning on becoming a military training facility, and that means their sole focus will be teaching sorcerers how to excel at war. And they've vowed to rid the earth of the world's greatest enemy: the dragonborn."

The words felt like poison in her ears. As if the world wasn't toxic enough, the University was now going to add strength to their hatred. Andie could hardly believe how cruel and unjust the world could be.

"There's already been a formal declaration of war," Yara said from the corner. "From what we can tell it was met with rousing applause in the streets. They've certainly done a good job of convincing the world of the dragonborn's evil. The only way to save us now is to reunite you with your people and try to convince the entire world that the dragonborn aren't a threat."

"Fat chance," Andie said with a humorless laugh.

"You don't know how right you are," Marvo said, squeezing her hand. "When we were running through the streets, we saw the city burning. Raids, attacks, more desperate people than I've ever seen in my life. Complete and utter carnage. And you wouldn't believe what kinds of hateful propaganda the University is putting out. The most awful things you can think of. They're calling you and your people a plague."

"We're running out of time."

"We may already be out of time."

"I guess I understand that. Where are we headed now?"

"To the True Isles. I know you've never been so I won't try to describe it to you, except to say that if you ever wondered what paradise looked like, you're about to find out."

"And what's in the True Isles? More allies?"

"Yes, and hopefully a way to get those icons out of you girls. For all we know the University could be tracking us now."

"True. Well, if we get rid of them that will be one less thing to worry about. How far are the isles form Michaelson? I want to see my dad."

"Andie," Marvo began, sitting up and looking away. "I can't let you go there."

"Are you out of your mind? What do you think they'll do if they catch him? They'll torture him for information!"

"Andie, calm down and think. We've been underground for months. If they had wanted your father, they could have found him and killed him by now."

Andie closed her eyes and shuddered. She couldn't bear the thought of anything happening to him, especially not after she had been so lax in staying in touch with him in the weeks before they went into hiding. She didn't know what she'd do if anything had happened to him.

"As it happens, I'd already sent people to get him the night of the battle. Hopefully, they're still at the safe location I established. We've already sent word for them to meet us in the True Isles. I know it's not ideal, but this is the safest way."

Andie nodded slowly. The slow sway of the ship calmed her, made her feel somehow grounded, strangely enough. "I understand."

"Speaking of safety, I've said all I can say to you about what's ahead for us."

"Meaning?" Andie crossed her arms and stared back at Marvo, a look of sheer indignation in her eyes.

"Meaning I trust that you're not our spy, but I don't

trust that you won't talk to Raesh and Carmen about the things you just heard."

She couldn't believe that not only was there a traitor among them but that Marvo could ever in a million years consider that Carmen and Raesh couldn't be trusted. Being thorough was one thing, but not trusting the two of them was ridiculous. Her anger was mitigated by how much it hurt her to see him laid up like that. Andie didn't even bother responding. She stood and was already out in the hall before she turned around to face Marvo and Yara.

"Fine. You sit there and be suspicious of everyone, of your own blood, and I'll go on trusting the people who have repeatedly risked their lives for me."

Marvo began to speak, but Andie was out of the room before he could say a word.

CHAPTER FIVE

ANDIE WALKED THE LOWER DECK SIX TIMES BEFORE SHE could bring herself to relax. She tried her best to see the situation from Marvo's angle, but she just couldn't wrap her brain around what he was doing. She finally settled towards the back of the deck and leaned over the rail, looking down into the roiling depths of the ocean they traveled through. The misty salt air made her skin itch, but she ignored the sensation and tilted her head back, basking in the warmth of the sun.

She tried to reason with herself, considering why Marvo might not trust those closest to him. It wasn't so uncommon for sorcerers to use spells to control people's mind and make them do whatever they wanted. Raesh and Carmen could be doing someone else's bidding against their will. She realized Marvo was probably right in his secrecy, as perhaps their traitor wasn't even intentionally betraying them. Someone could be acting against their will. Trapped in their own mind.

Andie sighed loudly and rubbed her eyes. The idea that one of her own, possibly even one of her closest friends, could be being controlled by the enemy made her stomach tie up in knots. She gritted her teeth in determination, clear at what she must do. She had to discover the traitor as soon as possible. She couldn't waste any time.

The winds picked up, and the water began splashing up more violently, and Andie began pacing again, trying to think back to when someone could have been spelled. If that was in fact what happened, it must have been an exceptionally powerful spell to have lasted that whole time. She didn't even know anyone powerful enough to have set such a spell, even at the University. She so desperately wanted to believe whoever betrayed them did it against their own will, but her instinct told her otherwise.

She finally settled down enough to realize how beautiful the view was. She stopped and leaned on the railing. She'd only seen the Spider Sea once before, but never from a ship. The sun was falling into the horizon, and the sky overhead was like a chest full of gold that someone had tossed across the black of space. And below, the sea was endless, already beginning to be dappled with the light of the trench spiders. They were coming up from the caves, where they rest during the day, to play near the surface of the sea during the night.

The water seemed ten times darker than it was when they came up and brought the incredible silver light of their bodies. Trench spiders looked similar to the spiders on land, only about twenty times bigger and their eight legs were like eight long feathers. Their thorax looked like a dandelion. Andie couldn't help but notice how stunning they were, thousands upon thousands of those little silver lights coming up from the trenches as far as the eye could see.

"They're kind of incredible."

Andie was startled by the voice, but it was only Raesh. He looked well, like he hadn't been hurt much during the escape, but Andie wasn't really surprised. Raesh's magic couldn't be controlled like hers could, but he was still extremely powerful, and he was learning how to use his particular kind of magic to his advantage. She was so busy looking him over for injuries that it took her a moment to realize he was smiling at her. She smiled back.

"I see you came out practically unscathed," she said.

"With the exception of a few bruised ribs and a smattering of completely not serious cuts. My dad got it a little worse, I think. But, he'll be fine."

"Speaking of your dad. I just spoke with him and Yara."

"And I can tell by the tone of your voice that he told you about the traitor and certain people who have yet to be ruled off his list of suspects?"

"He told you about that? You mean he actually told you to your face that he didn't trust you?"

"Well, it wasn't quite like that. You have to understand, he's being thorough. You and he are our leaders and, honestly, neither of you can afford to make any kind of move without thinking of every possible outcome. I know he wants to trust me, but he has to look out for so many people now. And, you know, for all he knows, I could be one hundred percent loyal to him, but be under a professor's spell or something."

Andie stared at him for a minute but eventually relented.

"I know," she said, running her hands through her hair in frustration. "I had the same thought, as well. I just can't believe this is happening. How could one of our own friends do this to us? It's unreal. And maybe Marvo is a leader, but Yara should know you two well enough to give you the benefit of the doubt."

"Maybe you should cut her some slack."

"For what? You gonna tell me she's a leader, too?"

"In her defense, she caught Carmen and me talking about some things."

"Like what? What could make her doubt you two? What, were you planning to capture me and render me powerless?"

Raesh looked away and didn't respond. Andie waited and watched him, feeling her joke lose its humor dramatically as the seconds passed.

"Raesh?"

"You have to understand, Andie. You're the most powerful person we know. Maybe one of the most powerful in the world."

"I think that's a bit of an over exaggeration, Raesh," Andie snorted.

"No, I'm serious. You're both sorceress and dragonborn. I've searched the records, and I don't think there's been anyone else like you… ever."

Andie blinked and stared at him a long moment, but she supposed she hadn't heard of another like her, either.

"And we don't even know the extent of what your dragonblood can do," Raesh continued. "Andie, you can fly. You can make lightning stronger, brighter, and hotter than anything I've ever seen. Your body can heal any injury. There might not even be a limit to your power. We know, beyond anything, you would never willingly betray us, but if you were ever to fall under the control of one of the professors or anyone else… I don't know if we'd ever be able to stop you."

Andie considered him a moment and then nodded. "I suppose you're right."

"It was only a list of possible contingency plans," Raesh said. When Andie turned to look at him, her eyes blazing, he quickly added, "None of which we kept, by the way. But, Yara happened to overhear us. I think deep down she knows we'd never do it unless we had to, but it really shook her up, and I guess I never realized how much."

"I see," Andie said, turning from him to the sea.

They stared out at nothing for nearly ten minutes, letting the silence fill them as they thought about the relationships and potential in their lives. Finally, Andie sighed.

"I'm sorry, Raesh. I know it's something no one wants to admit, but something we all should be worried about. If anybody ever figured out how to control me, it would be… catastrophic. And, if I'm being honest, I guess what really has me so freaked out is passing out during the escape."

"What do you mean?"

"It's humiliating."

"Don't even start with that," Raesh said, turning to her. "You're dragonborn. You need the sun to stay strong, and none of us even knew that. You'd been underground for eight months. If you weren't so powerful, you wouldn't have even been able to do as much as you did. You took out two of those Sentinels. You're the reason we survived."

"Well, in the interest of giving credit where credit is

due, you took out one yourself. What were those things anyway?"

"I have no freaking clue. No one has ever even heard of them. It did say it was from the Old World. Whatever they are, they're powerful. Incredibly powerful."

"I don't remember what happened after I took down those two. Who all did we lose?"

"By the time we made it outside, there weren't many of us left. We ran as fast as we could, and my dad and I carried you. The Searchers chased us and never stopped firing. We lost another on the way out."

"How did we escape?"

"We made it to SKY 6 and took over the train. We started down Brie and, for a while, we thought we were safe, but the Searchers had got on the train, too, and they brought five more of those Sentinels with them. We couldn't really fight them off. There weren't enough of us then, and you were unconscious."

"Raesh," Andie tried to make out the expression on Raesh's face, but he stared out at the setting sun, his face as blank as she had ever seen it. "I'm so sorry I wasn't able to help."

Raesh didn't even seem to hear her. He continued as if she hadn't even spoke. "We lost two more in the fighting. One of the Searchers set the train on fire with his gun, and then the train started to shake. The gravity control gave out. Before we knew it, we were all floating, but it gave us the upper hand. We managed to take out all of the Searchers, but the Sentinels were too strong. They killed two more of us and hurt my dad."

"I..."

"The only thing that saved us from them was the same thing that almost killed us. The train went off the rails. Yara and Carmen locked us all in a protective shell. The Sentinels almost broke through their magic, but they were thrown as the train cars tumbled, flipped, and raced down the mountain. Everything was tearing apart around us. Crashing, exploding, being ripped away. We finally landed at the bottom, half alive, but away from the Sentinels. Luckily, my dad's friends were still waiting by the sea. And we escaped."

"That sounds incredibly terrifying. Raesh, I'm so sorry I couldn't help. I'm sorry I wasn't strong enough to…"

"Andie, stop."

"I'm sorry."

"It was a nightmare. But we made it."

"Yeah, you did. And you saved me, too."

She gave Raesh's shoulder a squeeze, and he finally looked back at her as if he had been pulled away from a dream. He looked haunted, but he smiled back.

"I guess I did."

LATER THAT NIGHT as Andie was lying in her bed, restless beyond anything imaginable, she heard the door open behind her. She turned over to see who it was. Yara. Yara first walked into the room, and then took a step back and leaned on the open doorway. Andie could tell she had something she wanted to say, but after the cold shoulders they'd exchanged earlier, it was difficult for them to face each other.

Andie turned back over, hoping Yara would talk herself out of whatever half apology she was thinking up just then. For a long time, Yara sat staring at the wall, not speaking, not moving, hardly even breathing, and Andie lay in her bed, trying desperately to fall into the sleep she knew would never come when she wanted it.

"You think you've got it all figured out."

Andie grew angry almost instantly. If Yara had come to apologize, it would have been bad enough, but to come into the room in the middle of the night and accuse her? And exactly what was she accusing her of?

"You can lie there and pretend to be asleep or pretend that you can't hear me. It'll only make this easier. You think that because we're all here together and we have a history that we can all be trusted. Given the benefit of the doubt outright. Well, that's the definition of a traitor, Andie. Someone you trust. Someone you would never suspect in a million years."

Andie lay still, listening. The gentle sway of the ship rocked them back and forth, the sound of the ocean on the other side of the smooth wooden walls a muted rhythm that Andie hoped would lull her to sleep.

"The University is smart, so smart," Yara continued. "They know who matters to you most and who you would blindly put your faith in. All Marvo and I are trying to do is protect the more than five hundred lives on this ship, including yours. And I'll pretend I didn't notice when you forgave Marvo practically immediately and yet you won't even turn over now to look at me. Whatever."

Andie sighed and turned towards the doorway where Yara stood with her arms crossed. Her expression smoldering in the dim light. "Yara…"

"But it doesn't matter," Yara interrupted. "I'm still your friend. I'm still your ally. I'm still the girl you asked to come along on this impossible mission with you because you knew that I would always do the right thing."

"I asked Carmen, too."

"Well, Carmen isn't cleared yet. It's like you're not even listening to me!"

Yara pushed herself away from the door and paced for a bit. Andie curled herself up even more, grabbing the pillow up around her head in a fruitless effort to get more comfortable. After a few minutes of pacing angrily, Yara threw herself onto her bed.

"I've been in Arvall City for the last ten years. Since I was sixteen. But I wasn't always there. I was born on the other side of Noelle. It was a small town, a village really. It didn't even have a name. It was like it was the place that time forgot. That everything forgot. But we were happy there. We didn't have much, but we had each other."

Andie tried to read Yara's face, but she simply stared up at the ceiling, refusing to meet Andie's gaze.

"Actually, we were pretty poor. Unbelievably poor. But so was everybody else." Yara spoke slowly, as if recalling a painful memory that she had hoped to forget. "For a long time, I didn't even recognize that we didn't have money or nice things, but the older I got, the more I began to understand that we weren't okay, that we had nothing. And I remember I would get so angry when I looked around our house, or what was left of it, and see that we were living like… like I don't even know what. So, I started to steal. Little things at first. Bananas, potatoes, towels. Things we needed to survive. My mother would ask where they came from and I would lie, saying people gave them to me or I found them or I earned them from doing jobs around the village. But soon I grew bored. I wanted more. So, I started stealing other things. Money. Family heirlooms. Clothes. Things we didn't need, but I wanted. But that wasn't enough either."

"Why are you telling me this?" Andie asked, but Yara ignored her question.

"I started sneaking around the big cities that were to the north of us. And by then I was good. I was the best. You can't imagine all the things I had. Money, jewelry, more food and clothes and things than I could use in a lifetime. And then one day I decided never to go home again. To stay in the city and live the life I thought I deserved. I was only fifteen, but people care less about your age and more about what you can do for them when you have the skillset I did. And so, I left."

"Yara..."

"My parents came looking for me. My connections told me they were getting close, so I hid away where they would never find me," Yara continued. "A few months passed. I came out again, and I found out that they had never left. They'd stayed in the city, living in an alley behind the apartment I'd been staying in. Some gang was doing their business in the alley and my parents were just there and happened to see it. And so, they killed them. They slaughtered my parents right there in the alley like they were nothing. Of course, they did it with magic, and the police didn't have the resources to track that kind of attack. And it was days before anybody even noticed the smell and found the bodies."

"I'm so sorry," Andie whispered. She had no idea her friend's life had been so dark.

"It was strange. All I had to do was go down and see them. Talk to them. Tell them I didn't want to go home, that I could provide for all three of us there in the city. And it wasn't even them I was running away from. It was poverty. It was hunger and cold and fear. I just wanted to feel safe in my own life."

Andie didn't know what to say. Yara was opening up about her past for the first time, saying things Andie never could have imagined. She didn't know how to react. She loosened the ball she'd made of herself and turned over to her other side so that she faced Yara completely. Yara was still staring up at the ceiling. Her eyes seemed lost, her face blank and her eyes hurt. Andie was about to speak, even if it was just to mumble some trite expression, but she stopped herself, sensing Yara wasn't finished.

"By then I knew I was a sorceress and that I was pretty powerful, so I practiced my magic and learned as many spells as I could remember. It took me almost a year before I thought I was ready. And then I found them. The gang. With my connections, it didn't take long. By then I was sixteen and legal. I didn't have to sneak around anymore. I followed them to their hideout…"

Yara paused. The waves against the ship's hull below now nearly deafening in the silence that threatened to consume the room.

"…and I killed them."

Andie felt her entire body go tense. She wondered if she'd heard correctly. Did her best friend just admit to being a murderer?

"It was the worst mistake I ever made in my life. Even now, ten years later, it haunts me. Every time I do magic or think about fighting the University, I remember those men. The way they looked when I was finished with them. Andie, you have to understand that I don't think I'm above you or Carmen or Raesh. Or anyone else. I don't think I've earned your trust or your friendship. But I know what can happen to a person when they come under strain. True, honest strain."

Yara finally turned to look at Andie, her eyes darker and more haunted than Andie had ever seen. "You don't have to be evil to be capable of it. All I want is to make sure that every person on this ship is still intact and then find the one person on this ship who's broken. So, no, I'm not going to trust someone's intentions just because I know them. And yes, I will make it my duty to personally assess Raesh and Carmen before they're cleared. And you can hate me for that, but I don't really care."

Andie stared incredulously at her but finally nodded. Yara nodded back and returned her gaze back up to the ceiling.

"And one last thing," Yara added. "I abandoned my parents, and they died. I won't abandon this group. Not in any way. Not ever."

Yara leaned back in the bed, covered herself fully with her blankets, and lay there silently. Andie stared at her for several moments, trying to figure out what to say or if she was supposed to say anything at all. But before she could come up with anything appropriate to say, Yara had fallen asleep.

CHAPTER SIX

THE NEXT DAY WAS A LITTLE BETTER FOR EVERYONE onboard. The chaos of the escape was a little further behind them, but the traitor still had everyone terrified. They didn't know if the person was just giving information to the University, or if he or she had orders to kill them in their sleep. Everyone was suspicious of everyone except their closest friends, and so divisions grew up overnight. Even then, no one liked to be surrounded by more than three people at a time. Tensions were high, maybe even insurmountable. Rumors of who the traitor could be spread faster than wildfire, and Andie had had just about enough.

Andie was meeting with the captain that morning. They'd already docked in the True Isles, but the order had come up from Marvo that no one was to leave the ship yet. Andie had spent half the morning trying to comprehend the story Yara had told her and trying to separate how she felt about Yara's past from how she felt about Yara now. She'd spent the other half of the morning thinking of where the dragonborn might go for safety. Both dragons and dragonborn preferred mountainous regions if the history books were to be believed. She certainly felt like it could be true.

Brie was the highest mountain by far, but there was no way they would ever go back there. It would be too dangerous. They had been spotted most recently over Abhainn, which was almost the geographical center of Noelle. She hoped they would be smart enough to seek safety elsewhere.

"You don't have anything more specific than that?" the captain asked.

"I might," Andie said. "Where's your map?"

"Hanging up there."

He walked with her over to a wall-length window, and Andie saw that it was actually a massive map of the world. It was completely made of loveglass, and shimmered with an iridescent glow. The captain touched the map and the glass changed, zoomed in to show only Noelle. It was controlled by a combination of the user's magic and the geographic data fed to it through the comm station. It was fascinating, and Andie stared at it as if seeing loveglass for the first time.

"What, never seen a loveglass map before?" the captain grinned.

Andie shook her head and walked up to the map, narrowing it to the regions surrounding Abhainn with her own magic. "It's incredible."

"Pretty basic stuff, really," the captain said proudly. "But I've never seen a map so big as this one. Have had it in my care for the past ten years, I'd reckon."

Andie smiled and quickly steered the conversation back to the matter at hand. "The dragons were last spotted here," she said, pointing to the map. The captain deflated somewhat, but turned his attention dutifully back to Andie. She narrowed her eyes as she inspected the map closely. "Now it looks like there are at least six different mountain ranges nearby. We don't know which way they were heading, but these two here don't have the elevation they'd want, even in these circumstances. That one at the top is too far north; it wouldn't be warm enough for the dragons."

"Leaving the three to the southwest here," said the captain. "I know for a fact that middle one has been taken over by the Glycerinnds after they fled from Brie. Now I know pirates, even a few hundred of them, are no match for your people, but I'm assuming they wouldn't be looking to cause trouble or start something that could alert the public to where they are?"

"You'd be right. That leaves these two."

"So, which is it?"

Andie sighed. "I don't know. They both have the right elevation, the right temperature. They're secluded. It's hard to tell."

"How do we even know they're still in this region? They were spotted here, but they could've gone anywhere. Noelle is almost twenty-three thousand leagues from coast to coast."

"No, if they were spotted here it means they were coming down to land. Dragons can fly near the very outer layers of the atmosphere, too high to ever be seen from the ground. If someone saw them, it was because they'd found somewhere to land. But where?"

Andie and the captain sat looking over the map, but it wasn't long before an idea come to her.

"This one. That's where they are."

The captain tapped the glass and the mountain range Andie selected was brought up.

"That's in the Hot Salts of Mithraldia," he said. "I guess it'd be hot enough. But wait... lightning is constant there, sometimes several thousand times per hour. The clouds never clear there. Don't your people need sun?"

"Exactly. If these were the only two viable ranges in the area, they must've known that eventually someone would put the pieces together and go looking for them. Now both of these mountain ranges are large enough that it would take even a sizable team a long while to search the whole thing, but eventually someone would find them. No one would think to look for them near the Hot Salts, under a constant cloudy sky. They'll be growing weak, but they could fly above the weather to the sun whenever they really needed it."

The captain sat back in his chair, looking over Andie with a smile of pride on his face. When she looked back to him, he furrowed his brow and looked back to the map. "The lightning can be treacherous. Are you sure that's where they'd be?"

"They're there, I'm sure of it."

"Alright. I'll get the new heading into the system."

"Thank you, captain."

The captain nodded and immediately set to work inputting coordinates into the ship's navigation system. Andie watched him work meticulously at the wheel for a moment, and knew the ship was in good hands. With one last look back to the captain, she turned and left and went back out onto the deck, where Carmen was waiting for her with two bottles of something extremely bright.

"What is it?" Andie asked, taking the one Carmen handed her.

"Believe it or not, beer. It's good, take my word for it. I'm on my fourth."

"Your fourth?" Andie laughed, looking Carmen up and down. Carmen's legs wobbled slightly beneath her, but she quickly steadied herself on the nearby wall. The girls turned their bottles up and started walking back downstairs.

"So," Carmen began. "How long is it going to take us to get to this mystery location?"

Andie turned to looked at Carmen from the side of her eye.

"Oh, I see. No one can trust the spy. God forbid I send this top secret info back to my clandestine buddies at headquarters."

"Carmen…"

"Nope, understandable. Must keep everything in ship shape. Lips sealed, files locked, legs closed, the usual."

"Carmen…"

"But you should know now that I actually do plan on killing you slowly, painfully in your bed tonight. I mean, nothing personal, orders and what not. It's all very straightforward, really. Wouldn't do it if it weren't absolutely necessary. I mean, you are the enemy, after all."

"Carmen," Andie said, laughing. "You're being ridiculous. You know I trust you. And you know that deep down Marvo trusts you, too."

Carmen sighed and chugged the rest of her beer, wiping the dripping liquid from her lips with her sleeve. "I know. To be honest, it's kind of refreshing to not have some giant weight resting on my shoulders."

"You mean, minus the fact that we're trying to save my entire species from extinction and evil rumors. Not to mention we can't use magic because the University is tracking us using technology we're going to have to have surgically removed?"

Carmen grinned. "Yeah. Minus that. Thanks for the reminder."

The girls laughed as they continued down the hall together.

"So, is there anything you *can* tell me?"

"Well, Carmen… you're still pretty."

"Now we're talking."

Carmen put her arm around Andie's shoulder. They only had a few minutes before they needed to be at the meeting. Raesh had called a meeting to explain a system for the division of information so that no one person knew everything. The girls rounded the corner and passed two rooms before they reached the mess hall. They went inside and it was nearly completely full of Marvo's fighters. Andie hadn't realized there were so many onboard.

"Wow," Carmen said. "I guess we don't need to be worried about an attack. There must be four or five hundred people in here."

"Now if we only knew the *one* person who we can't trust."

Carmen looked at Andie and they shared a concerned look.

"That's funny, I just had an even more terrifying thought," said Carmen.

"What?" Andie asked, not really wanting to hear another reason to worry.

"How do we know it's only one spy?"

Andie shook her head, wondering why Carmen had even said that. She knew she wouldn't be getting any sleep when the time came, but she couldn't afford to worry about those things now.

"I don't see Yara," Andie said, changing the subject. "Although, I guess even if she was in here, it'd take me forever to find her. I can't believe how many people are on this ship. We've still got some time. Wanna check to make sure?"

"Yeah. We could probably find her with Marvo. She's becoming quite the introvert."

Andie and Carmen started off down the hall again. What Carmen had said was true; Yara had had lost all social skills and desire overnight, it seemed. Andie hadn't noticed it when she first woke up, but the more time she spent around Yara, the more she realized that her friend had grown to distrust everyone. The knowledge of a traitor among them had had a heavy effect on her, not to mention the conversation she'd overheard between Carmen and Raesh. She wouldn't eat in the mess hall or talk to anyone. Raesh said she had been like that ever since Marvo told her there was a spy onboard.

Yara was almost always near Marvo, discussing and planning, or up in the crow's nest looking down on all the passengers and taking notes on their groups, behaviors, preferences, etc. She talked to Andie and Marvo, seldom to Raesh and Carmen, and never to anyone else. Besides all of that, Andie was certain there were other things bothering her, too. Probably the weight of her circumstance finally catching up to her.

Andie and Carmen reached Marvo's room. Murakami was standing guard at the door. She'd sustained some injuries during the escape, but only one serious one that Andie could see. A grisly slash that began at her temple and ran down to her chest. Andie hadn't had a chance to speak with her since they boarded, but by the concentrated look on the woman's face, she suspected it wasn't the best time to chit chat.

"Murakami," she said, touching the woman's shoulder. "How are you?"

"A lot worse than the Sentinel who did this to me, but I'll survive. Glad to see you're up. It's better for the cause that you're conscious."

"Thanks, I think. Are you sure you don't want that bandaged? It looks deep."

"No medicine, no bandage. Where I come from stiches are enough. The pain is real. The rest of you can try avoiding it, but it reminds me of everything that's at stake."

"I understand. I know you're not doing this just because of me, Murakami, but I just want to say thank you for being here, and I'm sorry for the friends you lost."

"So am I."

Murakami didn't say anything else or turn away, but there was a certain kind of finality in her voice that told Andie the conversation should end there. She gave Murakami a smile as the woman moved aside. Andie opened the door and she and Carmen walked in. Yara was in there, so were three fighters who had been with them since the battle in the Archives. Their names were Kent, Sarinda, and Lilja.

Yara seemed her usual closed-off self, but Marvo was

finally on his feet again. In fact, there was another person in his bed. Andie moved to congratulate Marvo on being able to stand, but just as she was touching his arm she got around Sarinda and saw who was in Marvo's bed. She couldn't move. She couldn't believe it.

"Dad?"

CHAPTER SEVEN

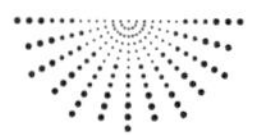

A RAGING, HEAD-POUNDING THUNDER PULLED ANDIE into consciousness.

It came again and again, relentless, so close but yet so far away. Something sharp was pressing into the side of her face and her leg was cold. Too cold. She tried to open her eyes, but when she finally did something immediately covered them. Her eyes started to burn. She tried to pick herself up, but she couldn't move her arms and she soon found she couldn't move her legs either. It was like she was frozen in the middle of something thick and strong. She couldn't breathe, there was no light, and no sound. She was all alone, or at least she thought she was. She couldn't tell. The booming noise got louder, and Andie thought it was perhaps an oncoming storm until she realized it was the sound of her own heart beat raging loudly in her ears.

She struggled and struggled, but could do no more than manage to wiggle a little. Before she'd thought she was lying down, but now she knew she was neither lying nor standing. She tasted blood and soil and an immense pressure built over her skin. She was suspended. In dirt.

Finally, it dawned on her exactly where she was. She was buried. Someone had tried to bury her alive. She felt weak, like she'd been out of the sun for a while. She considered, but it couldn't have been more than a few seconds. It was only moments ago that she was on the ship, surrounded by people she knew. Her father.

Panic threatened to overtake her, but she forced her mind to remain calm as she puzzled out her situation. Her thunderous heart beat grew louder still, and the pressure in her head built. She knew she didn't have much time before she suffocated completely. Her body could only heal itself so much.

Tears streamed from her eyes as she squeezed them shut as tightly as she could. She silently counted down from three, and when she hit one, she summoned as much strength as she could. Andie drew her magic inward, and, with one single explosion of release, she propelled it out from her in an effort to free herself from her dirt cage. It worked. The dirt around her exploded in every direction, and she flew up into open air.

She was suddenly and completely free, and she fell to her knees and coughed up dirt and small roots as her panic slowly subsided. She cleared her eyes. She looked back to see her leg and saw that it was so cold because it was bleeding profusely and was probably broken. She looked around her, her heart threatening to explode from her chest. Her eyes streamed and her breath came in ragged gasps.

It was mere moments before her dragonblood began to heal her, though, and the sight of her leg healing calmed her. She rolled over onto her back and tried to look up at the sun. The air was still clouded with dust from the explosion and the sky was completely clouded over. She lay there for a time, healing. When she was feeling better she stood up and took a look around. She couldn't believe her eyes.

She was standing on the side of a mountain. She was on one of the lowest peaks, but there were several others surrounding her and the tallest one was huge. There was no way she was seeing straight. She closed her eyes and opened them again only to find that the mountain was still there and she still wasn't where she was supposed to be. More than that, the sky was completely overcast and green lightning was pounding the earth incessantly in every direction she could see.

Now that she was above ground, the sound was almost unbearable, like cannons going off over and over and over. Though only the faintest suggestion of the sun came through the thick menacing clouds, the land was alive with the terrible, intermittent flashes of light from the lightning. Wherever the lightning struck, great chunks of land were sent spraying into the air and moderate fires were burning as far as her eyes could see. Far, far below, the earth itself was black and smoldering, completely devoid of any plant life. Lightning ruled the land.

"Well, crap," she swore under her breath. She could barely hear her own voice over the deafening sound of the thunder around her. She tried to process what could have happened, drawing on anything she could possibly muster from her own memory. But it was a fruitless attempt. The last thing she remembered was being on board the ship with her friends. The next, well…

Andie looked around, more frantically this time. "Raesh?" she called, hoping for an answer. "Marvo? Yara? Carmen?" Her calls were met with nothing but a haunting echo as her voice came back to her from the mountainside. When it became clear there was no one else around her, she fell to her knees and held her head in her hands. She opened her mouth and let out a frustrated scream.

But her screams were in vain. There didn't seem to be anyone around to hear her, and even if someone was there, there was no way she could be heard over the weather. She couldn't understand what had happened or why. One minute she was standing in a room with her friends—and her father—the next she was buried alive on the side of the mountain. She closed her eyes and tried to focus.

The last thing she remembered was seeing her father lying in Marvo's bed, looking a great deal weaker than the last time she'd seen him, but smiling up at her. They were finally back together and then they weren't. But no, that wasn't right. She began to remember something. The last thing she'd seen wasn't her father, it was a flash of light. A flash of blue light and blast of cold energy. For a moment she was suspended, then she was buried alive. A spell. That was the only explanation. Someone had spelled her there.

She considered the options. The blue light could have been an attack, and any one of her friends with magic could have sent her away in an effort to protect her. The thought made her smile. Someone must have known or sensed something was going to happen and had been quick on their feet. Quicker than Andie had been, that was for sure. She could barely remember the incident and could easily have been taken out had someone not acted.

"Someone saved me," she said out loud.

But as the words came out of her mouth, she realized that no one knew where they were headed except for her and the captain. He couldn't have sent her there because he wasn't a sorcerer. Carmen was on the deck with her, but she never went inside the captain's room. There was no one else in the area and the captain wouldn't have had time to upload the coordinates yet.

She then remembered the unfamiliar cold feeling of the magical energy, and knew it hadn't been anyone she recognized. She didn't know the magic she had felt. It was foreign to her.

But then she knew. It had to have been the traitor. But why send her exactly where she wanted to go? Not only that, but they also put her out of reach of themselves and the University. There was nothing to be gained from this. How did they even know where to send her? Maybe they meant to send her somewhere else. None of it made sense.

The only thing she could do for the moment was to try to remember who was in the room. Since she'd woken up in the ground, her mind was completely fuzzy. But she focused and saw it. Yara. Kent. Marvo. Sarinda. Her father. Of course, there was Carmen who came in with her, and Murakami who was standing guard when they arrived. And Lilja, one of the other fighters. Obviously, her father wasn't the traitor. He hadn't even been with them in the tunnels.

But that still left seven people. She wanted to trust Yara, Carmen, and Marvo outright, but this situation couldn't be taken lightly. If Marvo hadn't trusted Carmen, even for the most obvious reason, then maybe somewhere inside he knew something Andie didn't. After all, Andie hadn't even known Carmen for two years, and Marvo had known her all her life. Murakami had always seemed a bit odd to Andie. And maybe it was a little naive to trust Marvo just because he claimed to have been the first one to recognize that there was a traitor; there was no way to prove that. Even Yara—beautiful, sweet, wise Yara—might not be a true ally. No one had ever really explained why she couldn't be the spy.

What is happening? Andie ran her hands through her hair as she inspected the area surrounding her. It was so foreign, so wild. Thunder crashed overhead as another flash of lightning hit the mountainside not that far behind her. She had to move. It was too dangerous where she was. She could figure out the puzzle of the traitor another time. She couldn't do anything if she was killed by the lightning, anyway.

She stumbled on, not really knowing which direction to take. The lightning pounded the mountainside around her and she was constantly forced to change direction as entire cliffs and stretches of the mountain crumbled around her. She walked and walked and walked, and just when she thought she had made her way substantially down, she realized she'd been going up for the last hour.

But she kept on, looking for something, anything, to help her find her way. Hours passed and so did the day. Time went quickly and although her magic kept her from tiring, Andie grew exhausted in other ways. There didn't seem to be anyone on the face of the planet she could trust, and, worse still, whoever the traitor was, her father was with them. And a ship full of her friends and allies.

One person was about to ruin everything.

CHAPTER EIGHT

JUST WHEN ANDIE WAS ABOUT TO PICK A SPOT TO SETTLE for the night, thinking it was hopeless to try to find her way down with the sun nearly gone, she saw it. A dragon.

It was flying low over the nearest peak, dropping beyond the zenith and coasting along the mountainside. It swooped up and avoided the crags and came soaring across the gulf between that mountain and the one on which Andie stood, propelling itself with more grace in those fleeting seconds than in all the movements Andie had seen in her entire life. She gazed up at it in awe, frozen in place. It seemed to sense when a bolt of lightning was cutting through the air and avoided them with terrific ease. She blinked, her eyes not quite believing what she was seeing. It seemed to be getting bigger. It was coming straight for her.

The dragon flew up and soared until it was at Andie's level and then circled her. It seemed to Andie that the warrior on the dragon's back was looking down and surveying the area. Finally, the dragon landed near her and the warrior bowed from the dragon's back.

"You are Andie," he said, his voice accented with traces of a foreign dialect. He gave her a cautious smile. Andie couldn't help but stare. His hair was long and windblown, the same emerald green as the dragon's hide on which he rode. His eyes shone an even deeper emerald, reflecting the brief flashes of lightning that flickered across the sky above him.

"Yes," she finally managed to say. Her voice was hoarse and she still tasted dirt.

The green-haired man inspected her up and down, a curious look on his face. "Are you well?"

Andie blinked at him, then looked down at the muddy and disheveled state she was in. "I'm… fine," she croaked. She could hardly believe her eyes. "Are you… Are the dragonborn near? Are you all okay?"

She was having trouble wrapping her mind around what was happening to her. Where was she again?

"We're all quite fine," he said, smiling freely now that he was confident who she was. "We've been in these mountains for some time. We've grown happy here. No harm has come to us and we have yet to be spotted, though Saeryn doubts this peace will last."

"Saeryn?" Andie asked, her spirits instantly lifted.

"Yes. She's there with us, of course. Come. I will take you to her."

When the man didn't move, Andie realized what he had just asked her to do. "You mean, on the dragon?"

The warrior's expression looked sly, but he nodded. "Perhaps," he said as he slid gracefully from the dragon's back, landing on two feet next to Andie. He held his hand against the creature's side as he stood gazing at her.

Andie felt numb. She couldn't help but gaze back at the stunning beauty of the man and the dragon, their colors matching in perfect harmony. He wore shimmering armor made from the same scales of his dragon, a brilliant green with jewels and chains and engraved metal—she had never seen anything so stunning in her life. She had of course seen depictions, mostly illustrated texts in books she had secretly found in the University's archives, but seeing the dragon and its rider in person this close, so still, nearly brought a tear to her eye.

The man smiled and took a small step back from his dragon, motioning towards its massive back with one graceful hand. "Try."

Andie did not hesitate. In a world where her circumstances were constantly changing, where life varied by incredible degrees from moment to moment and where she didn't know who she could trust, the one thing she felt confident of was that these were the people she belonged with. These dragons weren't the evil beasts she grew up hearing about through rumors. She knew better than to trust blindly, but out of everyone she had met and everything she believed in, she knew in her heart that this warrior and his dragon were on her side. She walked over to the dragon, and the dragon turned it's long, scaled neck to look her in the eye. The warrior laughed.

"What's so funny?" Andie asked, turning to face the warrior.

He grinned at the dragon and then bowed his head slightly to Andie. "She says you look like you rolled in dirt."

Andie blinked and couldn't help but stare wide-eyed at him. "She talks?"

"In a way," the man considered. "We riders share a mental connection with our dragons. We understand each other."

"That's… Wow."

The dragon nudged her shoulder with its snout. Andie froze a moment then placed her own hand against its hide. It was not what she expected. She had thought the scales would feel cold, metallic. But they were in fact warm, the scales a smooth silk against her skin. The beast closed her eyes as she touched it, and Andie jumped when she let out a snort.

"She likes you." The warrior grinned, leaning casually against the enormous beast as he watched Andie with a curious look on his face.

Andie smiled at him then turned back to the dragon. "Hello," she finally spoke out loud. She didn't know what else to say. She secretly cursed herself for acting so simple, but her mind was so consumed with wonder and yearning, she didn't even care. All she wanted to do was ride the dragon.

The beast snorted again, small wisps of smoke billowing from its snout. She then knelt on her two front legs, lowering herself for Andie to mount.

"Alright," she said, reaching up to grab hold of the heavy leather harness that wrapped loosely around the dragon's neck. "Here goes nothing."

Andie let out one long deep breath then bent her knees and launched herself up onto the dragon's back. It was by no means a graceful maneuver, but she found her seating, and, when she realized she was actually sitting on a dragon, she couldn't help but let out a long, joyous laugh.

"Interesting," the warrior said, after she'd settled.

Within moments, she was riding a dragon for the first time in her life. She had imagined what it might be like hundreds of times, especially when she was trapped underground for all those months, but she could never have imagined the actual experience.

The dragon lifted from the ground with such power that it left Andie breathless for a moment. She could feel the massive muscles of the dragon's back as it moved beneath her. Its wide, thick wings pumped up and down powerfully and with a sound like two giant, elegant machines of their own.

The iridescence of the dragon's scales shimmered in the flashes of lightning like countless diamonds, and the dragon's entire body was warm and poetic. The head weaved from side to side in front of her. They danced through the lightning and Andie had never felt more exhilarated. It was the most amazing sensation she had ever felt. She closed her eyes and relished in the cool wind that blew her hair as they flew through the skies, an incredible energy coursing through her body like one she'd never experienced.

The warrior rode with a straight back and with the reins in one hand, a true paragon of dignity and patience. Even as the dragon performed swift and daunting maneuvers, he never faltered or gave the slightest suggestion of discomfort. He was totally at ease with the creature.

"Does she have a name?" Andie asked.

"Her name is Ronen," the warrior said. "She is not

the fastest or the strongest, but she is the most agile. And she is an even better friend."

As the warrior spoke, the dragon soared up and then allowed itself to fall, soft and graceful even in its descent, until it stretched its wings and cut the air once more. Andie gasped.

"She's showing off," the warrior explained, his voice partially lost in the wind as they soared through the skies. "Not only can we speak to one another mentally, but she can sense my intentions. My emotions. A dragon can read its rider through instinct. Dragons are incredible creatures."

Andie held on tight and marveled for the rest of the journey. For the first time in a very long time, she felt totally and utterly herself. She felt free.

The dragon took them to the tallest peak of the mountain range. Higher and higher they flew, until they cleared the clouds and left the earth and the lightning behind. As soon as they were above the clouds, the sunlight and warmth flooded them, and Andie knew they were in the right place. There were dragons everywhere. Flying, crawling across the side of the mountain, sleeping in groups of several dozen. It seemed there was a dragon in every color imaginable and each was as beautiful as the last and the next.

And moving around among the dragons, Andie could see her people, the dragonborn. They were moving all over the mountain to perform whatever daily tasks needed done. The scene before her took her breath away. She hadn't managed to comprehend just how many had come through the portal that night of the battle at the University. But, seeing them all there, going about their business as if the mountain had been their home for centuries, she couldn't help but marvel in shocked silence.

The warrior brought the dragon down into what looked to be the center of their commerce section, a kind of improvised market square on the mountain side. They had set up the market on one of the level grounds and there must have been three hundred dragonborn there, shopping and enjoying themselves.

When the dragon landed, few people even bothered to take notice of it. They were so use to dragons that one didn't even warrant their notice. But as soon as they noticed that the rider had a passenger with him, they began to stare at Andie and look her over.

"It might be best to give her some space," the warrior said. "She looks like she's already been through a great deal. I'm sure she's just as surprised and thrilled to see all of us as well."

"Who is it," some little kid asked.

"This is Andryne," the warrior said proudly, turning back to Andie. "She is the savior of our people."

"Andie," she corrected, although she wished she hadn't. She would have to get used to her real name now that she was with her own people and didn't have to hide.

Instantly, the clamor began. It was like the people had been waiting for her all their lives. The warrior did his best to hold them back, but one man was not enough. They flocked to Andie. They didn't run up screaming or pulling on her, but they crowded around her and all spoke at once in that calm, graceful way of theirs. They were grateful.

They carefully pushed their wares and baskets out to her, though she declined. It took some time, but the warrior finally extricated himself and Andie from the crowd. He led her back to the mountainside. The people followed. Andie saw that they were approaching a large cavern.

"We have been hard at work making ourselves at home in this new millennium," the warrior said. "Our old mountain no longer exists in the world, but this one will do for now. We have only just begun creating and connecting the caverns. It is slow work, as we do not wish to go too fast or too close together and destabilize the mountain."

"How did you do this?" Andie asked, looking up at the top of the cavern which was easily thirty feet above her.

"Some clever magic and quite a bit of dragon's fire," the warrior said with a grin.

They entered the cavern and walked a considerable way down into the mountain. Eventually they came to a clearing where fires were lit all around the area and a moderate sized group was meeting in the middle. Standing in the middle of the group was Saeryn. When she saw Andie, she threw up her arms to welcome her. Andie half walked, half ran over and hugged her.

"I'm so relieved," she said, still holding Saeryn. "I was so worried about all of you."

Saeryn was even more regal than Andie remembered. Wearing a flowing lilac dress with slits along the leg for easy movement, and magenta dragonscale and intricately-woven metallic armor and crown, she looked like a vision of fantasy. Her strong arms held Andie tight, the glistening scales reflecting the warm light of the surrounding fires. The armor was mesmerizing. Everything about the woman was mesmerizing.

"We're just fine," Saeryn said, beaming. "Though we were just as worried about you. How have you come? Where are your friends?"

"I don't know. One minute I was with all of them on a ship and the next I was buried alive on the side of this mountain."

Gasps went through the crowd as they all stood in shock and awe. Andie looked out at the surrounding dragonborn, her heart suddenly full. Her people surrounded her, gazing upon her with curiosity and kindness. She couldn't help but smile out at them as she took in the scene before her.

Warriors, workers, and children alike were gathered around the fires, dragons dozing peacefully around them. Andie noticed the men and women clad in various forms of dragonscale armor stood near their dragons, all of which reflected the same colors as their riders.

Blues, greens, golds, and reds glistened in the firelight, each unique set of armor different and more beautiful from the next. The eyes and hair of each rider the same matching hues as their dragon counterparts. Andie had never seen such a display. It filled her with such wonder. She had so much to learn about her people.

"Who did that to you?" the warrior demanded, his hand on his sword. Andie's attention was drawn back to the green-scaled warrior.

"I don't know. I was surrounded by my friends and then there was this flash of blue light and an incredibly powerful burst of cold energy. And then I was underground. I don't know exactly what happened, but someone in that room cast a spell on me. The day before, I had just found out that we had a traitor onboard.

Someone had been spying on us for the University, but I never learned who."

"They're cleverer than I thought," Saeryn said, her eyes narrowing with great concern. "But that is a matter for another time. Has your dragonblood healed you?"

"Yes."

"Good. How long ago was it that you saw your friends?"

"Earlier today. This morning."

"Did anything happen in the time you were on the ship?"

"No, nothing I can remember. We hid under ground for two hundred and forty days, beneath the University. We came up on the one hundred and ninety-first day of this year. That was two days ago. Since then—"

"The one hundred and ninety-first day?" Saeryn interrupted. "But that would make this the one hundred and ninety-third."

"Right. So, then we were at sea and—"

"But that's impossible," Saeryn insisted, with a look on her face that Andie couldn't understand.

"What do you mean 'impossible?'"

"Today is the two hundred and twenty-sixth day of the year."

Andie stared at Saeryn. That couldn't be. It was the same day, it had to be.

"No, that's not right," Andie said. "We boarded on 191 and this morning was 193."

"I'm sorry, but it's not. We've kept excellent track of our passage in this world and made every effort to stay appraised of the world's ways. Today is 226."

"But that means that... I've been... away... for thirty-three days. But how?"

"Your back," Saeryn said, suddenly overcome with nervous energy. "Let me see your back."

"Does she have the marks?" the warrior asked.

Andie turned around and allowed Saeryn to check her back. She heard more gasps from the people nearby and turned back to Saeryn. Andie began to feel her own back in a kind of mute and frantic terror.

"What's wrong with me?" she asked. "What's back there? What have they done to me?"

"This," Saeryn said, turning to show Andie her back.

Andie could see that Saeryn had a blue tattoo on her back, only more like a scar than something done on purpose. It looked like a hurried infinity symbol with a harsh L drawn in the exact center. The entire design was glowing blue. Saeryn turned around to face Andie again.

"Eitilt," she said. "The time curse."

"What?" Andie said, still feeling her back.

"We know it well. It was the spell the sorcerers used to trap our people. That spell was older, more powerful, and it stretched from the day they overpowered us to the day you freed us. Centuries. It would appear that the one that was cast on you was more hurried, narrower, but the result is the same. You were taken from your time and put down in the future. In this case—"

"Thirty-three days," Andie said, dumbfounded. "I can't believe this. What about my friends? Are they okay? Are they even alive?"

"I don't know. I'm so sorry, my dear Andryne.

"I believe she goes by Andie," the warrior mentioned as he strode past. He winked at her as she caught his eye.

Just then a powerful bolt of lightning stabbed the mountain and shook the cavern so hard that stalactites fell from the ceiling. Saeryn disintegrated them with a wave of her hand, including one that fell directly over Andie.

"What is this place?" Andie asked. "Where are we?"

"These lands were known by another name in our time, but I believe your era calls this the Hot Salts of Mithraldia."

"So, I was right. You came here to throw the University off your trail."

"Not merely the University, but the world. Andie, why didn't you protect yourself? You could have used magic to destroy that falling thing."

"I can't use magic. I still have my icon. It's a kind of monitoring device that all the students at the University have to wear in order to attend. We haven't been able to do magic since the night of the portal because the University can track us if we do and..."

Andie's hands flew to her head. She couldn't believe she'd been so stupid.

"No! I used my magic to pull myself out of the ground. The University will have noticed that. I'm so sorry, Saeryn. I don't know how I could have been so careless."

Saeryn moved forward and took Andie by her shoulders. She smiled down at her and just the expression on her face brought Andie to a calmer state.

"Andie, it's fine. We've covered these peaks with protective magic. And if by some chance they did monitor your actions and decided to come here, they would not find themselves very welcome. After the carnage of their last battle with us, I do not believe they would be so eager to attack again, not without some weapon or magic much more powerful than what they possessed last time. However, if there is a traitor among your company and if that traitor did indeed send you here, then the University already knows where to come for you. And us. But none of that is your fault, nor should it be your concern. You did an ineffable service to us in bringing us out of that portal. We know you would never willingly compromise us. It is not your fault that there is evil in the world."

Andie felt much better after Saeryn's words and she took a few deep breaths to calm herself. She looked around the group and everyone was smiling at her. No one was angry or concerned. She truly was among her own kind. As she looked at the faces, she saw one she remembered. Lymir. When he saw that she was looking at him, he came over to her. She hugged him.

"It does me a world o' good to see ye, girl," he said, holding her tight. "I hadn't been sure I would. Tell me, ye still carry the ole bracelet I give ye?"

"I haven't taken it off yet," she said, holding up her wrist. "But I'm confused. What are you doing here?"

"All in proper time," he said, smiling and turning to Saeryn.

"Andie, did anyone else on your ship know where you wanted to come?"

"Yes. The captain."

"And can he be trusted?"

"He'll follow the heading, of that I'm sure. But if you want the truth, Saeryn, I don't know if anyone on that ship can be trusted."

"Very well. If you were taken thirty-three days ago then they should be getting close to us by now, no doubt coming from the sea down the long belly of the Nathair River that runs behind the mountain. For now, we'll get that thing out of you. We have no surgeons, as dragonblood heals us, but there are those of us who are skilled in medicinal magic. We should have you free of the University's eye within the hour."

Saeryn had not lied. In a little less than an hour, the chief examiner of the dragonborn, Gordenson, had removed the icon from Andie. The process was slow and painful, and eventually revealed yet another deception of the University. The icon, once inserted into the palm, began to slowly burrow its way deeper into the host with each passing day. Eventually it settled up somewhere around the heart; it only appeared to stay in the palm because it was spelled to manifest its light and sensations there. Gordenson said that with time the University probably would have been able to kill the host with a mere whisper of a spell—an unbelievably deadly prediction seeing as to how more than a third of the sorcerers in Noelle were educated at the University and they all kept the icons for life. Gordenson finally removed Andie's through her back.

CHAPTER NINE

For the next three days, Andie lived among her people and began to learn their ways. She began to learn their language and customs, how they prepared their food and what life was like in the time from which they came. She learned a lot about the dragons, too, including what to feed them and how each dragonborn could develop an extrasensory relationship with their dragon. She never allowed herself to grow content or to forget the circumstances that she could never run from, but she was aware that she was dangerously close to being fulfilled.

However, countless things still weighed heavily on her. She couldn't stop wondering who the traitor was or if the rest of her friends had figured it out. She was worried about her father; she'd only seen him for a few seconds, but even then he looked weak, tired. And if there was someone onboard strong enough to cast a spell on her and land her in the future, then she had no idea what else that person might be capable of. She had finally calmed down enough to think rationally, however.

She knew Marvo couldn't be the traitor because he had no magic; she'd been so shaken and startled before that she hadn't even considered it. Her father was out. But that still left six people.

She was willing to give Carmen and Yara the benefit of the doubt after some thought, possibly even Murakami. Though, Andie wouldn't fully pull them off the list, she was so jarred by it all. She knew very little about Kent, Sarinda, and Lilja and at first that was enough for her to convict them. But the issue with that theory was that those three were essentially small cogs in the machine of the rebellion. Andie couldn't think of a single instance where those three had been included in major decision-making or had been privy to anything but the most obvious plans. How could they spy if they didn't have access to the pertinent information? Access that Carmen, Yara, and Murakami had plenty of. It was hopeless.

At least with her icon removed Andie could enjoy her magic again. She took advantage of the seclusion of the mountain and the knowledge of Saeryn and began to practice and to increase her power. Even Saeryn was impressed. Andie made many new friends among her people, most notably the warrior who'd picked her up when she first arrived. His name was Oren and he seemed to have taken an instant liking to Andie. He never crowded her, but always made himself available to her and was kinder and more attentive than anyone else. Andie greatly admired him and they spent a lot of time sharing stores about their vastly different lives.

On the morning of Andie's fifth day on the mountain, the two hundred and thirtieth day of the year, a ship was spotted on the Nathair. Oren saw it while out on watch duty and reported it to Saeryn. From the description he gave, Andie knew it was her ship. She was happy and devastated that they had finally arrived: she had no idea what to expect. For all she knew the traitor had taken over the ship and allowed the University professors and Searchers to board. Or maybe it was just the traitor and everyone onboard was dead. Or maybe the traitor had been discovered and contained, and everything was alright. She honestly had no idea what was coming up that river for her.

Saeryn suggested that a party be formed to meet the travelers at the ship, rather than allow the unidentified traitor to see their actual caverns. Oren, Saeryn, and a few others mounted dragons and pushed off from the mountainside to plunge down to the earth. Andie rode with Oren.

The dragons dove in perfect lines, curving only just enough to avoid touching the mountain. They met and cut through the black clouds and suddenly Andie found herself among the fierce lightning again. The sound was incredible, the vibrations and energy of the air were bracing. The dragons dove as if there was nothing in the world that could hurt them. They soared down, down, down, until they were mere yards above the river and then they leveled out and flew straight for the ship.

As they came closer, Andie could see that there were no people on the decks of the ship. Everybody was below deck, maybe because of the lightning. Andie couldn't tell. The riders made their dragons fly a brief circle around the ship for reconnaissance and then Oren and Saeryn landed on the upper deck. The weight of the two dragons rocked the ship and the deck groaned under their bulk. The other warriors decided to fly high and nearby to keep a watch over the ship and its surroundings. They flew up into the thunderous sky. Andie, Saeryn, and Oren dismounted and Andie led them toward the captain's room, but before they rounded the corner, they were met by two people. The captain and Raesh.

Before Andie could register that it was real or could get a word out, Raesh had her in his arms. She didn't know how long they stayed like that. She realized then that she hadn't known how badly, how deeply, she had missed him. And now that she knew for certain that he wasn't the traitor—he hadn't been anywhere near that room—it made the reunion that much sweeter. They finally let each other go, but couldn't stop smiling.

"What happened to you? Where have you been?" Raesh began. "How did you get here? How long have you been here? Are you hurt? Are your people okay? Did you—"

"I'm fine, Raesh," she said with a smile, grabbing his arms to calm him. "Everything is fine. Someone who was in the room with me cast a spell and sent me to the future. I landed on the mountainside five days ago and I've been with my people ever since. They're all fine. What about you? What happened after I was gone?"

"Chaos. When you disappeared, everything went into anarchy. Factions formed, suspicions grew, everyone was scared and confused. We almost had a civil war. No one could figure out what happened to you. We put everyone who was in the room with you in individual cells and spelled them so that they couldn't talk to anyone, including each other."

"What about your father?"

"Him, too. I know he doesn't have magic, but that doesn't mean he couldn't have been in on it somehow."

"Raesh, you can't be serious."

"Andie, I wouldn't have thought anyone in that room would ever want to hurt you, let alone be powerful enough to make you disappear. I love him, but I had to."

"A sacrifice I'm sure he understands," said Saeryn.

"I'm sorry. Raesh, you remember Saeryn from the portal. She's the Queen of my people. And this is Oren, one of the dragonborn warriors. Oren, Saeryn, this is Raesh and the captain."

Everyone exchanged greetings pleasantly, though Andie did not miss a certain hesitancy between Raesh and Oren. The captain led them back to the control room.

"It wasn't easy getting here," he said. "Coming from the sea to the mouth of the Nathair brought us through the Gray Fold."

"Yes, we know of that," Saeryn said. "Even in our time many ship would take a longer route than risk going through those turbulent waters. Most who attempted it did not return."

"We almost went around ourselves, but time was of the essence. Luckily for us, ships are a lot stronger these days. There was some contention about which mountain range to take, but I finally broke and told Raesh that you had picked this one, Andie, and so on we came."

"There's been contention about everything," Raesh said, his hands on his hips. "We're barely holding it together, but seeing you and your people is going to do everybody a lot of good, Andie. Everybody calmed down some when it was decided that the traitor had to have been someone in that room, though we still had no idea what happened. Narrowing it down to eight people out of five hundred helped. But you're what we need."

"I'll meet with them," Andie said. "But until we figure out exactly what happened and who did it, it's probably best that everyone stays on the ship. For the protection of my people."

"We should go down now and let you bring peace," Saeryn said. "Oren, wait here with the captain and we will try to be brief."

Oren bowed and took up a post near the map. Andie smiled at him, but he only barely returned it. Raesh led them out and then down to the lower decks where Andie began to listen for sounds of the passengers, but there was nothing. It was silent. They went down another level to where the cabins were and even there it was eerily quiet. Even Saeryn seemed ill at ease in the halls. Eventually they came to the large meeting room where the fighters had been meeting the day Andie disappeared. It was totally empty. The three of them walked in and up to the platform.

"We can wait here," said Raesh. "They should be coming in soon. The captain made the announcement to meet here when we saw the dragons approaching."

"What's taking them so long?" Andie asked.

"They didn't want to come until they were armed and ready to fight. I'm sorry, Andie, but we didn't know that you were here and we didn't know if your people would be friendly with us after we told them we'd lost you."

"A sound judgement," Saeryn said. "We would not have attacked you and we would have welcomed you with open arms, but it would have undone a great amount of trust to have come without our savior."

Andie cringed at the word—it didn't seem fitting.

She'd gotten them out of the portal, but that hardly counted for saving them. As soon as they were out, the dragonborn had to save her and her friends from being wiped out by the University. Moreover, the dragonborn had been forced to go out on their own and face the new world, and Andie hadn't been any help to them. They had saved her again on the mountainside.

"This is spinning out of control," Andie said. "We're supposed to be fighting the University, not each other. I can't believe one person could do this to us. Are you any closer to figuring out who the spy is?"

"If anything, we're starting to backtrack," Raesh said. "This morning one of the factions started talking about how the spell might have been cast from outside the room, meaning we're right back to having everyone on the suspect list. I don't know how we're going to do it, but we need to devise a plan to smoke this person out."

As Raesh finished, the fighters began to stream in. Those of them that were humans came in covered with ammunition and holding their weapons of choice. Those of them who were sorcerers kept their hands slightly clinched, ready to cast at a moment's notice. From the way they regarded one another as they came in Andie couldn't tell if they were more threatened by what the dragonborn might do or by each other.

They came in, cautious, and came down to the front looking as if they or the situation might explode at any moment. But then they saw Andie and the change came over them: pure relief. They came up to her and shook her hand or hugged her and asked her so many questions at once that she couldn't make any of them out. They didn't quite allow themselves to smile, but the whole room seemed to take on a new atmosphere when their eyes met her face. She could tell then, for the first time, just how scared they truly were.

More and more fighters piled into the room and the crowd rotated so that the newcomers could all see Andie and see that she was alright. Andie tried to give them as much hope and reassurance as she could. When everyone was finally present and accounted for, Raesh called the meeting to order.

"Alright, everybody," Raesh began. "For anyone who doesn't know yet, Andie is alive, she's fine, and she's back here with us now. She's found her people and they're on our side. Their Queen, Saeryn, is here with us tonight. Let's pay her our respect."

With his words, every fighter in the room bowed to the Queen. Raesh bowed, too. The Queen acknowledged them with a deft nod of her head.

"I'm glad we could all set aside our fears long enough to gather in the same room," Raesh continued. "And I know it's going to be a long, hard road back to trusting each other, but I think it starts here, today, with Andie."

Raesh turned to Andie and gestured for her to step forward and address the crowd, which she wasn't expecting. Andie moved to the front of the platform and looked out at the crowd. Most of those faces she didn't even know; most of the people she had never even talked to. But she understood that at that moment they needed her.

"I won't talk long because Saeryn has several things to tell you, but I want you to know that the true enemy is the University. Not us. Not each other. While it is true that there is a traitor onboard, I want you to know that I was in that room and the spell had to have come from someone who was in there with me. That means one of the eight people you have locked up is the spy. Everyone in this room can be trusted."

"What if there's more than one spy?" someone called out. "What happens if only one of them is in a cell?"

"What happens if the ship sinks?" Andie countered. "What happens if the lightning strikes the ship and fries the navigation system? What happens if the sky falls down? We can't afford to worry about problems we don't know we have. What we do know is that one person aboard this ship is a traitor. What we also know is that more than five hundred people onboard this ship are true allies. Which of those facts do you want to focus on?"

She paused for a minute to let the words sink in and the crowd seemed to think on it hard, as if they'd never considered it.

"I'm happy to be back with you and I'm still eternally grateful that you're all here willing to risk your lives for my people and me. But if we can't trust each other then we're dead already. We need to rebuild this unit or the fight will not go our way. And don't put all of your hope into me. Have faith in yourselves. I do."

CHAPTER TEN

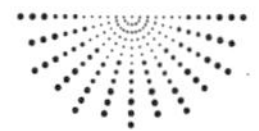

ANDIE BACKED UP, NOT WANTING TO PUSH HER LUCK with her crowd. She knew her presence was helping, but her followers had been through so much in the past few weeks that she didn't want to risk pushing them too far too fast. Instead, Saeryn stepped up to the front and her presence there was awe-inspiring, such grace and strength and peace.

"I would be remiss and shameful if I didn't first thank you for the sacrifices you've made in order to be here, fighting for my people. None of you are dragonborn and none of you have any obligation to us, and yet you've given up your comfort and potentially your lives in order that we might live. It is not a debt we can ever repay, but if you have need of us we will come without hesitation. I thank you on behalf of myself and my people.

"I don't know how familiar you are with the story of the dragonborn, so perhaps a brief recapitulation might be in order. We are a people out of time; we come from an era centuries ago, when the war between the sorcerers and the dragonborn was at its culmination. We fled to a safe haven in the mountains and Andie saved us by pulling us through the portal and across time, saving us by allowing us to take advantage of the very spell the University used to try to annihilate us. That is how we've come to your modern time. Very few were on our side back then, but there were some who fought for us. One in particular was a sorcerer who went to battle with us time and time again. He came through the portal alone some years ago. His name is Lymir."

At those words, Andie found herself almost breathless. She didn't know if she couldn't believe that Lymir was from ancient times or that he didn't tell her. It explained so much about his knowledge and the way he had looked out for her. It explained how he knew so much about the portal. Saeryn turned to Andie.

"The bracelet he gave you was to ensure that you didn't fall through the portal when you pulled us out. Lymir well knew the power of that door. It's quite a long fall from being a powerful sorcerer to running a tavern with questionable clientele, but do not underestimate him. We all owe him a great debt."

Andie could hardly believe her ears. She fidgeted with the bracelet on her wrist, realizing how much sense Saeryn's words actually made. She always wondered about the tavern keeper and how he knew so much about everything.

"Lymir was once head of your Council," Saeryn continued, addressing the crowd again. "In fact, he was the one who conceived it all those centuries ago. He was also the appointed instructor of a royal line of sorcerers during that time, a position which afforded him great access and influence. He joined our cause after that line began to commit crimes against my people out of fear and envy. That was when the entire world decided it no longer wanted to live with us. But I assure you, we are a peaceful race. Our dragons may be fierce and our magic may be formidable, but we have always abhorred conflict. We are a simple people with simple desires. The hate against us that persists in your time began in ours. The sorcerers wanted us gone so that they could command Noelle unopposed. They knew that despite our kind ways, we would never let them subjugate a single city, let alone the entire land. Just as ourselves when we came through the portal, Lymir was heartbroken when he arrived in your time and found that the sorcerers had not only won, but that the people didn't even realize what had happened. How they had been deceived and brought down. He lived among you disheartened, having only one piece remaining to him of the time he knew. That piece was the bracelet that he gave to Andie to protect her. In fact, that bracelet once belonged to me."

Saeryn looked at Andie with a smile. Andie suddenly felt extremely guilty, almost as if she had stolen the bracelet from Saeryn by force. Without even thinking, Andie began to take the bracelet off and give it to the Queen, but Saeryn held up her hand to stop her.

"Keep that, savior," Saeryn said, never losing her smile. "If it weren't for that bracelet, you might not have survived pulling our people through that portal. Only the strongest of us could have succeeded in that task, and only you could have succeeded in such a feat. Lymir would not have chosen you for nothing. He saw in you what I see in you. Our future.

Andie stared down at her feet, considering. Her fingers played with the bracelet as she listened.

"I feel I've spoken enough now. I just want you all to understand that this fight is an old one and is sure to grow ugly before its end. My people and I are at your service and rest assured, we will not leave you to fight our battles by yourselves. But I implore you to trust each other. Raesh and Andie have assured me that the traitor is indeed one of the people you've captured downstairs. They cannot hurt you from a cell. Be at peace and be together. The enemy is out there, not in here. Thank you."

It was quieter than ever when Saeryn finished. No one clapped or moved. They barely breathed. Andie never knew so many people gathered in one place could be so quiet. She could tell that they had been lifted, inspired, relieved, but they were so in awe of Saeryn—and of Andie, too—that they didn't seem to know what the proper response was. Saeryn descended the platform and went out into the hall. Andie and Raesh followed, leaving the fighters to conduct themselves.

"I'm so grateful for this," Andie said, indicating her bracelet. "It means the world to me."

"As it once did to me," said Saeryn. "It suits you."

"I've been thinking... I was thinking about all the things you told me about the dragons and the dragonborn. How all dragonborn people are born with a link to a dragon. How the scale patterns on our skin are a symbol of our dragon until we are united with them. I was just wondering if, perhaps somewhere, there was a dragon out there for me?"

"I'm afraid I do not have the answer to that. We have lost so many of the amazing creatures over the past centuries at the hands of the sorcerers. We once lived in peace and all dragonborn had a companion, but now only few remain and not even all warriors have a dragon bonded to them anymore. I do not believe there is a dragon living who is to be bonded with you. At least, not until the dragons begin to mate again and new dragons are born. When the sorcerers began their hunt for the dragons, long before my time, our people grew weaker. In turn, as our people were massacred, the dragons themselves grew sparse. They stopped reproducing, our people began to grow weaker, which is how the sorcerers first began to overcome us."

"Well, I have the scales," Andie said, hesitant. "What does that mean?"

"It means that perhaps someday a dragon will be born to you, but until then I'm afraid you will never be able to reach your full potential."

"I see." Andie tried to shrug it off, but she knew it was obvious how disappointed she was. "Saeryn, may I ask one more question? It's a difficult one to ask."

Saeryn smiled and placed her hand on Andie's shoulder. "You may ask me anything, always."

Andie paused for a moment to collect her thoughts. "Oren has green hair and green eyes. His dragon is the same color. I noticed all the warriors and their bonded dragons are of the same coloring."

Saeryn nodded. "Yes, it is a sign of their bond. A dragon is destined to pair with one unique dragonborn, and one only. From birth, the dragons already demonstrate the same coloring as its soul partner."

Andie wasn't sure how to ask her question without hurting the Queen. Her friend. Finally, she let out a deep breath and just asked. "I couldn't help but notice your dragon is of a different color."

A long moment passed in silence and Saeryn hung

her head in mourning. "Oriander, my dragon… Ori. He didn't make it through the portal when you pulled us through. He sacrificed himself to protect our people when that evil spell was cast. He hung back to ensure we all made it through the portal safely, but I'm afraid it closed before he was able to follow. He was a great dragon, and an even greater companion."

Sorrow struck Andie's heart at those words. "I'm… I'm so sorry, Saeryn. Had I known, I…"

"There was nothing you could do, sweet girl," Saeryn smiled. "You saved our people, and for that I owe you a great debt. You are our savior, and never forget that."

"Then who's dragon do you ride now?"

"My dearest friend, one I considered a sister, did not survive that final attack from the sorcerers. Raylim, her dragon, came through the portal just as she fell. Normally, a dragon would not survive the death of its rider, but I summoned all my strength to keep him alive. He bonded to me, in a way. We have become close, growing stronger from each other's presence, although it will never be the same bond that Ori and I shared. Or that Raylim and Katyara shared. Nevertheless, we endure. And I am eternally grateful for the strength and companionship he offers me."

Andie couldn't bear the sorrow in Saeryn's eyes, but she straightened her back and offered a smile to the Queen as best she could. "I am so sorry for your loss. Raylim is lucky to have you."

"And I him," Saeryn answered.

Raesh rounded the corner and came to stand next to Andie. He opened his mouth to speak, but quickly shut it as he recognized the emotion that hung in the air.

When Andie looked back down to her feet, Saeryn

lifted her chin with a gentle finger. "I know this disappoints you, Andie. Not having a dragon of your own. But this is a different time, and perhaps someday, when things are different, you will find your match. But, right now, we must focus on stopping the spread of hate and malice. We need to convince the world that the dragonborn are actually good. That we aren't the monsters the University has purported us to be. You know as well as I that the University is in the midst of creating something terrible. I suppose now we should go down."

Andie took in a deep breath and let it out slowly. Saeryn was right, of course. She shouldn't let the fact that she doesn't have a dragon of her own impede her mission. She had never grown up even considering it an option, so why should it bother her now?

Saeryn turned to Raesh. "I understand that Andie's father is down there as well?"

"Yes," Raesh nodded, wrapping his arm around Andie's shoulder. He always knew what to do and what to say. "We put him down there, but only to sort of save face. People were so on edge that they wanted all of them locked up, even though Eric had only joined us onboard and couldn't possibly be the spy. I'm sorry, Andie. But I've made him as comfortable as possible and made sure he was treated with respect from the beginning."

"It's okay, Raesh, I understand," Andie said, genuinely not angry. "Let's go down."

It was a short walk down to the brig. The place was clean and quiet, but there were thirty guards stationed around the room. They seemed highly on edge, though they all calmed considerably when they saw that Andie was alive and well. They came to the first of the cells.

"They start here," Raesh said. "On this end are the three fighters. First Kent, then Lilja, then Sarinda."

Kent was very amiable. He didn't seem upset at all, as if it all made sense to him.

"I'm glad you're okay," he said. "With Marvo locked up I know it must have been hard on Raesh organizing everyone and trying to keep the peace. Even before we knew there was a traitor it was hard to keep us all in check. We come from different backgrounds and cities. Some of them hate each other as much as they hate the University. The only thing that holds us together is the will to do what's right."

"You seem like a really sweet guy, Kent," Andie said. "If you're not the one who betrayed us, then I'm truly sorry."

"Don't be. I understand. The needs of the many outweigh one guy's kindness. I know you're doing what you have to do. Stay strong."

Andie stopped at each of the cells, but Sarinda and Lilja refused to talk to her and barely even looked in her direction. They did, however, show deference to Saeryn before going back into their reticent modes.

They came to Murakami next. She wasn't as belligerent as Sarinda or as cold as Lilja, but she was also the same woman she'd always been—terse. She didn't hold much conversation, though she was interested in what Saeryn had to say about the ancient relationships of the Raeynese empire. After her, they came to Andie's father, and, even though it was against protocol, Raesh opened the door and let her in to see him.

"Oh, I'm so glad to see you," she said. "I was so worried something might happen to you."

"I'm fine," Eric said. "I've been out of my mind worrying about you. You just disappeared. I didn't know where or how or why. Oh, my beautiful girl. Your mother would be so proud of you."

"Dad, are you sure you're okay? Can I get you anything?"

"Andie, I'm fine. Traveling at sea is a little rougher than I expected, but I'm completely—"

"Dad, I'm so sorry I stopped calling as often and that I didn't come home the last time we planned. I'm sorry I couldn't control my magic and avoid ever going to the University in the first place. I'm sorry I haven't been here to protect you and that I've been so selfish and careless and—"

"Andie, stop. I have never been more proud of you. I never doubted that you loved me for a second and I knew how much you needed to go to the University, and not just for your abilities. For answers. Honey, you're going to mean a lot of things to a lot of people, but you're also going to be the savior of your race. I know you can do it. Your mother knew it, too. Don't ever worry about me. Go and save the world."

"She has already made a fine start," said Saeryn, going down before Eric as he lay in the bed. "I am Saeryn, Queen of the dragonborn, and I want you to know that your daughter is more than we had ever dreamed. I regret so much that your wife cannot be here to witness the courage and the strength of your incredible daughter. I thank you for lending her to us."

"It is my pleasure. Thank you for welcoming her into her people. She's needed it her entire life."

They stayed with Eric for a long while, but eventually moved on. Marvo was sleeping, but even when they woke him, he seemed devoid of life. He was grateful that Andie was okay and that she'd found her people, but beyond that he seemed totally drained of the vitality that he had possessed the last time Andie saw him. Raesh turned to her after they moved on.

"Something happened to him when you disappeared," Raesh said. "It was like the traitor suddenly became... real. I think all that time he was hoping that he was wrong, that there was no traitor or that the person would truly come over to our side. But when whoever it was spelled you out my dad just... withered. I think he lost his faith in all of us, in all of this."

Carmen was beside herself.

"Are you freaking kidding me! The future? That's both cool and disturbing. Are you okay? How are you getting along with your people?"

"Everything and everyone is great, Carmen. I'm glad you're okay, too."

"Are you, Andie? I can tell from the way you're looking at me that you don't see me as the same girl you used to know. I can't imagine how all of this must make you feel. I know it must have seriously shaken your faith in people and in everything we're fighting for, but believe me when I tell you that I am *not* the traitor. Do you remember that story that I told you back in the tunnels?"

"Yeah, I remember."

"That's me. That's who I am. I'm not perfect and I'm not always kind, but I would die before I betrayed you or anything important to you. Remember that."

Finally, there was Yara. When Raesh waved his hand to clear the visibility between them, Yara jumped to her feet, but then she froze. Andie didn't know what the movement meant. Yara had a look on her face that Andie had never seen before. Andie didn't realize it, but she was standing just as still as Yara, with an expression just as confusing.

"Andie?"

Yara's voice sounded more like a little girl's. She almost looked as if she didn't know where she was or what was happening. Andie wanted to say something, but couldn't. She didn't know how she felt to see Yara again. She wasn't even sure if she knew who the girl in front of her was. Everything Andie had believed about the people in those cells had been turned on its head, with the exception of her father.

"Perhaps we should give them some time alone," Saeryn said.

Raesh nodded and the two of them walked off around the corner. Raesh cleared the guards on the hallway. Andie and Yara were left alone.

CHAPTER ELEVEN

"I WANT TO THANK YOU ALL FOR COMING IN TODAY. I'M sure there must be a plethora of other duties you need to attend to. Legislation, public relations, the fortification of your individual cities and regions. Thank you for taking time out of your busy schedules."

"None of us are here to endure your false gratitude, Myamar. This polite request for a meeting is only farce. It's you trying to mask your ego under a guise of friendship."

"Stefan, your verbal contributions are, as always, endearing, but—"

"Of all the people in the world, Myamar, I'm the last one you want to condescend to."

Chancellor Mharú went silent for a moment. Everyone knew that he hated Stefan with a passion, but was too incompetent and frightened of him to do anything. Stefan was very old and very powerful. When the terrorist attacks began in Taline all those years ago, it was Stefan who almost singlehandedly brought the city back to its feet and he who had been unanimously declared protector of the city. Stefan had been in a number of dangerous and legendary battles throughout the history of western Noelle—battles that stretched back at least one hundred fifty years. No one was really sure who he was or what he was capable of, but there was not a sorcerer in all of Noelle who would ever risk fighting with him. Not to mention Chancellor Mharú was, and had always been, a coward.

"Moving on," he said, turning his eyes from Stefan. "The abominations known as the dragonborn have eluded us for the time being. But I'm confident that we will find them soon and when we do I—"

"You won't find them, Myamar," Stefan said. "These people are an ancient, powerful race. The time may be different and the land may have changed, but their power hasn't. If they don't want to be found, then they won't be. Don't you have other things to focus on besides continuing this futile campaign of hate?"

"What's important is that the people feel safe and they won't be able to do that until every last one of the dragonborn and their dragons have been hunted down and exterminated."

"Okay, Myamar. Have your little hunt. Scour the ends of Noelle and the seas looking for the ancient, powerful, self-healing race who ride giant fire-breathing creatures whose claws could shred you with a single swipe. Spend all of that exorbitant tax you levied on the region in order to fund a journey that will yield nothing. Ignore the University that has been ruined in body and reputation. Strain what few political connections you have left. But you know what, I wish you the best of luck. I hope you find them. And when your mother comes to me, begging me to go and bring you home, I'm going to hand over to her the charred remains of your body. And I'm going to laugh."

With that Stefan stood and began to leave. The other dignitaries, chancellors, mayors, and politicians began to whisper nervously. Stefan was by far the most powerful among them and they desperately wanted him in their fight against the dragonborn. One of them stood and addressed him.

"Stefan, please," she said. "We need you to get behind this. Many of us only came because we assumed you would be as eager to hunt down these... monsters as Chancellor Mharú. Won't you fight for your people? Won't you represent the city of Taline in this great battle?"

Stefan stopped halfway out of the door. He was still for a moment and then he turned slowly, his eyes terribly focused.

"I fight for my people every day. You don't know what it's like to wake up and not know if your city is still going to be there when the sun goes down. Every day I watch and I wait and I fear for every soul in that city. Not a single year has gone by in the last two decades when we haven't had at least a handful of attacks. Bombings. Poisonings. Mass hexes. And you think I'm going to turn my back on them to help you hunt down innocent people who just want to live life after *your* ancestors tried to deny it to them? The dragonborn aren't abominations. They're people. They frighten you because they're more powerful than you, yet you're the ones itching to fight. Your narrowmindedness is unbelievable. I'm going home to look over my people. Do yourselves a favor and let this go. Otherwise... you're all dead."

Stefan left the room and there was a deep and wide

silence for a while. Even Chancellor Mharú couldn't get up the stomach to talk for a few moments. He knew that they were all reconsidering backing his ploy. It was different when they believed they were going to have Stefan behind them, but now they were being led by a coward whose only claims to prestige and power came from a family name that he wasn't smart enough to know he needed. Fortunately, they all possessed some idea of loyalty and wanted, at the very least, to see the thing through.

"Well, we all know how paranoid and close-minded Stefan can sometimes be," Chancellor Mharú began. "It doesn't change the fact that we need to find them, kill them, and take back Noelle."

"How?" asked one of the dignitaries. "I've spoken with some of the professors who were here that night and fought the dragonborn. They say the power of those people is unlimited, that they can heal themselves and fight like raging warriors. How do we defend against that?"

"How many of us will die in the fighting and never get to enjoy the freedom we fought so hard for?" another asked. "People need assurances."

"What can we honestly do about these people and their power?"

"Your eyes are on the wrong future," the chancellor said, looking more devious than they had ever seen.

Chancellor Mharú came down from the podium and walked over to the side of the room. All the people in the meeting turned in their chairs to follow him with their eyes. The Chancellor stopped in the middle of the space and clapped his hands. A door materialized in the wall and as it slid up silver beings moved into the room and stood stock still. They made no noise and the members of the gathering instinctively leaned away from them.

"Ladies and gentlemen, I give you the Sentinels," the chancellor said proudly. "Perhaps you've heard of them? Most of us were told bedtime stories as children about the incredibly power beings who worked for peace in the Old World. These are the original thirteen who worked so tirelessly to maintain order in the ancient days of Noelle. These beings are centuries old, dating back to at least the time of Hightowyr, maybe earlier. They are notoriously difficult to kill. So difficult, in fact, that in all these long centuries no one has been able to kill a single one."

"But I thought three of them were destroyed when the criminals escaped from the University?" someone asked.

"No, merely damaged. The best part is that the Sentinels were instrumental in taking down the dragonborn centuries ago and I have no doubt that they can be just as helpful today. And do you know what else?"

The members of the meeting were interested now, had forgotten the chancellor's poor history and were growing more and more intrigued by his current machinations. Some of them were even beginning to hope.

"To this day, Sentinels are the only beings in the history of the world to be able to kill dragons."

The joyous gasps rang throughout the assembly and the members began to smile, to clap, and even to nod their approval to Chancellor Mharú. The chancellor himself began to feel his pride swell again. He was no fool, he knew how badly he had sullied the family name and how far he had to go to regain his reputation and influence. The defeat in the Archives at the hands of the dragonborn had been a devastating blow to his political career. He was desperate, but he was clever.

"And if that's not enough..."

The chancellor clapped his hands again and seconds later, a man came out dressed in all black—a black purer and deeper than anything the dignitaries had ever seen before. The uniform was sleek, fitted, and muffled every move the wearer made so that nothing could be heard when he made his entrance.

"This is the final version of our ultimate weapon," the chancellor said. "This... armor, for lack of a better word, is unlike anything we've ever produced before. To be brief, it amplifies the natural ability of the user. Senses, instincts, agility, strength, speed, and of course sorcery. This is everything we've needed. Not only will this level the playing field, it will give us an extreme advantage. When we face those abominations again we will annihilate them."

"That sounds incredibly impressive, Myamar, but how do you know it works? Still more important, how can you be sure it will work against the dragonborn?"

"We know it works because we've tested it," the chancellor said, arrogant as ever. "We've been testing it for eighteen years."

"Eighteen years? Well, why haven't we heard of it?"

"You have. We've been steadily and systematically blowing up the city of Taline for almost two decades. All those 'terrorist attacks?' That was this armor, going through round after round of rigorous testing and remodeling to create the perfect weapon. For the perfect war."

"Myamar, have you lost your mind? If Stefan were ever to find out about this—"

"He hasn't discovered anything in eighteen years and I have no reason to believe that will change now. Besides, if he ever does find out I'll implicate each and every one of you as just as culpable as I am. If I go down, I'm taking all of you with me. Perhaps that's incentive enough to keep this conversation between friends."

"So, it's blackmail then?"

"It's self-preservation. And while the method may seem cruel, I assure you you'll feel differently when you're able to walk over the cold, dead corpses of our enemies. We know this armor will work against the dragonborn because we tested it on one who was enrolled here. Andie Rogers. We used her icon to steal bits of her DNA and although we were unsuccessful in turning her genes into a weapon, we did succeed in creating a weapon that disintegrated the specific dragonblood DNA sequence. In short, if you use this suit against a dragonborn, effectively, there won't be anything left of them.

"Now, I've sent out the herald. The seven great families of Arvall will finally be together again soon. It will be the first time in nearly two hundred years that we've all been in the city. Until then, my friends, rest easy knowing I've secured our future."

Myamar held up his arms to the assembly and they applauded him. Maybe from fear, maybe from genuine gratitude. They would have done anything to get rid of the dragonborn. Shortly after that, the meeting was closed and the dignitaries left, still smiling. The man in the armor followed Chancellor Mharú through the room and back to the chancellor's private office, one of many which the University kept for him.

"We're alone now," the chancellor said. "Feel free to take the cowl off."

The man removed the cowl and his long hair fell to his shoulders; he hadn't cut it in quite some time. He'd also recently started growing a beard, though it was only just long enough to stop being shadow. He was tall, lean-muscled, and had grown fiercer in the last months than he had ever been before. He'd become the leader of the chancellor's armored battalion and of the many things he wanted, perhaps the most pressing was his desire to serve Chancellor Myamar Mharú.

"I'm very pleased with your improvements," the chancellor continued. "When you first applied for the battalion, I was rather hoping you'd screw up so that we could kill you. Everyone wanted you dead. At first I marveled at your ability to transcend that and now I've grown to respect it. You've come farther than anyone in these last months and your efforts will not be forgotten."

"Thank you, chancellor," the man said. "Permission to speak freely."

"Of course."

"I wonder, chancellor, if the other dignitaries and heads of state would be so willing to follow you if they knew that this was all part of a much larger game. I mean no disrespect, but I worry what their reactions might be when they find that you've done these things in large part for personal reasons."

"You mean to satisfy my own political aspirations? My dear boy, they already know. Just as I know that they will follow me because they think it's best for their own futures.

Those men and women who just left certainly aren't the smartest you'll ever meet, but there are no illusions among them. Everything is a political ploy, every decision a carefully planned stroke, every word and handshake a play for future prestige. Politics is not a career, it's a lifestyle. True, I advocate hate against the dragonborn. However, it's not because they pose a threat or even because I personally hate them. I do it because they're a familiar evil that the people can unite behind and once the people are united I'll be there to step into the role of their savior."

"So, you don't think the dragonborn are dangerous?" the man said, unsure of which questions were appropriate to ask his superior.

"Of course, they are," the chancellor responded. "But every living thing is dangerous in its own way. My family has hated the dragonborn and their beasts for centuries. I certainly don't like them, but that kind of pervasive enmity is from another time. I'm an opportunist. If the dragonborn hadn't decided to come back I would've chosen some other group of people to persecute. I want you to understand something, my friend. Knowledge is important. It's why I worked so hard to turn one of Andie Rogers' friends against her to feed me information from the inside of their little rebellion. But contrary to popular belief, knowledge isn't power. *Power* is power. Never forget: we're not after the dragonborn. We're after control of Noelle."

"I understand, chancellor," the man said with the conviction and acquiescence of a true soldier. "I pledge myself to your cause."

"And will you die for my personal gain?"

"No, sir. There'll be no need for that. No one who

comes between you and your destination will survive me."

"Oh, I like you," the chancellor said, reclining in his chair. "We're going to make a great team you and me. Your name is... what, again?"

"Ashur, sir."

"Ashur. I like it. I apologize, I'll have to make a better effort to remember it."

"Nothing to apologize for, sir. I knew it would take people a while to learn my new name."

"And why did you change it?"

"Because who I was before wasn't good enough. That person was a failure. He's dead now. Ashur lives."

"Excellent. That'll be all for now, Ashur. While you're out today, head over to Taline and test the suit out some more. We wouldn't want Stefan to get bored."

Ashur gave a slight bow and then walked out, closing the door behind him and leaving the chancellor alone to continue his evil schemes.

"I like that name," he said to himself. "I'm glad he changed it. 'Tarven' was a rather stupid name anyway. I think I like the idea of self-reinvention. I may have to consider it myself."

The chancellor reclined in his chair again, arrogant, grinning, and thinking on all the evil he had planned. For quite some time, he had been planning for this. He'd made a series of very grave mistakes in the early years of his political career and all but tarnished the family name. The fact had never left him, had always been hanging over him like some dark curse. And so, many years ago, the chancellor began planning the events that would eventually culminate in a massive war.

Unlike most people, Chancellor Mharú knew

everything about himself and accepted it. He knew he wasn't the most well liked, or the bravest, or the best sorcerer. But what gifts he did have were equally as powerful if wielded correctly. He knew he was patient, heartless, and persuasive. More than anything he knew he was a coward, and, because he could accept that, he grew very close to the concept of fear. He knew what it looked like, how it operated, what potential it could have. He knew he'd never get where he wanted to go on his name or his ability, so he planned to capitalize on the fear of others. He had originally planned for a civil war a few years from then, but when he heard the portal that trapped the dragonborn was becoming active he adapted his plans.

He knew it was all a lie. He knew the dragonborn were a peaceful people. He knew it and his ancestors knew it, too, but they didn't care. The chancellor wanted to grind Noelle into nothing through its own fear, then rebuild it in his own image. He wanted control of the land and the people, from coast to coast. He knew what a dangerous game he was playing, but he also knew that he was the only one who knew all the pieces and all the moves. He wasn't coldhearted because of circumstance or necessity. He was simply evil.

CHAPTER TWELVE

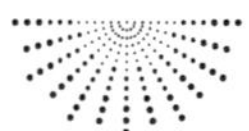

ANDIE AND YARA STILL HADN'T SPOKEN TO EACH OTHER. They couldn't—there was too much hanging in the air between them. Andie was thinking that she didn't even know the girl in front of her, didn't trust her and wasn't sure that the girl hadn't tried to kill her or transport her back to the University. As she watched Yara, Andie figured she must have been just as confused about this meeting. Yara must have doubted Andie's power, her ability to protect herself or more importantly any of the fighters who had signed up to fight with her. Andie knew that Yara had essentially always thought that Andie was invincible. Andie herself had thought that some days. But after seeing her sent from the ship so easily—maybe she had been the one to do the sending—Yara must have doubted Andie's ability.

Yara was the first to move. She took four cautious steps toward the door and then stopped, as if waiting for Andie to make the next move. Andie walked all the way up to the door. And then opened it. She didn't know what she was doing or why; all she knew was that the girl in front of her had once been her closest friend, her most loyal ally, and now she didn't even know if Yara wanted to kill her. Yara's expression seemed to suggest that she was thinking the same thing.

Without thinking it, Andie closed her hand into a fist. The fist started to glow and vibrations swam in the air around it. Andie hadn't meant to do it. At least she didn't think she did. When Yara saw the fist, she took a quick step back and began to emit her own light. And suddenly the tension between them was incredible, impossible. The gulf dividing the two girls had never been so vast, so insurmountable. Andie was hardly aware of what was happening. All she knew was that she felt so betrayed by the person across from her. The girl she'd recently found out had killed. Then, almost as quick as she could blink, Andie shut the door, brought the spell back up, and hurried out of the brig. Raesh and Saeryn were waiting for her at the top of the stairs.

"Good talk?" Raesh asked.

"Honestly, I don't know what that was," Andie said. "Are you any closer to figuring out who it is? Do you have any leads?"

"Nothing. I think it might be best to hand it over to someone more objective. Someone who doesn't know them as well and isn't related to two of them."

"Which among them is even powerful enough to cast such a spell?" Saeryn asked. "Casting a spell like that, even targeted at a single person, requires a massive amount of energy. I would suggest looking at the older ones first."

"The oldest one is my dad and he's a human. The next oldest is Andie's dad, and we know it wasn't him because he wasn't with us in the caves. Murakami has some magical ability, but her blood is not pure so I don't know how strong she is or could be. Carmen and Yara are both incredibly powerful. Kent has always been kind of ordinary, while Sarinda and Lilja are two of our best fighters. However, I can't say for certain what the three would be capable of if they'd gotten secret training. They're quick learners and fierce combatants. So again, we just come full circle."

"Whatever happened, it was serious magic," Andie said. "When I woke up, my body was weaker. It was like the three weeks I'd jumped had all been spent without sunlight. Like my body was confused."

"What really troubles me is how this imposter knew where to send you," Saeryn mused. She leaned against the wood-planked wall, her arms held casually behind her back. "I don't think I would be wrong in assuming your destination wasn't common knowledge?"

"Not at all," Raesh said. "It took me a week to even get the captain to tell me where we were headed. No one has been allowed in his control room except the first and second mates, and the captain is the only one with a key. And he never leaves the coordinates in plain sight. Not even the first mates should know where the ship is headed."

"Then the spy must have gone directly into Andie's thoughts. It is cruel and reckless magic, but it tells us that this spy is not to be toyed with. It would be very unwise to underestimate this person."

"We won't," Andie said. "Where were you planning to go after here, Raesh?"

"If we were able to find the dragonborn we were going to head back to the source. Arvall City. If we can stop the lies there, then we can stop the vicious rumors in their tracks. Overcoming the University and Arvall should be our top priorities. There's no way the University could go ahead with its designs if it can't get the support of its own city. And from there it's a domino effect."

"You make it sound simple, but it's going to be the hardest thing we've ever done. These people have been having nightmares about the dragonborn for hundreds of years. And the University took that fear and multiplied it. Every day we wait the lies grow stronger, become more real. I don't know what we're going to do."

"You're going to bridge the gap," Saeryn said. "Between your time and ours. You'll have to convince them that we're good, that we mean well, and that we seek the same peace they feel they now have to fight for. We want nothing but to find a new home and begin to rebuild. We are not the monsters and it's important that they understand that they are not the monsters either. Aside from a few obvious differences, we're really not so dissimilar. But I won't presume to teach you how to do your job, you're already sacrificing so much. I won't take your autonomy on top of it all. I have faith in you."

"So, Arvall?" Andie asked.

Saeryn offered a small smile. "To Arvall."

The three nodded and there wasn't much to say after that. Andie walked Saeryn back up onto the upper deck. Oren and the captain had moved outside and were discussing something in great depth. Oren looked thrilled to see Andie, and even happier to see that Raesh was not with her.

"I think our best bet is to go back on foot," the captain said.

"What?" Andie said. "Why? We can't go back on foot that would take too long."

"Oren here was telling me that the river turns south a few kilometers further."

"But I thought it went straight until it hit the coast?"

"I'm afraid that was our doing," Oren said. "In creating our caverns and tunnels we've had to displace a great deal of soil and stone. In addition, the erosion of the lowest peak has pushed the river into a new direction."

"But that shouldn't matter anyway. We can just turn around and go back the way we came."

"We can't, Andie," the captain said. "The Nathair has one of the strongest currents in Noelle. If we opened the ships engines to their max we could probably fight a good way back, but with the ship working that hard we'd run out of fuel before we even made it halfway. Even if we did have the fuel, I'd never try to push the ship through the Gray Fold coming from this direction. It'd be suicide. If we keep on the direction we're going now, at a moderately increased speed that will cut down time but not burn too much fuel, we could make the coast in two weeks, but then we have to sail all the way around the bottom side of Noelle to get back to the port at Arvall."

"Captain, are you telling me that there's not a single stream or river we can take to get back any faster?"

"This isn't a commercial river, Andie. The current is just too strong. Once you're on it you're on it until your reach the end. There are a lot of tributaries, but they're all flowing too strongly in the wrong direction, making too many delaying twists and turns, or too small."

"How long will it take to sail around Noelle, once we reach the coast?"

"At least three weeks. We've got to travel down the coast and then turn west to come around. We turn north when we pass New Carthage."

"I'm terribly sorry for our inconveniencing you," said Oren.

"No, it wasn't you. Even if the river was still running the way it used to, we'd be in trouble."

"How long would it take you and the passengers to cross on foot?"

"I would take a few days to cross these lands safely. After that it would simply depend on what kind of transportation we could get. I'm not familiar with the area, but this is the most rural part of Noelle and I doubt if anything is coming through this region that can carry all five hundred plus of us at once. So, I'm guessing we'd be walking most of the way."

"That's too long," Andie said. "We need to get back now. We've already waited too long."

But they were out of ideas. They knew that the University was already preparing to reopen soon as a military training ground and that would be the end of everything. The dragons could cover the distance easily and rapidly, but there was no way the creatures could carry the dragonborn warriors and the Council fighters. The dragons were strong enough, but there wasn't enough space. They talked it over a bit more, but when nothing viable came up they decided it was finally time to call it a night.

"Andie, we'll come back and speak with you tomorrow," Saeryn said. "Enjoy your time with your friends."

"Actually, I..."

Andie didn't know how to say what she wanted. She

missed her friends, all of them new and old, but there was no possibility of her staying on that ship overnight. She'd told Raesh that she would be staying the night, but she hadn't meant it. When he asked her, he'd had a look on his face that almost begged her to stay with him; he seemed as if he was either afraid himself or was totally against her going back up on the mountain with Oren. Andie wasn't an idiot. She'd noticed the looks they'd been giving each other, which was stupid because she didn't even know Oren, and Raesh was... Well, Raesh was Raesh.

Truth be told, Andie did want to stay with Raesh. Just to talk with him and laugh with him, and maybe pretend for just a night that things were the way they used to be when she was a scared first-year student at the Academy and he was the flirty-but-sweet boy who helped his father around the restaurant. But she couldn't stay on that ship, not with a traitor on-board who was potentially one of her closest friends. She didn't know who to trust. And if the traitor truly had as much power as they were beginning to believe that person did, then Andie couldn't risk getting others get hurt in an attempt on her life.

"I'm going to go back up with you," Andie said, raising her voice as several bolts of lightning came down nearby. "I don't know who to trust on this ship and every time I think about it, it just gets worse."

"But what about your... what about Raesh?" Saeryn asked.

"He'll understand," Andie said. "Will you tell him, captain?"

"Of course."

Andie mounted up behind Oren, and he and Saeryn

lifted off and cut through the flashing sky. As the lightning curled through the air around her and the thunder ripped through time and space, Andie began to seriously think about the future of the fight. For all she knew the traitor could have converted others by now, could have devised an entire plan to wipe them all out before they made the coast.

The spy had the advantage of anonymity and of knowing exactly what the University was planning. The only kink that had happened so far was that the person had been locked up because they got too eager and performed the spell in the same room with Andie. But if the person managed to find out Andie's destination without being in the control room, there was no definitive way of saying that they had to be in the room in order to cast the spell. She simply didn't know what to think.

When they finally made it back to the mountain, Andie went straight to the area that had been given to her to live in. She said some parting words to Saeryn and nodded to Oren, and then left in such a way that everyone knew she was asking not to be bothered again that night.

Andie tried to think of a plan, any plan with any outcome, just something to keep her mind busy, but she couldn't. All she could think of was the peace of mind she'd lost and all the lives on that ship that were suddenly susceptible at the hands of a traitor. She wondered how someone could be that evil.

It was easy to understand why Chancellor Mharú and his cohorts were so against the dragonborn: they had been raised to hate them. They had known nothing but that hate since birth and since the dragonborn weren't around to defend themselves, the people had no reason to change the way they felt. But the traitor had lived among people who felt otherwise, people who knew how kind and how beautiful the dragonborn were. This person had made a conscious decision to brutally betray everything and everyone surrounding them. They had put the lives of hundreds of Council fighters at stake and could potentially doom the dragonborn if not unmasked soon. And if the traitor was successful and provided the University with the things it needed to grow, that would be the end of Noelle as they knew it.

And the University itself was a whole different kind of evil. They were proud of the systematic genocide that had been carried out centuries before and wanted to bring it back again. They had no proof that the dragonborn were who they thought they were—they just wanted them dead, gone. Andie couldn't believe she had ever trusted that place to teach her, to educate her about her own people, her own power. Failing to get anything done, physically or mentally, Andie put out her light and laid down.

But sleep did not come. Her mind wouldn't stop working, worrying. And when she finally did manage to forget about those things for a moment, a crushing nostalgia set in. What she wanted more than anything that night was to make things revert to the way they used to be. She wanted to go back to Michaelson, before the Academy, before dragons, before the battle in the Archives, before that little room over Marvo's restaurant, before her father's accident, to the time when she and her parents were a family. When they were whole.

She wanted her mother back, the woman she was forgetting more and more as time went on. Sometimes, late at night when she was alone and pretending to be asleep, Andie could almost feel her mother's arms around her. She could hear her voice, smell her, and even see her there next to her, smiling. But most of the time that woman was a kind of void inside of Andie, something that had existed too long ago to leave as lasting an impression as she wanted. Andie wondered what her mother would have to say if she were there with her, if she could see the way the world was so eager to hate and slow to accept.

Andie knew the University wanted to win the unanimous support of Noelle before opening the military facilities. Raesh had told her about some of the news they picked up along the Nathair. The University had almost finished constructing the newest facilities and adapting the old ones. Soon it would become the perfect training place for killers driven by fear. It would also become the perfect fearmongering institute, undoubtedly the first of many.

The University knew how to manipulate fears—they had been doing it for five hundred years. She could almost see Chancellor Mharú sitting at his desk, smug and satisfied, thinking that the battle was practically won. The only thing that scared her where that coward was concerned was his resources. The chancellor may have been cravenly, but some of his associates and interests were not. He had access to hundreds of years of magical knowledge, relationships, money, tools, infrastructure, and more. All Andie had was her power and her allies, and the latter was in an unreliable state.

Thinking of the University made her think of Tarven, the other coward and traitor, though the only person he had betrayed was Andie. She would never admit it out loud, but she thought of him every night. She liked to think of him and some days she even looked forward to it—not because she felt in any way romantically linked to him, though. She thought of him in order to keep herself fresh, sharp, at her most aware. She never wanted to be caught in the open like that again, which was part of the reason why her current situation was hitting her so hard. Thinking of Tarven forced Andie to face her mistakes, her bad judgements, all the forgiveness she had heaped on him until the last possible moment when it was almost too late and almost cost her the lives of her friends. Tarven had played her like an instrument, had toyed with her and blinded her. She never wanted to feel that again or be the kind of person who forgave the unforgiveable, or ignored her own instincts just for the sake of preserving an illusion she knew in her heart wasn't real. As she thought back she realized just how far she had come in a short period of time. It hadn't even been a year since the fight in the Archives.

CHAPTER THIRTEEN

"I WANT TO TELL YOU A STORY."

Andie nearly jumped out of her skin. It was Saeryn. The Queen had crept up without a sound and was standing behind Andie, smiling and waiting patiently for the girl to respond.

"Saeryn, I didn't hear you coming."

"I'm a dragonborn warrior. You never know I'm there until it's too late," she said, taking a seat.

"Let me make a space for you—"

"No need. I may be a Queen, but I'm not spoiled. A little dirt is good for humility. Now, I want to tell you a story and I don't want you to interrupt. You can take whatever point you want from this story or you can forget it entirely. It will be your choice. I only want to share it with you because I genuinely believe it will be of some help. Also, you're a terrific listener, Andie, and your heart is full of hope, no matter how bitter you may want to seem on the outside. Do you accept my terms?"

"I do," Andie said, leaning back on her arms and waiting for Saeryn to begin.

"Well, good. This is a story about me. I wasn't always a Queen. In my time, I was just a girl. Truth be told, I was little more than a peasant. Much like you, my mother had been killed by fanatics from the University and I lived with my father. In those days, the dragonborn wouldn't think of hiding, even though we had already been scared into submission. Some cruel mind had invented the Sentinels, the only things I've ever seen that can kill a dragon. Our poor, beautiful creatures began to fall all over the regions.

"My father and I were farmers. We grew crops, raised animals, and did some modest pottery. We never had much, but we always had each other. It was rather nice, actually. But, of course, the University wouldn't be sated by any amount of carnage, no matter how terrible. Eventually they came to our region and enslaved or butchered everyone. The last time I saw my father I was being ripped from his arms. You see, though we were considered lesser, savages, the sorcerers sometimes kept the women and girls around for their pleasure. I didn't hear of my father again until some years later, but of course they'd killed him the same day they took me.

"I was fortunate enough to fall in among a group of older women who had been slaves for a while already. They took to me and protected me. For three years, they looked out for me and kept me from the filthy hands of the sorcerers. Those were dark times, Andie, and we suffered terribly. There was no relief for me even in avoiding the lechery of the sorcerers. Torture, starvation, humiliation. There aren't words for some of the things we endured. And the sorcerers just kept hurting us, figuring out new and innovative ways to bring us pain because our dragonblood kept healing us. But as you know, though we heal we still feel pain. We still feel every second of pain. I can't tell you how much it broke my heart to see those women going in my place, offering themselves for those nightmarish evenings instead of letting the perverted sorcerers have me. They would cover me in mud or rub me down with molded food to make me less appealing. They were my angels.

"I'd only passed seventeen winters, but I had no intention of being a slave all my life. I knew I need to escape and knew that somebody needed to unite my people, give them hope. I already knew that I came from a long line of royalty, but by the time I was born our people had been thrown into disarray. Even my mother never got a chance to sit on the throne. By the time I was enslaved, our people weren't concerned with royal lineage, only survival. In fact, there were many royal lines. I'm proud to say that mine was the kindest. Even dragonborn had cruelty in their history, but my royal line had always been fair and understanding.

"One day the guards came for me. I had made up my mind to go with them that night. I refused the mud, the rotten food, and all the other tricks the women had used to keep me safe. Three years was more than enough time in slavery. The women cried as I was dragged off, but I knew what I was doing. The sorcerer who kept us was so wealthy I don't think even he knew how much money he had. His palace was so large, it took twenty minutes to reach him from the slave gallery. When the guards dumped me at his door he looked me over, then made me bathe. I let him watch me, let his eyes drink me in. I relished the bath. I had not been fully clean since I'd left home. I washed my body, my hair, cleaned my teeth and feet. When I was ready I went to stand by the bed; I beckoned him, pretended I had accepted my fate. He did not know what I planned.

"I won't tell you how, but I will tell you that I disposed of him in a manner I thought fitting. I snuck back to the slave gallery, told the others what I had done, and offered them a choice. We found our strength and from then on, we fought back with everything we had. It wasn't long before we had completely overrun the palace. We left there and divided into groups, liberating our people in multiple regions. I grew in influence and my power grew as well, as I ceased to be afraid.

"Before I knew it, I was a general in our militia. We began to understand that the only reason the sorcerers had defeated us physically was because they had first defeated us mentally. We had let them frighten us. We had cowered in their shadow. But that was done. Soon we were uniting in the mountains we had previously called home and not long after I was given the great honor of being asked to reign among our people. I didn't want the throne at first; it seemed silly to stand on ceremony and call myself a Queen when we were fighting for our lives and didn't even have a permanent home. But I did as the people asked. If it had not been for Eitilt, that terrible curse, we would have taken back our world, yet that was not the turn fate had planned for us.

"I know you have many questions and concerns, not the least of which is why you were the one to hear our call for help. That answer is... complex. As are the many 'whys' behind your betrayer's actions. Such is life. You fret too much. I will go now, but I leave you with this: we are a powerful people, Andie, and there is no limit to our power when we choose to abandon fear and leap into hope."

Saeryn smiled and touched Andie's hand. They sat like that for a moment, not speaking, not moving, just understanding. When Saeryn finally stood to leave and Andie was left alone, she felt significantly better. At the beginning of her stay, Andie had felt special in having Saeryn spend so much time with her; she felt that she had been singled out by the Queen. However, the longer she stayed the more she began to understand that Saeryn treated them all that way; she genuinely loved her people. Then Andie had begun to wonder how she could have such grace under pressure when there were thousands of things that could go wrong and millions of people wanting their ultimate destruction. But now she was beginning to understand. Saeryn wasn't optimistic or willfully blind. In fact, she was acutely aware of the many ways in which their way of life could be ended, but she understood that her strength wasn't for herself. It was for all the people watching her, the people who depended on her in order to believe that what they were fighting for was worth it. And that's when Andie finally understood.

Pain was probable. Fear was merely possible.

THE NEXT MORNING, Andie was feeling better; she couldn't fool herself into ignoring her circumstance, but she realized that there was so much more than just her personal feelings involved. She also knew that no matter what was going on onboard the ship, she had her people, the dragonborn, behind her.

She straightened her space and then went out to see

what her people were up to. That morning the children were performing a piece they had been working on in their classes. Andie was amazed that the dragonborn had set up a school, markets, and a prototype of a financial quarter in less than a year. They had already mapped the entire mountain range and were fast approaching the initial phase of their building projects. They were going to take a group of the smaller peaks and break them down into materials they could use to construct buildings, aqueducts, and a number of other things as well, all of which would unite to create a formidable infrastructure. They had also already begun mining in the mountains and the valleys between. They had found a number of useful minerals, silver, coal, and even iron ore. One of the architects told Andie all of this and more as they sat and watched the children perform.

When the performance was over, Andie went to the market to get food for breakfast. The dragonborn didn't deal in money, at least not among themselves: everyone had a set of tasks and as long as everyone did their share the workload was light and resources were plentiful. She was amazed at their ability to share, at the evidence of their evolution beyond petty scheming to a kind of generosity and compassion that Andie could hardly describe. It was like being in the middle of one big family. One enormous, incredibly content family. Of course, they had arguments and disputes—in fact, Andie had witnessed at least four such instances since she had been living with them—but they resolved them with reason and love.

Michaelson had been her home her entire life. It had always been a paradise to her, with its gold and waving fields, the lake that stretched toward her like an old friend, the sky endless and open above her. And, for a time, she had called Arvall City home, with its glass and steel and opportunities, its history and its diverse people. She'd found a second home and a great system with Marvo and his family. But being up there on the mountain with her people felt more than right. It felt like destiny.

"Andie, one day you're going to have to leave this little place. It's not right for you to stay here, cloistered and afraid of the world."

"I'm not afraid, dad, I just don't see what the big deal is. You're a sorcerer. Why can't you just teach me how to control my magic? You lived with mom, she must've told you some stuff about how this is supposed to work."

"There's no way I could ever replace your mother or do the things she would've been able to do. She could've taught you everything you needed to know, and with ease at that. My magic is totally different from yours, Andie. Even at sixteen, you're already as strong as I am. This time next year you'll be more powerful than me and in ten years you'll have more power and ability than I could ever dream of. I love you and I wish I could keep you here with me forever, but you need to learn control."

"Fine. Then I just won't use my magic at all. I don't want to leave you here alone. And I don't like the city. It's loud and it smells and the people are rude and you can't see the stars at night and—"

"And you don't want to go. And I don't want you to go. But, Andie it's about more than just learning control. You need to learn about your history: who your people are, what happened to them, what your future could be like, what you're capable of. There's only so much I can

tell you and even your mother didn't know much about the history of the dragonborn. You have to know that I would do anything for you, but I can't make the world accept you or what you can do. You need to learn how to hide your magic. And don't argue because you know I can't handle the thought of something happening to you."

"I don't have to go now or soon, right? I can stay with you a little longer?"

"Of course you can. It's still a couple of years before the Academy will take you, but one day, sweetheart, you'll have to go. It won't be so bad. You can visit me and I'll visit you. but Michaelson is such a small part of the world. And you're meant to do great things. One day you'll find it."

"Find what?"

"Your destiny."

Thinking of her father almost brought Andie to tears, but she was also incredibly happy to have him back with her again. She was planning to talk to Raesh when she saw him again and make sure he understood that her father was coming with her, back up to the mountain. He wouldn't spend another night in a cell, not even to appease the other fighters. They must've known that he wasn't a spy. As she walked, she looked around her at all the life and happiness and she knew that her father would be happy there. The dragonborn might not let him stay long, but as long as the ship was in the vicinity and as long as her people would have him she wanted him to see what she'd found. She took her armful of items and set them down in a crook of the mountain where the sun was shining perfectly.

She began to put together a modest breakfast and

bathe in the soft light of the high sun. Not long after she began, a dragon landed not far from her and curled its huge self into a ball to sleep. Its steady, deep breathing was almost hypnotic and it helped Andie relax as she finished preparing and began to eat.

She was content. She looked around her, watching the stillness and the grandeur of the mountains. She looked behind her and saw a thin, climbing pillar of smoke, no doubt from one of the new caverns been blown out with dragon fire. For a happy people, the dragonborn were surprisingly hardworking. They understood the totality of requirements in order for them to preserve and protect their way of life—they accepted it and went on with the business of living. Andie finished her breakfast and got up to go find Saeryn.

They saw each other at almost the same instant. There were smiles, waves, and Saeryn turned her body and her attention to the approaching Andie. She was almost to the Queen when a mighty roar rang through the sky. As one, the dragonborn turned to the sky and so did Andie, all of them watching the dragon as it soared with a greater speed and a fiercer determination than Andie had ever seen. Everybody on the plateau cleared out of the way as the dragon landed so forcefully it cracked the ground. The warrior who was riding dismounted and looked as if he had seen something terrible. He turned left and right, searching, until finally his eyes landed on Saeryn and Andie.

"What has happened?" Saeryn said, her shoulders already clenching to bear the weight of the new burden.

"There has been an explosion," the warrior said. "We were out beyond the range, watching over the Nathair to see if anything had entered to region. We heard a noise, a terrible noise. It wasn't until we turned and flew back along the river that we realized it was the sound of steel being torn apart. The ship..."

And with that he looked at Andie and she immediately felt the knots forming and twisting in her stomach.

"The ship carrying your friends," the warrior said. "It's been ripped in half."

CHAPTER FOURTEEN

"EXPLOSION?" ANDIE SAID, BARELY FOCUSING. "WHAT happened? Is anyone hurt?"

"I'm afraid so. There were casualties. I'm not sure to what extent, but I don't have a good feeling about the outcome. I came back to alert you. The two who were on patrol with me have stayed behind to watch over the wreck from a distance. We couldn't go down, in case whoever or whatever did that was still there and still posing a threat."

"What do you mean *who*?"

"I'm dragonborn. I know fire and explosions. Whatever happened there wasn't an accident. No natural explosion could have done that. That was magic. Dangerous magic."

"We must go down at once," Saeryn said, taking Andie's arm. "Gather all the healers and tell them what has happened. Have them meet us at the ship immediately. Bring food and water. Gather blankets, clothes, and be as quick as possible. Where is the ship? Did it move at all from its position yesterday?"

"No, it's still there. What's left of it."

"At once."

Saeryn began to run with Andie still in her grasp. Andie could barely comprehend what was happening. All she could think about were the names. Raesh. Yara. Eric. Marvo. Carmen. Kent. Lilja. Sarinda. Captain Wolfe. Charles. Murakami. Sarah. Elizabeth. Mary Louise. Roderick. So many people who had aligned themselves to her cause and gave up their lives to be there on that ship, fighting for what they believed was right. Over five hundred brave souls who had given up a life of ease to fight what had never been a fair fight, and now they may have given up their lives entirely.

Before Andie could understand what had happened, she was on the back of a dragon riding behind Saeryn and they were plunging through the sky. Andie had meant to ride behind Oren, but had mistaken Saeryn's dragon for his; for a split-second, Andie thought she saw a strange look on Saeryn's face. But, of course, there was a strange look. There was a strange look on everyone's faces. They had just found out the people coming to help them were probably dead. Saeryn gripped the dragon differently, more purposefully, and the creature seemed to sense her desire. Andie had never experienced such speed and power before. The dragon was a living breathing knife in the sky and in seconds they had passed through the ominous clouds and left the sunlight behind.

Beneath the clouds, the lightning seemed brighter, hotter, faster than ever. The thunder sounded a thousand times amplified, so loud it was like each clap traveled down inside of her and split her again and again. The dragon flew like it was honing in on something, unaffected by the lightning, heedless of the thunder.

Andie had finally come around and brought herself back into her body, back into the midst of yet another horrible incident. This was all the University's fault. They had planted the spy and told them to wreak this havoc on the unsuspecting fighters. Andie just couldn't comprehend how anyone could be so evil, so hungry for other people's blood—at least, she hadn't understood it until right then and there as she was cutting her way through the sky.

Suddenly she was filled with a rage and a bloodlust unlike anything she'd ever known was possible. She hoped that of all the lives lost, the traitor would still be alive. She wanted to see them, touch them, feel their throat beneath her hands. She had never relished the thought of violence, and certainly not of taking a life, but she had reached her point and passed it. Whoever the traitor was, they had performed their last evil. She prayed for them to be alive. She prayed for the chance to end them.

As they neared the ship's position, Andie was finally able to see what the warrior had warned them about. The other two dragons were still circling above the wreck, but when they saw Saeryn and her group approaching they came down to join them.

The ship itself was a complete ruin. It was split open about a third of the way along its length. The wreck was lying on the edge of the shore where they had anchored before. The explosion had blown the steel back in sharp, grotesque tears. The shining grey steel of the ship abruptly became a smoldering black at the split, the long, jagged shards of steel point out from the point of the blast. Only a thin sliver of the bottom of the ship held the two halves together, but even so there was nothing that could be done for it. Andie was in a kind of sedated awe when she saw it, the great bulk of the ship lying on its side in the sand, the lightning running the sky above.

But as they came closer and closer, Andie began to see that there were survivors. Lots of survivors. They were standing or lying along the shore, wounded, anxious, looking up at the dragonborn in fear as if they thought they were being attacked. Saeryn turned the dragon to fly over the wreck to survey it from the air. Totally destroyed. The survivors were tending to each other and Andie searched desperately for a face she recognized. She searched for her father. Finally, the dragon touched down and Andie leapt off.

She ran through the people, looking at their injuries, their lacerations, their wounds, their blood. They reached out for her, tried to question her or garner some reassurance from her, but she couldn't stop. She simply couldn't ask her legs to quit moving until she had found a familiar face. Finally, someone seemed to understand what she wanted and pointed. She followed the direction of the finger, and, even when she didn't see anything, she just kept running. Hoping. And then there he was.

She couldn't tell who reached who first. All she knew was that she was in Raesh's arms. Or maybe he was in hers. There was one less person she had to worry about.

"Where are you hurt?" she asked, checking him over furiously. She spun him around in front of her, examining every inch of his body as he turned.

"Andie… Andie, I'm fine. I caught some shrapnel in the side, but I'm fine," he said, stopping his spinning and placing his hands firmly on her shoulders. "I've already been seen to. Andie, it wasn't an accident. It wasn't natural."

"I know, they told me," Andie tried to hide the frantic emotion from her voice. "What happened?"

"One minute everything was quiet. Then suddenly there was a horrible flash of heat and the floor began to rise. A moment later, the ship was ripped apart." Raesh's eyes were haunted, the memory clearly burned in his mind.

"How many dead?" Andie asked, already afraid and tensing to receive the blow.

"Eighty-seven."

Eighty-seven people dead, because of her. She hung her head, but Raesh pulled her in again. He held her, tried to comfort her. She could hear him in her ear trying to reassure her, trying to convince her that this wasn't all her fault, that he didn't blame her, that no one blamed her. But that didn't matter to her. She wanted blood. She pushed away from him.

"Who did this?"

"Come with me," he said.

He took her hand and led her through the crowd. The fighters still tried to get her attention, to get *her*. Andie was beginning to wonder if they wanted her help or her blood. Raesh led her to a clearing that she hadn't noticed from the sky, where a group of people lay together, side by side. But Andie's eyes went behind them, to her father. He was alive. She ran to him and threw her arms around his neck. Her heart was finally able to slow as she held him, knowing he was real and was okay. She leaned back to look at him, and, aside from a fairly serious wound above his eye, he seemed to be fine.

"Andie, I know you're going to want to make a fuss

over me, but I'm fine. I swear to you. Raesh moved me last night before any of this happened. He knew I didn't belong down there. And you have more pressing issues to attend to. All these people are looking to you right now and you need to give them something. Deal with this. I'll be here. Go."

Andie wanted to protest, but she could see in her father's eyes that he was serious. She nodded, kissed his cheek, and rose. She turned to look at the bodies on the ground. Carmen. Kent. Murakami. Sarinda. Her heart froze in her chest. She knelt down, prepared to mourn, but realized that they were still alive—breathing raggedly, but still alive. She could have died right then and there from the relief.

These few seemed so much worse off than the other survivors. As Andie pushed Carmen's hair back from her face, she saw that the face was covered in blood, a series of slashes cut across her beautiful face. Her breaths came slow and ragged, and she remained unconscious as Andie stoked her hair. It crushed her to see Carmen like that, but she felt a wave of relief to know that Carmen wasn't the traitor. That also meant that Kent, Murakami, and Sarinda were innocent. Andie looked around for Marvo, anxious to exonerate him as well, but she couldn't find him. There was a moment of fear as she realized that if he wasn't hurt there was a good chance he might be... She looked to Raesh.

"Where's your father?" she asked. "Please tell me... don't let... is... is it him? Is your father the traitor? Did he betray us?" She hardly recognized her own voice as she asked the questions, willing beyond anything for the answer to prove her wrong.

Raesh looked at her in a way he never had before.

She knew it was true when she saw his eyes. Raesh was broken, defeated, only holding himself together because he had the weight of the rebellion on his shoulders. Andie wanted to reach out for him, but she couldn't. She was broken, too.

"I can't believe this," she said. "I can't believe this."

"Andie," Raesh said, his expression indefinite, his lips fumbling, his hands shaking. He paused. "My father is dead."

Andie lost her breath. A kind of stasis took over her.

"We couldn't tell what happened at first," Raesh continued. "We thought he might have... escaped... but... we found what was left of him. He's gone."

Andie tried to will herself over to Raesh. She sent all kinds of commands to her body to get it to move, or think, or communicate, or do anything at all. But she remained suspended above herself, numb, and instead it was Saeryn who went to place a comforting hand on Raesh's quivering shoulder. He stood there, his shaking hand placed over Saeryn's, barely even strong enough to hold himself together. He then fell to his knees and buried his head in his hands as Andie and the rest stood there, watching their friend mourn his father.

And then Andie broke, again, but this time it was rage that bubbled up from the wound. She looked around and around and around until she found her. The traitor. The only one left. Lilja.

Andie walked over to her and Lilja saw her coming. Lilja stood up and curled her fists, ready for whatever Andie would do. Andie cast right at Lilja's face, but it was blocked and countered and a ball of red light collided with Andie's chest. That made her even angrier. As she and Lilja began their duel, the other fighters all backed away and cleared the area, ducking the stray spells that went streaking through the air. Lilja was more practiced than Andie had thought and provided a challenge. Lilja seemed to understand how furious Andie was and she refused to go without a fight.

Andie quickly grew tired of the annoyance. She raised her hand and slammed it into the earth, and it was hard to tell which was louder, the thunder or the sound of the earth breaking out from Andie's hand. Lilja was blasted up and off her feet, and, when she came back down, she landed directly on her spine against a stone. She cried out in pain, but before she could even roll over, Andie was already standing over her. Andie raised her hand, and, with her magic, took Lilja by the throat and lifted her into the air. She began to close her fist, which began to close Lilja's throat from every direction.

"Andie, stop!" her father called. "Andie, you can't do this!"

"Leave her be," Saeryn spoke kindly but raised her hand to Andie's father. "Too much has been lost this day. Justice is only right, though if you can, Andie, try not to kill her. She must pay, but there is a way she must do it. A duel is one thing, murder is another. You are not a murderer."

"Murder?" said Andie. "You're going to tell me that I shouldn't kill her? Look around you. Eighty-seven of our own are dead because of her. My friends are lying there near-dead. And Marvo... Marvo... She needs to die! This is the University doing everything it can to break us, to make us afraid, to crush us before we can even get on our feet. For weeks, we've been living in fear, afraid to trust each other, unsure of whether or not we would even make it. She cursed me into the future! She created chaos and split us all up! She needs to die and I'm going to kill her!"

"I'm sorry."

Andie turned her attention back to Lilja. The girl's face was beginning to change colors and she was kicking at the air, trying to free herself.

"Let me explain. Please," Lilja said in barely above a whisper.

"Andie," Saeryn said, her hand on Andie's shoulder. "Let her speak. She may have information we need."

Andie wasn't interested in hearing what Lilja had to say, but Saeryn put her hand over Andie's and brought down the arm and the magic. Lilja came back to earth and as Saeryn put Andie's hand down, Lilja was able to breathe again and began to take her air in gulps. Andie stood tense and furious, ready to exact her vengeance at the first chance.

"I didn't do this," Lilja said. "I swear it wasn't me."

"Liar!" Andie screamed and used her magic to push Lilja over.

"Andie, enough," Saeryn said in a new voice. "Calm yourself. Look at the girl. Can't you see she's terrified?"

"I didn't do this!" Lilja shouted. "I'm sorry for the thing I did, I know it was wrong, but I had no choice. Please, you have to believe me."

Andie watched the begging girl. She was thin, blonde-haired, pale, and beautiful in a classical kind of way. Ever since Andie had known her, Lilja had been frowning or scowling, completely loyal to the cause, yet still arrogant and conceited. But as she looked down on her there by the river, Andie realized what she was seeing. Lilja was afraid. No, not even afraid. She was petrified.

"Tell us the thing you did," Saeryn said. "And fear not. I will see that you are punished for no more than you deserve. If mercy is merited, it will be given. You have my word."

Lilja looked up at Saeryn with tearful eyes and swallowed hard as she rubbed her throat with both hands. She finally nodded. "I only helped them the one time," she pleaded. "Just the once. When we were hiding in the tunnels. I went up to scavenge with Sarinda and a group of Searchers caught us. They called the professors and one of them recognized me. They threatened my family. My friends. I might have signed up to fight this fight and to risk my life, but my family didn't. I couldn't just let them be slaughtered."

Andie took a step back as she looked down at the girl. She was trembling all over, her eyes glazed over with the horrors of what she had done. Andie took in a deep breath and let it out slowly then knelt on the ground next to Lilja. "Go on."

"The Searchers said they would let them live if I told them where we were and how they could find us," her voice was hoarse, barely a whisper. "I told them we were hiding in the tunnels under the University, but I never thought any of us would die. I thought that because we had you and Raesh and all the fighters that we could take them and make it out safely. I figured they didn't even have a chance against us. I swear, when we came out, I fought them with everything that I had. But that was it. That was the one and only thing I ever did for them, I swear. I've been trying to atone for it ever since. I've been doing my best to make this mission work."

By then, Lilja was in tears and Andie was relenting.

She could see that no one could have been harder on Lilja than she was being on herself.

"So, it was you and Sarinda who told them?" Andie asked.

"No, Sarinda never said a word. She didn't have any family so they couldn't make her cooperate. They wiped her mind. She doesn't even know she was with me. Andie, I know you and I have never gotten along, but I only did what I thought I had to do to keep the people I love alive. And when we were on the ship I did my best to stop the other one."

"The other what?"

Lilja held her head in her trembling hands as she held back a sob. When Andie placed her hand on her shoulder, she took in a silent gasp. Finally, her trembling stopped and she steadied her voice as she looked Andie in the eye. "The other spy."

Andie was dumbfounded, as was everybody else.

"There's another spy for the University here?" Andie asked. "How? Who?"

"I don't know. When they had me they just told me that they already had someone else working in our group and that it was only a matter of time before we imploded. They laughed about it. They said they chose this person because of you. That once you'd been brought down, you'd be easy to wipe out. I swear I thought I could figure out who it was and stop them. I never thought they'd be powerful enough to send you to the future or blow up the ship. I'm so sorry. I'm so, so sorry."

Andie turned from Lilja. She raised her eyes and scanned the crowd. That left one other who could possibly be the traitor. One other who happened to be in that room when Andie was blasted away. She didn't want to believe it, but she had no choice. She scanned the river side with keen eyes until she saw her lying still some distance away. Andie began walking over and a path cleared in front of her, fighters moving aside as they watched her expression. She made a straight line over to the girl and when she reached her, Andie just looked down on her.

Yara was covered in blood. And even though she surely knew that Andie was standing beside her, she wouldn't look up. Andie spread her fingers and pushed toward Yara. The blood that covered her began to disintegrate, turning into dust and then drifting up into the lightning-filled sky. Soon Yara's face was clean, as was the rest of her. Andie searched briefly with her eyes, but could see nothing.

"I don't even see a scratch," she managed to whisper. "You're not hurt at all, are you?"

Yara turned her face up toward Andie, slowly, methodically. She spoke in a measured whisper.

"No."

Andie dropped to her knees. She vaguely heard people talking behind her, someone giving commands, yelling, moving feet. She went numb, deaf, mute, immobile. Her eyes were frozen on Yara's face, as Yara's were frozen on hers. Eighty-seven dead. Hundreds injured. Lilja a traitor. Carmen gravely injured. Marvo dead. The ship in ruins. And Yara. Yara. Andie just kept watching her, unable to do anything else. Her skin felt like ice as she stared into the eyes of the girl who was once her best friend. Once a trusted ally. A traitor.

Then out of the corner of the sky a green dragon came diving right toward them. It was Ronen. Yara was totally oblivious of it. The dragon leveled out several yards away and flew straight for them, its great mouth open. Suddenly it had Yara between its teeth and it was flying away with her, straight up into the dark sky, weaving its way between the unremittent lightning.

Andie was aware only of her body falling over. Then darkness.

CHAPTER FIFTEEN

"EVERYTHING WILL BE READY IN THREE DAYS, Chancellor Mharú. The Sentinels, the army, the propaganda. All of it."

"Excellent, Ashur. I am completely in awe of your transformation. You've taken a fledgling program and made a master work of it. Your dedication will not be forgotten. When I come into my kingdom, I will remember you."

"Your praise is reward enough, chancellor. The only other satisfaction I need is to see the dragonborn eradicated. This entire plan is yours, from start to finish, has been executed masterfully. I'm just happy I was allowed to be a part of it. I'll go and bring them in now."

Ashur turned to go, and the chancellor prepared himself to receive his guests. The seven families had not been together in a very long time. Chancellor Mharú was the last of his line and had been under tremendous pressure to marry and continue his family. And he certainly planned to, but before that could happen, he needed to touch it. True power.

The other families had quietly ruled their respective domains for many years and never once had any issues; this fact had teased them into thinking they were competent and while they were certainly more effective than the chancellor, the truth was that none of the families had faced the challenges that Myamar had. They had never given a formal reason for their leaving, but he knew it was because of the portal. They knew their ancestors had barely managed to capture the dragonborn before and even then, it had cost the world greatly. They were afraid of the thing, afraid it would open up again and the dragonborn would wreak terrible havoc on their lives.

But the chancellor had never wanted to live anywhere else. His family had moved generations previous, but as soon as he was a man he moved back to Arvall. He had made it his responsibility to manage the city from which they all came. For many years, his staying was the only positive mark in his long list of embarrassing mistakes. But all of that was about to change. Just as he had settled into a pose he thought was welcoming, but also formidable, Ashur reappeared.

"Where are the families?" the chancellor asked.

"They're refusing to see you, sir."

"What?"

"They say you haven't yet proven yourself worthy of their presence."

"How dare they! Do they have any idea what I've been through? What I've done to get here?"

"I'm sorry, chancellor. I insisted, but they said it was impossible. They won't see you until you've done what you promised to do and eradicated the dragonborn. They say they don't believe you have the power or... forgive me, chancellor... the courage to carry through on your claims. They only came to see the University out of nostalgia. They're going to be staying up in the professors' quarters in the mountain. They've asked that neither you nor any of your administration bother them until the task is done."

Chancellor Mharú was so furious he began to get hot. He swiped his hand across his desk and knocked everything off onto the floor. He threw his hands up and magic cracked the ceiling and blew the windows out. He collapsed into his chair and buried his face in his hands. He wanted to issue orders to Ashur to bring the families forcibly down, but he was too full of rage to speak.

Ashur waited respectfully. He wanted to ask if there was anything he could do to serve the chancellor, anything he could do to make the situation more manageable, but he had seen the chancellor like this before and knew it was best to wait.

Suddenly a sound began to come up from the chancellor. It was a moment before Ashur realized what it was. The chancellor was laughing. He was actually laughing. The chancellor began to laugh so hard that for a moment Ashur wondered if the man was beginning to lose his mind, but then Chancellor Mharú looked up.

"Kill them," he said. "Kill them all."

"Right away, chancellor," said Ashur unhesitating and pleased. "How would you like it done?"

"Use the new armor. Hopefully, the irony won't be lost on them. And Ashur?"

"Yes, chancellor?"

"Make sure they suffer."

Ashur bowed, turned, and left the room. The chancellor twirled in his chair to face the window. With a casual wave of his hand he fixed the glass in the window, though he left the crack in the ceiling. Somehow it brought him joy. He spent a few moments fantasizing about the cruel, slow deaths of the other families. He was certain that from that day forward there would be nothing and no one to stand in his way. The old days were done and Myamar Mharú would never again be thought of as a coward.

Just that morning he had worked one of the most powerful spells he had ever performed. It was truly a masterpiece and only he and Ashur knew of its occurrence. The only thing that bothered the chancellor now was thinking about how the spell had affected its target. He had a specific goal in mind, but one never knew how these things would turn out. He thought about his spies living among the rebel fighters and he trusted that they understood their place in the plan. Of course, he was planning to kill them along with everyone else. There was no room for loose ends in the empire he was planning.

The chancellor stood and left his office. He greeted the aides sitting at their desk on his way out and walked down the long, shimmering hallway that lead toward the front of the University. The new banners and schedules had already been hung up for the fast approaching opening of the military training grounds. The chancellor smiled at the banners as he strode arrogantly past. The damage from the night of the battle of the archives and from the escape of the rebels had been cleaned up. The chancellor had his administration working around the clock to put away even the memory of the University's failure. He had even issued a gag order covering both the events.

. . .

THE SAME NIGHT of the battle in the archives, the chancellor had sprung into action. He may have lacked basic courage, but he was nothing if not resourceful. He knew with so many people fleeing the building and the dragonborn wreaking havoc in Leabharlann, it was the perfect opportunity to exact revenge. Most of the dignitaries in the mirror room had opposed some of his more extreme measures. They had called him everything from a demagogue to a fascist imposter. He grabbed Ashur, who still called himself Tarven then, and headed for the mirror room. As he suspected, the dignitaries had remained in place, doing their best to exude elegance and calm while the commoner folk were hurrying out. There was confusion and chaos all around, as nobody was yet sure of what was happening. All they knew was that there had been explosions and a group of professors had come running and screaming out of the library. One of the foreign heads of state approached Myamar as he entered the room.

"What is the meaning of this? The festival is being ruined by this tumult. Explain yourself."

The chancellor ignored him and moved on to inspect the room. He turned to Tarven.

"How fast will your plants work?"

"Almost instantaneous," Tarven said, still trembling in fear. "What do you want me to do?"

"I'm going to clear this room of everyone who hasn't pissed me off and then I want you to kill the rest. Give me a moment."

The chancellor hurried to the small dais set up at the side of the room. He grabbed the microphone.

"All students and guests need to leave the room immediately. Proceed down the hall and out into the front lot. There's nothing to worry about, just a small gas leak and we want to get it checked before things escalate. All foreign heads of state and dignitaries need to remain here for a moment, as we have special evacuation protocols for you."

The chancellor waited patiently until everyone unessential had cleared the room. Just as the last of them were leaving, the other dignitaries from outside were being brought in by the professors. The chancellor had asked that they be rounded up. When he finally had them all in one place, the chancellor looked out to survey the crowd. He was performing a last check to see if any of them were worth saving. He saw several of his friends among them and even a few of his distant relations, but he was not a man to be swayed by that. He smiled.

"If you'll all just wait here for a moment, we'll have someone come in who will show you a quicker, less bottlenecked path. Wait here for your much-deserved treatment."

With that, Chancellor Mharú stepped down from the dais and headed for the door. He nodded to Tarven, who was still struggling to pull himself together. Tarven turned and waved his hand at a section of the flowers he'd placed earlier. The petals began to blacken and disintegrate, and as they turned into Ashur a white smoke began to flow from them. The chancellor, Tarven, and the remaining professors exited the room. The dignitaries, who were no fools, saw the smoke and immediately tried to follow the chancellor out, but they found themselves blocked by an invisible wall. The chancellor turned to smile at them as his spell trapped them inside the room.

"I'd like to give you a dramatic, fitting goodbye," he said. "But you're not even worth it."

He turned to leave and the people in the room looked up at the flowers; all the way around the top of the room the flowers were turning black, becoming Ashur, and pouring the white smoke over them. There wasn't much time after that. Soon they were all dead. The chancellor's only regret was that he hadn't had all of the dignitaries in the room at the time. Apparently nearly 300 had already left the building before they could be rounded up.

AS THE CHANCELLOR rounded the corner, the screams began to reach him. Ashur and his battalion must've caught the other families before they boarded the train to leave. The chancellor relished the sound of death and magic. He was more confident than ever that the new armor would prove more than a match for the dragonborn if it could defeat the families. All seven of the family lines were extremely old and extremely powerful, not to be taken lightly if one valued your life. If the armor could best them in an honest battle, it just might defeat the dragonborn.

"Chancellor! Chancellor!" screamed one of his assistants as they came running through the hall. "Something is going on at the train. The battalion... they're killing the families!"

"Killing them?" Chancellor Mharú asked. "As in defeating them? Murdering them?"

"Yes! There's blood everywhere and the families are

trying to escape, but the battalion won't let them. It's a slaughter!"

"I understand your sentiments, it's very distressing," the chancellor said, trying desperately to hide his smile. "But the battalion is only performing its duties. Evidence has recently come to light proving that the families are actually traitors in league with the dragonborn. I asked them here to give them a final chance to come over to the right side and they attacked us. The battalion has no choice but to eliminate the threat to the University. It's to protect us, all of us. Even you."

The girl still seemed anxious, panicked, clearly not used to seeing much blood or violence. She was shaking uncontrollably and by now had begun to cry. Chancellor Mharú took her gently by the arms and looked into her face.

"Go back to my office. Have one of my aides make you some coffee and try to settle down. Don't think about what you saw or heard at the train, okay? Put all of that behind you."

"I can't forget that. I can't stop... hearing those voices..."

"Listen," he said through gritted teeth, grabbing the girl hard and giving her a violent shake. "If you want to work here you need to get used to seeing these kinds of things. People will die here. A lot of people. There will be torture, pain, suffering, dark magic. There will be blood. If you can't handle that then maybe it's time for you to do a little suffering of your own. Now get out of my sight."

He tossed the girl aside and kept walking, not even looking back to see if she was alright. The cruelty made him feel powerful.

Once he was outside, the chancellor walked straight across from the University to the very edge of the precipice and looked down on the city. The whole vast grid was under his influence, his lies, his propaganda. All he need to do was make the people afraid and after that they belonged to him. They would support anything he wanted, as long as he could kill the dragonborn and their beasts. And if he actually did manage to kill the dragonborn, then all of Noelle would be his.

Just then he heard a scream and the sound of running feet behind him. He turned. It was Rasputraenir, current head of the House of Urania. He had managed to escape the battalion and was running, running, running, straight for the chancellor.

"Myamar! Myamar, you have to help me!" the man cried. "They're going crazy in there! They're killing us, they're—"

But before he could finish, the chancellor waved a hand and the man was lifted into the air, flipped, and thrown over the side of the mountain. The chancellor didn't even bother watching the body fall. Instead, he simply enjoyed the sound of the man's final scream.

"Everything is mine," he said, his eyes on the city.

CHAPTER SIXTEEN

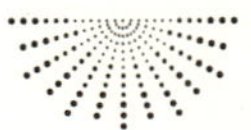

WHEN ANDIE WOKE, SHE DIDN'T KNOW WHERE SHE WAS, at first. Her mind was clouded, her head hurt, and she felt nauseous. But within seconds everything that had happened came rushing back in. She bolted upright and found she was lying in her living space, on the mountain. Someone had spread her bed out for her and there were two little cups beside where her head had been. She threw the cover off and jumped to her feet. As she turned, she came face to face with Lymir. It startled her.

"Lymir," she said. "What are you doing here? How did I get back on the mountain?"

"Well, it's a hard tale," he said, taking a seat. "The way I heard it was ye fainted down there by the river. I don't blame ye, not after what happened. They gathered ye up an' flew ye back up here for a good rest. I haven't left your side since. I give ye some tea to make ye sleep an' I've been wi' ye ever since."

"Where is she?" Andie asked. "What have they done with Yara?"

Lymir looked down at his feet and for a moment he

refused to meet Andie's eyes. She moved closer to him and lifted his face.

"Lymir, tell me what happened."

"They've sentenced her to death, Andie. I'm afraid..."

Andie felt like she should have said something, anything. But she knew there was no point. She turned from Lymir and began to straighten up her area. He watched her and tried to talk to her, but she responded to nothing. Then he tried to help her clean up, but she refused and asked to be left alone. Hesitatingly, he left.

About a half hour later, Andie emerged from her space and went straight for Saeryn.

"How soon can we be ready to leave for Arvall?" Andie asked.

"Are you sure that's the best thing for now?" Saeryn asked. "I agree that we need to leave as soon as possible and make great haste, but you have quite a situation at hand. Hundreds of your friends are injured, some dead, and of course there's the issue of the traitor."

"I understand it's not ideal, but you know as well as I do that we need to stop the University. That's what all of this has been for. All the suffering, and enduring, and betrayal, and lives lost, everything was leading us up to this moment."

"But Andie your people—"

"Knew what they signed up for. I'm not happy to see them like this: broken, injured, betrayed. But they knew the risks. They understood that they might not make it home again or if they did they might not be the same people who left. We are at war, Saeryn. This is the cost. And while I am beyond grateful for everything that they have given and sacrificed, they are not my people. You are. The dragonborn are."

Saeryn did not look convinced, but she gestured for Oren to come.

"Oren, have the warriors prepare. We leave within the hour."

Oren nodded and disappeared around the bend of the cavern. Saeryn remained and watched Andie, looking her over from head to toe. Andie felt herself being watched, but she wouldn't meet Saeryn's eyes. She could feel everything Saeryn wanted to say, every emotion she was feeling. Pity, compassion, sympathy, fear, anxiety, love. Saeryn had told Andie that when two dragonborn were especially close, they could sometimes sense each other's emotions. Andie hadn't realized until just that moment how much she and Saeryn meant to each other.

"Andie, I already know what you'll say, but you should be here for it."

"For what?"

"The execution."

Andie gave a small gasp. The word made her feel cold. Numb.

"She made her bed and now she needs to... They can do it without me. I don't need to be a part of it."

"You know, there were traitors in our time as well," Saeryn said. "And many of them were friends and people I trusted. It was hard to have to watch them die, but somehow I knew it was my duty to be there. Betrayal never ends, not really. They turn their backs on you, betray you to your enemies, and then force you to have to kill them. That's the worst part of all because then you feel guilty for punishing them, even though you know you had no choice. And you continue to feel guilty for the rest of your life."

"Saeryn, I can't. I just can't. You and the rest of the dragonborn call me your savior. You lift me up on a pedestal and act like I'm some kind of miracle. You say I'm the one who can bridge the gap between our people and the rest of Noelle. Let me focus on that. Give me the chance to be everything you and the rest of our people already think I am. Let me earn your trust. But, please, please, don't ask me to stay here and watch her die."

"As you wish," Saeryn said, touching Andie's arm. "I'll call for you when we're ready. You will ride with me."

Andie bowed and turned to leave. She went outside to be alone and found herself in the very corner of the mountain where she had been when the ship exploded. But she didn't think about that. She didn't think about Carmen and Murakami and the others lying unconscious in the sand. She didn't think about her father's terrible wound. She didn't think about Marvo's death or Raesh's pain. She didn't think about the ship, the victims, the blood, the unbelievably agony and blackness of that entire circumstance. She didn't think of Lilja. And she didn't think of the traitor.

Not much later, Saeryn found her. She took a seat beside Andie and they simply sat there in the sun, in silence and uncertainty.

"Raesh can handle things down at the ship," Andie said.

"And your father?" Saeryn asked. "I think his wound may have been more serious than he let on. With him already being in such frail condition, I fear for him."

"I just want to get out of here," Andie said, standing.

Saeryn gave up after that, though she seemed hurt. She led Andie to where the dragon warriors were gathering with their dragons. Lymir tried to get Andie's attention, but she ignored him and mounted up behind Saeryn. When all the warriors had mounted their dragons, they all left the ground behind. Oren was to stay behind and oversee the execution, but would join them after the deed was done.

A faction of warriors and healers had also been left behind to watch over those who were staying on the mountain. The scientists, thinkers, teachers, farmers, and other important contributors were to remain behind, as well as the children. They weren't terribly concerned about being defeated in battle, but Saeryn was a wise and careful ruler, and she did not want the future of her people to be left to chance. She wanted to be prepared for any outcome and to ensure that the dragonborn would never again be in danger of extinction from the earth.

They flew like they had never flown before. They soared so high in the sky they couldn't be seen from the ground. Andie held on tight and every time she thought the dragons couldn't go faster, they surprised her. They truly were incredible beasts. Before the sun set they had left the Hot Salts of Mithraldia behind and were making great haste over vast rural regions that Andie didn't recognize. The sun sank behind the horizon and still they flew on, as efficient at night as they were in the day. Andie allowed herself to be filled with the energy of flight. It kept her mind from going to places she didn't want to think of.

The dragons were flying as fast and deliberate as ever, not the least bit tired, but the dragonborn treated their dragons like they treated their family and so they soon came down to earth and landed in a field that had recently been harvested. The bent stalks were a perfect place to lay for the night. The warriors all dismounted and saw to their dragons, then everyone went to sleep almost at once. They would need to rest and be back up in the sky before the sun came up. They couldn't risk being seen and spreading fear before they reached Arvall. They had no plan, not even a definite beginning of one, and the last thing they needed was for their surprise appearance to be ruined. Neither Andie nor Saeryn slept at all.

In the morning, just as the sun was beginning to lighten the sky, the dragonborn took up again and rose to their usual height. On and on they flew, passing mountains and valleys and woods that sometimes seemed to go on forever. They passed a lake so blue and deep and dark that it looked like the night sky had taken liquid form and fallen to earth. They flew over small villages that could barely be seen from the sky and they came to cities whose building were so tall they had to circumvent the city just to be safe. Shortly after midday, they settled in another field to rest and were soon off again. They mounted up again and followed a narrow but seemingly endless river. They flew as if a demon chased them, cutting the sky with blinding and confident grace. Never once did they break their formation, they were so disciplined and focused. Andie was certain that whatever they met in Arvall would be no match for them.

Night came again and they settled to earth once more to rest. The dragons were able to drink from the river and some of the warriors washed their faces before eating and lying down. Saeryn laid down and was asleep instantly. Andie watched her, knowing she must have been exhausted from the stress alone. She knew that as much as Saeryn valued her help and support, she wanted more for Andie than just fighting for a cause. But that would have to wait. There was too much going on at the moment, but the most pressing issue was the University and its inability to let the past go, to stop spreading lies and leave the dragonborn to live in peace. Andie felt her own body warning her it was becoming dangerously low on energy, but as long as she kept getting enough sunlight in the daytime she would be fine. Besides, she couldn't possibly think of sleep at a time like this, when the soul of the whole world was hanging by a thread. The University couldn't win. The chancellor couldn't win.

When they woke up in the dark of the morning, Saeryn said that they would arrive in Arvall just before sunset. By flying in a straight line and taking advantage of the dragons' incredible speed, they would do in three days what would have taken the ship more than six weeks to do. Andie didn't respond when Saeryn said it, she just went to the dragon and loaded up again. For the first time in days, she was excited. She was ready to fight the University, to meet them in the street or in the hallway and hand them over to destruction. They had killed so many people and caused so much pain, not only in the past weeks, but in all the centuries that they had been in power. Andie was full of mixed emotions and she relished the opportunity to vent them. She had no intentions of holding back or showing mercy.

The dragons mounted up from their final rest and they took to the sky. They would not touch the ground again until they reached Arvall City. They did not know what they would find there, but they went to face their destiny bravely. Andie looked down on the lands they passed over, knowing they were probably filled with people who hated them, who wanted to see their blood running in the street. It had never occurred to her before that it might not matter to the world if the University had been spreading lies. For all she knew, the rest of the world hated the dragonborn as much as the University and would want them dead anyway. It was no secret that the dragonborn were incredibly powerful; people tended to fear things more powerful than themselves, regardless of whether or not those things or people posed an actual threat. And though the dragons were sweet, calm creatures by nature, their great size and intimidating appearance would put people off. What if the world didn't care that the dragonborn hadn't done anything? What if they were just looking for an excuse, any excuse to slaughter the dragonborn? And if a fight did break out, the dragonborn would have no choice but to defend themselves and then the world would see the true magnitude of their awesome power. If that happened, if the dragonborn were forced to take even one life, the world would never forgive them. Everything would be at an end. They would go to war and the dragonborn would kill thousands, millions, of the sorcerers and common folk in an attempt to save their way of life—and in the eyes of Noelle the dragonborn truly would be monsters.

More than that, there was always the chance that the people would be willing to relent, but simply wouldn't believe Andie. The loose, ill-conceived skeleton of a plot they did have revolved around Andie's ability to persuade people that neither she nor the dragonborn posed a threat. She had to erase centuries of hate, propaganda, and engrained teaching. Even Andie didn't believe it could work. Hatred of the dragonborn was one of those things that simply was. She had no idea what she was going to say.

The land slid away underneath them. Rivers and lakes disappeared somewhere behind them. Things too small and far away to be distinguished flashed by, instantly forgotten. The sun fell lower and lower into the sky until it finally touched the land in the distance. Across the horizon, the great towers of Arvall City were coming into view, shining silver and blue against the land. The sky began to darken as they flew closer. The energy and the mood among the warriors seemed to change as they began to get close to the city. Everyone was bracing for the inevitable, whatever it might be. They slowed gradually the nearer they came and began to drop lower over the city. As they slowed, the sound of the wind and the dragons' wings lessened considerably. Saeryn turned to speak over her shoulder.

"The outcome doesn't matter," she said.

"How can you say that?"

"Because I only just realized it. No matter what happens, Andie, we are forever grateful for you being with us. Thank you."

Saeryn turned back around and then the dragon plunged. The phalanx of warriors followed closely and they were all diving through the air, descending on the city. For a moment, Andie was perfectly calm: the wind raced past her, the massive wings of the iridescent creature pumped up and down on either side of her, the city rushed up with its lights and actions, Saeryn's long dark hair danced in the sky. And just for a moment, before they knew the result and before the conflict started, Andie felt the future was theirs, one way or another.

But suddenly there was an explosion in the air and one of the warriors was knocked off of his dragon. The dragon quickly maneuvered itself back under him and he caught hold, but the first explosion was quickly followed by several more. The explosions were erratic and incredibly powerful. Because the dragons couldn't see the explosions coming, they couldn't maneuver around them and the situation quickly became dangerous. What was most terrifying was that the explosions were black and as cold as a freezing winter. It was smart. Any regular explosion wouldn't have been able to distract a dragon or the warrior on it. Heat made them stronger. But a cold explosion could seriously harm them and with the sun going down it would be harder for them to heal.

The dragonborn began evasive maneuvers, but they were all for nothing as the University's trick continued to plague them through the sky. Andie noticed that there were less explosions the lower they went and pointed it out to Saeryn. Again, the dragonborn dove through the sky. The dragons flattened their wings against their bodies and the warriors flattened themselves on the dragons' backs. They fell through the sky, hoping to reach safety. They finally broke the level of the city's highest buildings and the explosions gave out. The dragons leveled out and headed for Brie. For the University.

The explosions must have doubled as a warning system because as they came closer to the ground, Andie could see people in the streets below panicking and running inside. Cars were racing away, barely missing each other as they sped for safety. And then a horn began to blare. What should have been a quiet landing was turning into a fearmongering nightmare. Saeryn and the dragonborn warriors remained calm and pointed the dragons for the mountain. Andie grew less certain by the minute. Soon they had reached the foot of Brie and were beginning to incline as they began their ascent. The moment was almost upon them now and Andie couldn't think of anything. Nothing at all. She was simply in expectation.

But the University had planned ahead again. Slots opened in the mountainside and sorcerers behind shields of energy began casting spells. As the ill-aimed spells flashed by, Andie could feel the chill coming off of them. They really were beginning to learn. But the dragons easily dodged the feeble attempts and the warriors only cast defensive spells to protect their ascension. Andie was filling with energy. Her mind and heart were still blank, but she was suddenly aware of her own power. She'd stopped trying to understand why and how the University could be so evil, but if they wanted to go to war with her, with her people, she was prepared to do so.

They cleared the precipice and found that the large lot in front of the University was completely full of people. The civilians screamed and ducked as the dragons came soaring up over them. The warriors did a single lap and then landed wherever they could: on top of the University, away on the side of the mountain, and some stayed flying above. Andie and Saeryn dismounted and walked to meet the crowd.

"Saeryn?" Andie whispered.

"Yes?"

"I think I'm afraid."

"So am I."

CHAPTER SEVENTEEN

AS THEY APPROACHED, THE OTHER DRAGONBORN warriors began to fall in behind them and the more they walked, the larger their group grew. The crowd that had already gathered began to back up, to clear out of the warriors' way. Andie and Saeryn each kept a wary eye on the people, unsure of what they might do now that they were face-to-face with the threat they had heard so much about. The response was exactly what Andie had suspected: absolute fear. Andie looked around, trying to gather information about why all the people were gathered, but it wasn't hard to discover. There were massive banners strung up all around, posters, and signs with the event. They were there to celebrate the reopening of the University.

Andie looked over and noticed for the first time that all the damage that the University had sustained was fixed and the black marble looked stronger and more sinister than ever. She hadn't realized before, but even SKY 6 had been replaced with a new model and the rails had been repaired and burnished. There was a gated area not far from where they were, and she could see a massive collection of fireworks waiting to be released for the ceremony. There were heads of state standing on a platform in the direction they were heading. And so was Chancellor Myamar Mharú. He didn't seem at all surprised to see them and only then did Andie realize that they had played directly into his hands. He had planned all of this from the start, knowing that blowing up the ship would force them to escalate their timetable and come to face him. Andie felt like a complete idiot.

"I told you they would come," the chancellor began. "I told you they couldn't resist the opportunity to show themselves, to menace us, to do everything in their power to end our way of life."

"I believe you have that backwards, Melpomene," said Saeryn, in that authoritative yet gentle voice that only she could manage. "It is my people who have been hunted and slaughtered, and I am ashamed to see that nothing has changed in the centuries that have passed."

The crowd began to grow enraged, afraid, at the very sound of her voice.

"We did not come here for war, though we are prepared for it if that is what you prefer. We have only come to expose your propaganda for what it truly is: a snake pit of lies. We have been in this world for months and yet you cannot name a single crime that we have committed."

"A *single* crime?" the chancellor mocked, feigning disbelief. "The list of your horrific accomplishments has no end. You broke the laws that govern our world and breached time through an illegal portal. You slaughtered the innocent people working in this University who only tried to reason with you. You murdered hundreds of dignitaries and heads of state in the mirror hall—the great leaders in this land. You came back again some weeks ago and wreaked even more havoc and how are we supposed to know what chaos you've been creating around the world?"

"If we were truly so bloodthirsty would we have landed our dragons and come to walk among you?"

"It's your own arrogance that put your feet on the ground."

"More lies, I'm afraid. We escaped that portal because your ancestors trapped us in there and our entire race was almost exterminated from the face of the planet. Once we were out, we were immediately under attack and though we wish there had been another way, we had no choice but to defend ourselves. Since then we've been living in the mountains, far from here. If we're so horrible why have you heard nothing of us for months? And we never returned to this mountain until right now. The people who were here were rebels fighting to bring peace and you slaughtered most of them while they ran for their lives. I believe that is what you meant to say."

The crowd continued to bubble and get angry. Andie kept her eyes on them and the warriors were always ready for anything.

"My name is Saeryn. I am the Queen of the dragonborn. I assure you, my people do not want war. As you can see, we haven't even brought all our ranks. This is only a small party that has come here seeking a resolution."

But the crowd seemed to have hardly heard her. They did not see a Queen, only the embodiment of every nightmare and cautionary tale they had been told since they were children. And those who hadn't heard the stories were afraid because everyone else was. Someone in the crowd threw a stone, but Andie blocked it with her magic. More stones followed, but the warriors kept them all at bay until the crowd died down again.

"They will not hear me," Saeryn said, turning to Andie. "I pass the torch to you, savior. If you cannot placate them, it will mean war."

Saeryn took several steps back and let Andie come forward. The chancellor laughed.

"What kind of Queen lets others fight her battles? Are you afraid?"

"I find it hard to believe that you of all people are going to stand there and accuse someone else of cowardice," Andie said. "All of Noelle knows that you lack the courage of a child."

"Remind me again who you are," he said, grimacing. "You seem... inexperienced for a rebellion."

"My name is Andie Rogers and I was once a student at this University. My father was a sorcerer, but my mother was dragonborn and she passed that magic to me. I am a part of both worlds and I can assure you all the true enemy here is not the dragonborn, but the University. When I was a girl, they came to my house and they beat us. They took my mother and nearly killed my father. I never saw her again. Some years later, they arranged for my father to have an accident and nearly killed him again, though that time he never fully recovered. Does any of this sound familiar? Have any of you ever had someone taken from you, threatened, killed? I know they try to wipe our minds when they're finished, but at least some of you must remember."

There were many uncertain mumblings coming from

the crowd. They hardly seemed convinced, but at least they were listening.

"These are the misguided and troubled thoughts of a child," the chancellor said, not losing a step. "If we've ever come to your homes it's only been in service of you. You saw the devastation of the University. Many of you were there that night when we lost so many lives. And it was all because of them."

"Really?" Andie sneered, nearing the platform. "Tell me, if the dragonborn had only just escaped the portal, how were they able have that room filled with poisonous flowers a week before?"

There were gasps in the crowd. They seemed to genuinely want to hear the chancellor's response, but he did no more than smile.

"What's happening now is the same thing that happened hundreds of years ago," Andie continued. "You're letting yourselves be driven by hate and other people's greed for power. Ask yourselves: what have you ever seen the dragonborn do? What evil have you witnessed? Nothing. Everything you think about them was told to you. I know we've all grown up hearing the stories and fearing the legends, but that's all they are is stories. I have lived among you and now I live among them, and though the cultures are different, neither is evil. We could have had our dragons rain fire from the sky, but we didn't. Our magic is stronger than yours and we could have come and started casting instead of talking, but we didn't. That kind of violence is not what we want. All we want is to carve out a piece of the world for ourselves and live in peace. We don't want anything from anyone, especially not a fight."

"That's a very moving speech, little girl, but I hardly

think that stories could persist for hundreds of years if there weren't truth to them. Now, people you've seen what kind of carnage results from a world with dragonborn. Read your history books. Look at the painted walls of our corridors. These dragonborn are an ancient evil and they've returned to finish us. Don't be fooled by this simple child's inability to know right from wrong."

"I noticed that in all your aggrandizing, you've never once given definitive proof that my people have done something they shouldn't, or that they've done anything at all."

The chancellor tried to hide his frustration, but his political mask was cracking. He hadn't planned to be caught out like this, exposed. Andie looked at him and could tell that his plan was beginning to falter. He was losing his footing.

"No one has known where the dragonborn have been for months," Andie continued, growing more confident. "We could've attacked you, burned your lives down while you slept and gotten away with it, but we came here looking for a better future. We don't want to have to hide. If you don't want us living among you, we understand, but please allow us to live. There's so much we could teach you, so much we could learn from you. My people have come from a time when everything was different. The new world is foreign to them and they're afraid. We've done nothing, nothing at all."

Much to Andie's surprise, it seemed the crowd was actually listening to her. She paused, afraid to go on and ruin the goodwill she'd garnered, but also afraid to stop before she had them fully. She decided that the best thing to do was tell them not about what the dragonborn *hadn't* done, but about what the University *had* done.

"It might interest you to know that Chancellor Mharú turned two of our friends into spies. He consistently had them place us in danger. Just a few days ago, one of them blew up the ship we had been traveling on. Eighty-seven of my friends were killed and all because this man's greed was insatiable. If you don't stop him, there's no telling what he might do."

Andie leveled a finger at Chancellor Mharú. Before anyone knew what was happening, the crowd had turned to the chancellor and was waiting to see what he would say in his defense. But all he did was stand there, his eyes locked wide in surprise and rage, his legs beginning to shake in front of all the people. Andie almost smiled —the faces of the crowd began to change and the murmurs began to build. She could tell they weren't yet fully convinced, but the longer the chancellor stood there dumbfounded, the worse his chances grew. Andie looked to Saeryn and the two shared a hopeful look. Then the chancellor began to laugh. Andie nearly toppled at the sound, confused as to how he could find anything funny about this situation.

"You know, I really couldn't turn him," the chancellor said with a smile. "I had to resort to more... arcane methods."

"Him?" Andie asked, confused.

"Yes. Your traitor. Oh, wait... do you mean to tell me you still haven't figured out who betrayed you?"

"It was Lilja and... a girl I used to believe was my friend."

"No, no, no, no, no. I always knew you'd catch Lilja sooner or later. She never wanted to cooperate, you know. But once we threatened her family and her friends, well, she started to see things from our side."

More gasps went through the crowd. The chancellor paid them no attention and though Andie was glad the tide was turning, she was hardly able to focus on anything outside of the chancellor's words.

"But the other one wasn't a girl. It was a man. The one with that godawful name. Something so short and stupid I always forget. Marvo. That's it. You see, I knew he would be perfect. Old, human, ridiculously likeable, and an intensely close friend of yours. Not to mention the leader of your little rebellion. The absolute perfect candidate. See, I captured Marvo long before you ever even saw that stupid portal. We were watching you from the beginning, Andie, and when we got wind of what you were searching for in Leabharlann I started making a plan in case you ever managed to free those abominations. Me and a few of my associates kidnapped your Marvo and performed some very old magic on him. It allowed me to periodically act through his body, influence his decision-making, even make him perform spells on occasion. Things like having him decide to stop looking for a way out and bring you all into an ambush. Or having him read your mind whenever you touched him. Or sending my magic through him to send you back here to the University, though, admittedly, that particular spell backfired. Or, my personal favorite, exploding him with a wave of collective magic too large for his body to handle and killing scores of your friends in the process."

Andie couldn't even respond. All she could do was stand there and stare at him, her whole life over the past week being unfurled and rewritten. Marvo. Yara. She'd had it all wrong. And poor Marvo had been used as nothing more than a pawn and then disposed of in the most brutal way possible. All to get to her.

"So, you see, the girl is right," the chancellor said, turning to the crowd. "I am the villain of the story. I did lie and deceive and murder. These ignorant dragonborn may be powerful, but they're essentially harmless, probably not all that different from yourselves. And I did lure them here with a rather intricate plan in order to have my battalion murder them. And I think I'll murder you, too. After all, you're only a few hundred common folk from the city. No one will miss you. You're going to be slaughtered just like those eight hundred people I killed in the mirror hall."

The crowd began to panic and turned to escape, but the chancellor's battalion had slowly been enclosing the entire area while Myamar and Andie had been talking. Now Andie looked around and saw that they were surrounded. She'd expected there to be some kind of opposition waiting, but this was far more than she'd thought possible. The slow-moving, sleek armored men were closing in from all around. The dragonborn warriors tightened their ranks and moved to protect the Queen, but Saeryn waved them away. She wasn't afraid to fight.

"Whatever happens, do not attack," she said. "Only defend."

As if in response to her words, the chancellor clapped his hands and the battalion began their attack. As the first spell hit her defensive shield, Andie could tell that something was wrong. The spell had nearly taken her off of her feet. She knew there was no way a sorcerer's magic could be so strong, so fierce. She looked around and she could tell by Saeryn's face that she noticed it, too. All around her the dragonborn were struggling to maintain their defenses. Their shields were giving out faster and their footing was less stable; the closer the men in black came, the tighter the dragonborn had to retreat. Andie and Saeryn were also using some of their power to shield the crowd from any stray spells.

"Something is wrong," Saeryn said. "They cannot be this strong naturally. It is impossible."

"It must be the armor," Andie said, ducking. "Another one of the chancellor's little ideas. We have to figure out a way to stop them or else defending won't be enough and this is going to turn into a full-fledged battle. What about the dragons?"

"Perhaps. If it comes down to that. But I want to avoid that as long as possible. Seeing the dragons breathe fire will only frighten the people and the dragon fire is so strong I fear it may injure the innocent."

Andie began watching their attackers, searching them for weak spots, mistakes, anything that could give them the upper hand. Then she noticed how all the men were facing them directly, their shoulders squared to the dragonborn. They were absolutely refusing to show their sides or backs. Andie curved a spell between two of the attackers and hit one in the side. There was no affect and it only seemed to make the man that much angrier. She aimed another spell and this time purposefully missed by a wide margin, but she caught the spell once it was past the men and brought it down again so that it caught him square in the back. The man lurched forward and collapsed. However, it was only a moment before he regained his feet and resumed the attack. But the secret had been seen.

"That armor is incredibly strong, but it's vulnerable from the back," Andie said.

Saeryn nodded and cast a spell that bounced off of the ground and curved, catching a soldier in the back. As he was thrown forward, Saeryn cast again and threw him backwards.

"Curve your spells," she called out. "But don't hurt them. Remember who we are."

CHAPTER EIGHTEEN

THE DRAGONBORN TOOK THE QUEEN'S COMMAND AND began a fiercer defense. The chancellor didn't like that. He began to see just how wrong he had been about those people. Still, the dragonborn had their work cut out for them. Saeryn's command not to hurt the battalion members greatly restricted what the types of spells the dragonborn could do and the battalion was incredibly strong. Andie was struggling to fend the men off, as their attacks just seemed to get harder and harder to defend against. But just when things were beginning to look down and Andie was about to suggest they begin their own attacks, a wonderful thing happened.

The people joined the fight. They began attacking the battalion, fighting alongside the dragonborn. At first, Andie didn't know what they were doing and she nearly attacked one of the people as they stepped forward, but then she saw how they took up ranks beside the dragonborn and began to defend against the attackers. The battalion was certainly a force to be reckoned with, and the increase in the number of magical attacks against them didn't seem to daunt them, but it did make a difference. At the very least, it stopped their advance. Not all of the people joined the dragonborn. Some of them remained unconvinced of the lies they had believed their entire lives and took up with the battalion.

Soon, everyone on the mountain was fighting. The air was thick with flying spells that lit the night with their color and energy. Explosions, whistling, and breaks rang through the night as the spells hit home or missed. Only the chancellor remained on the outside of the fight, hiding behind the platform like the coward he would always be.

Andie and Saeryn were fighting back to back and drawing a strength from their proximity to each other. Andie soon realized that they were actually synced and feeding one another through a magical connection that could only be felt between two dragonborn. The fight raged on and on, and some of the civilians from the city proved to be surprisingly powerful casters. But the University's armor was a formidable thing and the battalion soon figured out what the dragonborn were doing. They closed ranks, tightened, and realigned so that it was nearly impossible to get them in the back. and then they unleashed an attack more vicious and determined than anything Andie had ever encountered. They advanced with a maniacal method, refusing to back down or be swayed by the faces of the people they were attempting to kill.

Andie knew that something needed to be done. The air was growing thick and cloudy with the flying spells, the dust, the stones and earth being blasted high into the air. And the dragons were getting restless. They sensed their riders were in danger and they began to crawl about and circle the confrontation while their mouths began to smoke as the opened their great and terrifying jaws. The situation was quickly spinning into something so dangerous it bound to end in a massive loss of life. Andie began to push herself, to think of something that could stop this before it took a turn for the worst.

"Battalion!" one of the men called. He had a red star on his chest. "Attack formation Delta! Offensive maneuver Zero Hour!"

"What is this?" Saeryn asked.

"I don't know, but let's stay close together. I don't like where this is going."

The man who had called out the order stepped forward and took off his mask. Andie had been shocked more times than she could count over the last week, but as she saw Tarven's face for the first time since the night of the battle in the Archives, she couldn't help but to be shocked again. And, this time, all the way down to her core. From what she could remember, Tarven had been in deep with the University and had failed them one too many times. She always assumed that he was executed shortly after the battle and she never thought she would see him again. She never wanted to. Yet there he was, looking stronger and more menacing than ever. He'd clearly left his plants behind to take up the University's new armor, as well as the mantle of leader of their battalion. He looked right at Andie.

"It's been a long time," he said.

"Not nearly long enough," Andie replied. "Honestly, I'd kind of hoped you'd died."

"I almost did, but I've been reborn. Remade into something stronger, faster, more powerful. I'm a thousand times better."

"Well, that's very cute, Tarven, but I'm in the middle of something right now. I'll deal with you later."

"Tarven is gone. My name is Ashur, taken from the transformation of the flowers that killed a room full of useless diplomats and impotent demagogues. And, as it happens, I think you'll deal with me now. Form!"

The battalion took its stance in a single, totally uniform movement.

"Mount!"

The battalion interlocked, arms around shoulders to create an unbroken chain. They also grabbed something on each other's backs and turned. Blue veins began to run through their armor and the temperature within the massive circle of soldiers began to plummet. Simultaneously, black tendrils of smoke stretched forth toward the dragonborn and Andie began to feel herself grow week. It was like she hadn't seen the sun in days, weeks, months. The tendrils of smoke were leeching the energy of the sun directly from their bodies.

"Begin!" Ashur shouted.

All at once an almost blinding blue light rose up from the battalion as the soldiers began to chant. The cold and the tendrils were still draining the dragonborn and it was a moment before anyone could distance themselves from their own pain to pay attention to what was happening. Saeryn was the first to realize. She spoke in a whisper.

"Eitilt."

"The time curse," Andie finished, as they both looked up to the sky.

The wave of blue light from all sides met in the sky above them and merged, creating a dome that covered all of the dragonborn. Terror was quickly passing through the dragonborn and even the fiercest of the warriors looked panicked. Andie was afraid, too, but she was almost too concerned with trying to find a way out to notice her own fear. Almost. Just when she thought the situation couldn't get any worse, they heard a great rumbling sound. They looked up again and a tear was opening above them. It wasn't like the portal Andie had saved the dragonborn from. In fact, now that she saw it with her own eyes, she remembered that she'd seen it briefly, for less than a second, when she had been sent to the future. But as she looked up into the tear she could see something. A great, rolling cloud of death coming across the land. It was the same cloud that had almost killed the dragonborn before Andie pulled them out. They weren't sending them to the future, they were sending them back to the moment before the cloud hit. They would be killed instantly.

And then the panic really began to spread, not merely among the dragonborn who had experienced this before and knew exactly what would happen if they got taken up, but also among the civilians who were trapped in the dome and had no idea whatsoever what was going on. Even Saeryn, who had always been calm and elegant under pressure, was struggling to maintain her peace. Andie wanted so badly to resolve it the way Saeryn wanted, to show the people through sheer force of will that the dragonborn did not pose a threat, but the time for peace was over.

"Saeryn, we can't do this," Andie said, on her knees from cold and the smoke. "Your way won't work. They're too strong and too ruthless. If we don't fight back, we're never going home again."

Saeryn turned to Andie and looked in her eyes.

"Saeryn, please. You were right. Our duty is to our

people and right now that duty is to make it back home to them. We tried to reason with them, but it's over. At least now the people have seen what the University truly is. Now we don't need to convince them. We need to save them."

Saeryn looked around at her warriors, her people. She also gazed around at the civilians who had come over to stand with them. They would all be dead in minutes. She turned back to Andie.

"Then let us do it your way."

She turned back to face their attackers and took a deep breath. As she exhaled, she pushed a massive blast of hot, magenta magic out. The chain of soldiers stumbled and one of them slipped. The tear above them shrunk a little.

"Attack the battalion!" Saeryn commanded.

With that the dragonborn rose to their feet again and began to mount an attack. The soldiers were strong and they were well trained, but the dragonborn were from a time when everything was decided by battle and blood. As they moved out to cast at closer range the battalion began to retreat, the chain began to break as they were forced to defend themselves.

Andie and her people fought through the cold, the smoke, the pull of the space-time tear in the sky above them. They did not cast at any civilians, but their mercy toward the battalion was at an end. Soon the soldiers had quit Eitilt and were fighting to defend themselves on a personal level. The smoke and the cold also retreated. Yet Saeryn was not satisfied by this. She moved back to stand in the middle of her people and once there she threw her arms up into the air and began to radiate warm and rejuvenating light, as golden as the morning sun. As she did so, Andie and the dragonborn began to fill with energy, power. Saeryn was sacrificing her own power to refuel her people.

"Protect the Queen at all costs!" Andie yelled.

Some of the dragonborn warriors formed a tight circle around Saeryn to shield her from any attack. Before long all the civilians were fighting alongside the dragonborn, finally convinced of their innocence. The front of the University had turned into an all-out warzone —makeshift weapons had appeared and people were fighting in brutal hand-to-hand combat—and more members of the battalion were coming up from the University. Andie knew what to do then.

"Call the dragons!" she cried.

As one the warriors each called their specific call and then they all waited for the dragons to swoop down and bring the terrible fire. But when the dragons didn't show, they began to get worried. Andie made her way through the pandemonium to the edge of the crowd and looked to the mountainside where they had left the dragons. She couldn't believe her eyes.

The dragons were under attack. It was the Sentinels. Andie had completely forgotten their existence. The Sentinels were racing back and forth over the terrain, slashing and morphing and pounding almost too quickly to be seen. The dragons spit their fire as ferociously as they could, but the Sentinels moved too well to be hit by such passionate attacks.

The silver beings liquified and launched attacks that couldn't even be quantified. Andie and the dragonborn had been so preoccupied facing the threat they could see that they hadn't once looked back to make sure the dragons were okay. They had essentially abandoned them and played into the chancellor's plans once more. The riders who had been circling in the sky had gone down to help the dragons, but they had come under attack themselves. Andie wanted to go and help them, but there wasn't much she could do. She remembered what a threat the Sentinels could be, but she also knew that dragons were terrible foes to pick a fight with. They would have to care for themselves for the moment.

"The dragons are facing their own attack," she called when she got back to the center of the circle. "We'll have to do this on our own."

But just as she was about to relaunch the attack, she caught sight of Chancellor Mharú. He was lifting his hands into the air.

"I've anticipated every course of events," he said, grinning maliciously. "And I've been practicing this spell for almost forty years. Normally one needs a network of other sorcerers to help power the spell, but in special circumstances, much like this one, sacrifice works just as well."

The blue light began to emanate from his hands and in a matter of moments the tear had reopened in the sky.

The battalion closed ranks in front of the chancellor to protect him. Almost as soon as he began the spell, civilians began to drop all around. Andie raced to the nearest one and tried to save them, but their veins had already turned a dark blue and their skin was going loose on their body. Dead before they hit the ground. They were dropping in groves.

The dragonborn and the battalion all seemed fine. The spell must have been feeding on the energy of the weakest among them. Andie stood and began casting in the direction of the chancellor, but she couldn't even get close to him. And his spell was growing rapidly.

"You know the greatest thing about being a coward?" the chancellor called. "You're afraid of everything. And so, you plan and you scheme and you get really good at being clever. Before you know it, you're a master manipulator who has plans, and backup plans, and backups for the backups, and so on. Would you like to know what I'm talking about?"

"I'd like you to stop talking and come down here to face me," Andie called, never stopping her attack. "I see you've surrounded yourself with super soldiers and innocent people. Anything to avoid the fight."

"Obviously. I am afraid, after all. Try to keep up. Watch the next phase of my plan. Remember that psychic link I was talking about earlier, with your friend —sorry, dead friend—Marvo? I've been practicing on it for months. And once I have one person I can move from conscience to conscience. But why don't I just show you?"

The doors of the University opened and as more of the battalion began to come out Andie switched sides again and had her hand raised to cast a particularly nasty spell, but she stopped herself. She looked closer. It wasn't more members of the battalion coming through the doors. It was more civilians. They walked in a brisk, uniform way, not looking at anything in particular, just staring straight ahead. Andie knew instantly what the chancellor was planning. She turned to the dragonborn.

"We have to stop those people," she shouted. "He's luring them out here so that he can sacrifice them as fuel for his spell, we have to stop him."

The dragonborn began to cast on two fronts: one an

offensive, fighting back the battalion and their invulnerable armor, the other a defensive, casting sleeping spells at the waves upon waves of people flowing out of the University's doors. Fortunately, the people were moving slowly enough that the dragonborn had soon stopped the flow and Andie collapsed the doorway so that no more could come out. She looked back at the chancellor, feeling victorious, but was surprised to see he was still smiling. More than that, he was laughing.

"You still don't understand, do you?" he asked, unbuttoning his shirt. "I don't need them to be awake. And as for the ones inside, I may not be able to see them, but the connection is already there. Look again."

Andie turned and saw that all the bodies they had put to sleep were already dead. The dark blue veins. The loose skin. It was a massacre. Chancellor Mharú's evil laughter made Andie turn around again. he had fully undressed and now she could see that he had been wearing the new armor under his suit.

"Now you should begin to understand," he said. "There is nothing you can do to stop this spell. I may not have the power to kill your precious dragonborn, but I can send them to a place that will do the killing for me. Which reminds me... my spell needs more power."

With those words the chancellor ran for the train, which Andie hadn't noticed was already beginning to move. A handful of the battalion followed him, including Ashur. Andie turned to ask for help, but with the insane number of battalion members, the space-time tear beginning to pull on all the dragonborn, and the dragons fighting for their lives against the Sentinels, she knew she couldn't take anyone with her. Even Saeryn was busy providing the energy of the sun. But the chancellor couldn't be allowed to get away—there was no telling how many lives he would take if he reached the bottom.

She turned and ran for the train. It was almost out of reach and she had to push herself to run faster than she ever had before. As the train slipped over the precipice and began its vertical descent, Andie leapt off the mountain after it.

CHAPTER NINETEEN

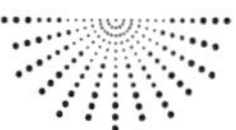

SHE WAS FALLING WITHOUT ANYTHING TO HOLD ON TO. She was directly behind the train, but it was quickly picking up speed and was pulling away from her. She struggled and kicked, trying to maintain her focus, her orientation, but she was freefalling and the train was quickly escaping.

She stretched her hands out in front of her and with her magic she pulled at the back of the train. The entire back ten feet of the final car ripped off and splintered into a thousand pieces. The largest parts of the debris missed her, but some of the smaller pieces cut her badly. But she was still trailing the train. She used her magic to give her a violent forward push, and she shot right down into the car.

But the gravity component was damaged because of the loss of the back part of the car. She caught herself on a sconce and began crawling down using whatever she could grab. All around her objects in the train were being ripped out of the car by speed and suction. She had to duck more than once to avoid being hit. When she finally reached the door, she grabbed the handle and settled her feet on the sides of the door.

When she turned the handle and opened it, half of the objects in the next room came rushing up. She evaded them and then flipped herself around to the other side of the door, closing it with a desperate slam. She was quick getting back to her feet: she'd gotten a good view of the room and knew there were at least two soldiers in it. As soon as the door closed, the gravity corrected and Andie leapt up. With a deft wave of her hand, she blew two of the soldiers out of the windows. But there were still six more, Ashur, and the chancellor.

"You know the best part of the spell, Andie?" Chancellor Mharú said. "As long as you can avoid being attacked yourself, you don't even have to stay with it for it to keep going. That spell will keep building and when I reach the city at the bottom of this mountain I'm going to find all the fuel I need. All I need to do is put myself around life and the spell will do the rest."

Andie glared at the man before her. "You talk too much."

She cast right at his face but it was blocked by the battalion. The chancellor and Ashur raced into the next car. They were followed by all except two soldiers. Andie didn't have time for anymore pleasantries.

"Saeryn, forgive me."

Andie channeled her power into a ball of black fire so hot and so powerful that it melted one of the soldier's armor. Her magic always amazed her, and even still, she hardly believed she was capable of the things she had managed these past few months. She stared after the black fire with wide eyes, a strange mix of sorcerer's and dragonborn magic. Her own strange brand of whatever it was. She wasn't exactly sure what to call it, apart from terrifying.

She tried to ignore the screams as the suit melted onto his skin and he collapsed. Not dead, but certainly wishing he was. She swallowed back the bile that crept up her throat at the smell of burning flesh as she pressed forward. She couldn't allow herself to be affected by such thing. Not when the survival of her entire race and the entire city of Arvall relied on her succeeding at her task.

The other soldier began a panicked attack that betrayed his fear and Andie easily avoided his incompetent display. She began to swirl her hand around and around, focusing her energy on the soldier. Soon a vortex began to gather behind him and in a matter of moments he had been lifted and was spinning and tumbling out of control.

Andie spun her hand faster and faster until the vortex was a miniscule tornado, whipping everything in sight into a fury. She flung the soldier and the tornado over her shoulder and the man hit the back wall so hard Andie heard his spine crack. She'd never wanted violence, not really. But if trouble was what they wanted she was going to give them as much as they could handle.

As she burst into the next car, the group of villains was just moving through the door at the other end. She cast a bolt of lightning and hit one of the soldiers, but only succeeded in knocking him into the next room and closing the door. She rushed across the car and flung open the door. The man she'd hit was already up and running. She chased him down easily, as his wound was slowing him, and at the same instant her hand met his back she sent her magic into him, paralyzing him totally. He hit the floor and Andie never stopped moving.

In the next car, the first thing she did was throw a wall of magic. All the furniture, fixtures, appliances, and other objects in the room were hurled forward ahead of the chancellor. The great field of debris collided with the door and totally blocked off the escape. But the chancellor was quick on his feet. He spied an emergency ladder leading to the roof and he and Ashur quickly went up and out, followed by three of the soldiers. That left two soldiers she hadn't seen before, obviously already stationed on the train.

Her spell with the furniture had broken all the lights in the car and so, with the exception of the moonlight and other sources flashing by outside, the car was totally dark. In fact, all Andie could see were two glowing pairs of hand. They began casting immediately, terrible and deadly spells that only served to further remind Andie how ruthless the University was. Her advantages were the dark and her ability to stay calm when her opponents were clearly frantic.

She used her stealth to close the distance in the dark and then cast a low spell at one of the soldiers' legs. He leapt to his left to avoid it and landed right where she wanted him. She got in close and took him with hand-to-hand. During their months in the tunnel, Marvo and Raesh had taught her much. The soldier was stronger and faster because of his armor, but Andie had the better training. She laid him out flat in less than two minutes. When she turned to the other soldier, he crouched down and threw up his hands in surrender.

She rushed past him and jumped on the ladder, but just as she was about to climb up to the roof, the soldier grabbed her. Unfortunately for him, she'd figured it was a trick. In one deft movement, she kicked him off and threw herself up on the roof. As soon as he stuck his head up through the hole, Andie caught him with a hook in the center of his face. He went crashing back down.

She was using her magic to hold herself upright, but with the incredible speed of the train it was a difficult job. Not to mention the train was traveling vertically at that point. She started walking forward and could already see the chancellor and his battalion ahead. As soon as she stepped onto the next car, she disconnected all the ones behind her and the train soon left them behind.

"You're very good," the chancellor called through the night. "If only you weren't dragonborn, and fought for me. Ah well. Disappointment abounds."

"Why?" she screamed through the violent wind that lashed her hair across her face. The roar of the train flying through the cold air muffled her cries. "What possible good will come of all this bloodshed? They'll never accept you now, never give you the power you want so badly. You've killed so many people, and for what? To keep spreading a lie?"

"I want what all men with power want, Andie. More power. You are part of the new generation that wants nothing, does nothing, is satisfied with sand when you could have diamonds. But not me. I'll never stop, I'll never have enough."

"It's power you don't need! You're the chancellor of western Noelle. Half of this entire continent is under your control. Why can't you—"

"The world has lost its way! We've stopped trying, stopped striving! I want it all! Everything!"

He and Ashur continued on, leaving the final three

battalion soldiers in Andie's path. She looked around and saw that they were nearing the end of the line. Soon the chancellor would be in the city and if he made it that far there would be no stopping him. The three soldiers looked skittish as Andie approached, no doubt wary of her power now after seeing her plow through all their friends.

Andie stopped, eyed them fiercely. "This man is on his way to suck the life out of Arvall. That means that in a matter of minutes everything and everyone you know will be gone. They will be dead. Your friends, your family. All of them."

They froze in place as they listened to her speak. She took it as a sign to continue.

"You don't need to do this. You owe him nothing," she pleaded. "Are you really going to stand between him and me? Your lives are worth more than this."

The soldiers looked at each other and even with their faces covered, Andie could tell they were reconsidering. She took another step forward and they took one back. One of them removed his mask and relaxed his battle stance.

"We're not from around here," he yelled over the sound of the rushing wind. "None of the battalion is. We don't know these people. They mean nothing to us."

"I'm not from around here, either. I'm from Michaelson, a small farming village near Gordric's Pain. But these people... they mean something to me. If the chancellor sees that he can only get his way by mass murder, how long do you think he'll stay calm? How long before it's your cities and your people that he's massacring? I'm going to stop him and I'm going to do it now. The only question is, do I take you down with him?"

The larger soldier looked at Andie and then back at his peers. They each nodded to him and he put his helmet back on and charged his suit. Andie clenched her fists and prepared to attack, but just as she raised her hands the soldier nodded to her, and he and his friends jumped from the train, covering themselves in bubbles of protective magic to break their fall. Andie let out a long breath she had been holding, turned her attention forward again, and carried on.

Tarven and the chancellor had reached the front of the train and run out of places to run or hide. Andie finally caught up with them and nearly had her head taken off by a white bolt of lightning thrown back by Ashur. The bolt missed her by an inch and hit the car behind her. It split the entire roof apart. He had come a long way since she last knew him.

Everything about him was different. His expressions, his body, his energy. She sensed he had done terrible things since the last time they saw each other. A lot of terrible things. What shocked her most was his power. Before, he had merely been talented with hortological magic, but now his speed, power, and casting ability were off the charts. Even better than his comrades. He must've been good, because he was the last line of defense between the chancellor and Andie, and the chancellor didn't look worried at all.

"You truly are a marvelous thing, Andie Rogers," Chancellor Mharú called. "I've never seen anything like you. Well, almost never," he said, patting Ashur's shoulder.

Andie couldn't help but roll her eyes. "You'll have to

do better than that to impress me, I'm afraid, Chancellor."

He ignored her. "I'm feeling rather ecstatic, and so I'll offer you your life this one time. Join me. Come over to my side and see what real power feels like. Touch it, possess it, relish it. If you were ever to put on this armor there would be nothing on this earth that could stop you."

"Are you out of your mind? You're trying to eradicate my people! You killed my friends, tried to kill my father, and have proven yourself to be nothing but pure evil."

"Those are just people, Andie, and the world is full of them. Find a new home, adopt a new culture, reinvent yourself. Take the things you want. Don't let anything stand in your way."

"Take," she repeated, beginning to almost glow with rage. "Take. Like you took my mother?"

"Fine, Andie. You want to be a martyr, then let us help you die."

Ashur began moving forward toward her. The train began to gradually level out as they neared the bottom of the mountain. This time, Andie cast first and although her aim was perfect, it only caused Ashur to stumble a little.

He retaliated with a spell that wrapped her in super-cold air, and she had to catch her breath quickly in order to defend against his next attack. He cast again, but she caught it and flung it back at him, bringing him to his knees. As he stood again, he conjured a long chain in his hands, but instead of steel, each link was made of freezing energy. He lashed out and missed her twice, but the third time the chain wrapped around her arm and caught her, and the pain was so intense she wanted to scream.

Ashur pulled on the chain and the armor gave him such strength that Andie was pulled off her feet. As soon as her feet left the train, Andie flew up and away. The train was still traveling at an incredible speed. The only thing that kept her from flying away was the chain wrapped around her arm. Using her magic, she cut the chain and brought herself back to the roof. But before she could stand, Ashur lashed out with the chain again and this time it wrapped around her body, pinning down one of her arms. She steadied herself, but the freezing cold was draining the energy right out of her. Ashur was strong, so much more powerful than she'd imagined.

But she couldn't fail. She accessed a deeper part of her magic and released it, engulfing herself in flames and melting the chain right off. Ashur lashed out again, but Andie burned so hot the chain evaporated before it reached her. She almost melted through the roof. When Ashur discarded the chain, Andie returned to her normal state and cast a flurry of spells at Ashur that even his armor couldn't block or absorb. When they hit, she heard his arm and his ribs break.

She had assumed the fight was over and began walking past him to get to the chancellor. The train levelled out completely as it began to slow and pull into the station. Andie was only a few steps from the chancellor when a hand grabbed her and flung her back twenty feet. She very nearly slid off the train entirely. Ashur was back on his feet and moving his arm as if nothing had happened. Andie couldn't believe it.

"That's impossible," she said. "I heard the bones break."

"Did you really think the University wouldn't figure it out?" he asked. "They've been experimenting on people with dragon's blood for years. They finally figured out how to mimic your healing abilities. This suit will never work as well as an actual dragonborn body, it's a lot slower and can't heal completely, but it does the trick. You can't win, Andie."

"I have to."

"Then you'll die trying."

"This isn't you, Tarven."

Tarven glared at her, a fiery light illuminating his piercing gaze. "Tarven is dead. My name is Ashur."

CHAPTER TWENTY

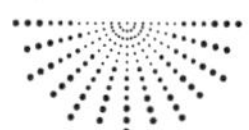

ANDIE COULDN'T BELIEVE WHAT SHE WAS HEARING. SHE cried out and shook her head, her eyes clouded with angry tears that threatened to spill from her lids. Tear of rage. "No, you're wrong. Your name is Tarven and this isn't you! I know you wanted to impress them, to be accepted by them, but I can't honestly believe you're this evil. Think about what's happening around you. He's about to go into your city and take innocent lives. Are you honestly okay with that?"

"I am completely loyal to him. I swore my allegiance and I will do nothing, *nothing*, to jeopardize the work that he is doing. He is building an empire greater than anything you can imagine. A continental kingdom governed by a single, infallible power. And he chose me to lead his battalion, and, one day, all of his legions. The future is now, Andie. The future is Myamar Mharú."

"What happened to that boy who tested me my first day at the University? That cocky, but sweet boy who spent all those afternoons teaching me, helping me, showing me magic I'd never even dreamed of? Where is he? All he wanted was to show the world how special his plants were. What happened to him?"

Ashur was silent then. He seemed to be trying to think of a suitable response, but couldn't. Something about his expression then made Andie pause; she couldn't quite tell what was happening inside of him, but the expression on his face was almost one of regret. She thought then, seriously, that he might not truly be loyal to the chancellor, or the University, or any of it. He might be just as trapped and threatened as Lilja was. He might just be another pawn in the chancellor's vast and ever adapting game.

But Ashur clenched his fists and the suit began to glow, and Andie knew that either he was too brainwashed to stop himself or he truly had gone over the edge of reason. He flung another bolt of lightning at her, this time grazing her side. Behind him, Chancellor Mharú was jumping onto the platform, as the train had almost completely stopped moving. They'd arrived at the station.

"So, you want to trade lighting?" Andie asked. "Let's see what you can do."

Ashur cast another white bolt and Andie met it in the air with a black one. And back and forth they traded lightning, black and white, hot and cold, like a miniature copy of the Hot Salts of Mithraldia. Ashur was well trained, methodical, precise. Andie was organic, intuitive, powerful. The bolts flashed through the air with a terrible sound as loud as any real lightning in the sky. As the bolts sailed by, they hit the train, the platform, various parts of the station, and anything else in their path. Andie and Ashur were destroying everything around them. Andie looked for the chancellor, but he was already gone. She needed to move, fast.

Ashur reached back to conjure his next bolt and Andie did that thing she only did in times of great distress: she reached into the deepest reaches of her magic and released it. A black bolt of lightning erupted from her chest and shot out with such force that she slid back on the train. The bolt was so wide it seemed more like a stream of energy that was wrapped in violent purple flames. Ashur was blown away so hard and fast that Andie couldn't see where he landed or if he was even still alive. She leapt off the train and ran to find the chancellor.

She cleared the station and was running down the nearest boulevard when she stopped. She had no idea where he'd gone. The city was huge, sprawling, and he'd gotten a considerable head start and could have been anywhere by then.

Andie wracked her brain trying to think where he could go to get the quickest access to a large, dense population, but there was no end to the possibilities. The arena, the pier, any of the six boulevards in the publishing district, the financial district, the baseball stadium—Andie could hear them cheering from the train station—and on and on. She was at a total loss. For all she knew he had already started his mass sacrifice. She looked up toward the mountain and saw a tiny dot of light that was almost invisible from so far away. The tear. It had grown.

Just as Andie was about to lose her mind, the screaming began. She turned and began running toward the sounds. She could hear cars crashing and explosions as complete and utter chaos spread in the distance. She ran as fast as she can, wishing the entire time that she had a dragon who cut the air and have her in the area to save people. The closer she got, the more she heard, the more she feared, the more she pushed herself to run faster and harder. When she finally reached the intersection where everything was happening she was met by two things: fear and death.

There were bodies everywhere. There were far too many to count and even the people running were tripping over the corpses that littered the road in every direction. Even as she looked up at the buildings, Andie could see bodies collapsed in the windows. As the people ran, fled, they were killed in midstride. Andie turned and turned, trying to find any sign of hope or salvation, but there was nothing there except carnage and sheer terror.

The chancellor was moving down the street ahead of her. He was standing on a section of the pavement that he had ripped up and it was floating him along at an increasing speed. Andie began chasing him, but he was moving too fast. She could hear him laughing as the bodies continued to fall all around him. As he turned to watch the destruction, he saw her.

"You simply won't die, will you?" he asked. "No matter, the spell is already begun. It's self-sustaining now. All I have to do is wait."

"You're killing the entire city! This is madness! Please, stop!"

"It's too late for your pleas, little girl. Although, if it makes you feel any better I was never going to stop. The plan was always to get rid of the dragonborn by sacrificing the city and then blame the mass destruction on your people. Then the world would be in a constant state of fear, hiding from a threat that didn't even exist."

"That's sick," Andie managed to spit out.

The chancellor laughed suddenly. "No, brilliant I think is the correct word."

"You're only—"

"Stop trying to reason with me, girl."

The chancellor turned and began floating even faster. Andie stopped running. There was no way she could keep up with him on foot. Again, she wished for a dragon. Then she remembered a conversation she'd had with Saeryn. She'd told Saeryn about that night in the archives when, for a few moments, she'd levitated while fighting against the University. Saeryn had told her that it was possible for a dragonborn to levitate and even fly if they had the power, the concentration, and the will. She said it was a rare and powerful trait.

Andie had practiced some on the mountain without much luck, but now she was out of options and the dragons were too far away. She closed her eyes and went to that deep recess of herself, where her most incredible power resided. She focused all her energy, all her power. She tried to picture in her mind what she wanted to do, but although she felt the power she didn't feel the change.

Yet when she finally gave up and opened her eyes, much to her surprise she found she was hovering. When she blinked and refocused her eyes, she noticed she was actually at least five feet above the ground. It had worked. She couldn't believe it. For a split second, she allowed herself to laugh. A nervous sound that erupted from her lips, so foreign after the darkness she's endured these past months. But her momentary thrill caught her off-guard and she slipped suddenly from the air. Fortunately, her will and determination froze her in mid fall and she propelled herself back up, an air of defiance on her face.

She steadied her hands beside her and began to will herself forward. It took a tremendous amount of concentration, but she found herself flying toward the chancellor, moving faster and faster. He was so busy enjoying the sight of the bodies falling that he almost missed her, but when he did see her flying toward him, a change came over him. For the first time that night, Andie could see that he was afraid. The sight of a powerful dragonborn flying toward him with only one goal in mind terrified him. He cast more magic at his pavement and the chase began.

They weaved through the streets of the city, moving faster and faster. Andie had some issues controlling her flight and she more than once knocked against buildings and lamp posts. The chancellor was so busy trying to escape that he stopped looking back, refused to see the girl coming for him. For her part, Andie was as exhilarated as she was afraid.

Time was running out and as they weaved in and out and between and around she was aware that the spell was spreading at an incredible rate. The magic followed the chancellor, but it also spread out from wherever it landed. The more Andie chased him, the more she helped him spread his poison. And, of course, she never forgot that her people were back up on Brie, fighting for their lives and the culture of their entire people. The dragons, too, were locked in battle to the death. And the innocent civilians of Arvall were the collateral damage of a senseless and profitless war.

There was no time. Everywhere around her was death and screams and fear. The chancellor had created something so terrible Andie's heart was breaking more and more each second. She thought of the millions of people dying across the city. She thought of her people dying, perhaps already dead, on Brie. She thought her friends, the fighters, wounded and broken in spirit thousands of leagues away. Marvo. Carmen. Her father. Her entire world. Enough was enough.

She pushed herself like she had never done before and soared forward so rapidly she closed the distance between herself and the chancellor in less than a second. She collided with him, taking him off his floating ground and through the window of a skyscraper they were passing. The crashed through the glass and tumbled across the tiled floor, hitting the ground so hard they lost their breath. By the time Andie looked up, the magic had killed everyone on the floor and she was sure the magic was spreading up through the building as she stood there. In fact, the magic had grown so strong and so vast that even Andie was beginning to feel the effects; she simply hadn't noticed before. The chancellor looked as though he were still having trouble catching his breath as he rolled over on his side and pulled a large piece of glass from the side of his face. As the blood ran down over his mouth he looked up at Andie, smiling.

"Well, even I couldn't plan for this," he said, undaunted. "I didn't know you could fly."

"I can do a lot of things. Including showing you what real pain feels like if you don't stop this spell."

"Oh, I think it's too late for that. Look around you, the spell can't be stopped. Most of the city is already dead and soon the rest will be, too. Lucky for you, you're nowhere near the gateway to the past. I would have loved to watch you be sucked away."

"It is not too late. You can still save whoever's left. You can put a stop to this!"

"You mistake me for someone who cares about these people, girl."

"How can one person be so evil? What is wrong with you?"

"Me? I just wanted power. Respect. I wanted to walk out in the sun and not be thought a coward. And now I've failed. I think I've performed the spell incorrectly. Look..."

The chancellor held up his hand and Andie saw that the veins were beginning to turn dark blue. The skin was dying, beginning to wither even as she watched.

"You're dying," she said, in disbelief. "No! Who's going to stop the spell?"

He began laughing manically then. "Oh, stupid girl. It's not the spell you should be worried about, but our one greatest weapon that I leave behind."

"Weapon, what weapon?" Andie pleaded, falling to her knees. "What can possibly be worse than killing an entire city?"

Mharú tried to push himself up from the ground, but he immediately fell back, his body too weak to even lift his head. "This spell is tied to me. I'm dying, but there the true power still lives." His laugh transformed into an eerie cackle that made Andie take another step back from him. "He lives. And so long as he lives, so long as the weapon is alive—and I promise you, girl, that suit of his will keep him alive—the world has no hope. You think me killing a city is bad, just you wait until you see the destruction my Ashur can do."

Andie shook her head in disbelief. "You're a fool if

you think Tarven will carry on your evil plan for you. Besides, I don't think he's even still al—"

"Stupid girl," the chancellor snapped, bloody spittle spraying before him as he spoke. "You're missing the point. It's not about the spell. It will stop when I die, which seems to be any moment now." More red spilled across the floor as he rolled to his side and coughed up more blood.

Andie stood frozen, staring down at the man before her. She had never wanted to kill anyone so badly in her life, but there he lay, dying before her. Part of her was grateful she wouldn't be forced to let Saeryn down by becoming a murderer. Another part of her was angry that he took that task away from her.

"You know I never hated your people. Not really. Not until tonight. When I woke up this morning the whole world was soon to be mine. And now I'm dying by my own hand and the only person here to say goodbye is a girl I tried to kill."

"Don't do this. Don't let it end like this. Do the right thing, please."

His voice was barely a whisper, his breaths coming in slow, gurgling wheezes. With one final effort, he looked up at her and spoke. "You'll never understand the allure of power, little girl. But no matter. You lost, anyway."

With that, the chancellor laid his head back on the floor and clenched his fists. The suit began to charge and glow. Andie took several uncertain steps back before she realized what he was doing. He was going to give the spell one last wave of magic to sustain it. Enough to kill anyone left in the city. She dove for his body, her hands outstretched before her, but she was too late.

Chancellor Myamar exploded right before her and she was met in midair by a wave of magic unlike anything she'd ever experienced. The armor had amplified his final spell immensely. Andie was thrown back out toward the street and across it, until she crashed through the window of the next building and collided with the floor. The last thing she saw was the wave of blue magic traveling out across the city and the building where she'd been thrown from collapsing in an unbelievable cloud of smoke, debris, and noise.

HE WAS JARRED awake from the unbelievable pain. It felt as if his entire body were burning and as he looked down at himself, or what was left of him, he nearly fainted from the shock.

One of his hands was gone, as was most of his arm below the elbow. His legs were so badly burned they were undistinguishable as legs and one of them was totally numb and wouldn't move. Every time he twisted his body, the discs in his back grinded against each other. Both his arms were in excruciating pain. He lifted his remaining hand to feel his head and felt that not only was his hair completely burned off, but the skin of his face was totally melted. And he could only see out of one eye. He was so shocked and was in so much agony that he could hardly move.

The only thing that remained largely undamaged was his torso. As the leader of the battalion his uniform had a thicker, more advanced chest plate so that his suit could harness more energy and deliver a more powerful performance. The torso of his armor remained largely undamaged and was the only thing that had saved his life.

The enormous bolt of black lightning that Andie had used against him had thrown him over two hundred feet away. It took him quite some time to comprehend his world through the pain and figure out where he was. He looked into the sky and saw the blue wave of magic. Chancellor Myamar Mharú's final desperate act. The man he'd sworn his allegiance and life to was gone, had failed.

He rolled over onto the chest plate with a grunt of pain and began to crawl. He didn't make it very far before he stopped, in so much terrible agony that he wanted to cry, to give up and die right then and there. He had never known such pain, such desperation. His skin was peeling off on the ground as he crawled and his back, more than likely broken, felt like it was tearing apart.

He gathered his strength and continued. The pain grew worse the farther he went, but with his goal in mind he knew he could make it to a safe place, somewhere he could meet up with other members of the battalion and regroup. This was only the beginning. And though he was broken, burned, and defeated, he was not without his rage.

CHAPTER TWENTY-ONE

"HOW LONG WILL THEY STAY LIKE THAT?" OREN ASKED.

"As long as we need them to," Saeryn responded, looking at her work. "We gave them every chance we possibly could, Oren. There was nothing left but this."

When the final blast of magic had gone out from the chancellor, Saeryn had looked down on the city as its entire population was wiped out in one, maleficent move. Her heart had broken to see such unadulterated evil and she grew tired of it. She grew weary of battle and destruction. She ended her spell of light and went to face the battalion. As they converged on her, she rose into the air and began to revolve, sweeping her arms all around her, casting a spell that even the University's armor couldn't withstand. By the time she came back to the ground, the entire battalion was frozen still—those near her, those in the University, even the ones spread out around the mountain. Her spell was that powerful.

"What about the tear?" Oren asked. "It has closed for now, but how do we know it won't be back? We have to find the chancellor and stop him."

"Andie went after him," Saeryn said. "And I'm afraid she caught up with him."

"What do you mean?"

"That wave of magic. It had to be the chancellor. And even with his new armor there is no way a sorcerer could survive an expense of magic like that. He is surely dead. Even the Sentinels have ceased to attack and they would only stop if their commander were defeated. I fear what Andie may have done when she caught him. She may have... perhaps..."

"No," Oren said, his voice filling with fear and doubt and other things. "I know I don't know her as well as you do, but I've spent some time with her and I don't think... I know she's not capable of something like this. Not Andie. She couldn't. She wouldn't."

"I don't wish to consider it either, Oren, but what else is there? What other explanation? The chancellor would not have gone through all this effort and scheming simply to take his own life. What would you have me believe?"

"I say we should give her the benefit of the doubt. Wait for her return and ask her. Whatever happened, she would not lie to us. But she couldn't kill. Not Andie."

"Regardless, we have more pressing things to attend to. Look at all this carnage."

As she spoke, she indicated all the bodies lying around the entrance of the University and throughout the lot and the precipice. All the bodies were darkly veined and the skin hung loose on the corpses. There were hundreds of them on the mountain alone and Saeryn knew that with that blast of radical, unmonitored magic from the chancellor every soul in the city would be dead. Millions of people sacrificed to feed an all-consuming spell that had ultimately failed. Not a single dragonborn warrior or dragon had been taken up into the tear. The chancellor's grand design had failed. And all the wounds and breaks the dragonborn had sustained were already beginning to heal. The dragons, too, were improving with each second—only three of them had sustained serious injuries, but they would be healed within the hour.

Saeryn and Oren walked toward the precipice and looked down toward the city, thinking of all the bodies that must have littered the streets, buildings, stations, boulevards, parks, and every other space. Bodies killed in midstride or in the middle of eating. Bodies sucked dry of all vitality while they slept or woke. Bodies silenced and broken forever without ever having done anything to deserve their end. Saeryn hid her face in her hands, momentarily overcome by the unbelievable sadness. Like Andie before her, she couldn't believe or understand how anyone could be so evil, so careless with the lives of millions of people they had claimed to protect. Oren rested a hand on her shoulder. And for a moment they just stood there.

Sometime later, when Saeryn had composed herself, she decided on a plan of action. She understood that life had a balance, that once certain events took place they couldn't be erased or altered. Or at least they shouldn't be. There was a course to things, a flow and current of life and death and everything in between that went on its way unobstructed, and Saeryn knew that that was simply the way things were. But suddenly that wasn't good enough for her anymore. Not then. Not that night of all nights. Time and death were very dangerous things to toy with, whether one was skilled in magic or not, and there were rules and structures to the handling of each. Saeryn was prepared to break one of the highest of those rules.

"Oren, I need your help and the help of our people. It is not right that all these people should die for us. They came here tonight with one goal in heart and by the time they were brutally murdered they had come to see the error of their ways. And even if they hadn't, it isn't right to leave them here like this, broken and forlorn. I want to save them. I want to do what only our people can. It will be harder without the rest of our people here, but we can draw on the University's battalion for strength. What say you, Oren? Can your Queen count on you?"

"You can always count on me, Saeryn. But, what do you intend to do?" He glanced out at the broken and scattered bodies, uncertain at what she was implying.

"I intend to bring them back."

Oren's eyes grew wide as he stared at his Queen. "But that's impossible. You know we don't have the power to return people to life."

"Perhaps not, but I would rather die than not at least try."

Blinking rapidly, Oren finally bowed. "Of course. I cannot think of one thing I wish more than to return these people back their lives, though I'm afraid my reasons pale in their honor next to yours. I was thinking that they were the only people on the face of this planet who could tell the whole world that we weren't evil. They saw with their own eyes how evil and callous the chancellor and his men were. I will round up our people."

Oren went off to apprise his fellow dragonborn of what Saeryn wanted to do and gather them for the event. Saeryn directed some of the men to bring the unconscious battalion members to a central location to create a point of focus. Once these tasks were all complete, the dragonborn kneeled around the bodies of the frozen battalion members and then bowed their heads. They began to link with one another, holding hands and placing hands on shoulders. Saeryn began the spell and each of the dragonborn warriors picked it up until they were all chanting in unison. She knew there was hardly a chance in the world the spell would work, but given the dark and evil nature of the people's slaughter, she knew she at least had to try.

The chanting grew louder as the dragonborn worked as one. Their efforts appeared for naught, though, as hardly a glimmer of life returned to the people. But then something incredibly happened. The dragons had finally rejoined their riders and they lay down next to the group, encircling the dragonborn and lending strength and comfort. The magic amplified, a new and strange energy washing over the city. One so strong and so new that Saeryn hardly believed what she was feeling. She closed her eyes and let it consume her, offering her very being to aid the spell.

The mountain went still, quiet as the night sky. It had already become eerily calm after the unspeakable massacre, but this was new, unique. The spell had stopped all motion and sound on the mountain, and had even stopped motion and sound in the city below. All of Arvall, for the first time since its conception, was in a state of peace. The dragons inched closer to the dragonborn and nuzzled their backs.

The dragons' eyes began to shimmer and then the iridescent skin around the eyes began to shift through innumerable pearlescent shades of color that had no name. This was something the dragons hadn't done in a very long time. In fact, none of the living dragonborn had ever seen it, not even Saeryn. Their eyes began to behave that way when the dragons needed to provide the strength and magic a dragonborn needed to save a life. It was an ancient magic, one long lost to history. One Saeryn had thought lost forever.

They worked as one until nearly all their magic had depleted, but it was not enough. Saeryn could feel the magic wane. She squeezed her eyes shut and willed every fiber of her being into the spell, drawing on the ancient magic of her royal house, pushing as much of that energy out into the souls of the people around her. But it wasn't until Raylim—beautiful, strong, and selfless Raylim—flew down before Saeryn and cast his own life's energy out into the world, that the spell finally took. With one final effort, Raylim raised his silver head high up to the sky and let out a powerful breath of fire. The flames flew so high, they penetrated the clouds. For a moment, the entire city glowed in Raylim's warm light, and then the dragon softly laid down his head and gave his life to save those around him.

Saeryn held onto the spell, gazing down at the creature who had just sacrificed himself for the cause. Tears streamed down her face as she harnessed the last magical energy that emanated from his body, letting the heat from his flames fuel her magic, and blasted it out over the city streets. A silver, beautiful magic that offered exactly what was necessary for the spell to succeed. Saeryn fell to her knees and wept. "Thank you, my friend."

Not many minutes had passed before the first sign of the spell's efficiency appeared. Saeryn didn't believe her eyes at first, convinced her vision was deceiving her. She blinked through her tears to clear her eyes. She saw a man lying dead near the dragonborn begin to change. The dark blue color in his veins receded. His loose skin tightened on his corpse. Before long, his fingers started to move and not long after that the man was on his feet, confused but alive. He was soon followed by a woman and then another man, and before long there were bodies rising all around them.

Inside the University, the people that the chancellor had tricked into coming there to sacrifice themselves began to wake and roll off each other. They had a vague recollection of having a voice inside their heads asking them to come up to the University and to go along with whatever happened there. As they began to wander out into the night they saw the dragonborn and the dragons, kneeling in a circle and chanting in a beautiful, solemn rhythm.

Below the mountain, in the city itself, the people began to live. They revived in the exact positions they had died in, sometimes with a cough or a gasp. They couldn't believe it. The last thing they'd known they were having all the life and memories sucked out of their bodies; they remembered feeling cold, then numb, then nothing. But now they were back again, standing on their feet and breathing the sweet, clean air. They began to cheer and pray and cry tears of joy for being back, for being saved. And they knew exactly who had saved them.

Everyone had seen Chancellor Mharú floating through the streets and spreading that horrible magic everywhere. They remember his cruel smile and the way he enjoyed watching them perish. Some of them had lived long enough to see that final wave of magic as it rushed for them and took their lives. They had no doubt about who had done this to them and because of that they began to rethink everything they had feared, thought, rejected, accepted, and wanted. They also knew who to thank for their salvation. Saeryn wasn't just casting a spell, she was broadcasting a message. She was sending a telepathic message to everyone in the city telling them exactly what had happened and letting them know that there were witnesses to prove it—witnesses who had come to the top of the mountain to see the dragonborn dead, but then found themselves fighting beside them.

Even with the strength of the dragons and the battalion members, the dragonborn began to grow weak. It was a massive spell and the amount of power and skill it took were tremendous. As the final slain civilians came back to life, Saeryn and the dragonborn let go of each other and sat down to relax. It was the largest, most taxing spell any of them had ever done, though it would have been so much easier if they had all their people, even the children, helping. The dragons were the last to quiet, each laying its head on the floor in exhaustion. They had spent every ounce of their magical energy, but it had worked. Their magic had saved the city.

The civilians began to close in around them and one man stepped forward from the rest. "You saved us," he said, stunned, trembling. "I can't believe it. We were so wrong about you, about all of you."

"It was not I, but the combined efforts of my people and our dragons," Saeryn replied, pushing herself from her knees. "Raylim here, in particular. He sacrificed himself so you can live."

The man gaped down at still form of the massive dragon.

"Such a beautiful creature." Tears welled in the man's eyes. "I have never seen such a thing. To think, I believed them evil my entire life. Such lies, such evil. We almost went along with that lunatic."

"He was a cruel, manipulative man," Saeryn replied. "I fault you not for believing what had been told as truth for so long. But he is gone now and he can no longer hurt anyone. The real truth is now clear, as you can now see. I see no reason for us to be enemies."

"I'm so embarrassed. I think we all are. We almost agreed to wipe out you and your entire people, and all because we listened to a man we started out not trusting in the first place. I guess we were desperate. Afraid. Can you ever forgive us?"

"There is nothing to forgive, my friend," she said, rising to her feet, although she was still incredibly tired. "He tricked you. And although you all did make the decision for yourselves to believe him, I would never hold a grudge against you for acting out of fear. It happens to the best of us. I would simply ask that we move forward in peace. I hope now you all understand that my people and I are not dangerous. We've found a place in the mountains, far away from here, and I can assure you that you will never see us again. We can be happy and whole there, leaving you to enjoy your homes and your lives in peace. You have my word that there is nothing to fear from us. We're not so very different. Our abilities may differ and our histories may have diverged, but we are all people, after all, and we all want the freedom to live and be happy."

The man turned to look at the other civilians and see

what they thought. They all nodded vigorously, though they seemed sad. The man looked sad as well as he turned back to face Saeryn.

"What's your name?" he asked.

"My name is Saeryn."

"Queen of the dragonborn," Oren announced as he stepped forward.

"Well, your Grace, we have no intention of harming you or standing in your way, though you and your people have proven here tonight that even a small group of you is formidable. But I think it would be reckless of us to send you away to some distant mountain. Unless of course that's what you want."

"The dragonborn thrive in mountains," Saeryn said. "It would not be a punishment or a hardship. We would simply be going home."

"I see. Well, we won't ever spread these lies or this hate again. We'll never blindly follow another leader, either. We'll do better from now on. I promise. But... I wonder... if you might consider staying for a while? Or maybe visiting periodically? It's just that we've been so wrong for all our lives and I think I can speak for everyone else when I say that we'd like a chance to get to know the real dragonborn. We'd love to live with you and learn from you. Like you said, there's no reason for us to be enemies and if we're not enemies then perhaps we could be allies. We completely understand if you want to go or need to get back, but I want you to know that the door is open and we want you here. Also, this new world and its technology must be so foreign to you. They hadn't even discovered electricity yet in your time. And since you came through a portal here in our city, it's the responsibility of the citizens of Arvall to show you how to survive and thrive in this new world."

"You're genuine about wanting us around?" Saeryn asked, humbled by the man's kindness and soft-spoken way.

"More serious than I've ever been. We all are." Murmurs or agreement erupted around him, an endless stream of people approaching and thanking and crying their appreciation.

Saeryn looked up and around at all the people. They were all nodding their heads and smiling at her. All the dragonborn warriors gazed around themselves and met with smiles and handshakes and tears. The people had truly changed, had finally come to understand that it was never the dragonborn who had been evil or manipulative. It was never the dragonborn who had lied, murdered, stolen, and deceived every inch of the way just so that they could amass an invulnerable stockpile of power. It had been the University. It had *always* been the University. It wasn't long before the dragonborn themselves were beginning to smile and respond in kind. Saeryn's heart was filled to bursting with happiness and relief. She reached out her hands to the man and brought him closer to herself.

"Very well, then," she said. "We shall be allies."

A collective cheer went up from everyone there. Civilians, sorcerers, and dragonborn alike. They began to embrace each other and welcome each other. It was the most joy that any of them had experienced in a very long time. Saeryn looked all around her at the people celebrating and hugging each other. It was what she had always hoped for, but never expected to ever actually come to pass.

She was absolutely overwhelmed by the sheer and unfiltered mirth. But as she turned around and around she realized that there was someone missing. Someone who had worked as hard as she had and sacrificed even more so that they could be standing there on that precipice, arm-in-arm with their former enemies. Andie. She strode to the edge of the precipice and looked down over the city.

If anyone deserved to see the result of this hard and dangerous work, it was Andie.

"So, what happens next? By now they've reached Arvall City and they've either managed to convince the people that they're not a threat or a lot of people are dead. What now?"

"Well, captain, the only thing we can do until they get back or until we get word is wait. The ship is completely destroyed and I don't think any of us is familiar with this area so if we start just walking there's no telling where we'll end up. Besides, too many of us are injured or unconscious. It would just be too much chaos to do anything now."

"I understand. And what about the bodies of all the ones we've lost? I didn't want to say anything in front of the group, but if those bodies are left out much longer the smell is really going to be a problem. We need to arrange a mass funeral. I know it's not the right way and I know it's not what any of us wants or deserves, but that's what we're going to do. It's dishonorable to leave them out like this. They sacrificed too much for the rest of us."

"You're right. Honestly, captain we should've buried

them by now, but I just haven't had the will to face this yet."

"Raesh, I'm sorry about your father. I truly am. I've known Marvo since we were kids and he was one of my closest friends. I didn't hesitate for a second when he told me to be at the port and be ready to take him and his people to safety. He was only human and yet he was one of the bravest and strongest men I ever met. He died an honorable death, fighting for a cause that meant something to him. To all of us. He died a brave and honorable man."

Raesh sighed and offered a smile to the captain. "I know. He was a great man. I'm proud to have called him my father. It doesn't make this any easier, though."

"There will never be another like him. Still, you can't keep putting this off. It's time for you to face this and to give your father's memory rest. I know you wanted to wait for Carmen to wake up to be there with you, but it doesn't look like she's going to wake up soon. Almost everyone else has, but she's... just not responding to any of our medicine. You'll have to do this without her."

Raesh nodded his head and began walking back across the shore. The river flowed quick and dark beside him, almost two hundred feet wide at that point. He greeted the fighters as he passed them and stopped to check on some of the more seriously injured ones. Everyone had calmed and cheered up considerably since the traitor was discovered and executed, though they were still on edge about the future. At least, they felt, the worst was over. Hopefully.

Raesh moved on to where Carmen and a few others were lying, still unconscious. Most everybody had woken up and been seen to properly, but Carmen and two other fighters had yet to respond to anything, although the other two did show signs of waking soon. Lilja and Kent were sitting behind Carmen's head, watching over her as they did day and night whenever Raesh way away. Sarinda had woken not long after Andie left, but after finding out the truth about Lilja she had refused to be seen with her. It had been a bitter scene.

Many of the other fighters, most of them in fact, had forgiven Lilja. They understood that she was truly loyal to the cause and had only done what she did in order to protect her family. They understood that they would have done the same. Kent was still his kind and helpful self and had done everything in his power to help Raesh restore some kind of order to the group. Neither he nor Lilja felt at all angry or vengeful about being locked up. They just wanted to help. Raesh sat down beside Carmen and took her hand.

"You better not be thinking of sleeping too much longer," he said. "I need you here. We all need you in ways you can't imagine. You're the only family I have left. I don't know if Andie and the others are coming back and I don't know what news they'll bring if they do. You have to wake up. You have to help me."

"It's hard seeing friends like this," Kent said. "Sometimes I think I don't want them to wake up, because, when they do, all they'll find is carnage. The ship destroyed. Eighty-seven dead. Well, eighty-eight now. Us stranded in the Hot Salts and the future more uncertain than it's ever been. And to wake up and figure out that the traitor was Yara... and that she's dead..."

"It's horrible," Lilja said, looking down at her hands.

"It's horrible and it's all my fault. I should've just said no."

"From what you told me it sounds like the University had already turned Yara before they came for you. None of this is your fault," Raesh said. "Any of us would've done the same to protect our family. All you can do now is your part in getting us back on track. That's how you earn our trust back."

Lilja nodded, but never raised her eyes. Raesh knew she'd still be beating herself up for months to come. Kent rubbed more of the balm on Carmen's forehead that the dragonborn had given them. He seemed to want to say something to Raesh, but couldn't figure out how or if he should say it.

"What is it, Kent?" Raesh asked, not angry, but curious.

"I'm just wondering how she'll take the news. Andie, I mean. About what happened."

"I don't know, but I wish I could be there with her when she finds out. I sent a coded message with the bird, like Saeryn asked. Just enough information so that Andie knows what's going on, but not enough so that if anyone on the other side intercepts it, they won't have one up on us."

Kent nodded. "Smart. Have you heard back yet?"

Raesh shook his head. "The message should be getting there soon. I sent it not long after they left. The night that Oren dealt with Yara's execution. I'd give anything to be there by her side when she reads it. After all, I know how devastating it can be to lose someone you love."

CHAPTER TWENTY-TWO

SHE WAS THINKING OF YARA. YARA. YARA. HER BEST friend who she'd turned on at the first sign of trouble. Her best friend who she'd refused to give the benefit of the doubt and never even given a chance to explain herself, defend herself. Her best friend who had turned on them all and was now likely gone. She remembered that Carmen had introduced them. She remembered that Yara had been so kind and helpful when she'd first arrived at the Academy and Yara had also been the first to figure out that she was truly a dragonborn.

They had been immediate and true friends, and Yara had literally gone to the ends of the earth with her, had fought with her, suffered with her, been afraid with her. They'd been hiding in the tunnels under the University for months and she was beginning to lose her mind, her calm, but it was Yara who had reassured her and Yara who had forced her to maintain her hope. She couldn't believe how she'd treated her friend, her ally, her fellow soldier. And now she was gone. And there was nothing anyone could do about it. She still hardly believed Yara had been the one to turn on them. That she was the traitor.

The last sight of her—the final image that would have to suffice for the rest of time and pain—had been her being carried away in the jaws of a great green dragon. A huge, fire-breathing dragon, more fearsome than Andie had ever seen her. It had been the one she rode with Oren, and she shivered thinking about how vicious she had appeared when she came to collect Yara in her jaws. She had seemed such a gentle creature when they flew together before.

She wondered what fate Yara had met. Had the dragon simply dropped her from a great height, somewhere along its way back to its cavern? Had it tossed her into the path of lightning and let the legendary bolts of the Hot Salts do the work? Or had it swallowed her whole, condemning her to darkness and a slow death? Did it burn her alive with its terrible, unquenchable fire? Or did it simply crush her in its jaws, just break her irreparably and then never give another thought to the deed? Did she really want to know? She kept repeating to herself in her mind that the dragonborn were a peaceful race. Perhaps the dragon hadn't hurt her at all. She clung to that thought as fiercely as she could. Surely, they wouldn't have harmed her without Andie's consent.

Andie opened her eyes. She was lying on her stomach on the floor and she hurt all over. This was the fourth time in recent days that she'd woken up like this, but this time her mind was perfectly clear. She knew the reason she was hurting so badly was because she had been standing so close to the chancellor when he made his final attempt and blew himself up.

She lifted her face and found that her neck hurt tremendously, too. She looked straight ahead and she could see glass on the carpet. The hole she'd made in the window after the blast hit her was huge and there was glass everywhere. She began the slow process of picking herself up and it was excruciating. But she knew she needed to get back to Saeryn and the others. If they were still there. For all she knew, the spell—with all its millions of sacrifices—had worked perfectly and the dragonborn on Brie were no more. She needed to get back up there to see it for herself.

And even if Saeryn and her people were still alive, millions of people were dead. The chancellor's spell had killed everyone in Arvall, and, regardless of how they had hated the dragonborn or wanted them dead, she knew that they deserved better than the fate that had found them in the end. She was frustrated, confused, and angry with herself for not being able to stop him. She had failed.

She had no idea his hatred could run so deep or that he had been hiding such power and such evil. She knew she would never be able to come to terms with the horror that lay outside. And there was still everyone back in the Hot Salts to think of. A part of her wanted to lie back down and stay there forever. It was all too much.

"We thought you were dead."

Andie sprang to her feet, momentarily disregarding her pain, and spun to face the voice. It was a woman. She was dressed in a knee-length gray skirt and a pink blouse that was almost see-through. She had her hair up in a tight bun and she wore glasses with a thin frame. Just a regular woman. And all around her there were other people dressed in regular, office appropriate clothes. The room was full of people and they were all staring at Andie.

"Who are you?" Andie asked, her hands up and ready to defend herself.

"We work here," the woman said cautiously, backing up a few steps. "We were working last night when everything started turning to chaos. First, there were a lot of screams and then there were these terrible crashes. And then we died. All of us. But a few hours ago, we woke up and we've kind of just been too freaked out to go outside. We were going to wake you, but we didn't know if you were hurt or how badly. And, well..."

"Well what?" Andie shouted.

"Well, you weren't exactly... here last night. And we just wondered where you came from. Who you are..."

"My name is Andie," she said, calming down a little. "I was knocked over here by a blast of magic. I was trying to save you all, but I failed. Which is why I don't understand how you're all alive right now."

"It was the dragon Queen," the woman said. "She brought us back."

Andie stared at the woman for a long moment, trying to process what she had just been told. "I don't understand. Saeryn saved you? How? Is she here? Is she alive?"

"She's not here, but I'm pretty sure she's still alive," the woman explained. "It's kind of hard to explain, but it's like we all got this transmission in our brains. A woman's voice. I just remember hearing this soft voice, chanting in my ear, coaxing me back towards life in a language I didn't quite understand."

Andie sunk to the floor to steady herself. Had they actually won? She had no idea Saeryn was capable of such magic. Part of her didn't believe what she was hearing. But, the woman was alive, so she must be speaking the truth.

"The magic was so strange, so unfamiliar." The woman bent down on the floor near Andie, smiling softly at her as she recounted her memories. "I remember waking up and feeling like my soul was flying, like my mind was on the back of a dragon or something. It was breathtaking and terrifying all at once. But then, when I opened my eyes, I was alive. Your dragons gave back our lives after Chancellor Mharú tried to sacrifice us all for a spell."

"The dragons brought you back?" Andie spoke the words softly, only mildly believing it.

Another woman came to join them, placing her hand on Andie's shoulder. "Not long after we woke, we heard voices from the streets. People are saying the dragon Queen saved us and gave us back our lives because they had been taken away from us in an act of such immense evil."

The two women helped pull Andie to her feet when she didn't respond. They led her to the nearest chair and kindly waited for her to collect her thoughts.

Andie tried to think things through. If the women spoke the truth, and she had no reason to doubt them, it meant the dragonborn were still alive. It also meant that the chancellor was truly dead and that everyone else had died but been brought back. The truth was finally about to be exposed. She was confused at first until it finally dawned on her. It was good news. Something good had finally happened. They'd won.

"Can I have some water?" Andie finally managed to say.

"Sure," the woman said, grabbing a bottle off of her desk. "Are you okay?"

"Yeah, it's just," Andie began. "I don't know. It's over. I'm not sure if I believe it."

The woman who handed her the water smiled. "You look confused."

Andie nodded. "I am. I think… I think I'm happy."

"Is that unusual?"

"For my life? You'd be surprised."

Andie drank the water and rested for a moment while her body began to heal. When she felt stronger she stood, thanked the women, and then led all of them outside where they met a huge crowd of people standing in the street. An excited chatter filled the streets, hundreds of people gathering together and speaking frantically, each looking around and above them, searching for something. Andie walked up to the first person she saw.

"What's going on?" she asked.

"We're waiting for her to come back around again."

"Who?"

"The dragon Queen."

Andie gasped and grabbed the man by his shoulders so abruptly that she startled him. "What do mean 'waiting for her to come back around again?' What is she doing?"

"She's been flying around the city for hours now. She's looking for someone, I think."

Andie let him go and started making her way through the crowd. She pushed through until she made it to the center of the intersection and then she cleared a small circle around herself.

"Everybody stay back!"

She raised her arm straight in the air and sent up a

beam of purple light that soared so high it touched the soft, morning clouds. She held it there, burning bright but not hot, the beam itself buzzing slightly as it blasted through the sky. She knew that if Saeryn was still in the city or anywhere within ten miles she would be able to see the beacon. And sure enough, Andie soon heard the powerful sound of pumping wings and as she turned she saw the dragon beating through the sky toward her, Saeryn leaning low on its back.

The crowd backed away, leapt away, and cleared the entire intersection and when the dragon landed it had all the space it could want. Saeryn had jumped from its back even before it hit the ground and at the same instant Andie was rushing toward her. They threw themselves into each other's arms, rejoicing that the other was alive and that there was finally peace.

"You never came back and we had no idea what had happened to you," Saeryn said, still breathing heavily. "And I came down to find you, but I had no idea where to start. I've searched for you for hours. Are you okay? What happened?"

"I'm fine. I'm so sorry. The chancellor blew himself up as a last measure to ensure that everything died and I got caught in the blast and didn't wake up until just now. But all these people should be dead. You should be gone. What happened?"

"I don't know. This many people dying in sacrifice should have been enough power to fuel the spell a hundred times over. We should have been torn from the earth, but instead the fissure closed. We lived. All I can think is that he performed the spell wrong. Andie, what happened to him? What did you do?"

"Nothing. I took him down, but that was all. I swear.

He wasn't wounded in any way that he couldn't have healed from. He just didn't want to accept defeat. He ended it."

Saeryn exhaled a sigh of relief. Andie saw in her face what she had feared and how much she had feared it.

"Don't worry, Saeryn," she said. "I won't deny that I wanted to kill him, to kill everyone in the battalion, but I know it's not in our nature to kill. And I also know that you would never have looked at me the same if I had done something like that."

Saeryn touched Andie's face and they hugged again, now totally free.

Whispers began getting louder around them. Andie couldn't help but smile as she heard people asking their neighbors excitedly if that was the dragon Queen, if she was the one who they heard in their head when they were brought back to life.

"Excuse me," a shy-looking man mumbled softly as he stepped towards Andie and Saeryn. "I'm sorry, but… Are you the dragon Queen? Are you the one who brought us back?"

Andie turned to the man and placed her hand on his shoulder. "She is. This is Saeryn."

The man chewed his lip as he looked to be searching for the right words. He wrung his hands together and then finally knelt down and bowed his head. Others did the same as whispers of thanks began echoing from the buildings around them.

"It was not me," Saeryn spoke to the crowd. "It was not my magic that brought you back. It was the magic of the dragons and of my people, as a whole. It was the magic of good that grew stronger than I had ever seen it grow. A magic that came together to vanquish evil. It is not me you need to thank, but my people and our dragons."

The man looked up with wide-eyes, tears brimming his lids. He then spoke with a quiver to his voice, but he spoke loud so all could hear. "I'm sure I speak for everyone when I say, thank you. Thank you to you all. Thank you for saving us. How can we ever repay the debt?"

Saeryn bowed her head to the man. "We ask no repayment. We did what was right, and we had luck on our side. All I ask is your acceptance of our people. We would like to stay in your city for a time."

Everyone in the crowd grew silent for a moment, and then excited cheers erupted through the crowd as far as Andie could hear. They seemed to really be coming around.

"But what about the University?" someone asked. "The professors and all the people who work for them? What are we gonna do about them? We can't just let 'em go, this would start all over again."

"They'll be taken care of," said Saeryn. "For now, they are no longer a danger to any of you. I understand you're angry and if you decide to execute them, my people and I will not interfere with your laws, but I would urge caution and wisdom. It is compassion that separates us from them and if you sacrifice that then you may as well align yourself with the enemy. I believe you have a very fine prison in this city and I think it would make an excellent permanent home for those who tried to rob you of your freedom and your lives."

There was some hesitation in the crowd. Many of them seemed to really favor execution, but Saeryn's words appeared to be having the desired effect. After some more deliberation, they seemed to agree that it was probably best, but they wanted to hold a formal tribunal soon to be thorough.

"And what about the University itself?" a small, elderly lady asked. "Is it still going to be a military training facility?"

"No," Andie said immediately. She had thought this through long and hard in her months below ground. Her dreams of a new University where all are welcome. "We're done gearing up for war. I think we can do something better with it. We'll build it around new ideas. Truth. Safety. And everyone, absolutely everyone, will be welcome to attend. I know that together we can rebuild this world. The hate for my people has spread far and fast, but we can end that. And we can end hate for everything else, too. I know we don't live in an ideal world and lofty wishes aren't always practical, but there's more to life than this and I think we all know that."

"Will you lead it?" a young boy asked from within the crowd.

"No. But I'd like to attend it," Andie smiled down at him. "I have a friend who'd be perfect for the job, though."

The voices around her grow louder as people began speculating who this person might be. Andie raised her voice and spoke clearly, for all to hear. "His name is Lymir. He is a great and wise man, and we should all be lucky to have him as a leader at the new University. We will, of course, consult the public officially before appointing him, but I can assure you there is no one greater to lead us into our new time of peace."

"Who is this man? What has he done to have earned

your trust?" the mother of the boy stepped forward, her arms held firmly on her son's shoulders.

"That is a story for another time," Saeryn answered. "But trust me when I say, Andie is correct. There is no greater person to lead everyone into this new era."

Shouts of Lymir began echoing through the streets as the message passed on. Saeryn turned to Andie.

"What will you do?" the boy called up to Andie.

"I guess I could head up the hortological magic department. Someone's gotta make it right."

There were some laughs among the crowd and Andie herself smiled, though it did make her think of Ashur and where he'd gotten off to. She turned to Saeryn and without a word expressed to her all the gratitude and belief that was piled up inside of her. Without a word, Saeryn returned it.

The two of them were about to mount the dragon and leave when the people they had been talking to kneeled. They were both surprised and were even more so when they saw that many others were following the example. Andie turned to look behind them and saw that everyone was beginning to kneel down. In all four directions, as far as the eye could see, all the people were kneeling low. Andie was humbled and warmed by the sight.

"I think they truly respect you," she said, turning to Saeryn.

"I think so. But make no mistake, Andie... they are paying homage to you, too."

CHAPTER TWENTY-THREE

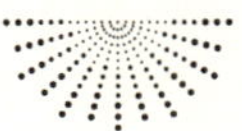

OVER THE NEXT FEW WEEKS, THE DRAGONBORN remained among the citizens of Arvall City. The people were happy to have them, though there was a transition period when people had to convince themselves not to be afraid and to accept that everything they had been taught over the course of their lives was nothing more than a pack of ugly lies.

Saeryn was elected to a special board that was put in charge of the city until a formal government could be established in the region. The board was responsible for creating new legislature and carrying out a total restructuring of the city's cultural and historical institutions. The civilians made an honest effort to erase everything that disparaged or lied about the dragonborn. And since the dragonborn had been pulled from a past centuries before, they were perfect for helping to rewrite the history books to present the absolute truth.

The professors, Searchers, monitors, battalion soldiers, and even the Sentinels were tried for high crimes against the city, the region, the dragonborn, and all of Noelle. The professors were stripped of their degrees and titles, banned from ever being in positions of power again. The Searchers were forced to hand over all weapons and to provide the special board with any and all knowledge of the kidnappings, disappearances, murders, and memory erasures they had perpetrated over the years.

The result of those interviews was a harrowing collection of volumes listing too many evils to comprehend. The white fire and the deighilt were taken from the hooded monitors, who were also banned from any positions and forced to write detailed confessions. The battalion soldiers ceded their armor to the city. The Sentinels were shut down and hidden away where they couldn't hurt anyone ever again.

The trials took place over the weeks and the information that came out during those days was sickening. All of the people who had been willingly involved in Chancellor Mharú's crimes were sentenced to prison, without any possibility of ever being released. In fact, they were sent to a holding facility until the dragonborn could help the city finish constructing a special prison with defenses that couldn't hope to be outsmarted. Where they were going, there was no hope. Yet many thought they were still getting off easy; after all, if it hadn't been for Saeryn all the conspirators would have been guilty of the murder of an entire city. Approximately six million people. In an odd turn of events, the dragonborn and members of the local police force had to protect the conspirators, lest the civilians have their way with them.

The city had a hard time rebuilding itself. Saeryn and the dragonborn had given them back their lives, but there was still a lot of physical damage to the city. The chancellor's final wave of magic, having been amplified enormously by his armor, had destroyed and completely blown out a number of buildings and he had already begun a widespread demolition of parts of the city in order to expand the new military University. Much had to be reconstructed and much could never hope to be salvaged.

The University also had to be remodeled, stripped of all its propaganda and military aspirations. The chancellor had certainly left his mark on everything he touched and there was no denying that the people had a long way to go before they could rediscover normal.

Chancellor of West Noelle, Myamar Mharú, became a name no one even whispered. His image and likeness was taken off of every wall, tossed out of every building, burned in the middle of the streets in large piles that burned all night and smoked all morning. His many laws and edicts were struck from the books and every office he had in the University or the city was cleaned out, destroyed and redesigned. Everything he'd left his mark or imprint on was destroyed and they performed this action again and again and again, all throughout the University and the city, until every trace of him was removed.

The board decided to keep a special section with files on the chancellor and the horrors he had committed—they never wanted history to repeat itself. The costs would be too high.

A search began for the soldiers that got away. Some of the men Andie had fought on the train were caught and imprisoned, but according to the battalion's register quite a few got away. Some men had escaped during the night, but a large group of others had already been stationed at the edge of the city. By the time the dragonborn got there, the building was empty.

A wider search began throughout the region, but no one had the first idea about where those men had gone. Many feared that Ashur would lead them back and another war would begin. It was made an even greater fear by Saeryn vowing to never again abuse the magic of blood and dragons to tempt fate. If anything like this ever happened again, the city would be in huge trouble.

Yet the hardest chore of all was trying to decide how they would convince the rest of Noelle that the dragonborn were not only not a threat, but were allies. Saeryn was asked to send more telepathic messages, but she declined—she knew that the messages only worked the first time because those people in the city had seen firsthand what kind of man the chancellor was and she had brought them all back to life. Without those particular circumstances, the messages would only be seen as more lies.

They thought it might be a good idea to send ambassadors, a mix of dragonborn and the most respected citizens of Arvall; perhaps a delegation of that composition would be well received, or at least *received* in the first place, and have a fighting chance at changing people's mind. There was also talk of simply inviting people to Arvall to see the dragonborn in-person, get to know the people and see that they were completely kind and did not have wickedness in their nature. Many more plans were also put forth, but so far nothing had been selected as especially promising.

Raesh and the others from the Hot Salts of Mithraldia had not yet arrived, but were hopefully only a few days out. It had taken so long because a sturdy ship had to be found that could survive the Gray Fold. It took that ship four weeks to reach the group where they were and would take even longer to get back. Several messages had been sent with the crew of the ship for the fighters, and news of the dragonborn victory elated them to no end. Instructions were also sent and Lymir began to prepare in earnest for his new position.

Many of the fighters were ecstatic to be going home and to not have to fight, but there were still some concerns. A faction of them decided to go off on foot and look for the remainder of the battalion, taking some supplies from the new ship and saying goodbye to their friends. Kent and Lilja were among those who left. Lilja feared what might happen to her if she ever went back to Arvall; she was not convinced that she would be forgiven or pardoned, even though Raesh gave her his word. Kent went with her to keep her company and keep her strong.

Everyone else who had been seriously injured in the explosion had woken up by the time the ship arrived. Except Carmen. Her condition was stable and her health hadn't deteriorated any further, but something was clearly wrong. Everyone else was awake and for some reason Carmen simply wasn't responding. They were hoping that something could be done for her in Arvall or that Saeryn might be able to help her.

They set sail from the Hot Salts loaded down with provisions from the dragonborn people and a flurry of good wishes. The dragonborn were sad to see them go: the two races had learned a lot from each other in the weeks the fighters were among them.

Since the University was going to be all-inclusive

now, Raesh had offered himself as an instructor. He thought he might teach classes for people without the gift of magic—though he himself was a pearlblood, he'd spent most of his life pretending to be human and was probably the most qualified to teach those classes. He wanted to help people, but he also wanted another direction for his life. Fighting and secrets and death had had a hold over him for too long. He wanted to be something his father would have been proud of. He wanted to do something good, something worth remembering.

He also wanted to finally publish his books, something he knew he should have done long ago, but hesitation was behind him now. The only other thing he wanted was Andie. They had been apart so much lately and it was as painful to him as watching his friends die. He needed her in ways he couldn't explain and he only hoped she felt the same way.

There was peace all around.

The only person who wasn't doing well was Andie. Not long after they'd defeated the chancellor and his battalion, a messenger bird arrived from the Hot Salts. It carried a torn tear-streaked letter addressed to Andie written in Raesh's messy scribble.

My cousin has yet to wake up.

The traitor has been executed.

Your father has passed on.

Andie had to reread the message multiple times before she could fully comprehend what the letter was telling her. Her vision swam and her mind worked a league a minute as she processed her thoughts. Carmen was in a coma and Marvo had been executed. Well, not really, she thought, as he had blown himself up in his attack. But her eyes filled with tears as she read that last line over and over. Her father was dead. Her chest felt like it was going to implode. She wasn't sure her body was able to take the news. Grief filled her very core and she began to shake, not wanting to accept the words as true. She had just lost a part of her.

Your father has passed on.

She didn't want to believe it. He had looked to be doing so much better. No, she couldn't believe it. She… Andie then read the line before it and dropped the letter on the floor.

The traitor has been executed.

Andie flustered, trying to recall the events of the past few days. Everything had happened so fast. The attacks, the magic, the death, the new life. She tried so desperately to remember her interactions with Raesh back at the ship, but she quickly realized she hadn't communicated with him or anybody else since discovering the truth.

"Yara," Andie whispered as she fell to her knees.

Marvo was the traitor, not Yara. Marvo was the one who betrayed them all, although not knowingly. It had been he who had been spelled, or so the chancellor had said. Raesh wouldn't have known the truth. But everyone at the ship would still think Yara to be the one who betrayed them. Yara wasn't the traitor. Yara was innocent.

Yara was dead.

For days on end, Andie refused to come out of the room they'd set up for her in the city. She couldn't face herself after what she'd done. Her best friend was killed because Andie was too blinded by anger to bother confirming her suspicions. She had been killed for nothing. Andie couldn't look herself in the mirror, let alone face anybody else. She felt broken. Betrayed by her own actions. She could never forgive herself.

What was worse, is that beyond the anger and grief and self-loathing, she had an irreparable sadness for the loss of her father. A sadness she felt was unfair for her to feel, as how can someone who had done something so terrible be allowed to feel sorry for herself like she was. But still, despite her fierce determination to not allow herself to feel the sorrow that came from a parent's death, she still mourned.

Her father had been seriously injured, and he had given her the signs. She could have done something to prevent him from getting worse, but she didn't. She left. He mentioned something about a headache and dizziness. Now he was dead, too, and it was all because of her.

Carmen was just as tragic a thought. She should never had been in that cell, anyway, and if she hadn't been so close to Marvo, she would still be conscious. Maybe even unharmed. She had taken Andie under her wing at the Academy and had shown her how to have fun and enjoy life. Now she was lying in a coma and there were no signs that she was ever going to wake up.

Andie cursed herself for ever even doubting Carmen, for not believing in her and in the person that she had already proven herself to be. It was far, far less than a true friend and ally deserved. And now Andie was left with nothing but a collection of bitter memories that was made even more painful by how sweet and beautiful they were.

Andie couldn't stand herself. She felt sick, trapped inside the body of someone who had betrayed her friends and family. It was her fault that they were gone. She could never forgive herself for it.

The days passed. And then the weeks. Soon enough a new year had come around and the University was getting very close to its reopening. The rebuilding of the city had come quite a long way, though there was still much work to be done.

Still, the city was alive again. The people were happy, excited about the future. The dragonborn were still living on Brie, for the time being, and the ship was only a few days out from arriving at the port. Everything seemed to be advancing. Everyone seemed to be moving on.

Everyone, part from Andie.

CHAPTER TWENTY-FOUR

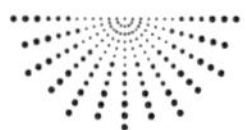

"THIS ISN'T HEALTHY," OREN SAID, PACING BACK AND forth. Since arriving back from spending some time on the ship with their allies he had been trying to speak with Andie, but she hadn't allowed any visitors. He was growing impatient. "I've worried for her before, but never like this. When it came to the University and the chancellor's many plots, she at least immersed herself in the support system around her. She allowed each of us to do our parts and in the end we succeeded. But she's changed. It's as if she thinks she's alone now and she won't speak to anyone. She barely even looks at you, and you're the one person she looks up to."

"It was a victory for us, Oren," Saeryn said softly. "But it was hard-won. The people of Arvall were all dead, she'd failed to save them. We managed to give them back their lives, but at great cost to our strength. Even I didn't think we could have managed such a feat. Our beloved dragons gave them a second chance, despite the hate and evil that they had harbored for us before. But Andie's friends, the fighters who left home and aligned themselves to our cause, they all died. And no one was there to revive them."

"She must surely see the good in what she's done, though?" Oren finally stopped pacing and faced his Queen. "Surely she knows the deaths are not her fault."

"Her own father died," she replied. "Her best friend is lost. Another is still sick. It must be hard on her to understand how all this was fair. She must also be thinking about how awful things would have been if the chancellor won, which he very nearly did. And now she's supposed to teach in the very same building that housed the people who hated her most?"

Oren slumped against the wall. He wore casual linens now, no longer requiring his dragon-scaled armor his people were renowned for. He was growing used to the simple life among the people in their strange, modern time. "I suppose it has been far harder on her than on anyone else."

"She still believes it's her responsibility to save the world. She's only just learning that we can't save everyone, even if we're only trying to protect the ones we love. Even in a war with an outcome as favorable as this there are consequences. I only wish she wasn't the one who had to suffer them. She still believes she failed in regards to her father and her friends."

"Is it her father that has gotten to her the most?"

Saeryn shrugged. "Perhaps. Although she does not seem one to lose herself to grief so strongly. No, I suspect it is her involvement in the loss of her friend that is eating away at her. Yara, the girl we punished for being the traitor."

"I must speak to her about that," Oren said suddenly. "She knows not the truth of what happened."

Saeryn considered. "Perhaps that is wise. But not just this moment. We have things we need to attend to."

Saeryn and Oren turned and headed back into the University to finish overseeing the new design. Saeryn was met almost immediately by one of the other members of the board. He name was Stefan. He had been invited to Arvall City from Taline to the north. Now that the chancellor's personal files had been opened and reviewed, it had been revealed that the University was responsible for every terrorist attack in Taline for the last twenty years. Chancellor Mharú's unbelievable crimes had nearly destroyed the city that Stefan had worked so hard to protect. The other board members thought it only right that Stefan should be invited to the city to help define its new direction. He and Saeryn had become fast friends.

"It's a relief to know that something good is finally going to come from this place," he said. "I've spent so many years wondering if or how Myamar was responsible for the tragedies that have plagued my city. Now I know."

"That one man did a great deal of evil against us all," Saeryn replied. "But he's gone now."

"And for that I'm grateful. I understand that Andie Rogers is the girl I should thank for finally setting the world back on course."

"Indeed, she is."

"I was once on the council of Taline with her father. He was a good man. I was sorry to hear that he passed. I'm afraid I was once as nearsighted as the rest of the region. I regret it, but I had been taught that the dragonborn were evil, not to be trusted. I nearly harmed him and his wife once. You can imagine my shock and sadness when I learned later that she had been taken that very same night."

"The fact that you are here now tells me everything I need to know about you. My people and I are not in the habit of holding onto past grudges."

"That helps me a great deal to know. But I wonder about Andie. I can't imagine what stories her father told her about me. I was never very open with him, but it was only because I took our sworn duty so seriously. I always thought very highly of him. And I never forgot the face of his wife, that beautiful woman who was so atrociously mistreated. I never met Andie. I'd like to meet her now. Soon, if she'd be up for it."

"I'm sure she will in time," Saeryn said with a heavy sigh. "But right now, she is coming to terms with the terrible weight of her losses. Many lives and many dreams had to be sacrificed for this victory, and no one has had to bear the brunt of that pain more than Andie. But I will make sure she knows your intentions."

Stefan gave Saeryn a terrifically honorable bow and then disappeared down another hallway. Saeryn continued forward, lending her expertise wherever it was needed and stopping every so often just to encourage and reassure people. It was hard work and had taken a lot of effort, and would require still more later.

Saeryn had offered any number of times to assist them, to help in any way she could, but the citizens thought her position as Queen was too majestic for menial chores. She tried explaining to them that among the dragonborn not even the Queen is above contributions and that she was no stranger to hard work, but they wouldn't listen. They were just trying to pay her back in the only way they knew they could. And so, she fulfilled the role they crafted for her and made sure she was always around to boost morale.

The dragonborn and the citizens were learning so much from coexisting, from leaving behind hate and moving forward in peace. The new spirit of cooperation would be reflected in all of the new paintings, decorations, and especially in the course selection for the new classes. Some dragonborn had even been asked to remain in Arvall City and teach classes at the University, while some of the scholars and researchers from Arvall had been invited to the Hot Salts to live among the dragonborn and learn more.

Saeryn continued down into the very bowels of the University, where the corridors were. They were still in the process of removing the University's heartless celebration of all the death and pain it had caused. Instead, the walls would be covered in an iridescent mural telling the history and struggle of the dragonborn people. The mural had already begun in some parts and when it was finished would be leagues long. She stayed to watch some of the painting and then left, on to supervise other tasks and lift other spirits.

Saeryn was happy. She knew she was happy and she knew that the only thing that could make it better was to see Andie happy. Her people were finally safe, finally accepted, and she wanted Andie to share in that more than anyone, because it was Andie who had lived alone all those years, without her mother, without her people, and it was time she knew the life she should have had all along. When she was done in the University, Saeryn boarded SKY 6—which had been rebuilt for a second time and hopefully the last—and rode down Brie.

Traveling on the dragon was faster, and, like all

dragonborn, Saeryn loved the open air and the sun on her skin, but she was also in awe of the modern technology. When she reached the bottom, she walked directly over to the place where Andie was staying—the place she hardly ever came out of. Saeryn walked right up to the door and rather than knock, she simply spoke.

"Andie, it's me. May I come in?"

"Why not?"

It was as melancholy an answer as she had ever heard, but perfectly in line with what Andie had become. Saeryn opened the door to the building and was immediately met with the smell of soldering ash. She quickly looked around to make sure nothing was burning, but when she saw Andie sitting calmly in the middle of the floor she calmed some. She walked further inside and looked around. The room was filled with books, almost the entire floor was covered with them.

Andie had no furniture, no appliances, just books in every direction. There were piles on the stairs and piles in the kitchen. Andie herself was surrounded by small piles and individual books laid out with their insides exposed. The books looked ancient, so old in fact that some were showing warnings that they were preparing to fall apart. Saeryn's first instinct was to ask what Andie was doing, but she could well imagine what kind of answer that would get her. Instead, she sat down beside Andie and said nothing.

"To what new catastrophe do I owe this visit?" Andie asked, never looking up from her book. "Another one of my friends die?"

Saeryn didn't say anything. She merely kept sitting and looking around her.

"Look, if you're here for another heart-to-heart I appreciate it, but it's not what I need right now."

Still nothing. Andie began to get annoyed.

"I know you only want the best for me, and I know that seeing me in pain isn't easy for you, but please... Saeryn, you're really freaking me out just sitting there looking around like that."

"You have my blood."

Finally, Andie looked up. She thought she'd misheard Saeryn or maybe misunderstood what she meant.

"What?" she asked. "What did you say?"

"You have my blood."

"What do you mean?"

"It is common knowledge about our heritage among the dragonborn, but perhaps that knowledge got wiped away as the years passed and the sorcerers destroyed our books and our histories in your world. It is the coloring that gives it away."

"Coloring? What do you mean?" She was curious but also disinterested. She ran her fingers along the floor as she listened, partially lost in her own thoughts.

Saeryn reached out and stroked Andie's unkempt amethyst hair. "Each family shares a coloring, Andryne."

Andie's attention snapped back up at the sound of her full name. She considered what Saeryn was saying and realization slowly dawned on her. She gazed forward at Saeryn's beautiful, silken magenta hair. "We share the same coloring."

Saeryn nodded and smiled. "Not only that, but a dragon does not just let anyone ride it. There are only two instances a dragon allows a rider on its back who is not its rightful pair. The first, is if you are family, related to the rider."

Andie considered a moment and nodded. "That explains why I rode your dragon, I suppose. What about Oren's?" The mere thought of Oren's name send a shiver up her spine. She tried to push the thought of him and his dragon away, but all she could see now was the memory of his beast taking Yara away.

Saeryn tilted Andie's chin up so they locked eyes. "The second, is if that rider is of royal blood. A dragon will allow the royal lineage to ride its back, regardless of who their true rider is. I'll admit I don't fully understand it, but it dates back to the earliest days when the dragons first roamed the earth and we first bonded with the magnificent creatures. I believe our family, the royal line, were the first to bond with the dragons."

Andie stared wide-eyed at Saeryn, her thoughts working wildly as she tried to grasp what she was hearing. "But I don't understand. How can that be?"

"I believe we are from the same lineage."

"I… What? But you're from over one thousand years before. What does this even mean?"

"It means, my sweet Andryne. That you are born to be the dragonborn Queen. You are my heir."

Andie swallowed hard and shook her head. "Impossible. I'm no Queen. I'm a murderer… I couldn't even save my friends. I have no right to any throne."

"Andie, you are my blood. Whether you chose to accept this or not, you are a dragonborn ruler. One day you will be the Queen of the dragonborn."

Andie was dumbfounded and she almost fell over from the shock. She wasn't exactly happy or sad or angry or anything. With all the joy she felt at having beaten the University and the pain she felt at having lost so much and so many, she hadn't really known how she felt in weeks. She was completely convoluted inside. And now Saeryn was telling her that she was royalty and would be Queen someday. Queen. She wondered if it was good news, if it was bad news, or if it was just one more thing she had to consider her duty to fulfill.

"Andie, the first thing you need to understand is how happy I am to know that you are my blood and how proud I am of everything that you have done, every trial and hardship that you have battled through to be here today. You are so strong it makes my heart burst to look at you. But the time for your self-pity is at an end. I have allowed you to grieve as much as I felt necessary, but now you must hold fast and gather your courage. There is a long road ahead and millions of people in this city and in this region will be looking for someone to lead them, someone to make them believe again. The dragonborn want someone to be a link between their world and this new one that we find ourselves flung into. I want with all my soul for that person to be you.

"I know what you've lost and I know that it hurts unlike any other pain you're ever likely to feel again, but what is done cannot be undone. We have all suffered a great deal. The other dragonborn suffered these same losses centuries ago when the war against us first began. Yet here we stand. You are royalty. And, far more than simply a silly title, being royalty means leading, inspiring, and protecting. You cannot allow yourself to be this person that you've become. You mean too much to too many people. I need you too much to watch you whither like this."

Saeryn touched Andie's face and wiped the tears that

had begun to fall. Andie was hurting so deeply inside that there didn't seem an end to the pain, but she knew Saeryn was right. She had known it for quite some time now. She recognized that none of her pain would ever fully be healed, but there would come a point when she would have to focus, to pick herself up and go on with the business of living. That point had come. If the dragonborn needed her, if Arvall City needed her, she would be there.

"Of course," Andie said. "Back in the Hot Salts, Oren looked shocked when his dragon let me ride her. It all makes sense now. But I still don't think I…"

"You are the strongest person I've met. Not only that, but you are unique. You represent everything this world needs right now. You are sorcerer and you are dragonborn. There is no one better to represent our people in this new era of peace."

The words were too much for her to handle, but Andie knew it was her duty to stay strong. To stay true to herself, and part of her always knew there was more to this life than what she had grown up believing. Finally, she nodded. Accepting her fate as best she could, given the circumstances.

"So, what happens now? Do the rest of our people know that I'm your heir?"

"Well, I haven't made a formal pronouncement, but I'm sure once they saw you riding my dragon they figured it out. I can assure you, this news will please them all. I don't know if you yet understand how much the people love you. You've done more for them than you know."

"I'm just glad to have them."

"Good. Now that we've come to an understanding,

there are things we should talk about. But first, Oren wants to speak with you."

Anger flashed across Andie's face at the mention of his name. "No, I will not see him."

"Andie, he has information you need to know. Information that I think will lighten your heart and help you move on from the darkness that has bound you to this room for all these months. You must hear him." Saeryn placed her hand on Andie's cheek as she spoke, and when Andie didn't respond, she turned to leave the room and Oren stepped through the door in her place.

"Say whatever it is you have to say and then leave," Andie said coolly. "I have nothing I want to say to you."

Oren narrowed his brow as he looked down at Andie on the floor, but he quickly closed door and joined her in the center of the room. It took him a long while to collect his thoughts, but when he finally spoke, his voice held warmth and compassion.

"Andie, about Yara," he began.

Andie's heart beat wildly in her chest as she listened. Her best friend, Yara. Mistaken for a traitor and wrongfully executed at the hands of the man before her. She hated him almost as much as she hated herself. "Speak."

"It is not the dragonborn way to kill. It was my duty to deal with the traitor, but when the time came, I was unable to see it through."

Andie sat up straighter, frozen in place. What had he just said?

Oren continued, "I sent her through a time spell. I couldn't be responsible for killing one of our own, so I sent her through a portal, back towards where I once came."

Andie's mouth hung open. "You didn't kill her." She could hardly believe her ears. She pushed herself up off the floor and began to pace the room, repeating the words to herself. She turned to Oren abruptly and froze again in place. "So, she's alive?"

Oren nodded solemnly and held his hand on Andie's shoulder. "She is. Just not in our time. Andie, Yara is gone. It is best not to dwell on it, but I hope that knowing she was not killed brings you some peace."

Andie's eyes filled with tears as she flung her arms around the man before her. He stood there, awkward for a moment, but then wrapped his arms around her and held her close as she wept. The two stood there in their embrace for many long minutes until Andie finally regained her breath and wiped away the tears.

"Thank you, Oren." She unwound herself from his arms and stepped back from him, letting out a deep breath she had been holding. "Thank you."

Oren nodded and turned to leave. He turned back to look at her as he held the door open. "You will make a great ruler, Andie. I am honored to serve you." And with that, he walked out of her room and Andie listened to his footsteps as they disappeared into the silence.

A moment later, Saeryn rejoined Andie in her room. Andie beamed at the Queen, the weight of guilt finally lifted from her heart. But her smile was short-lived as she recognized the pain in Saeryn's eyes.

Saeryn took a deep breath and looked down at her hands for a moment. It was a thing she rarely did, a gesture of hesitation. Generally, she was a woman of action and conviction. If there was something she was having trouble saying to Andie, it couldn't be good.

"As you know, we've sent out warriors to track down

the rest of the battalion, but so far we haven't had any luck. However, this morning those warriors came back with news of a different problem. As they were flying back over the String Fields to reenter the city, there was a message burned in the fields."

"What did it say?"

"*Fhealltóir Fola*. It means blood traitor and it is from a language that is no longer spoken in your era. I think convincing the rest of Noelle is going to be a much larger issue than we initially believed. Before the University attacked us, there were others who either envied us or sought our power. And none of them was so darkly vicious as a certain group from the north. They haunted us and tormented us in ways the University couldn't even dream of. When the University finally did begin to come after us, this group disappeared. We assumed they'd moved out of Noelle or died off. But this message was their calling card once upon a time and it is a phrase only they or a dragonborn would know."

"Do you think they've been hiding all these years?"

"Why not? The world assumed we were dead and yet here we are. Why should they be any different? Andie, if these people are still alive, then there are no doubts about it. There will be war. And much of it."

"That's the last thing we need. They've got to be close. The String Fields border Arvall on the eastern side. That's just outside of the city."

"And make no mistake. They will come."

Andie looked around her at her books. She looked back up at Saeryn with a devilish grin.

"Then let them come."

"What?" Saeryn said, shocked. "Andie, I don't think you understand."

"Look to your right. Pick up one of those thin volumes in the far pile."

Saeryn turned and reached for the book. She brought it into her lap and began to study it. It wasn't until she opened the cover that she gasped.

"This is a journal from the House Erato, one of the seven founding families of Arvall!" she said, turning it over in her hands and observing every inch of it. "This is incredible. Where did you find such a thing?"

"In Leabharlann. Now that we have unrestricted access, I'm finding all kinds of things you wouldn't believe. I have journals from all seven of the founding families and I've been studying them. You won't believe the secrets they were keeping, even from each other. Even within the families there was strife. But what's most interesting is that of all the visits they made to study the past and to visit different places in their contemporary time, they only made one journey to the future. And you can't imagine what they found."

"What?"

"That's a long story. But look around you again and this time look closely."

Saeryn began to look at the books again, everyone within reach. She peered closer and began to read the names and the dates. As she did so, she began to move faster and faster getting more and more excited and falling further and further into disbelief. Her heart was racing and Andie could hear her breath changing. Finally, Saeryn looked back at Andie.

"They're grimoires! Our grimoires!"

"These were stolen from the dragonborn and they date back almost a thousand years," Andie said. "And the University wasn't just stealing from us. They stole from dozens of different tribes and cities. There's more knowledge and power here than any one group of people could ever amass on their own. It's part of why the University became so powerful and they could've been totally unstoppable, but they could never utilize anything from the ones they stole from us. Only someone with dragonblood could use these spells. And more still, there are hundreds, thousands of books in the archives that can tell us everything we need to know to rebuild, to unite, to be as we never were before."

"Andie, why haven't you told anyone about any of this?" Saeryn asked, still pouring over the books. "There's so much knowledge and wisdom here. So much beautiful information."

"I was afraid, at first. Knowledge corrupts, warps. But with your help I can control this. Saeryn, we need specific things to move forward with this."

"Like what?"

"First we'll need professor Marcus Iceubes. He once taught folklore at the University, and he's one of the good guys. Then we'll need salt paint—it's going to help us a long way in our preparations. And finally, I need you to tell me everything you remember about the Old World. We have a lot of work cut out for us, but with the chancellor dead and his weapon destroyed, we have every chance at rebuilding this world into what it was always meant to be."

"And what is that?"

"A place where all races can live together in peace. And a place where dragons can once again fly free in the sky."

EPILOGUE

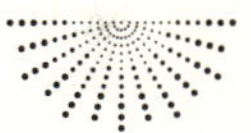

"I THINK HE'S DEAD."

"He's not dead, he's just unconscious. No one is stronger than he is."

"He's dead, look at him. His heart isn't even beating."

"Shut up. We will save him. We just have to get north."

"This is ridiculous. Why are we slowing ourselves down dragging a dead body?"

"I told you, he's not dead. We just need to get there as soon as we can."

"Even if you're right, he's as good as dead. He's been gone for weeks. All I'm trying to say is that we're wasting valuable and limited resources on him and we don't even fully understand what they can even do for him if we get there."

"What they're going to do is save him. They'll put him back together, and between their magic and the power of his suit, we'll save our greatest weapon. He's our leader. And if there's even the slightest chance that we can save him then it's a chance worth taking. And we can always scavenge or take more supplies when we need them."

"He wouldn't want us to be this careless. We're supposed to move every night, but we can't do that and drag him around with us at the same time. So, we move every three nights and that puts the entire group in danger. They've got dragonborn, Council fighters, and who knows who else out looking for us. You really want to try to save a guy who could die from too much motion?"

"If you're so sure he's dead, then why don't you just dump his body and be done with it? But if you're wrong and he does wake up, and he finds out you tried to ditch him, do you think I'm going to stick up for you?"

The other man shut his mouth and looked around himself peevishly. The entire battalion was watching.

"Now, I think you'll agree that it's best to give him a chance. Even if his body is broken and his breath has left him, we saw what their strange magic did to the people of Noelle. It's not impossible to bring someone back from the dead. We need to get him up north where the forces are, or else we have no hope of defeating them and taking back the world. We're done talking about this. Everybody listen up. Get your gear together and let's get on with it. We have a long journey ahead of us if we're going to make it north and have any hope of defeating these damn barbarians and their dragons. I need three guys to help me carry the bed."

"This is ridiculous. I can't believe we're risking our lives dragging his dead body with us."

"He's not dead, I tell ya. Even if his body is, we'll bring him back. We have to. Without him—without our greatest weapon—we have no chance at destroying those beasts once and for all. We have to try."

"I still think we're wasting our time. That suit can only do so much, and his body is barely in one piece. He's gone. We've lost. It's done. The bloody dragonborn have won."

"Shut up and lift the damn bed. Alright everybody, move."

As the group moved onward in the darkness, the form lay wrapped tightly in bandages, his suit barely clinging to what was left of his body. The battalion marched in silence, the echo of their footsteps the only sound in the dark night. On and on they marched, barely stopping to regain their breath and fill their water canisters.

Throughout the entire night, the men pressed on, determined to get their one final weapon to safety. They would bring Ashur's destroyed body to their allies in the north. Their hopes had faded, but not necessarily lost. If they could only make it in time to have him brought back, they had a chance. If anything, they could salvage the suit and create a new weapon, perhaps, although most had already given up that hope.

But as they marched, a shadow stirred. Under the tightly-wrapped linens, the power from the suit reached Ashur's very core. His heart began to beat again, and the silence of the night was pierced with his scream.

Their weapon was alive.

CALLED BY DRAGON'S SONG

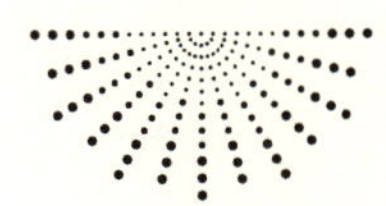

PROLOGUE

SIX JOYFUL YET TRYING MONTHS HAD PASSED SINCE Chancellor Myamar Mharú and his enhanced battalion nearly wiped out Arvall. The city had since been in a state of complete overhaul after learning the truth about the dragonborn and slowly welcoming them. Elections were held and new leaders and officials put in office all over the region. Trials had taken place daily, resulting in a wide range of sentences and revealing just how evil and cruel the University had truly been.

The destruction to the city was unimaginable, and the escaped members of the Chancellor's battalion periodically set off bombs around the city to inspire fear. But things were slowly beginning to improve. Delegations comprised of both Arvall citizens and dragonborn ambassadors were sent out on regular diplomatic assignments to spread the truth about the dragonborn and win people to the cause. Arvall had spent millions of dollars in promoting tourism, inviting people to the city and the region to experience firsthand the magic and kindness of the dragonborn. Though some found it hard or impossible to stop a lifetime's worth of hatred, many hearts were changing. Thousands of hearts were changing. Perhaps even more.

The University was soon to be reopened. Lymir and his entire staff worked tirelessly since their appointments. They were making every effort to make the University a welcoming place to both magical and nonmagical people. New courses and professors were added, and while they've ensured that the University's cruelty will never be forgotten and that future generations will always be taught about the atrocities that the University committed, all courses propagating hate of the dragonborn and dragons were removed. The damage to the building was repaired and the halls were alive with excitement and comradery. The hideous murals celebrating the bloodbath of the dragonborn slaughter had been removed and a new mural celebrating the feats and power of the dragonborn had been painted.

Most promising of all was the integration of the dragonborn into modern society. Since the revelation of the University's lies, the citizens of Arvall had gone out of their way to make the dragonborn feel safe and welcome. Though the home of the dragonborn was still in the Hot Salts of Mithraldia, they frequently came down and sojourned among the citizens to learn and grow. Many dragonborn live temporarily in the caves along Brie Mountain. The citizens have also learned a tremendous amount of knowledge and wisdom from the dragonborn. There had been skirmishes when visitors balked at the idea of the dragonborn coexisting in the modern world; several small factions from other parts of Noelle had come to Arvall City to attack or otherwise provoke the dragonborn and prove that they truly are evil. Yet, for the first time in nearly a thousand years, dragons and dragonborn lived among everyone else and could do so freely. Happily.

It was widely known as "The Great Peace," the first time in the history of Noelle that so many cities and regions have ceased competition and came under one banner of understanding.

CHAPTER ONE

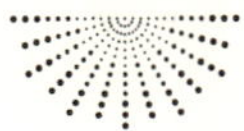

A battalion soldier held him under either arm as Ashur took his first steps since that fateful night six months prior. He grew furious with each step, knowing that the soldiers at his sides were doing most of the work, but he could barely hold his own head. His legs felt like lead weights and the pain was indescribable. He only had the strength not to scream; the last thing he could afford was to look even weaker. The battalion was incredibly loyal to him, but he didn't want to test that. It had already been months since they'd had a decent meal, shelter fit for human beings, and even longer since they'd been able to lead normal lives.

"Great work, my leader," a soldier said. "You'll be doing this unaided soon."

"Yes, very admirable, my leader," said another.

Their praise made Ashur angrier because he knew they were lying. He shoved them both off and fell to the ground. They tried to pick him up, but he held up his hand to stop them. Then he began the slow process of standing up, which he hadn't done in months. The pain was agonizing and his head ached so much he thought it might split. His arms and legs shook under the strain of trying to raise himself and already he sweated heavily. But, one thing he could not allow himself to do was quit. He focused his mind, drawing a picture to himself of his goal, his most desperate desire. He let that picture fuel his body. He pushed himself up and with a final furious heave, he stood on his legs by his own power.

"Incredible!" someone said. "The doc said he wouldn't be able to stand on his own for weeks!"

"No doctor has a clue what our leader is capable of," said Lucas. "He is the future."

The battalion saluted Ashur as he trembled on his feet. He felt some small amount of pride return to him as he balanced there, thinking that this weakened state was not him, but Tarven. It reminded him of who and what he used to be. But he focused again, envisioning the picture in his mind that had driven him since he first opened his eyes on the operating table. A field covered in the bloody corpses of the dragonborn, Andie Rogers' head in his hand.

ANDIE STOOD in the May Cave, high in the mountains in the Hot Salts of Mithraldia. The day of the ceremony finally arrived and she was more nervous than she thought she'd be. She lived among her own people for a while, but still felt like an outsider. They had welcomed her with open arms, but their experiences had been so different she still found it hard to relate to them sometimes. That aside, she felt more at home than ever. She opened herself to every aspect of their way of life and she learned and grew so much among them. On this day they honored her, again, for her actions the night of the confrontation in Arvall, which most of Noelle now called the "Night of Revelation." All she knew about the ceremony was that the dragonborn presented her with a very great, very precious gift. Apparently, it was extremely rare and an honor of the highest degree. As Andie stood, waiting, she saw Saeryn coming toward her.

"Saeryn," Andie called, giving a low bow.

"Princess Andie," Saeryn responded with a smile.

They hugged and Saeryn led Andie through the crowd, toward the center of the cave where a dais had been set up.

"I'm sure you must have a lot of questions," Saeryn said.

"I always have questions about everything the dragonborn do, but what I'm really wondering is why I'm being honored... again."

"I know it must seem a bit... overzealous of us, but you quite literally saved our lives, Andie. Again. There's no amount of gifts or honors or ceremonies that could repay that debt, though I assure you this is the last. At least until you save our lives again. The dragonborn are a respectful and thankful people. Admittedly, we do tend to overexert ourselves in our gratefulness. But I want you to know that no matter how uncomfortable you feel and no matter what you may think of the ceremony or your own worth, you have earned this honor. It is rightfully yours and you should embrace it."

"I'll do my best. To be honest, I wish I could honor you and our people. You're telling me about unpayable debts, but you and the dragonborn have finally given me a home, finally made me feel like I belong. For years I lived in fear, in a world that hated me and would have executed me if they knew what I was. When you and our people came, you saved me. So as far as incredible debts go, I think we're even."

The two of them arrived at the dais just as the elders did. All around them were the dragonborn who gathered with smiles of joy to see their princess honored. Many had come back from Arvall just for this occasion. A buzz of expectation and low chatter hung over the setting. While she waited, Andie glanced around the cave.

When a person heard of the dragonborn living in a cave, their first reaction is bafflement. No one understood how a people as powerful and beautiful as the dragonborn could allow themselves to live in caves. But the caves were just the beginning. Not only do the dragonborn spend countless hours making perfect networks of tunnels, they also improved the caves; it wasn't quite decorating, but a dragonborn cave was no dank, dark cubby.

The dragonborn used their magic and traditions to smooth and shape the walls, level the floors, and purify the air. They spent countless days casting spells against cold, sickness, insects, weak foundation, and more. The dragonborn were also gifted craftsmen and artisans, and could make the most beautiful fixtures, ornaments, and furniture. One of the greatest tools they had was the fire of their dragons. They brought the dragons into the caves and had them breathe fire against the walls while they cast magic at the same time. They called it "waking," literally bringing the cave to life. Waking left the cave walls pearlescent and color-changing. The first time Andie saw it she nearly cried from the beauty.

The May Cave was the central cave, the largest and highest in the network, and the only cave that could hold all of the dragonborn at once. It was used for ceremonies, meetings, and other important events. Andie gazed at its shimmering walls and perfectly smooth surfaces. Its absolutely clear air and the brilliant, yet soft light that emanated from the walls. It seemed a crime to call it a cave.

"I believe we're all here," Saeryn said. "Perhaps we should get started."

Silence followed her voice as if she had released a command. Every eye looked up at the Queen, who looked as beautiful and regal as ever. Saeryn turned to Andie and gestured for her to join her at the front of the dais. Andie went over, nervous. A vigorous applause sounded as she took her place beside the Queen.

"We have gathered this afternoon to pay homage, yet again, to our princess and hero, Andryne Rogers. She's lived among us for a while now and I believe I speak for every soul here when I say we are proud and humbled to have her. Today the elders and I would like to bestow a gift, one of the rarest and most powerful we could ever give. This is one of our most sacred and heartfelt gifts. Elders, if you will."

The elders moved forward, carrying a chest between them. Regardless of their age, they seemed to handle the large chest with minimal effort. They sat it down beside the feet of the Queen and opened it. They lifted the gift out and held it. Andie couldn't take her eyes off it. A collective gasp made its way through the cave.

"Yes, it is quite extraordinary, if I do say so myself. Such beauty." Saeryn's voice echoed through the cave, overwhelming the silence that fell upon the room. "This is the Aethrailaer. Armor that has not been seen or made in many centuries. This kind of armor is made by taking a few scales from every living dragon and combining them on a gold and iron frame. Only scales that have naturally fallen can be used. As you can imagine, in the old times all the dragons were hardly ever in the same place and scales disintegrate so easily if they are not quickly preserved. We started on this as soon as we landed in the Hot Salts after leaving the portal and now it's finally ready. Andryne, this is from all of us."

The elders presented the armor to Andie. She reached out to take it, her face a reflection of pure awe and joy. It was heavier than it looked. The scales had been tightly, seamlessly woven together over a golden frame. It was clearly magical craftmanship, unlike anything Andie had ever seen. The gold frame had been enchanted and was not only flexible, but also shimmered in response to Andie's touch. The scales themselves were the same beautiful, iridescent sheen as when they were on the dragons' backs. The working and design of the armor was flawless, the most exquisite she'd ever seen.

"Thank you for this," Andie whispered through a clenched throat. She was speechless. Tears threatened to spill from her lids as she stared down at the remarkable beauty of the armor. It took her a long moment to collect her thoughts enough to speak. "I know you all want to congratulate me and praise me for bringing peace to our world. And maybe I did. But I owe you just as much, and I plan to repay that debt by being worthy of this armor and never failing you. It'll be a dark day if I ever need this, but it's a beautiful and peerless gift. I'm going to display it near my office at the University. Thank you."

Everyone applauded. Andie did, too. She had never

felt prouder. Saeryn hugged her again and then each of the ten elders shook her hand.

"Alright, everyone. I promised Andie this would be a brief, yet sincere ceremony and I believe we've thanked her enough for today. Thank you all for coming out and please go in peace."

The dragonborn gave their last smiles to Andie and drifted out of the room. The elders offered her some encouraging words and they left, too. Andie and Saeryn turned and descended the dais, heading into the tunnel that led out high onto the west side of the mountain. They came out into the open air. Dragons swooped above them and below was a field of clouds hiding the raging storms that ceaselessly plagued the region.

"Now that we're alone, we need to talk about Arvall," Andie said. "I just got another letter from Marcus. He said 'Fhealltóir Fola' is beginning to show up a lot more around the city and its outlying districts. The more they look into it, the less sure they are about who's really setting off these bombs. It might be the battalion or it might be the ancient enemy of our people. The Beautiful Dead. I think it's safe to assume that they're still around and still angry."

"Yes, it seems that for all our kindness and patient ways, we dragonborn cannot help making the worst enemies imaginable. Make no mistake, though the name of this group may sound attractive, there is nothing gentle in their methods. They are a darker enemy than anyone should have to face."

"Why do they call you blood traitors?"

"We share a common ancestor."

"Another ancient people?"

"Dragons. You see the University became so

obsessed with rewriting history in order to eradicate our people that they left out the other half of our origin story. A second group of people were descended from the great dragons. The Beautiful Dead are actually somewhat older than us. When their people came into existence, they had no magic. They were incredibly strong, fast, agile. They had heightened senses and hunting abilities. While we obtained our magic from the dragons, the Beautiful Dead acquired physical attributes. They are absolutely lethal.

"Then the dragonborn came along and were given the gift of magic. This drove our older brothers insane with jealousy. They didn't just want physical abilities, they wanted the power to cast spells as well. It wasn't long before they discovered that by drinking our blood they could obtain our magic. The Beautiful Dead are aggressive and belligerent by nature, and we knew that if they ever obtained our power there would be no stopping them. They would consume the world. So, we fought them. For centuries. It wasn't until my great grandfather came along that we finally defeated them. He was a powerful sorcerer and he devised a spell that would bind their blood, so that even if they drank from us they would never obtain our magic. And that spell is never-ending so long as the corresponding bloodline in our people is protected."

"Let me guess... that bloodline is ours?"

"I'm afraid so."

"Super."

"Whoever is left of our line must be protected at all costs."

"The whole blood traitor thing makes sense now. Looks like we have another battle on our hands.

Fortunately, you and I have been studying the grimoires for months."

"And learned a considerable amount."

"So, there's the Beautiful Dead, the Battalion, and a host of other smaller threats, and we have no idea where any of them are or what they're planning. It's going to be a long year."

A messenger came running from the caves. He bowed and handed the letter to Saeryn. After reading it, Saeryn looked at Andie solemnly.

"It's another warning from your Professor Marcus," she said. "They're still finding bombs, though thankfully no more have gone off. He's also warning us that the city has been getting a lot of rather serious threats from eastern Noelle."

"Well, we always knew we had our work cut out for us," Andie said, gripping her armor tighter. "We'll deal with them as they come. Right now, we need to get ready to fly to Arvall. If we leave by dusk we can make it to the ceremony."

CHAPTER TWO

ANDIE, SAERYN, AND LYMIR STOOD WITH THE REST OF the faculty and staff of the University. The day had finally come to reopen the institution under its new mission.

Lymir stepped forward and began his speech, but Andie was too busy to listen. She and the other high members of the University had received an onslaught of angry, vengeful letters in the preceding days. Some had been mere reminders of how eastern Noelle felt, but others had been too evil to ignore. Precautions, both tactical and magical, had been taken to make sure that nothing happened on the first day. The police force of Arvall were also called to help keep the peace. Still, just that morning Andie received a letter demanding they close the school or risk being attacked. The letter threatened that the dragonborn and dragons would be eradicated for good. It was signed by the battalion.

Andie knew that wherever he was, Ashur was plotting his revenge. Saeryn thought it best not to tell the people about the letters. The other members agreed. They all believed it was high time they opened the University and set the world back on the right track. Enjoying the era of the Great Peace was just as important as protecting it.

"…which is what we've always wanted," Lymir said. "Finally, the citizens of the world have begun to welcome the dragonborn to live among them and to teach them. I believe the coming days will be the best the world has ever known. While it would be foolish to assume that we can change every heart, I know we can still make this world the place it always should have been and that starts today, with reopening of the University. Once a stark symbol of oppression and murder, this institution will now be dedicated to helping any and all who walk through its doors. We will educate…"

Andie couldn't leave her place on the podium, but she focused all of her attention on surveying the crowd and the area. She was almost certain this was a mistake; they'd risked all these lives and the reopening of the University just so they could show that they were strong. She wondered if that strength would be enough once the bombs began. But before she knew it the audience was clapping, Lymir was done, and the ribbon was cut. The ceremony was complete and confetti and balloons rained down.

Andie turned to Saeryn, who looked just as concerned as she was, and then motioned for them to leave. They smiled and waved to the crowd before hurrying off. Everyone else headed to the front doors to see the University. Oren found his way out of the crowd and over to them, with Lymir close on his heels.

"I can see you were just as anxious as I," Saeryn said to Andie. "I seriously doubted our decision."

"Yeah," Andie responded. "I was sure something awful was going to happen. And I still don't feel comfortable enough to feel safe."

"I have been extremely watchful all morning," Oren said. "I haven't been able to relax for a fortnight and today I seem more suspicious than ever. I don't care to have so many enemies about and to not know where they are or what they want to do."

"I think we're all a little anxious today," Lymir said. "And for good reasons. At least with the University we knew exactly who the enemy was, where they were located, and what they were capable of. We still don't understand the full extent of the battalion's armor or of how the Dead have adapted in the last centuries. And we've received threats from at least two hundred other smaller groups."

"Two hundred?" Saeryn asked.

"The danger is far from over. I still believe Arvall City and the Hot Salts are safe, but for how long? I think it might be best if we sent a party to investigate."

"I would second that," said Oren. "It's time we became more proactive. Our enemies won't dare to show their faces yet, but the more we let them get away with, the more they will attempt. I could lead a party out now."

"I'll go with you," Andie said. "And we can get a couple more dragonborn to fly with us. Saeryn and Lymir could get the Arvall police to increase patrols, at least for tonight. We could leave now and fly north. That seems to be where most of the letters are coming from and the field burnings are in the northern tracts of the String Fields."

"Be careful, princess," said Saeryn.

Saeryn and Lymir turned to search for the police, and Andie and Oren made their way to Oren's dragon. Andie still found herself disappointed that there was not a dragon for her yet, but she had been told to give it more time. She and Oren mounted the dragon and Oren signaled three nearby dragonborn. They all took off. Andie looked back and just before the people were too small to make out anymore, she saw him. Raesh.

THEY FLEW NORTH TO TALINE. They landed at the edge of the city and go on foot. Since the Chancellor and his men were stopped, Taline had finally experienced peace and been allowed the chance to get back on its feet. The city thrived with Stefan's leadership. Andie and Oren met with him to see what news he has.

"We've received some rather cruel sounding missives, but nothing like what you're getting in Arvall," Stefan said. "Honestly, things are quiet here. Without the bombings and destruction that Mharú subjected us to, the city was finally able to rest and come together. We have taken precautions, though. We've strengthened security along Gordric's Pain and set up watchtowers along the silver cliffs. We conduct weekly patrols as far south as Michaelson and as far North as the Church of Stone and Sea. We've tried our best to catch whoever is burning the messages into the String Fields, but they continue to elude us. If you're looking for my opinion on the matter, I agree with you. Whoever your enemies are, they lie to the north. I would suggest you visit the Church. I don't often go on patrols myself, but I happened to go on the last round. I wasn't at all satisfied with their behavior.

The Church has always been... odd, but this was something else entirely. You could do worse than to investigate there."

THEY LEFT Taline and flew all night and all morning until they reached the Church at dawn. Andie had heard many stories of the Church, but nothing could have prepared her for it. The Church of Stone and Sea was exactly what its name described. A sacred house of worship built from the red sand of the very beach on which it stood. Its foundation was made from the last of Noelle's Voldredarian stone—a material as hard as steel, more valuable than gold, and enchanted to sing persuasive hymns to all passersby. Many who stay too long around the Church never leave. The red sand made the Church one of the most beautiful buildings Andie had ever seen, perhaps the only structure that ever rivaled the dragonborn caves. But what was most impressive about this building was not its vermillion walls or even the songs of its stones. It was the sheer size of the structure. The Church was the largest manmade structure in history. It stood at over two hundred meters tall and was more than twenty kilometers long and as many wide. It took over a thousand years to build. Andie was speechless.

"I never knew men could make such things," Oren said.

"You and me both," Andie said, craning her neck. "You never came here before?"

"No. The Church was already completed by the time I grew of age, but the dragonborn have always stayed away from this place. One hears stories of terrible things.

Our people believe this place isn't enchanted, but cursed."

"But it's a church. Right?"

"No, it is much more than that. Inside those walls is an entire culture. They are an entirely different race, completely self-sustaining. Many people who go in never see the light of day again. No one knows what happens to them. And the priests, if they can be called that, are said to be the most dangerous of all, hardly the holy men you might anticipate."

"What's so dangerous about them?"

"I've only heard stories and perhaps none of them were true, but be on guard here, princess. We don't know anything about these people. Can you hear it? The hymn?"

Andie turned her ear to the Church and focused; not only did she hear the hymn, she realized she had been hearing it since she landed. In fact, she even knew the words. The Church had been singing to her ever since she came into its range. Suddenly, she knew exactly what the Church wanted and what part she could play. What part she *should* play. Before she could hear anymore, Andie cast a spell to block the hymn. Instantly, she felt her autonomy and her own mind return.

Andie and the others walked toward the Church, entering its unbelievably massive shadow. The Church was the most beautiful and dazzling building she had ever seen, but without its hypnotic hymn in her ears, Andie was able to think clearly and stay focused. As they came to the gargantuan front doors, they opened without warning. It was a triple door. The two side doors swung slowly inward and the middle door swung inward and up. Oren and the others hesitated for a moment, but Andie beckoned them forward.

"It's unsettling, I know," she said. "But somebody seems to be expecting us. I don't know how I'm supposed to feel about that."

They entered and found themselves inside a cavernous foyer, totally alone. Once they cleared the path of the doors, the triple doors close behind them, completely soundless. Andie and Oren shared a look. Andie looked around and if it hadn't been for the knots in her stomach she might have been floored by the total, genius beauty of the place. The fixtures and furniture were expertly crafted in red and gold, gothic style, with the posts and points so sharp they could be daggers. Now that she was closer to the red sand walls, Andie could see that they were also reflective. She could see herself looking back. Right before her eyes, a line appeared in the wall.

The line, at first, looked like a split, but then it grew and began to separate the wall. As the split grew, the sand lost its fixed state and began to spill, but did so in a predesigned pattern, falling to the floor and running into two neat piles on either side of the new opening in the wall. Soon after, a perfect rectangular opening had appeared and six men moved toward Andie and her friends. The men were clad in translucent robes so that you can see their bodies beneath, but couldn't make out details. It unnerved Andie. The men's faces, however, were covered with the same red sand as the walls, leaving only a space for their mouths. Andie was incredibly tempted to ask them if they could see. Her curiosity was quickly replaced by a mix of wonder and dread as the men came to a stop just in front of her, forming a perfect line, side-by-side.

"Welcome..."

"Travelers..."

"To..."

"This..."

"Our..."

"Church."

Each man spoke one word and allowed the next to continue. Of all the things Andie had seen in the Church so far, this was by far the eeriest. For a moment neither she nor Oren could speak.

"And we thank you for your welcome," Oren finally said. "Might I be right in assuming you are the famous priests of the Church?"

"We..."

"Are..."

"But..."

"Six..."

"Of..."

"Them."

"I see. We ask your forgiveness for our intrusion here, but we are of the dragonborn people recently brought to your world from another time. What we seek is knowledge of our enemies, who seem to increase by the day. We have received a series of threats and—"

"Do..."

"You..."

"Charge..."

"Us..."

"With..."

"Machinations?"

"Certainly not. We're only here to inquire if you have

heard anything that might help us gauge where our enemies are or what they might be up to. Many of the letters we've received seem to have come from your region. We accuse you of nothing, but we have heard of the admirable watch you keep over this region and its movements. Have you heard anything that might be of assistance to us?"

Oren waited for an answer, but the men simply stood there, facing straight ahead without moving or making a sound. Andie got the distinct impression that they were doing something deliberate that she and her friends couldn't see.

"Wise priests," Oren began again. "My comrades and I mean you no harm, nor do we wish to interfere with the workings of your Church. We ask nothing of you but information. Here with me today is someone very important to our people. This is Andie Rogers—"

"Don't..."

"Lie."

"It..."

"Surely..."

"Cannot..."

"Be."

"It is," Andie said. "My name is Andie Rogers, princess of the dragonborn. I wouldn't have come here if this weren't something critical to the survival of my people."

"Please..."

"Follow..."

"Us..."

"Most..."

"Revered..."

"Princess."

The priests turned and began to walk back by the way they came. Andie followed without hesitation, hoping the sooner she found out what they knew the sooner she can leave this place. Oren and the four dragonborn warriors that accompanied them followed. The priests led them deep into the Church, through more hidden doors that spilled open and rooms massive and brilliant. So far, they'd seen no other people besides the priests, but soon they came to a room that must have been at least a kilometer wide. The room was filled with wonderful, warm smells and Andie realized that the entire room was a kitchen and the thousands of people there were all cooking. Her eyes wandered over the dishes and she saw foods she could neither describe nor comprehend.

"What is that?" Andie asked, pointing to a peculiar looking dish.

"Our..."

"Specialty."

"A..."

"Serving..."

"Of..."

"Cloud."

Andie took a closer look and, sure enough, the dish was translucent and waving sedately. Yet it wasn't just a piece of cloud. They'd done something to it. Andie shuddered and turned. She noticed the cooks' faces were covered with the same red sand as the priests'.

"How do they see?" she asked.

"Our..."

"God..."

"Shows..."

"Us..."

"The..."

"Way."

Andie looked at Oren, who already had his hand on his sword. The priests hadn't done or said anything untoward, yet Andie felt something off about them. Something sinister. Andie had learned to trust her instincts and just then they were telling her to prepare for an unpleasant surprise.

The priests led them out of the kitchen and into a room considerably smaller than the others. The priests abruptly stopped and turned toward Andie, who nearly drew her sword she was so startled. She took a quick glance around the room, but there was nothing to see. It was completely empty. For a moment, the priests just stood there, their translucent robes billowing around them, which was odd because there was no wind.

"What..."

"Did..."

"You..."

"Expect..."

"To..."

"Find?"

"Nothing," Andie said, stepping back in response to their tone. "We told you all we want is information. We know nothing about you and your Church."

"That..."

"Much..."

"Is..."

"Clear..."

"Little..."

"Princess."

Andie realized that something was different about the room, something beautiful. It was the hymn. Her spell wasn't working there. She could hear the hymn and it was louder, more persuasive. It was hypnotizing.

"If there's something you want to say then speak up," she said, finding her courage. "We're not here to fight, but it seems you want to provoke us. I suggest you start talking or show us the way out, but if you continue like this I can guarantee you won't like how it ends."

"Finally."

"The..."

"Future..."

"Queen..."

"We..."

"Seek."

Andie was about to ask them what that meant when the men began to levitate. As if that wasn't troubling enough, the men began to merge. All six into one body. And still the hymn flowed into her ears. As she looked at her fellow dragonborn, she could tell the song was getting to them, too.

CHAPTER THREE

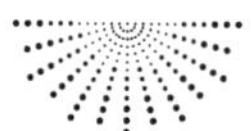

"AT THE CHURCH OF STONE AND SEA WE SEEK ONE thing and one thing only: the unity of all people." The new entity spoke with the voices of all six, its voice hollow and layered and echoed throughout the surrounding space. "All people believing as we do. All people united under our banner. All people wearing the red sand. We felt your power from afar, Andie Rogers. The very walls here desire you. Only you can realize the dream that we have dreamt for centuries. Too long have we subsisted on merely taking the chance passersby who get caught in our hymn. We want the world, which you can deliver. You ask if we know of your enemies and the answer is yes. We have been in contact with all groups that wish you ill. No one passes through our region without our knowledge. We have made promises to each, but we wish to deny them. We wish you to be our ally and spread the seeds of the Church across the lands. Imagine: one people, one mind, one goal, one Church."

The hymn pulsed in her ears. It brought her to her knees. It was so beautiful, powerful, and true. Yes, it was true, it must be. Nothing that poetic and melodic could be false. Andie began to see, to understand her place in the coming days and movements of the church. Everything could be so much better, so perfect, if she would only bow to their will.

"What will you say to our proposition princess? Listen to the hymn, the dream. Believe in us and our loving purpose. We only want to bring all people together under a better truth. The broken, crumbling world from which you come does not need to be the world in which you die. Join us. We will take you into our arms and provide the home you desperately seek. We love you already. Be our vessel. Help us, Andie. Save us."

Andie rested on her knees, happy, crying, finding peace within the red sand walls. But the priests' last words sounded similar, reminding her of something. Something she had heard before. Voices calling out to her from some place. Voices in need, crying for her to help them. Save them. The dragonborn. Her people.

The hymn was so beautiful, so strong, but it was false. It was merely a subliminal ruse meant to attract her to their terrible cause. She began to wake.

"Impossible," the entity said. "No one resists the magnitude of the hymn in this room! Kneel! Join these ranks and become us!"

"Clearly, you've never messed with a dragonborn before."

Andie regained her feet and cast her spell again, only this time she made it infinitely stronger. The hymn left her and her clarity returned. She faced the entity, but before she could raise her hand, he drifted backwards and disappeared into the walls. Andie was about to help the other dragonborn to their feet when the whole room began to tremble. Within seconds, the room began to morph. Andie and the other dragonborn were borne in the air on the red sand. A face appeared in the wall in front of her.

"If you will not join us, you will fall," it said. "We anticipated you would become one of us, but we made other arrangements as well. An army of thousands lies within these walls. The Church of Sand and Stone has offered asylum to all your enemies and they have gathered here to prepare for a battle that will shake the very foundations of your peace. This army grows daily and soon it will be too large for even the dragonborn to defeat. Feast your eyes upon your end."

A large opening appeared in the wall and as she looked through, Andie could see into a room full of soldiers. There were different factions and different races. Andie knew that her worst fear had come true. All their enemies across Noelle had joined together to form one massive army. The opening closed, protecting the soldiers from the spell Andie just cast.

"You've chosen wrong, princess," the entity said.

"No. You have."

Andie raised her palms and emitted wind and light so powerful, the face in the wall blasted away and the room was pushed out from her. She and the dragonborn fell back to the ground, but the others were still under the influence of the hymn. She had to find a way to get them out.

Suddenly, something hit her face so hard that she was thrown across the room. Just when she was about to catch her breath, something hit her again, and then again while she was in midair. She landed on her back and had just enough time to draw her sword and protect herself from the next strike. It was the red sand, acting as if it had a mind of its own. The very walls of the Church were striking out at her. She fought it off with her sword as best she could, but it was nearly impossible to defend herself on her back. She felt the sand of the floor come up around her throat. Then her arms and legs were trapped and sunk into the sand. In the ceiling above, a large point formed in the sand, extremely sharp, and began to descend toward her.

But she wasn't afraid. She and Saeryn had been studying the grimoires for months. Andie learned a few tricks. She exhaled and clenched her body. Instantly she became fire, her entire body turning into a humanoid flame. The sand all around her superheated, turning to glass. She broke it easily and regained her feet. Before the room could launch another attack, Andie raised her arms and sent a pulse of flames out in every direction. The entire room was turned to glass, stuck in its final movement. Andie cast a spell to make the dragonborn float beside her and she levitated herself up with all the force she could muster, sending her heat out above her first.

Several moments later, they burst from the top of the Church into the warm sunlight. The minute the light touched them, the dragonborn regained consciousness. Andie put them down on the roof of the Church and it was only seconds before their dragons came. They all mounted up and took off as fast as they could, thankful to finally be rid of that place.

CHAPTER FOUR

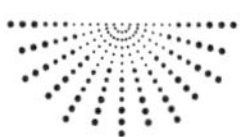

"YOU DON'T UNDERSTAND," ANDIE SAID. "THE ARMY IS massive. It already numbers in the thousands and is still growing."

"Oren," Lymir said, still confused. "What did you see?"

"I'm afraid the allure of the hymn was too much for me and my comrades," Oren replied. "It completely overpowered us. If Andie had not been there, my friends and I would be at the mercy of the Church. Andie is the only one who was enough in control of herself to see what was hidden in those walls, though I can assure you the Church is no friend of ours."

"There were always rumors of their megalomania, but never proof," Saeryn said. "We always assumed the rumors were false and that the Church had no enemies, though now it's obvious that it never allowed its detractors to leave. But I don't understand why they think this army will help them achieve their goals."

"It's likely both the army and the Church are using each other." Andie rubbed her temples as she processed the memory of what she had experienced in the Church. "The Church thinks the army will help it convert the world. The army probably thinks the Church's only goal is to help them take us out. But they're both our enemies. Not only is that army composed of all our enemies, but it's so much closer than we ever imagined. I doubt they have transportation for an army that large, so they'll be walking. It's only a few days by dragon, which means maybe a month on foot with a large army. And I have to be honest they looked like they're starting soon."

Everyone was quiet. Andie, Saeryn, Lymir, Oren, and several of the high members of the University were in the meeting hall of Lymir's department. Andie and Oren had only been back for an hour, but they wasted no time in warning the others.

"We only just opened the University," Lymir said. "But maybe we should consider closing its doors again. I'd rather postpone and save lives than risk people getting hurt just to prove we aren't afraid."

"We cannot close those doors again." Saeryn's spoke with a finality in her voice. "This university is not just for education. It is a symbol to Arvall and to the world of a new era. It means a great deal to my people as well."

"Saeryn's right," said Andie. "We can't close the doors. We can't give in. Even if we did, it wouldn't change anything. That army isn't for show and it's coming no matter what we do. Closing the school only takes away the hope we just gave everyone."

Lymir leaned back in his chair and locked his fingers. Andie couldn't stop thinking about the Church. She realized that their enemies were greater than they ever thought before. Lymir began to nod his head and everyone knew what he would say.

"So, we stay open. Classes go on as usual and the celebrations will continue as scheduled. We'll tell the people nothing, but we'll take every precaution possible. I want our professors trained harder than ever. I want our defenses increased and expanded. Not just magic, but computers, too. I want every security measure we can think of and when we run out of ideas we're going to call in other people to think up some more. If we're going to keep these doors open, we're going to do everything in our power to protect these people and give them a chance."

"We must," said Oren. "These people have welcomed us into their lives and their city. They've risked a great deal to help us and they've made a new world feel like a home. We cannot lead them into slaughter."

"We won't."

The voice belonged to Raesh. Andie didn't see him come in. In fact, she hadn't seen much of him at all over the previous few months. But as he entered the room and neared the table, Andie focused her eyes elsewhere.

"I promise you, Oren, no one is going to be forgotten or abandoned. I agree we have to open the school and keep this army a secret, but don't worry. We've learned a lot in fighting the University. We're ready, and if we're not then we will be."

A kind of ease passed through the room. Raesh had a way of reassuring people. The meeting ended. Andie was almost gone when Raesh called to her.

"Andie."

"Hi," she said, facing him. "Something wrong?"

"I want to talk to you."

Raesh left the room through the other door and Andie followed, wondering what she was supposed to say to him. They hadn't had a real conversation in over six months and whenever they did talk it was only a passing greeting. She followed him down the long main hall, past Leabharlann, and she almost broke off and ran several times, but she didn't. She couldn't. Truth be told, she wanted to talk to him more than anything. So much was going so wrong so fast that she needed someone to confide in.

Saeryn had been a terrific friend, but Raesh got Andie in ways she didn't even get herself. More than that, there had always been something in their way—an enemy, or battle, or catastrophe, or death. Maybe now they could begin to change that. Soon they exited the University through the front doors and walked to the cliff facing the city.

"I don't know if you've been avoiding me or if I've been avoiding you," he began. "What I do know is that sooner or later we're going to have to talk. I want it to be now."

"Raesh, I don't know what you expect me to say," Andie said, berating herself for being so cold. "Whatever this is or was, whatever we are, there just isn't time for it right now. We have enemies all across Noelle. Some of them pretty close to our front door. That's what we need to focus on."

"Is it?"

"Yes. We need to look for ways to root these threats out."

"Do we?"

"Yes."

Raesh simply stood there, watching her in that way of his, that way that no one else on the face of the planet watched her. Andie didn't want to admit it, but she felt a host of emotions she hadn't been forced to deal with in months. After the attack on the city, there was so much chaos and death that she had easily put her personal feelings aside. But now, even with the army in the north, the dragonborn and the citizens of Arvall have gotten control of their lives. There weren't enough distractions.

"There aren't enough distractions to keep you occupied," Raesh said. "And there's nothing out here but us. I'm going to make this as simple as I can for you."

Raesh took two steps toward her, closed her in his arms, and kissed her.

"YOU'RE STRONGER, MY LEADER," said Lucas. "Soon you'll be stronger than you ever were, even before the fight. Now that pieces of the armor have fused with your body, you're going to be more than you ever dreamed. Nearly unstoppable."

"What are we doing here?" Ashur asked, continuing his pushups. "This is a complete and total waste of time. If I'd known this is what you had in mind—"

"Be patient with me, my leader. I'd already sent scouts ahead to speak with these people and the way seems clear. I would've come myself, but I didn't trust your care to anyone else. I've done my research on these people."

"Lucas, tons of people hate the dragonborn, but that doesn't mean we can trust them."

"My leader, you're right. Many people and factions across Noelle are no friends of the dragonborn, but most of them have only ever hated them on principle. Because that was the way they were raised and told to feel. Few people truly hate the dragonborn and their dragons, and my gut tells me that the only people in the world who hate them as much as we do are these people. We're here because we need their numbers and their experience. Chancellor Mharú was smart enough to only show part of his forces that night of the attack. He had battalion members stationed all over Noelle, but even with all of them, we still don't have the force to take on the dragonborn and western Noelle. I believe these people can help us."

Ashur stopped his pushups and stood. He paced, then he turned to face Lucas. Lucas was his second, his most trusted. While Ashur was too injured to command, Lucas intuited his every need and coordinated the battalion in his stead. He aided Ashur in his recovery and never, not even once, gave Ashur any reason to distrust him. Ashur placed a hand on each of his shoulders.

"Forgive me, Lucas. You've been a true ally to me and I've repaid you with mistrust. I'll meet with them."

Ashur and Lucas walked out into the sun. The top captains of the battalion lived in the largest of a series of cabins the battalion built when it was settled. Just that morning they relocated there, to the Unnamed Lands in east central Noelle, too far for the dragonborn to hear rumors. The sun was going down behind them, and, in front of them, at a distance of two kilometers is the Hushed Forest, so named for the quick and silent death that usually meets those who enter. The trees there were huge, as tall as fifty meters, and more beautiful and lush than any other forest in Noelle. So many have died by thinking that nothing so enchanting could be deadly.

"Are you sure this is where they are?" Ashur asked.

"And if they're so deadly, then why did they send our scouts back alive?"

"Three scouts came back."

"How many did you send?"

"Six."

"Maybe we're on to something."

"My leader," said one of the captains. "The information you requested about the Hot Salts has come back."

"The Hot Salts?" Lucas asked. "What could we possibly need there?"

"I started this investigation long before we confronted the dragonborn that night in Arvall. The Hot Salts is a very inhospitable land: hardly anything grows, most of the water is undrinkable, even the wildlife escaped there in the last age. The only thing that lives in the Hot Salts are criminals, vagrants, and some other undesirable specimens of Noelle. I began to get reports saying they were fleeing the land by the droves, leaving all their possessions. I wondered. What's terrifying enough to displace an entire community of criminals? I started studying topographical maps. There are mountains in the Hot Salts, some of the only mountains around that are high enough and large enough to hide an entire race of people who don't want to be found."

"But the weather there is too unforgiving. The lighting strikes make permanent habitation nearly impossible. Even the criminals only lived at the borders."

"That almost deterred me, but then I realized that those mountains are huge. So huge, in fact, that their summits breach the clouds. If someone were to settle in the mountains above the clouds, no one would ever even think to look for them up there. I've been trying to figure out where the dragonborn have settled since they came out of that portal. They've been careful, but I think I've found them."

"That's excellent news, my leader. These people will be glad to hear it."

"I'm sure they will. What did you say they call themselves?"

"CAN YOU SEE THEM, OLTHRION?"

"Yes, my liege. They can be no further than two kilometers. Do you take them at their word?"

"I trust no one. This so-called battalion claims to hate the dragonborn. They say they wish to see the end of them. I think they also intend to use us."

"What a pity for them, my liege."

"What a pity indeed. No one uses the Beautiful Dead."

CHAPTER FIVE

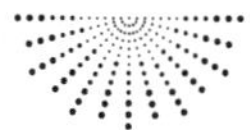

ANDIE STOOD IN VICTORY GARDEN ON THE SIDE OF BRIE, waiting for her first class to arrive. She wasn't as nervous as she thought she'd be. At least not about teaching. She and a few other dragonborn worked to reorganize the gardens and introduce some of the plants the dragonborn brought from the past and from the Hot Salts. She was a little worried about the Church, the army, and the battalion, but today those threats seemed far away. Today she was thinking about what happened yesterday and what it felt like to finally be with Raesh. She'd essentially given up hope. She'd even stop trusting that they belonged together. But that was over now. And for the first time in a long time, she was happy.

Soon enough her students arrived and surrounded her. It was time for her very first class to begin.

"Good morning, class. I'm Andie Rogers. Welcome to Modern Horological Enchantment."

Her students stared at her as if she were a celebrity. That was something she hadn't anticipated.

"Excuse me, Ms. Rogers," a girl asked. "Is it true you

took down both the Chancellor and the leader of the battalion single-handedly?"

"No. Well, yes, but I learned a tremendous amount from the dragonborn and I had a whole network of people who helped me along the way. Taking down the University was more than just one fight."

"But you're, like, unstoppable."

Several of the students nodded and looked as if they might burst from excitement. Andie felt proud, but also a little overwhelmed.

"No one is unstoppable," she said. "But you can fortify your mind and your abilities by knowing about the options available to you, which is one of the things we'll do in this class. Plant magic might seem lame or uninteresting, maybe not even worth learning, but consider this: when the Chancellor wanted to kill those eight hundred diplomats at the Winter Festival last year he did it by using a crossbred plant species. I know because I helped breed them."

The students finally settled down and their faces become completely sober. Andie didn't want to scare them, but to impress upon them the gravity of what they could learn there and of the world they lived in.

"Ms. Rogers," another student began. "Are we learning how to fight so that we can take on the enemies threatening Arvall?"

Andie looked at the boy, who couldn't be more than sixteen and who was so fragile-looking she feared a strong wind could blow him over. He looked anxious, unsure. They all did. Andie realized that by taking away their excitement, their joy to be learning from her, she'd exposed their fear. It was the same fear the whole city was trying to mask. But she knew she couldn't tell them the truth. They'd decided in the meeting that they would keep everything secret. She must lie.

"Don't worry. No one's coming to the city. You're perfectly safe."

She turned their attention back to horological magic and introduced them to the topics and books they would be studying. She gave them a tour of Victory. She found herself ashamed to be so good at misleading them, at giving them hope that will more than likely prove false. Yet it also felt good to see them smile and hear them laughing and looking forward. The class soon ended and Andie took a moment to celebrate her first teaching experience. Then the next class came. She had to begin lying all over again.

Soon the day was done. Andie grabbed a few things from her office and boarded SKY 6 to the city. Once the train reached the bottom, she boarded another train to cross the city, then another to Michaelson. Once there, she paid a visit to her old home. She didn't have the heart to sell it or have it taken down. Instead, she paid to have it cleaned regularly, though she knew she would probably never live there again. The house was all she had left of her parents, though. Her mother who was murdered for being different and her father who died because Andie was too angry to take care of him properly. She shed a few tears and then boarded the Sud to Taline.

By the time she reached the city, night had fallen. She caught a cab in front of the station. Her cell rang.

"Hi," Raesh's voice echoed through the receiver. "I didn't see you leave today."

"I'm sorry. I just wanted to get over to Taline before it got late. I wanted to make visiting hours."

"It's okay. I was just there a couple days ago."

"It's not fair."

There was a moment of silence while the weight of the situation hung.

"I love that you're still going," Raesh said. "I know it's hard and I know how much you want a miracle. I want one, too."

"Let's talk about something else. How was your first day?"

"Great," he said. "I think the students really responded to the lesson. I wasn't sure about giving them an assignment on the first day, but they seemed really into the idea of research. I can't believe I taught four classes today. You?"

"Well, us mere nomags can only handle two classes a day, but it was pretty amazing. I never thought I could warm to teaching so easily. I feel honored to be responsible for someone else's knowledge."

"I'm sure you're going to have a great year. You're kind of like royalty there. Everyone wants to know you. Professors, students. I heard some janitors mooning over you..."

"Ha. Ha. I didn't ask to be famous."

"True, but you do it well. I snuck in your class to see you this afternoon."

"What did you think?"

"I thought you were amazing and that you looked more beautiful than anyone or anything I've ever seen."

"As far as compliments go, that's definitely a top contender."

"I mean it. I'm so happy you stopped hiding the color of your hair and eyes. And not just that, but your energy.

Your drive. Everything about you. You're perfect, Andie."

"If I say it back now it's just going to sound stupid," she said.

"Don't worry about it. I already know I'm perfect."

She laughed as the cab pulled up at The Letter, the largest hospital in western Noelle. When Andie was a child it was destroyed in a terrorist attack, but had since been rebuilt and made bigger and stronger than ever. It was rebuilt out of the most advanced loveglass, and was virtually impossible to infiltrate or attack. Andie felt a weight coming over her heart as she looked up at the massive structure.

"Okay," she said. "I'm here."

"Alright. Call me when you're done."

"Okay. I'll probably just stay at a hotel tonight. It's too late to take a train back and I probably won't feel like making the trip anyway."

"No problem. I'll just see you tomorrow afternoon. Talk to you soon."

Andie hung up and exited the car. It was a slow walk because she was thinking of all the things that place represented. She had to go through a few security checkpoints, but it was really a quick process, especially since everyone in western Noelle knew who she was. She caught the elevator to the seventy-seventh floor and walked to the end of the hall. When she entered the room, it was as if the breath had left her body. It happened to her every time.

Carmen lay in bed, unresponsive, as she had been since the explosion in the Hot Salts. The doctors said her coma was unlike anything they'd ever seen. They'd tried so many treatments and methods that Andie had lost count. The problem was due in large part to the fact that no one was quite sure what spells the Chancellor was sending through Marvo's body. The spellwork was foreign to them, and, with both the Chancellor and Marvo dead, there was no way to test. Carmen had been lying in that bed in Taline for months. The doctors said that if she didn't wake up on her own, she'd never wake up at all.

Andie walked around the bed to the side facing the window. She sat down on the bed next to her friend and put another chocolate bar in the top drawer of the bedside table. She brought Carmen's favorite candy every time she came to visit. All three drawers were almost full. She saw the new flowers that Raesh brought the last time he was there. Overwhelmed by thought of how much Raesh himself must be handling the loss of his family, her stomach clenched in tight knots.

Andie took Carmen's hand and kissed her cheek, trying to remember what the old days were like before the University ruined everything.

"Oh, Ms. Rogers, it's you." The calm voice of a nurse spoke through the doorway as she carried in a small tray of medical supplies.

"Hi, Alecia. Long day?"

"They're all long. You? You look pretty chipper tonight."

"First day teaching and it went surprisingly well. Has she had many visitors today?"

"Not today. Most days she usually does. Dragonborn, council fighters, old friends from Arvall. Actually, there was someone here earlier. They didn't stay long. Kind of creeped me out to be honest."

"Why? Did they do anything?"

"Not particularly. They were just... odd. They were dressed in all black and stood in the far corner without saying a word. They didn't stay long and didn't say anything, but they seemed, I don't know, dangerous. More like they were spying on her than checking on her."

"I'll keep an eye out. Send word to me if you see them again."

"I sure will, sweetheart. You have a good night. And don't worry about visiting hours, stay as long as you like."

Alecia left and Andie bagan to wonder about who could be spying on Carmen and why. It was one more thing she never thought of. Carmen was a huge part of the resistance, and she fought fiercely alongside Andie and the others. If anyone wanted revenge, they could simply come to The Letter and kill Carmen while she lay there defenseless. Or worse yet, they could take her and hold her for ransom, allowing them to get almost anything from Andie and her friends. She made a mental note to increase the security on Carmen's hallway.

"Hi, gorgeous," she said, stroking Carmen's hair. "I know, I was just here the other day, but I missed you. I was kind of hoping you'd take pity on me and wake up. I'm sure you've got a whole host of insults and blunt talk you've been storing up while you rest. I don't think I can take it all at once, but if you spread it out evenly over, say, a week, I'm sure I can handle it. What do you say? You up for a reunion?

"I get it. No hard feelings. You're just not ready yet. I mean, honestly, I wouldn't be in a hurry to get back here either, not with all these... never mind. That can wait. I don't know if Raesh told you this, but... we're together.

Together together. I know what you're thinking: why did it take so long? I just wanted you to be the first to know it and to know that I'm happier now than I've ever been. I know there's so much going on in the world, so many things to watch out for, but he makes me so ridiculously happy. And I trust him completely. Which is why you need to wake up so you can berate me for still not having told him I love him when I've known it for so long now.

"Where are you now? Somewhere peaceful, I hope. You deserve it. It's hard to imagine where we came from and who we use to be. Almost as hard as it is to imagine where we're headed. I don't think you realize how much we need you. Not just your skill and your power, but your light. Your determination. Your mostly inappropriate jokes. I never realize how much I need you until I'm here. But hey, no pressure. You come back whenever you're ready."

She held Carmen's hand. Minutes passed, then hours. Nurses and doctors came and went, having brief and hushed conversations with Andie and giving her updates on Carmen's condition, if they could even really be called updates. The moon came up in the night sky and Andie tried to watch the stars, but the lights of the city were too bright. Instead of getting a room in the city, Andie stayed in the room with Carmen.

CHAPTER SIX

THE NEXT MORNING, SHE KISSED CARMEN'S CHEEK AND said goodbye. She made it back to the University just in time to receive her first class of the day. Tuesdays and Thursdays she taught Plant-Based Poisons to the 3rd and 4th Cycles. The students seemed to like the material and her teaching, and the day went by without a hitch. She had two more classes, and, aside from the students' inability to get past her celebrity, she'd consider her day a success.

After class, she walked to the second east wing of the University and waited for Raesh to finish his class. He came out looking pleased.

"Good day?" she asked, kissing his cheek.

"Yeah. Do your students stare at you like you're royalty?"

"Oh, so you have that, too…"

Together they walked to the main hub and caught SKY 1 up through the mountain to the faculty living spaces. The train went much slower than SKY 6, but Andie enjoyed this ride more. Everything on the train was free, and rather than going straight up through the rock of the mountain—which would have risked the structural integrity of the entire summit—SKY 1 went a few hundred feet straight up and then exited to the side of Brie, where it ascended to the top by traveling around and around the summit at a steady incline. They'd caught it at just the right time because the sun was just going down over Arvall. Raesh held Andie's hand as they watch.

"Quite a view," he said.

"If you're into gorgeous sunsets and vivid, sprawling colors."

"I already know the answer, but—"

"No change. She's still in a coma and they still have no idea what to do for her. But she looks good, if that means anything."

"It means enough."

"I can't believe you tricked me into moving in with you," Andie said, grinning.

"Tricked? You and I remember things very differently. But if you truly feel that strongly about it, there's plenty of other spaces available on the mountaintop. Feel free to move along."

"I never said I had an issue with being tricked. Unless you think we're moving too fast?"

"We should've been together the day we met. Let's be honest: the lives we lead aren't the safest. When I think of all the time we've wasted and the people we've lost, the things we've seen and the enemies that are still coming... no, I don't think we're moving too fast. I don't think we're moving fast enough."

He kissed her cheek and Andie didn't say it, but she agreed with him completely. In a world where so much was out of her control, Raesh was at least something that she wanted that she could have. No matter what threats showed themselves in the future, nothing could change the way she and Raesh felt about each other. The train continued its journey around the mountain until it finally reached the summit. Andie and Raesh descended and made their way back into the mountain through the tunnel.

The professors' living spaces were, in a word, sumptuous. No expense had been spared in the construction, decoration, or furnishing. They had the best of everything, despite Andie's instruction to allocate resources elsewhere during construction. The University may have been completely heinous, but they took care of their instructors, and now all of that luxury belonged to the new professors. Any dragonborn-hating propaganda had been ejected, but there was still enough luxury to go around. Everything was made from gold, silver, and even jewels. The rugs and paintings and fixtures had been brought from the farthest and most decadent corners of Noelle. Even the floors were made of platinum loveglass, a material so expensive and so rare that most people never came within a hundred kilometers of it in their lives. The opulence truly couldn't be overstated.

"I still can't believe we live here," Raesh said. "I know we got rid of all the propaganda and anything that even remotely resembled sympathy or acceptance of the University's actions, but, I don't know, sometimes I just feel like…"

"Like we should burn the whole place down and dump the ashes in the Spider Sea? Yeah. That idea was discussed. In depth. But ultimately this is just stuff. Really, really nice stuff that has nothing to do with hatred or evil. Actually, we checked the records and most of this stuff was actually sent as gifts. Regardless, I see no reason to be mad at diamonds. They didn't do anything to me."

"Fair."

"Now let's talk about the meeting with Lymir and Oren."

"Oren's getting ready to fly back to the Hot Salts and get the dragonborn army ready. He's concerned the location of the dragonborn might not be secure. To be honest, I agree with him. I think it's safest to assume that nothing is safe anymore."

"Tell me about it. Alecia was telling me last night that some stranger was spying on Carmen. Don't worry, I had them increase the security detail and keep a closer eye on the camera, but I'm beginning to realize that we have too many people who are important to us spread over too great a distance."

"Agreed. Oren and Saeryn decided it might be best to move all the dragonborn to Brie until further notice. It should work out fine, since half of the dragonborn are already here or in Arvall anyway. They would've consulted you, but—"

"They knew I'd agree anyway."

"Right. Lymir's working on a new training program for the professors. He'd like to train a few students, too. Anyone who shows promise and proves themselves to be discreet. We've reached out to some militia in western Noelle, but we haven't heard back yet. Taline has promised us whatever we need, including soldiers. I think we've got as much of a handle on this thing as possible right now. Have you been in contact with Marcus Iceubes?"

"Yeah, I spoke with him between classes today. He's still pouring over the journals I found. I was worried there might not be as much in them as I thought, but, apparently, he can't research fast enough. He's pulling out hundreds of secrets every week. I know there's got to be something in there that can help us in this war. He's going to give his classes over to a colleague so he can spend more time with the pages. He seems hopeful. And Saeryn and I are still studying grimoires, at least those we can read. We need a translator, but it has to be someone we trust. I know we hoped things might be worked out diplomatically, but I think it's safe to say that's never going to happen."

"We never have time to celebrate one victory before it's right back to battle."

"Yeah. Life sucks like that."

In their apartment, they dropped their things by the door and made their way to the couch. Raesh laid down and then Andie fell in his arms, her face against his chest.

"Well," she said. "Let's get ready to win a war."

THE DAYS PASSED SLOWLY. Andie, Raesh, Lymir, and the other professors began training at night on the summit. Many of them were smart, driven, and fully aware of the danger they faced, but few of them had ever been in a fight. Raesh called all the fighters that once fought alongside his father to help train the professors and select students.

Before the fighters returned to Arvall, they had been on assignment in and around the String Fields. Their mission was to gather intelligence on any threats in the region, but the Beautiful Dead and anyone else who'd been hiding near the border had evaded capture. The fighters had not learned much other than that the Beautiful Dead had taken every man, woman, and child from several small towns nearby and taken their resources. News of the deed spread quickly, and the city, the entire region, began to get suspicious. The fighters did succeed in wiping out several small factions on their way to join the army in the Church of Stone and Sea. They'd brought back one from each faction and the professors had learned a great deal about the army's capabilities and attack methods. Andie had been right. The army was already on its way and would reach Arvall in less than a month. The fighters also caught the trail of the battalion, but it was deemed too risky to follow. No one really knew what the battalion was up to or what it was capable of.

Lymir and Saeryn worked tirelessly to keep peace and hope in the city. Thankfully, the people still trusted the University and the dragonborn. Lymir instituted programs to make the citizens of the city aware without forcing them into fear. Saeryn sent word to her people to prepare themselves and not to take the secrecy of their location for granted. Saeryn spent her days as a liaison between the humans and sorcerers of Arvall and the dragonborn, though relations had never been better. She spent her nights pouring over the grimoires and the histories, trying to learn what useful spells she could and to decipher where the Beautiful Dead were. As a Queen, her integrity and strength were unparalleled, especially since she now bore the burden of not just her people, but the city of Arvall as well.

Oren remained among the dragonborn in the Hot Salts of Mithraldia. Not a day went by that he didn't worry about his Queen and princess so far away, and about all the dragonborn and the terrible fight they face with the Dead. More than that, his experience in the Church of Stone and Sea haunted him. It was a very rare thing for a dragonborn to be overcome by tricks, enchanted stone or not. He questioned his ability to command his dragon, to protect his people. He knew that Andie could not always be around to watch out for him. Or for anyone else. He spent a great deal of time preparing the dragonborn for their exodus and fortifying the mountaintop, so that even though they must eventually leave, they would still have a home to come back to.

In Taline, Stefan prepared himself and his city for the attack he knew would come. They had only just been able to breathe again, finally rid of the University's theft and terrorism. Now they found themselves plunged right back into life and death circumstances. But Stefan was no fool, and he had been around long enough to know how to defend himself with the utmost fury. He left no stone unturned in his search for the threats to his city, and he made sure of every bit of his considerable knowledge to make the city as safe as possible. As a personal favor to Andie, he had increased security measures on the seventy-seventh floor of The Letter and he went over himself every afternoon to ensure that Carmen was protected.

Raesh practiced controlling his magic. While he did improve some, there was only so much control a pearlblood could hope for. His biggest accomplishment was finding other pearlbloods in western Noelle. There weren't many—in fact, there were likely less than a hundred in the entire world—but they were strong. They appeared to have been practicing their magic in secret. Raesh found comfort in being surrounded by similar people, but he never stopped thinking of his father and how much he had to live up to. He knew there was nothing he could have done, but in saving other lives he could make his father proud.

Classes continued as usual and the professors were careful to keep the secret. The students seemed to truly love everything they were learning and—besides the usual lethargy, tardiness, and excuses that plagued every campus—the new and improved university was running better than ever. Andie and Raesh's classes were going well and Lymir's leadership steered the institution in a new and promising direction. If it weren't for the threat of impending doom, life might just have been perfect.

CHAPTER SEVEN

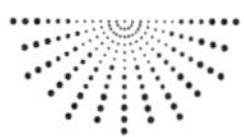

"YOU'VE MADE US WAIT FOR DAYS," ASHUR SAID. "I understand you don't know us or our agenda, but I would think the least you could do is show us some common courtesy. We're here to offer you the help you so desperately need."

"Forgive me, Ashur, but—"

"Where I come from, Olthrion, the lesser address the superior by their proper rank. Call me commander."

"And where I come from, such disrespect can lead one rather quickly to an early deposition. As I was saying, we made you wait not out of pettiness, but security. It would be foolish to pretend that we were afraid of you, but we do nothing without knowing who we're dealing with and what they're capable of. We know who you are. What are you capable of?"

As he turned from Olthrion, Ashur grinned. He motioned for his battalion to stand aside. He tensed his body and felt the power of his magic being amplified and focused by his new armor. He raised his hand and then slammed it into the ground. The moment his palm collided with the soil, an explosion flowed through his hand and split the ground for fifty yards. It was so wide and deep that several of the gargantuan trees lost their balance and topple over inside.

"That's just a taste of what I can do. My entire battalion is powerful and highly trained in combat. And more than anything else, we hate the dragonborn."

"Do you?"

It wasn't Olthrion who spoke, but another, deeper voice. Half of the battalion took a step back just at the sound of it. The man made his way to the front of the group and stood directly across from Ashur. He was tall, wrapped in impressive muscle, and his hair and beard were long and sleek. He carried no weapon, and yet he seemed more dangerous than any other person Ashur had met.

"You must be the King," Ashur said.

"There are no Kings here, commander. We follow the strongest and I have been the strongest for a very long time. My people have followed my lead for nearly a century."

"That's impossible," Ashur said, taking a closer look at him. "You can't be more than thirty years old. Men don't live that long."

"But I am not a man. Even if I look like one. My race is very old and very powerful. We've made it our mission to be invisible and there are precious few people living who know what we are and what we want. I'm curious as to how you know of us."

"Chancellor Myamar Mharú. Before he died he told me that his family had been keeping up with your people since the beginning of the first age. The secret was passed down through generations in case you were ever needed. He would have come himself, but he was murdered by the dragonborn. I know what you want and how you can obtain it. An army grows in the north that will march on the city of Arvall. We won't be able to make it back in time for the battle, but that's not what matters. By the time we get there the army will most likely have failed, but the dragonborn and the city will be weak. And from there we'll crush them."

"I cannot claim to dislike the strategy. Letting the eager fools go in first to weaken the foundation and die in the process, and then you and your battalion come in to knock down the house the dragons have built. Admirable. But I think you underestimate the men marching from the Church."

"Do you honestly think a group of poor, half-trained guerilla fighters can really band together and take out Arvall and the dragons? They have the numbers, but I've fought the dragonborn. It'll take more than numbers. It'll take fierce training and unimaginable power."

"Which is why I sent a dozen of my greatest warriors there months ago. By the time that army leaves the Church they will be worthy of a battle with those blood traitors. Make no mistake, commander, my people and I have hoped for the day when the dragonborn would return and be within our reach again. We've left nothing to chance, not even you. You think it was your idea to come here? I had spies slip information about my people into your Chancellor's office. All we had to do was wait for his greed and corruption to engulf him. He sought us out long before his death. I promised him an end to the dragonborn in exchange for his battalion and his resources. You didn't seek me out, young Ashur. You're here because you were promised to me, because you're part of a much larger and older game than you realize. Did you really think that fool Mharú would have been capable of all the things he accomplished if I hadn't given him the ideas? Who do you think convinced that elitist, xenophobic Church to harbor the army in the first place?"

"You're saying you've had a hand in everything that's happened?"

"Nothing has happened since the dragonborn stepped out of that portal that I haven't known about. We were the ones who told the factions to join as one."

"Then I'm in the right place. But I know something you don't."

"And what's that?"

"I know where the dragonborn home is."

A guttural breath traveled through the man, Olthrion, and all their people. The battalion members looked up and around them, finally noticing they were surrounded. The people were not just in front of them, they were in the trees, peering down with fierce frowns and keen eyes. They were impressively built, agile, strong, men and women alike. More than that, the people were surprisingly beautiful. In fact, it was hard to look away from them. They were wild and fierce and terrifying, but also breathtakingly perfect. Even the silver-haired elders had no problem hanging among the branches.

"Now you have my attention, commander," the man said.

"Your people go by many names and countless legends follow you. I know now I wouldn't have found you unless you wanted me to. This isn't even where you live, is it? Just another smokescreen."

"Bravo."

"The truth is that no one really knows anything about you anymore. You're nothing more than a myth. I'll gladly give you the location of the dragonborn and then follow you into this great war, but I need to know you can deliver your end of the deal. I know you're intelligent, cunning, intimidating, and apparently great at aging well, but what can you do for us?"

The man didn't look offended, but rather like he was glad to have been asked to exhibit his skill. His fellows cleared the space around him and he smiled.

"We are an ancient race, filled with the might of gods and beasts."

He ran to a tree almost too quick for Ashur to see and smashed his fist in a swiping strike, cutting the tree in half with absolute ease.

"We are the terrors between night and day that frighten time itself and break the hands of fate."

He leapt into the air and kicked his feet against the tree trunk, knocking the tree backward and flipping through the air, catching himself on another tree by punching his hand through the bark.

"We are strong, agile, fast, our senses keener than all the fiercest natural predators combined. We can hear conversations a whole town away, see through two kilometers of darkness, smell blood across mountains, feel the weather change even before the clouds change. Nothing we hunt escapes."

He released the tree and landed with a force that shook the ground.

"We live for centuries. We are the true children of the dragon. The beasts that bred us can no more hurt us than they can the blood traitors. If a dragon were to breathe fire on me this very moment, I would not even feel the flames. We are the greatest threat to the world. The true question is not whether we can deliver, but whether you can keep up."

"Impressive," Ashur said.

"We find you impressive as well, commander. We would not have invited you here if we didn't. I kept a close eye on your training and the battle in Arvall. Your strategy, intelligence, and leadership are impressive. Your combat and magic are remarkable."

"Speaking of magic, where's yours?"

"Don't worry. We shall have it soon enough."

"I think we're on the same page. With my battalion and your abilities, I think the dragonborn, the traitors, are as good as dead. Only one thing is left. What do I call you?"

"My name... is Beladorion."

"WE NEED MEDICAL ATTENTION. NOW!"

Andie heard the yelling from Victory. She told her students to stay put and rushed to the hallway to see what had happened.

"We couldn't take him to any hospital in the city. We were afraid of spreading panic."

Andie finally made it to the commotion and saw who was talking. It was Sarinda. Andie hadn't seen her since the day of the explosion in the Hot Salts. Raesh told her that Sarinda had been on assignment in the Dark Tundra, and, since she left there, no one had heard from her. Andie felt like hugging her, but Sarinda was one of four people carrying a bloodied body and there were more bodies following. They headed down the hall and through the main hub until they reached the medical wing. The doctors came out and took the bodies in. Sarinda turned to Andie and gave a little sight of relief. They threw their arms around each other.

"Come with me," Andie said.

She led Sarinda back outside and over to a secluded area where they could have some privacy. Sarinda was still breathing irregularly and sweating, but she looked as if she'd be fine.

"Are you hurt? Do you need a doctor?" Andie asked.

"No, just a few scrapes and bruises. I was lucky. We never saw them coming, Andie."

"Saw who?"

"I still don't know. It was a small phalanx, roughly a hundred soldiers, probably a scouting party. Is there something going on I missed?"

"We're about to be at war, Sarinda. There's a massive army marching down from the north right now. Didn't you see them?"

"No, we only saw those hundred."

"Tell me everything that happened."

"We left the Dark Tundra two months ago. We'd chased the battalion all over the north of Noelle, almost across the pole to the Old World, and finally defeated them. Or at least the faction we'd been chasing. We left the cold and came by ship down along the coast, but we were delayed because of icebergs in the Pauper's Sea and attacks from marauders. That's why we've been out of touch for so long because they destroyed our communications. We finally got free and then went full steam ahead to make up the time. Near the Church of Stone and Sea we saw a lot of movement, but we just figured it was another one of their mass rituals. We hit the Spider Sea and decided to dock in King's Harbor. But as soon as we stepped off the ship, we came under attack. They had weapons we'd never seen or heard of before. It was a bloodbath, but we killed three times as many of them. There were only about thirty of us, but we defeated them, barely. We had no idea what was happening."

"Did you get all of them?"

"All except one. Andie, I don't think he was human. He was strong and fast. He moved unlike anyone I've ever seen before. It was like he was driven by pure hate. We almost had him pinned down, but he escaped. He said something odd."

"What?"

"He said he wouldn't die before he'd killed his share of blood traitors. I don't know if he was crazy or if he was playing a part in a larger game than we realized."

"Sarinda, that was no fluke. That was an advanced party for the army that's marching on us. They must've thought you were an advanced party, too. And if that man was who I think he was, he wasn't crazy. He's one of the Beautiful Dead."

"The what?"

"They're the other race descended from dragons and they want to kill every dragonborn and drink our blood so they can obtain our magic. And the Church of Stone and Sea isn't just a neutral spectator anymore. They almost killed me and Oren, and now they're giving all their resources to an army of thousands that's coming to kill every last soul in Arvall City."

"I see I've got a lot to catch up on."

Andie and Sarinda talked for a long time while they waited for news. Sarinda received some attention for her wounds. The half dozen other fighters who survived were being treated somewhere in the hospital, but their condition wasn't critical. Andie sent one of the professors to take over her classes for the day. Eventually, the doctor came to speak to them.

"I'm sorry," he said. "We did as much as we could, but we simply don't have the knowledge to treat this kind of damage. We might have been able to do something if they'd arrived sooner, but by the time they arrived the symbiote had already taken to great a hold, I'm sorry."

"The what?" Sarinda asked.

"The symbiote. It's not fully alive or sentient, but the magic behind it is formidable. The sand has been animated so that it gets in an orifice or laceration and expands as it moves deeper. It absorbed their blood until their hearts stopped."

"The sand?" Andie asked.

"Yes. Red sand. It was hard to tell at first, because of all the blood, but it's definitely red sand."

The doctor turned to leave and Andie and Sarinda immediately ran down the hallway to the operating room. The sight of their fallen comrades lying withered and lifeless made them both halt in place, their bodies unmoving yet their minds racing wildly. Andie could barely comprehend what she was seeing.

While the limbs on the bodies before them were wasted and the skin hanging loose, their midsections were grotesquely swollen where the sand accumulated and soaked up all their blood. Sarinda's tears began to fall as she moved closer to the bodies. These were the people she'd traveled and fought with for months. Andie was close to tears herself as she leaned to inspect the wounds. Some of them looked as if they were cut or stabbed first and the sand got in afterwards, and some looked like they were wounded by the sand itself. But there was no mistaking what has happened.

"I'll kill them all," Andie said.

"What?" Sarinda asked.

"The Church. They've figured out how to weaponize the sand."

CHAPTER EIGHT

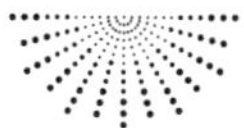

Later in the evening, after yet another meeting, Andie stood beside Saeryn in silence, thinking of all the ways the world they knew could end. They stood in the Archives, staring down into the portal that brought the dragonborn to the future. This portal has done so much for them and might still do a great deal of trouble.

"I still believe we should destroy this thing," Andie said. "Even the University's founding families were afraid of it. That should tell us all we need to know."

"I fear it, too, Andie. If we are not careful we may be sent back through this doorway just like we came from it. I fear, too, that Sarinda's run-in with the army's advance party will only make them march on us faster."

"Definitely. Now that they know they can not only stand their ground, but kill us, I don't see why they wouldn't want to speed up. They've been planning this for months. We're unprepared. They have an army of thousands and we have a city full of people who've never had to fight."

"I share your worry. Lymir is recruiting more

students and now he has all the professors in training, but our numbers are nowhere near where they should be. We certainly have experience and power on our side, but they could overwhelm us with sheer mass."

"It doesn't help that the Dead are with them."

"Actually, I don't think they are, or at least not completely. The Beautiful Dead are cunning and the greatest hunters and warriors the world has ever known. They were already master strategists before our race was even born. It seems...unwise to march with this army. The Dead are certainly bold, but they would never be so guileless as to attack us head on. I don't know how to describe it other than to say they would consider it a bad hunt. No, whatever they're planning you can be sure they won't march with the army, with the exception of a few lesser lieutenants for distraction."

Andie leaned against the wall and looked over at Saeryn.

"I don't understand how you can both be descended from dragons and not have the same abilities."

"Look at the scales on your arm, princess. They're very light, almost imperceptible, but if you look closely you can make out their shape."

Andie raised her arm and observed her skin as carefully and closely as she could. Before long she saw the pearlescent sheen and the beautiful scales. Upon looking closer, she saw that the scales were not the same shape as the dragons'. They were perfect heptagons.

"They have seven sides."

"Because we were born from the blood of seven dragons. The Dead are descended from only five. And, of course, our progenitors were centuries apart."

"No matter how many times I come face to face with

it or how many different shapes it takes I will never understand it."

"What?"

"How much people can hate us."

"Well, we knew something was coming, right?"

"Yes, but not this. Jacobi of House Clio wasn't terribly specific. She wrote that the founding families only used the portal to travel to the future once, to this time, and that they saw a city consumed by war. The journal said that the descendants of dragons destroyed everything."

"Well, at least now we know it was not us they saw, but the Beautiful Dead."

"The journal described the war as the worst and most deadly they'd ever seen. The founding families were monsters who had thousands of men, women, and children killed for no reason at all and even they said this war was horrific. They described it as the end of all things."

"The End of Days," Saeryn said. "Amanna Deireadh. It all makes sense now. The families returned to their own time and told their descendants what they'd seen. Over time the story made the descendants angry and more afraid until hate was all they knew. The mistaken future fueled everything they felt because they thought we were going to end the world. The story itself got twisted and grew into legend so that instead of 'the descendants of dragons' it became 'the dragonborn.'"

"The so-called end of times wasn't the descendants of the dragonborn restoring their race and taking revenge, it was the Dead restoring the power they think we stole from them and taking revenge on us. Are you telling me that the history of Noelle was forged because a few families didn't know how to tell a story?"

"It would appear so."

"Super."

Andie and Saeryn didn't stay in the chamber with the portal any longer than they had to. It was the only room in the entire university that hadn't been repaired. Everyone thought leaving it to carry the signs of the first battle would be a fitting memorial to everything that followed. She and Saeryn made their way out and moved slowly through Leabharlann, Andie reminiscing on the days when all she had to worry about was searching for a book on the dragonborn. As they exited the massive library, they ran into Marcus in the hallway.

"Professor Iceubes, hello," Saeryn greeted him.

"Your grace," he said. "Andie, I'm glad I've run into you. Both of you, actually."

"Have you found something?" Andie asked.

"Let's take a walk," he said, turning. "The question is what haven't I found. The founding families were keeping secrets from everyone, even each other. You wouldn't believe the people they've had killed, the petty jealousies, the secret wars, the unbelievable amounts of gold and silver they stole from the mint when they took over this building. I can't stop finding things, but I haven't come across anything on the Beautiful Dead. It's almost as if the families didn't even know they existed. But I do have good news. I've found the instructions to operating the portal."

"You mean we can control it now?" Saeryn asked, lighting up in hope.

"I mean we can do whatever we want. Turn it off,

turn it on, use it for past, future, teleportation. We can control it, instead of it controlling us."

"That may be the best news we've had all year," Andie said. "Thank you, professor, so much."

"There's more. The families didn't destroy the portals. Collectively they all claimed to have taken responsibility for destroying their appointed lot, but secretly each family kept one and hid it."

"You mean there are six more portals out there?" Saeryn asked, crestfallen.

"Seven," Marcus said. "At least seven. They're all over the place. There's one in New Carthage, one in Thabes in the True Isles. I haven't been able to find them all."

"Great," Andie said. "One step forward, seven steps back."

"I know it's not the news we were hoping for, but it gets worse. I'm not quite through the journals yet, but I doubt there's much more. I know we were hoping for something major, but I think it's essentially a dud."

"But there must be something."

"I'm sorry, Andie, but the truth is the later generations of the families weren't as cunning or ambitious as their ancestors. They didn't seem to have any interest in anything except wealth, prestige, and promiscuity. They certainly don't have any secrets that are going to give us any sort of magical or tactical advantage."

Andie sunk her fingers in her head and closed her eyes. It was not even close to what she was hoping to hear. She felt Saeryn's hand on her shoulder, comforting her. She opened her eyes, so frustrated she was almost crying.

"It's okay, Marcus," she said. "We'll just have to find another way. Thank you for all your help. Just learning how to control the one portal we do have is a help."

"I'll let you know if I find anything else."

Marcus left. Andie turned to Saeryn and put her arms around her. They stayed like that for a moment, comforting each other.

"I was really counting on those journals," Andie said.

"As was I, princess. But there is an aid for us out there somewhere."

"I'm sure you will. I think I'm going to take a walk and clear my head. I'll see you later."

Andie was only walking for a minute before she realized what must be done. It was time. She made her way deliberately, not stopping to talk to anyone or look at anything, just moving forward with her purpose. Everything they'd tried so far had failed. Visiting the Church, hunting the battalion, protecting the city. There were still bombings along the edge of town and messages still appeared in the fields. Every time they poked their heads out, it was only to find they have a new threat. Every line they'd held for hope had dropped them. The journals, the grimoires, their scouting parties. Even the training seemed doomed to fail because the recruits simply weren't tough enough. The enemy army was fast approaching, and, after the skirmish with Sarinda and the fighters, the army was no doubt invigorated, spurred on by the small victory and by the promises of the Church and the Dead.

Andie checked the time on her phone, a slow smile threatening her face. She knew that Lymir's office hours and classes were over, and sped toward his office without a look back.

She found him sitting in his chair, lost in thought.

"Lymir, it's time."

"LADIES AND GENTLEMEN, citizens and dragonborn, thank you for coming," Lymir began. "I want to thank you for your unconditional support and the way you've trusted each other and the University. What I'm going to tell you today is both shocking and unsurprising. It's no secret that people outside of western Noelle aren't happy about the dragonborn return. They haven't had the opportunity to live among the dragonborn and befriend them like we have. They still believe in the old lies and they have no intention of letting go of that hate. My staff and I, as well as the dragonborn warriors, have done our best to keep you sheltered and to protect you from a truth we didn't think you were ready for, a truth that we weren't sure would even come to pass, but it is my sad and heavy to duty to tell you this truth. Factions of heinous people from eastern, northern, and central Noelle have come together to form an army the size of which has not been seen in many cycles. With the help of the Church of Stone and Sea and another very old and powerful enemy, this army intends to make its way to us and destroy us. I ask you to forgive me for keeping this from you. We thought we were doing the best thing to preserve hope, but it is no longer prudent or helpful.

"I don't know if I still have the right to say this to you, but rest assured. The University has already been stocked with weapons, food, and supplies. We started stockpiling necessities before these threats even arose, just as a precaution. I urge you to take refuge in the

University and its walls where you will be well protected. If the University reaches capacity, we have shelters and bunkers set up across the city and each and every one of them is well-equipped to withstand a siege. The rest of the dragonborn warriors should be arriving soon and you'll have all the protection you need. I can see you're scared and I won't tell you not to be, but don't for a second think we've abandoned you. Your safety is always paramount. Know, too, that the professors and a large number of students have been receiving specialized training and will be prepared to defend you. I urge you all to do your best to learn what you can in the coming days. We'll need all the help we can get. Work on defending your families, your neighbors. We can survive this.

"I know the future must seem dark and believe me, I am just as afraid as you are. But I'm not going to give in and I'm not going to run. For those of you who wish to get out of the city, do so only if you can do it safely. The enemy is everywhere and they will not hesitate to kill you and everyone you love. I won't lie to you: we face the battle of our lives. But this is far from over. Our great city will not fall. The new university will succeed in its mission. No army of any size will take what is ours. There is always hope."

"If any warrior is left standing mount your dragon and fly for the west! Save whom you can and flee!"

The mountain peak was completely overrun with the Beautiful Dead. They climbed the mountain in the night, unbothered by the lightning and the storms, and breached the clouds just as morning dawned. They were so silent and quick they'd already taken down fifty warriors before the alarm was sounded. They moved with a speed and agility the dragonborn were not ready for. They had forgotten how capable and how terrifying their old enemies could be. Once roused, the dragonborn warriors put up a remarkable defense, but then they were surprised by the appearance of the battalion. Ashur showed no mercy.

Now every warrior left standing raced for their dragon, many being cut down in their stride. Oren was the last line of defense, doing his best to hold off the Dead and the battalion so that his friends could escape to warn the city. Only three dragons managed to take off from the mountain and of those three only one was allowed to escape. The dragonborn could not believe their eyes when the Dead were able to ride their dragons. A single dragonborn warrior became a dot on the horizon as he flew west. Oren continued to fight, cutting down battalion fighters and the Dead alike. He was truly a spectacular warrior, the best and strongest of all the dragonborn army.

But Beladorion appeared. His strength, his speed, his instincts were too much for the already exhausted Oren. With a deft move, he caught Oren on the back of the head and smashed his face into the mountainside. He picked Oren up and landed a series of strikes so fast and fierce and powerful that it was all the bloody dragonborn warrior could do to stay conscious. Beladorion dragged him by his throat across the ground.

"Have any of them died?" Beladorion asked.

"No, my liege," answered Olthrion. "We've managed

to take them all without killing them, though this one has murdered four of our men and several battalion soldiers."

"Yes, he is quite the warrior. Truly exquisite and precise. He would have made a remarkable Dead. Gather all the captured and take them into the mountain. Help the battalion tend to their wounded. Have some of our men gather the dragons and break them in."

"Right away, my liege."

"That was glorious," Ashur said, still covered in blood from his destructive rage. "I want more."

"And you shall have it, commander," said Beladorion. "I have here a man who has killed both your people and mine. A superb warrior. What shall we do with him?"

"I would say torture him, but I don't think he's got enough life left in him for that. Do you want to drink from him?"

"It won't do any good until the spell is broken. Besides, I don't think I'd like the taste of him."

"Then it sounds as if you've already made up your mind. I'm going to plan our next movement and interrogate some of the dragonborn. I'll start with the women. That should get their attention. If we leave now we should reach Arvall by—"

"We must wait. I know the exact time that we should arrive in the city and we can't come a moment before."

"Big plans?"

"Enormous."

Ashur left Beladorion with Oren. Beladorion kicked the proud warrior down and stood with his foot on his chest, grinning.

"It would appear you've reached the end," Beladorion said, slowly increasing the force behind his foot. “There is but one thing left to say to you as you take the sleep of your fathers. Fhealltóir Fola.”

And with that Beladorion put all of his weight into one swift movement and crushed right through Oren’s chest.

CHAPTER NINE

"REPORTS SAY THE ARMY IS EVEN CLOSER. THEY'RE moving fast and at this rate they'll be here within two weeks," Lymir said.

"They're ahead of schedule now," said Raesh. "Even if all of Noelle came to our aid, they would never get here in time. We're going to have to work with the forces we have."

"That was a great speech you gave, Lymir," Andie said. "There's not much hope to go around these days, but what's left of it definitely spread through your speech. Also, I just noticed that you lost your accent. What happened?"

"I just figured that if I was going to lead the University and speak on its behalf it was probably best that I work on my oratory skills."

"Lymir, your leadership is going to help in the next fortnight," Saeryn said. "I've been to the city just this morning and while the people are banding together to help each other, it's all they can do not to panic. I've been trying to resist the urge to take all the responsibility for this attack. If it weren't for me and my people no army would be marching on this city."

"If it weren't for the dragonborn it wouldn't be an army threatening the city, but the University," Raesh said. "And not just Arvall, but all of Noelle. People would still have hate and prejudice in their hearts. And anybody with dragon blood would be living in fear, just because of what they are. No matter what happens when that army arrives, the dragonborn saved us."

"I agree," said Lymir.

"Your words comfort me," Saeryn said. "But my personal feelings are of no matter just now. I've had the chance to look over Sarinda's report from her voyage. She wrote that a curious epidemic of Maeludrax disease was beginning in the True Isles. Thabes is almost completely shut down."

"That's the last thing we need," said Raesh. "The True Isles are supplying forty percent of our weapons and armor. Since when are there outbreaks in the True Isles? I thought their waters kept them disease free?"

"Precisely," Andie said. "It sounds like another trick of the army or the Church. If they can weaponize the red sand, then why not disease? The True Isles would be the perfect testing ground: a healthy population, secluded environment, almost nonexistent military presence. We can't let this go on. The True Isles are close enough to the Church that the priests would have known the isles were supplying us. Attacking them with this weapon makes perfect strategic sense. We have to help them."

Everyone nodded in agreement.

"I can leave this evening," Andie said. "I'll take a small party and we can be there by morning."

"And what will you do?" Raesh asked. "I'm all for

helping them, but the cure for Maeludrax isn't something we can make or buy in Arvall. Taline had the last remaining vials in western Noelle, but they sent them across the continent last year to some poor villages. They haven't synthesized anymore and the process would take at least three days. What can you do?"

"I can give them my blood."

"What?"

"Saeryn and I have been reading over the grimoires. Before they were executed by the University, some of our third cycle ancestors were scientists. They were experimenting with the healing properties of our blood. Up until that point, they'd all been so scared of the University and the hunting that they suppressed their abilities and pretended to be normal. But they found their courage and ran countless experiments over a decade. Their work was cut short by their deaths, but before that they hadn't come across a single disease that their blood couldn't cure."

"Don't tell me the University killed a group of scientists who could have potentially eliminated disease from the world."

"They didn't just kill them. The scientists were based right here in Arvall on the mountainside. Remember that thing they taught in school? 'The Great Erosion of the Third Cycle?' The University bombed the mountain, killing all seventy scientists and causing the top thousand feet of Brie to slide down in an avalanche, which they diverted away from the University and instead let fall on the city. They ended up killing almost a thousand people that day."

"There's never an end to the evil, is there? But about

your blood... even if that works, you can't give hundreds of people your blood."

"I don't need to. Not per se. I'll take a sample and amplify it by magic. Then I'll follow the instructions in the grimoire and distribute it. At least we can save some until the cure can be found and sent for. If the outbreak started days ago, there might not be many of them left."

"Go as swiftly as you can," Lymir said. "Our allies deserve to know that if they risk their lives for us we'll do the same for them."

"Okay. Saeryn, I'm sorry to ask this," Andie began, "but I need you to come with me. With Oren out of the city I won't have a dragon to ride. You up for an adventure?"

"Certainly."

Saeryn and Lymir left the apartment and Andie and Raesh were alone. Raesh stood and walked a bit, while Andie waited for him to say what she knew was on his mind.

"Okay, I'm not going to be that guy," he said. "The guy who said you can't go or starts worrying for your safety just because you want to go on a mission, no matter how insane. I won't doubt you or belittle you like that. You're the bravest, most powerful, most intelligent person I know. You're more capable than any of us. I'll just say be careful and that I'll be waiting for you when you get back."

She stood and went with him. She kissed him in a way she hoped thanked him for always doing the right thing, for always saying what needed to be said. He held her.

"I want you to do something for me," she said.

"What's that?"

"I want you to open something."

She turned and walked to the spare bedroom. She returned with a briefcase, but not just any briefcase: it was Marvo's. It was the briefcase Marvo kept his recipes in. Raesh's eyes widen when he saw it. Andie saw him struggling inside.

"Where did you find that?" Raesh asked. "I've been looking for it for months."

"I've been looking, too. Your father really hid this thing. I finally found it behind two secret compartments and a pretty tough safe. I wanted you to have it. And I want you to open it. Not for me, but because it's yours now and you should embrace it. Your father would have wanted you to have it. Marvo always bragged about how it would be yours someday. You don't have to cook anything or run the restaurant, but all of it is yours."

"It seems like someone else's life," he said, gently taking the case from her. "I've only been back to the restaurant a handful of times. It seems so small now, so old. There was a time when I looked forward to owning it. I had so many plans and ideas for how I was going to make it better and make it one of the greatest places in Arvall. And now I can't even..."

"You'll figure it out in your own time. There's no law that said you can't walk away from the restaurant if you want to. All of this is up to you and no one's going to judge you either way, as long as you face this. And the truth is... it *was* someone else's life."

Raesh stood there looking at the case for a few moments before he lowered his hands. He and Andie walked down the hall to the bedroom and he placed the briefcase in the closet. They lay down in the bed, in each other's arms, without saying a word, spending a few moments together before Andie began to start preparing.

A COUPLE HOURS LATER, Andie was stroking the head of Saeryn's dragon. It wasn't as big or as strong as her previous one, but Andie could tell this new dragon adored her just as much. He had claimed Saeryn as his own the moment his own rider had died. No matter how long Andie was around them or how many times she had ridden them, she's was always astounded. The creature responded to her touch, curling toward her and giving that deep rumbling purr that only dragons can make. Soon Saeryn exited the University and the two mounted up. They had four other riders alongside them. Andie double checked she had the right grimoire and the ingredients they would need for the spell—it was very old and very precise spellwork.

They flew in perfect chevron formation, high above the city and the people they had sworn to protect. With the dragon's great speed, it wasn't long before they were over the Spider Sea and it was a sight Andie would cherish for the rest of her life. She had never flown over the sea before and it looked even more beautiful from above. The soft light of the moon fell over the modest, coursing waves and created a new kind of perfect light. The silvery trench spiders were already near the surface, with their feather-shaped legs and dandelion bodies. It was devastatingly beautiful.

But even that incredible sight could only distract Andie for so long. She thought of the suffering Thabians in the True Isles. They had been a neutral party since the beginning of time. No one can remember when the

Thabians fought a war or did anything other than help those in need. They were skilled fighters and excellent blacksmiths, but their supplying weapons to Arvall was only one of three recorded instances of them ever choosing sides in a conflict. While it made perfect sense to cut off the weapon supply, Andie couldn't believe anyone could be so evil as to infect the entire isles with that terrible disease—a disease that is extremely painful and fatal if not treated quickly. If they had known the Thabians would be attacked so heinously, they never would have set up the arrangement.

She was confident her blood and the blood of the other dragonborn would suffice as a cure; she'd checked and doublechecked and triplechecked the grimoire. She worried that they were too late. Maeludrax disease is a horrible sickness: it begins benignly enough, as most illnesses do, with a fever. But overnight the body becomes covered in black rashes so painful that even the blowing wind causes severe pain. Next the senses go: sight, sound, taste, touch, smell. By the second night the body's immune system is almost destroyed and only luck can save a person from dying from some common illness that normally wouldn't be an issue. By the third day the bleeding begins and the lungs begin to shut down. Some people, especially those with magic in their blood, can survive past that point if they're strong enough and are closely monitored. But most people didn't live longer than four days and no one lived past a week. Andie could hardly imagine it: an entire civilization dying.

The dragons flew all night since there was nowhere to stop and rest. They reached The True Isles when the morning was still black. All the isles were surrounded by the cerulean water that never darkens, not even when the sun goes down. It was an old and powerful magic that allowed the waters of the isles to touch the other seawater without mixing. They flew straight for Thabes, a beautiful city lit by the evanescent glow of its wildlife; every animal and insect in the True Isles glowed. It was never truly dark. The inhabitants had sworn off modern technology and instead lived off the land and in huts made from sand and clay. Andie had been overwhelmed with beautiful sights in her life and this was yet another one.

They landed on the beach and hurried toward the only place in the city where the torches were still burning. Even before the dragons touched down on the beach, Andie could smell it: the scent of countless rotting corpses. They arrived at a large clearing and were halted by the shock. As far as the eye could see in front of them were bodies. Men, women, children, the elderly, even some of the larger animals that were mammals lay dead or dying. There were a few of the city's healers still moving around, helping where they could, but not nearly enough. Andie couldn't begin to count the people. As they moved forward again, Andie stepped in something and then pulled her foot back with a jerk. The sand was soaked in blood.

One of the healers saw them and came racing over. When he reached them, he began to speak faster than Andie could keep up with She realized he was speaking another language entirely. She tried to signal to him that she couldn't understand, but Saeryn grabbed the man and turned him toward her. She seemed to listen to him intently and then she turned to Andie.

"He said he welcomes us in the name of Alqwedelades, the god of him and his people. His begs for our help if we can offer any. He said all of the people who speak our tongue are dead or dying."

"How can you understand him?" Andie asked.

"He speaks High Thabian, a language older than our people. It was once well-known across western and central Noelle and I learned it as a child."

The man began to talk again, his arms and hands were waving wildly in his begging gestures. Saeryn asked him something in his language and he responded.

"He said the sickness has been on them for nearly six days. Over half of the population is gone. I've asked him if there is any healer left who has magic and he said there is one woman beyond the trees, but she has come down with the illness just hours ago. She may still be strong enough. We must hurry."

Saeryn turned and said something else to the man. He motioned to her face and to Andie's and then said something back. Saeryn responded and the man dropped to his knees and began bowing over and over.

"What happened?" Andie asked. "What's he doing?"

"I think he's... worshipping us. I asked him to take us to the healer so that we could help them, but he said we needed masks. I told him we are dragonborn and don't get sick, and then he began to bow."

Saeryn leaned over and raised the man up. She spoke to him so soothingly that Andie was almost calmed herself. The man made a final half bow then began hurrying toward the trees, with the dragonborn following. When they reached the woman, they could see that she had the fever and a few small rashes, but was still able to walk and lend assistance. Saeryn spoke with her and the woman exhaled a sigh of relief.

"Okay, princess," Saeryn said. "Let us begin."

Andie got the grimoire and began following the instructions for the spell. She cut her hand and caught the blood in a bowl. She finished the preparation and then said the incantation. She drew the blood into a syringe and gave the woman a dose. They waited. It didn't take long before the woman's complexion improved and the rashes began to slowly recede.

"That's amazing," Andie said. "I read the grimoire, but I don't think I actually believed it would work until just this moment."

"There have always been tales about the blood of our people," Saeryn said. "It's nice to know that some of the good ones are true. I wonder that no one has exploited these properties before."

"According to the pages, our blood can cure most known diseases, under most circumstances, but it can't cure wounds. It can't cure serious medical conditions, so nothing neural, spinal, circulatory, or anything like that. It's powerful, but not all-powerful. Still pretty amazing."

Andie filled another syringe and gave the man a shot as well, to protect him.

"Do you think you can do the spell?" she asked Saeryn.

"Yes, it seems simple enough."

"Good. I have another mission I need to attend to. You and the other dragonborn will have to take care of these people. Teach her the spell."

"But where are you going?"

"To take back our destiny."

CHAPTER TEN

ANDIE LEFT THE GROUP AND TOOK OFF THROUGH THE woods. When she was far enough away that was sure no one could see her, she took out the journals. She had gotten them from Marcus before they left the University. She flipped to the page she was looking for and it didn't take long to find: the location of House Terpsichore's secret portal. She would've told Saeryn what she wanted, but she didn't trust that Saeryn would understand. It was simpler that way. The Thabians needed the blood of her people, but her people needed the portal. Andie closed the journal and began her trek through the forest.

Everything about the True Isles was unusual and contained, including its climate. No matter what the weather on the ocean was like, the skies were always warm and clear over the isles. The climate was perfect along the beaches and huts, but deeper inland it was that of a jungle. Hot, humid, heavy. The wildlife was exotic, and Andie couldn't finish being surprised by one creature before she came across the next. It was not difficult to make her way because the foliage there was gently controlled by the Thabians to be a perfect balance that provided shelter for the animals, but also made hunting easier. The glowing creatures lent plenty of light, almost too much, and while Andie made her way with ease she also worried about being seen. But worry was pointless. Most of the inhabitants were dead.

She walked for some time, her hand was level with her face and ready to cast at a moment's notice. She was not convinced some of the army didn't stay behind to make sure everyone died. But she saw no one. In fact, the closest she had come to other people was passing three mass burial sites where she couldn't even begin to count the dead. She'd cast a spell over her nose and mouth so that the stench of the dead didn't make her sick. Yet there was no spell for the sadness. There was nothing she could do to stop her tears when she saw the sight of all those bodies that would never live or love again. They were just more reasons that fueled her anger and determination.

The journal said the portal was hidden beneath a Wellensbard, a trap from the old days. Wellensbards were objects that created optical illusions that only dissolve once the riddle they represented had been solved. The journal gave the general location of the Wellensbard, but because the author feared other families finding the portal, there were no specific instructions. The journal didn't even give a hint. Andie arrived in the area and had no idea where to start.

"Great. Tease me with the location of an ancient portal that can be used to get rid of my entire race and then leave me hanging."

She walked back and forth over the area, which must have been fifty square meters. She checked tree trunks, both sides of the small creek that splits the area, and anything that looked like it could have been in the wrong place. But all she saw was trees, plants, and a perfect night sky. Nearly two hours passed as she wracked her brain and poured backwards and forwards through the passage in the journal. She hadn't missed anything in the pages. She decided to try something. She raised her hands over the ground and prepared.

"*Solas revelati*—"

She had only just begun the revealing spell when the entire fifty square meter area exploded in a cloud of dirt, rocks, and tree roots. Andie was blasted off her feet and into a tree trunk. Hard. The dragon blood healing began immediately, but she had broken some ribs and she could feel the blood trickling down the back of her neck from a cut on her scalp. She had to lie there for a moment to catch her breath and heal. She knew she should've been smarter; Wellensbards were notorious for being spell-proof and extremely dangerous if messed with. If Andie wasn't dragonborn, she would've been in serious trouble.

"Well, at least I know I'm in the right place," she said, sitting herself up against the base of a tree. "That hurt. That really hurt. But I've got to find this thing. There's no way we can find them all before that army gets here, but I can get this one. I just have to think. Come on, Andie. The journal doesn't give anything specific, but there must be some clue. House Terpsichore would never run the risk of its descendants not finding the portal. They thought they were the only family who had one. Think. What do you know about them..."

House Terpsichore had been the most jovial of the seven families. They were the most ambitious and energetic at the parties and loved to hold competitions and pageants. They were no richer or poorer than the other families, though they had as many secrets. The seal of their house had been two lovers in dance, wreathed in some other smaller details that Andie couldn't remember. Over the last thousand years, the family didn't seem to have changed at all. She still heard stories about the extravagant parties they threw in east central Noelle. But that was as much as Andie could remember, and though she'd read the entire journal front to back there was nothing in it that could help her. All she saw was their pageants and their seal.

"Wait," she said. "That's it."

Before she'd even completely healed she hurried to her feet and began to dance. She was not quite sure of where the precise spot was so she moved all around the area, dancing as best and as truly as she could to a beat she didn't hear. If anyone had walked up they might have thought she was losing her mind. She danced across the jungle floor. Finally, she saw the land around her begin to disintegrate. When the illusion was finally revealed, she had to move quickly to avoid falling in.

"Well, would you look at that..."

The portal looked exactly like the one in the University, except this one was half buried and turned itself off. The automatic activation must have been a final security measure for anyone who found it that shouldn't have. Andie ran her hand over the smooth surface. She'd never seen one inactive before. The face of the portal was smooth, almost too smooth. A hard surface with absolutely no friction. Andie couldn't even begin to fathom the magic that went in to creating it.

"One down. Six to go."

. . .

By the time Andie made it back to the dragonborn, they'd already made considerable headway in healing the Thabians. Many of the bodies that were once lying prostrate were now sitting up. None were walking yet, but Andie figured the longer they were sick, the longer it would take them to heal. She was just glad it was working at all.

"Andie, where have you been?" Saeryn asked, looking half panicked. "You've been gone for hours. I almost sent people to look for you."

"I was sure you would after the explosion," Andie said sheepishly.

"I trust you're referring to the explosion that frightened us all to death. I almost went myself, but these poor people needed help. I trusted you to survive whatever it was and come back with a spectacular reason for your abandoning the mission, which, I feel it not inappropriate to add, was your idea. People are dying by the hundreds here and you're off exploring in the jungle. Disappearing, explosions, cryptic excuses. I expect more from the princess of our people. I have never been so disappointed with you."

Andie didn't want to admit it, but Saeryn's words almost cut her in half. Not once since she came out of the portal had Saeryn ever said anything like that to her. Andie could not have been more hurt if Saeryn physically tried to kill her. She simply stood there, weighing in her mind whether or not her excursion would be enough or if the truth will get her back in Saeryn's good graces. Regardless, the Queen of the dragonborn needed to know.

"I'm sorry, Saeryn. And I'm so grateful to all of you for helping to save these people. I know this was all my idea and that I took off without giving you a good explanation, but it was only because I didn't think you would understand and if you did I didn't think you would let me go."

"I think it's best you be honest with me now, Andie."

"I went searching for the portal. The one that's been hidden here for centuries. And I found it."

Saeryn and the other dragonborn turned their full attention to her and gawked. She had rarely, if ever, seen the Queen speechless. She took it as a good sign.

"House Terpsichore buried their portal here centuries ago and left a trail for their descendants, never knowing of course that it would be us, the dragonborn, who'd find it. I got the journal back from Professor Iceubes just before we left. When I finally got to the area, it took a little deductive reasoning, but I uncovered it. I'm not afraid to say I got lucky and the rest probably won't be so easy to unearth, but we're one step closer to controlling our destiny."

Saeryn continued to stare at Andie, almost as if she couldn't understand what she was being told. Andie stepped forward to take her hands.

"We shouldn't have to live in constant fear of these portals being used against us or anyone else. These things are incredibly dangerous and I don't trust them in anyone's hands but ours. I made arrangements for a ship to leave the port at Arvall and follow us here. It probably won't arrive for another day or two, but they can load the portal and get it back safely. Please tell me I've done a good thing."

Saeryn still couldn't speak, but she threw her arms around Andie and held her close. A weight fell off

Andie's heart. But when Saeryn let go of her it was a severe face, not a relieved one, that faced Andie.

"You've done a superbly good thing, princess. But you need to remember who you are. You're one of us and nothing you undertake is undertaken alone. Trust your people. Trust me. And never, no matter how great the possibility of reward, abandon those in need. It is not our way. The portal had been buried and undisturbed for centuries, and I doubt a few more hours would have hurt it. I am so very proud of you for your continued efforts to protect our people. We all know you love us. But we are a strong, resilient people. And you must promise me that from now on you will put others first."

"I promise."

"Good. Now, we still have work. Let us work to save some more lives and then you can show me the portal of House Terpsichore."

They worked tirelessly for as long as they could without resting. Eventually, they had enough of the Thabian healers on their feet to continue the work. They gave as much blood as they could afford and then the Thabians fed them and let them drink from their private waters. The food replenished them, the water made them better than they'd ever been before. Andie could try for the rest of her life and never be able to describe the taste and effect of that water.

After Andie showed the portal to Saeryn and their dragonborn warriors, it was time to take off again. Saeryn insisted that the city would need them for the preparations and the citywide evacuation.

"I can't imagine the chaos of all those poor people clambering up the side of the mountain to seek shelter in the University. There's certainly enough room for them all. The University's rooms, tunnels, and corridors go deep into the mountain. But it will take the next two weeks just to get them all up there with only SKY 6."

"That's the beauty of having this portal," Andie said. "It can be used for transportation. Marcus has all the notes on how to control the portals and set them up. As soon as the boat comes and carries this portal back to Arvall, it'll speed everything up."

"Excellent news. I confess I'm also worried for Oren."

"He's the best warrior the dragonborn have. I'm sure he's just being thorough."

"Yes, but he should have returned by now. One day when you're Queen, you'll learn that your people are your children and your job is as much to worry for them as it is to love them."

"I don't know what kind of Queen I'll make. I don't think I'll ever be ready for that."

"Well, we dragonborn live long lives, but we are not immortal. One day I will pass on and you will be the new leader. In fact, I may even step down if I think you're ready. And I'll tell you a little secret."

"What's that?"

"No one is ever ready."

They smiled. They gathered their belongings and trudged through the jungle to the clearing. They said goodbye to the Thabians and had to work hard to keep them from bowing. They reached the sands of the shore and mounted their dragons, ready for the flight home. The sun had been up for hours and the sunlight had done them all good.

"Saeryn, wait," Andie said.

"Is something the matter?"

"Not exactly. Look, we're already out here, a full afternoon and evening's flight from home, why don't we just keep going?"

"To where?"

"Most of the portals are out of our reach, at least for the time being. But we have more than enough time to fly to New Carthage and look for the portal of House Thalia. I know you want to get back to help, but there's nothing we can do back there other than train professors or stock food. There's plenty of people who can help with that. The Beautiful Dead, wherever they are and whatever they're doing, they seem to know more than we gave them credit for, and if they're as cunning as you suggest, they might even know about these portals. They and the Church have been one step ahead from the start."

"I don't know, Andie. The army has sped up its movements."

"Even if they ran nonstop we could still be back long before they arrive. I won't lie and say I'm sure of anything, but I trust you, Saeryn. I'm asking you to trust me."

"I've trusted you even when you didn't trust yourself. To New Carthage we go."

CHAPTER ELEVEN

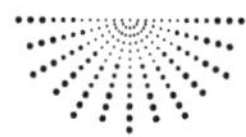

RAESH AND LYMIR SAT IN THE MEETING ROOM, GOING over battle plans and supply lists again. Many of the other professors had left or busied themselves with some small correspondence on their laptops. Everybody was startled back to the room when a bloody man rushed in, breathing hard and barely able to stand.

"They've found us! We need help! Please, someone must help us!"

"What's wrong?" Raesh asked, catching the man as his legs gave out. "You're dragonborn. But you're hurt. Why aren't you healing?"

"The Dead have found us. They captured them."

"Captured who?"

"Everyone. Men, women, younglings, the old. And they can ride our dragons."

"Why can't you heal?" asked Lymir.

"Their weapons. I've never seen such blades. They have swords that can hurt us in ways I've never seen. They didn't kill us, but it would have been only too easy."

"What do they want? Money? Land? What?" Raesh asked.

"The only thing the Dead have ever wanted. Our blood."

"How many got away?"

"Only myself. Two others were with me, but the Dead mounted our dragons and took them."

"Where's Oren? Did he get captured? Have they hurt him?"

"Oren... Oren… My general…"

"Where is he?" Raesh asked again, desperate.

"He's dead."

TWO DAYS LATER, Andie and her party flew in over the walled city of New Carthage. The original Carthage had been completely washed away in a flood, six cycles previously. New Carthage was built upon the ruins of its predecessor, but, even all those years later, it had yet to be complete. It had been called the City of a Thousand Laws because of the bureaucratic red tape that constantly delayed the city's completion, including the writing and rewriting of countless laws, tax revisions, and an intricate maze of zoning permits that had yet to be sorted out.

The New Carthaginians were a friendly enough people, much like the Thabians, without the beauty or seaside resorts. New Carthage was an extremely secretive city, and one of the most attractive and baffling things about it was its collection of godhearts. Dehydrated hearts of an ancient race of beasts that used to roam the region. Godhearts were one of the most sought-after commodities in all of Noelle. They had no practical use, but, as time passed, they came to be bought and used as jewelry. Jewelry of a kind that most would never be able to see, let alone afford. A single ounce of godheart, properly preserved, could easily sell for a solid ten-pound gold bullion.

While Arvall was arguably the most influential and well-known city of Noelle, New Carthage was without doubt the richest. Andie and the dragonborn party landed just outside of the city, not wanting to frighten the citizens or cause a commotion. Their mission would be faster if they could maintain a degree of secrecy. They got the dragons to lie down behind a thick group of trees and bushes and then began their approach, carefully.

"Remind me," Saeryn said. "Where exactly do the New Carthaginians' loyalty lie?"

"No one's sure," Andie answered. "We've reached out to them several times, but they've never reached a decision."

"What do you mean?"

"Well, apparently they take the whole democracy thing pretty seriously. The whole city votes on every major issue. Becoming our ally was a major issue. The vote wasn't heavy enough either way to make a firm decision and their city council didn't want to risk a move that could divide the city. The last I heard, they were conducting another vote and couldn't decide, but that was weeks ago. I'm pretty sure they're just ignoring us now."

"You said they voted before? Which way did they lean? More toward befriending us or more against us?"

"They wouldn't say."

They walked some distance before Saeryn stopped them and motioned for them all to hide. A trio of armed men marched by. Andie groaned audibly. There hadn't been any sorcerers born into New Carthage for years and so the city had to either hire people who had magic or hire people who use guns—the old-fashioned kind, not the terrible ones from the University. Andie was rather hoping security would be lax there, but they had just run into an armed, competent patrol before they'd even entered the city. That didn't bode well for what they'd find inside.

"Anyone who takes this long to come to a decision about a move so critical to not just our, but all of Noelle's survival, can't be trusted," Saeryn said. "Everyone knows what lies horded beneath these streets."

"Godhearts," Andie replied. "I thought the same thing. They don't want to pick a side because they don't want to risk losing their precious treasure. These people are not our allies."

"Agreed."

"But how far does that go and what do we do if we get caught? There's a big difference between just not being our ally and actively being our enemy."

"I suppose we could never answer that sufficiently by ourselves. My suggestion would be to not get caught."

Andie turned to Saeryn and saw that she was smiling. Saeryn reached down into a pocket of her bag and pulled out something thin and soft. Craiceann.

"I haven't seen any of those in a while," Andie said, taking the one Saeryn handed her.

"I had a feeling you had other plans when we took off from Arvall," Saeryn said. "One of the many cliché maxims that prove true when you become a Queen: always be prepared."

"Especially when your princess is always up to something."

She and Saeryn put the gossamer masked on and waited while the magic of the craiceanns changed their entire appearance. They got a good look at each other so they wouldn't forget what the other looked like, and Saeryn instructed the dragonborn warriors to stay with the dragons and be ready to leave or come to their aid at a moment's notice. She and Andie began walking toward the city gates.

"I've spelled these to give us the darker skin and exotic habits of the New Carthaginians," Saeryn whispered. "We should pass for them quite easily. Once we are past the gate we'll be fine, but if they stop us here then the mission is over before it starts."

Andie gave a slight nod and continued smiling, as if Saeryn were telling a funny joke. They waited in line at the gate until it was their turn. The guard took a long, odd look at them, but eventually waved them past. But as he waved his watch fell and Saeryn bent over to pick it up. She handed it back to him.

"*Gaeree*," the guard said, putting the watch on again.

Before he looked up, Andie was already raising her hand to cast. She had no idea what language he was speaking and knew it was only a matter of seconds before he figured out they were the imposters. She was about to blast him away when Saeryn speaks.

"*Praegio*."

Saeryn turned from the guard and moved through the gate as if nothing had happened. A stunned Andie was left standing stock still until she realized that everything was okay. She took a few hurried steps to catch up with Saeryn.

"How many languages do you speak?" she asked.

"Quite a few. You will, too, one day. The leader of any people should always speak multiple tongues so as to show respect to other leaders and their people. Cities will deal with you much quicker when they realize you've taken the time to learn their language. Come."

The streets of New Carthage were much the same as the streets of any major city, only cleaner and more expensive. When you have a seemingly unlimited supply of godhearts—which couldn't be found anywhere else in Noelle—it seemed you could afford a more beautiful city. The people even seemed more beautiful, somehow. The market district was alive with shoppers and patrol guards, though the police presence was far less intimidating within the city walls. Andie thought hard about where the portal should be, trying to remember the exact instructions in the journal. She wanted to pull out the journal to doublecheck, but she didn't want to risk anyone seeing it.

She and Saeryn walked for some time. The journal said the portal was buried near the center of the city. Luckily, the never-ending construction of New Carthage was a huge tourist attraction in Noelle and there were sightseeing maps placed regularly. Andie and Saeryn stopped at one, then continued toward the center of the city. As they walked, Saeryn told Andie stories of her reign as Queen and some of the sacrifices she's had to make. She told Andie about the heartache and how the responsibility was severe when necessary, but also about the loyalty, the hope, the love.

It had been apparent to Andie for months that Saeryn had been grooming her to take the throne. She hadn't been too worried about it, because it would clearly be years before she was ready, but she did wonder about some things that she couldn't bring herself to broach with Saeryn, not the least of which was whether or not her relationship with Raesh was suitable. She hoped it was okay, because if not there was no way she'd ever ascend to the throne. For all she knew, she wouldn't be allowed to have relationships at all. Saeryn certainly didn't seem to have any love interests, not that that was an appropriate detail to bring up in casual conversation.

As they walked, Saeryn tapped Andie twice on the inside of her elbow. Andie tapped Saeryn back twice, then tapped her four times on the shoulder. All the gestures were quick, precise, and done with smiles. Saeryn gestured again and they turn right, into an alley. Andie bent down, pretending to tie Saeryn's shoe. They stayed that way until a man in a pea coat and white slacks turned into the alley, walking very deliberately. As soon as he was close, Saeryn stopped feigning ignorance and stuck him with a punch so hard and fast that even Andie leaped back. The man collapsed to his knees.

"I don't know what's more impressive. The languages or that," Andie said.

"You don't fight as many battles as I have and not pick up skills. Does he have any identification? Any papers at all?"

"No, there's nothing. Wait."

"What?"

"I… I think I recognize him."

Andie stared hard at the face, trying to place when and where she saw him. His pale grey eyes were rare and distinctive. The longer she looked at him, the closer she came to remembering.

"Hurry, Andie. I don't like the feeling of this alley.

We should finish our mission and get back to the dragons as quickly as possible."

"Jasper Forlet," she said finally. "I took a class with him at the University, before everything happened. What's he doing here and why did he attack us?"

"I believe I can answer that."

Saeryn bent down and pulled at that top buttons of Jasper's shirt. It revealed battalion armor underneath.

"Great," Andie said. "Just what we need. Let's go."

They hid the unconscious body and returned to the street. No one seemed to have noticed. They relaxed. They walked for some time in silence because as they passed out of the market district the crowd thickened. Andie looked around her, trying to figure out why the crowd had become so dense. She grabbed hold of Saeryn and pulled her through until, at last, they reached the front.

"We must be near some major attraction," Andie said. "At least if anyone else is following us we can lose them in here. How did the battalion even find us?"

"They must have already been here. He was probably stationed outside of the city and saw us land before we changed our appearance. There's no telling what they were up to."

"Oh, I think I know exactly what they were up to and why the crowd is so big here. Look."

Andie pointed through some bystanders and Saeryn's gaze followed her finger. There was a massive hole in the center of the intersection. Nearby was a sign for tourists:

YOU ARE NOW STANDING ABOVE THE LOCATION OF

THE SINGULARE AND UNFATHOMABLE
COLLECTION OF
THE GODHEARTS
OF THE CITY OF NEW CARTHAGE.
WELCOME.

"Well, that was dumb," Andie said. "Who puts a giant sign above the exact location of the world's largest collection of the rarest gems known to man?"

"The battalion, the Dead, and the Church could fund their war for a century with only a handful of what's down there."

"Yeah, and I'm betting they took more than a handful. We're never going to catch a break."

"Well, at least we can locate and secure the portal. The exact center of the city, correct?"

"You want to know what else is at the exact center of the city? This giant crime scene where the battalion stole the one thing this entire city is obsessed with. This place will be crawling with patrols and investigators for months."

Andie ran her hands through her hair, frustrated to be so close to the portal. It hurt. And it made her exceedingly angry.

"Be calm, princess. We'll get what we came for. I refuse to leave this city without it. First, we'll find somewhere to avoid suspicion until nightfall. Then we'll come back and I'm sure that two powerful, intelligent dragonborn of royal blood can find a way to get what we want."

Some hours later, night finally fell over New

Carthage. The hole left by the battalion's heist was still uncovered and the godhearts below were exposed to the moonlight. The light of the crescent moon reflected off the jagged, unrefined surfaces of the godhearts in a dazzling, speckled pattern that danced across all the nearby buildings. By the time Andie and Saeryn returned, the city authorities had already pushed the lines four blocks back to keep away tourists and preserve the crime scene. Growing somewhat desperate, Andie tried out her feminine wiles on one of the patrol officers. Unfortunately, of the many gifts she had, flirting wasn't one of them. Saeryn couldn't help but laugh.

"It was a noble effort, princess. I'm sure if you were here in your true appearance we would have a different outcome."

Andie felt mortified, her cheeks tinging with a soft shade of rose. "I appreciate you trying to make me feel better. I might have another idea, though. Something my father taught me."

She took a breath and cast her spell. Everything around them slowed down.

Saeryn seemed shocked. She looked around herself at the passerby who appeared to barely be moving, his front foot suspended in mid-air as he stepped forward.

"This is incredible. Is this a variant of *Eitilt*?"

"I don't think so. It doesn't stop time, it just makes you move faster. A lot faster. Follow me."

Andie ran toward the massive hole and over the edge, Saeryn at her heels. They moved so fast they could run along the cavern walls, though the path was rough and slippery. They only just managed to make it to the ground when they hit a sort of wall and were knocked back. It took them a moment to catch their breath. The moment they were on their feet, they were surrounded by officers. Andie looked over at Saeryn. They'd been caught in a trap, which was one reason Andie never used the speed spell. It was great for some instances, except when defenses had already been put in place. It was too easy to protect against.

"Hands up, thief," an officer yelled, leveling his gun on them.

Several other guns came up as well, and the cavern filled with the sound of clicks as nearly thirty hammers were cocked.

"Actual firearms," Andie said. "A little outdated, don't you think?"

"Still kills just fine. We knew you'd come back. Nobody who gets their hands on one of these ever loses the taste for it and you got your hands on a lot of these. Where's your stash? Is this all of your gang?"

"There's been a misunderstanding," Saeryn tried to explain. "I realize we are here under suspicious circumstances—"

"You mean you were caught trying to sneak in using magic?"

"Yes, but we are no thieves. We came here in search of something else. Something of far greater value to us than godhearts. What we seek has the power to save or destroy, and we have no need of your precious stones."

"What is it you're looking for? Huh? Who are your people? You better start giving me some answers or the city council's going to have you in front of a high judge in the morning."

Saeryn seemed at a loss. The look on her face matched Andie's thinking. They'd been caught. The officer turned to Andie.

"How about you?" he asked. "Do you speak?"

"Yeah, I speak."

"Then start talking. Who are you and what do you want here?"

"Unfortunately for you, your city is indecisive. Which means I don't know which side you're on. Which means I can't tell you anything because it could become a diplomatic nightmare if you know who we really are and what we're after. That's all just a long way of saying that this is really going to hurt."

CHAPTER TWELVE

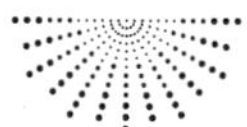

ANDIE STRUCK FIRST, HITTING THE TWO NEAREST officers with a bolt of lightning that didn't kill them, but threw them backward into the small mountain of godhearts. Saeryn went next, removing her scarf in an awesome flash of speed and magic, the fabric suddenly a solid yet flexible steel. She whipped it back and forth like a double-edged sword, taking out officers all around. On the other side, Andie got in close for hand to hand combat, taking the officers down without seriously injuring them. They were stronger than she was, but she was faster by far and had been trained by several of the greatest fighters in Noelle. In no time at all, she and Saeryn had the authorities put down. But they knew they don't have much time.

"Which way?" Saeryn asked.

Andie quickly pulled out the journal and opened it to the marked page. Once again, there wasn't much to go on, just like back in the True Isles. Andie was forced to think of everything she could remember about House Thalia. Unfortunately, she remembered even less about this house than she did the last. She turned to Saeryn.

"Tell me everything you know about House Thalia."

"Searching for the portal?"

It was not Saeryn who had spoken, but another female voice behind them. Andie turned and saw a police officer aiming a gun at them. The woman must have just arrived. Saeryn moved to pull her scarf off again, but Andie was quicker. She shot magic into her legs and launched herself at the woman. They both slammed into the ground. Saeryn rushed forward to help, but suddenly stopped. Andie got to her feet and looked over, but Saeryn didn't seem to see her. Andie gestured to her, but did not get a response. Saeryn was pacing and seems to be shouting, but Andie couldn't hear her. Then Andie looked over to the woman, who had her hand up, casting a spell.

"You first, then her," the woman said, practically snarling

"That's impossible," Andie said. "The police in New Carthage don't have magic. Who are you?"

"An imposter like you. The difference is I'm leaving here alive." Faster than Andie thought anyone could cast, the woman sent out a spell that sucked up all the oxygen around them. Andie fell to her knees, feeling her lungs collapse against themselves. But she had enough strength to raise the earth around the woman and trap her arms. Barely. Andie motioned with her weak hands as she suffocated, and the woman was pulled over and down, the earth around her arms remerging with the ground and trapping the woman up to her chest. Andie broke the spell and breathed a painful, ragged breath, but the woman cracked the ground and got up again. They traded spells, Andie hitting her with a ball of purple fire and being hit with a flurry of cuts from invisible knives in return.

The woman conjured a pair of long daggers made of the very wind and rushed in. Andie used every bit of her considerable training to avoid her; the woman was superb with the daggers, as if it was a dance or a work of art. Andie managed to land a few hits, but took just as many. The woman finally managed to cut Andie on her arm and the force of the wind dagger slicing her arm spun Andie on her feet. Furious, Andie reached up to her face and pulled the craiceann off, revealing her true face and body. She drew the sword from her hip and took a stance, prepared to end this.

"Andie?"

There was a slight delay while Andie realized that the woman had called her name.

"Who are you?" she asked. "How do you know my name?"

"I didn't think I'd ever see you again."

Andie stared into the face of the woman, noting her eyes, mouth, hair, build, but had absolutely no idea who was standing in front of her. The woman twisted her arm through the air and removed the spell blocking Saeryn. As soon as she could hear and see them again, Saeryn spelled her scarf and moved to attack the woman.

"Wait!" Andie called.

She moved to Saeryn and pulled her craiceann off as well, revealing the Queen of the dragonborn in all her glory. The woman's eyes went wide as she saw the face. She knelt and lowered her head.

"Forgive me, your grace," she said. "I would never have attacked if I'd known who you were. I'm sorry to tell you that you're too late. The portal is gone. I came looking for it, too, but it was already gone when I arrived. I came to claim it for you, I promise."

"Rise, stranger," Saeryn said. "I am not opposed to forgiving you if you will say how you know us and who you are."

"It's me," the woman said, with an expression not far from pleading.

The woman stood and her hand moved to her face. She pulled off a thin mask and the face she was wearing slid away. Another craiceann. And the face revealed was one that neither Andie nor Saeryn could believe. Andie can only manage one word.

"No."

Blackness.

"FHEALLTÓIR FOLA."

Beladorion stood over one of the dragonborn warriors, only just finishing beating the man until he almost died. Now the leader of the Dead waited for the dragon blood to kick in.

"I've always loved beating you blood traitors. As long as I don't kill you, the dragon blood heals you and we can begin again. But enough for today. I'll say one thing for you, you're not easy to break."

Beladorion left the man in a pool of his own blood and moved toward the front of camp. Along his way, he passed the rows and rows of dragonborn in cages. The dragonborn were a dignified people; they neither screamed nor pleaded. They were all confident their Queen and princess would find them and exact terrible vengeance. Beladorion locked his eyes on Ashur, who was doing some interrogating of his own. Although he was almost a hundred meters away, Beladorion could see and hear Ashur as if they were standing next to each other. He could smell the sweat of the dragonborn Ashur was beating. His senses and the senses of his people were unimaginable. Beladorion rushed forward and in seconds stood between Ashur and his victim.

"Commander," he said. "I'd like to go over our plan once more. I assure you, you'll be able to return to your plaything momentarily."

Beladorion headed to the front of the army. Most of the battalion soldiers and almost all of the Beautiful Dead were there, except those Beladorion dispatched with a special purpose. There may not have been a single army throughout all of time who could have stood against this force. Ashur followed Beladorion until they reached a small clearing.

"Is this supposed to be private?" Ashur asked. "No disrespect, but you and your people can hear across valleys. I don't really see what a few meters is going to do."

"I didn't bring you hear for privacy. I don't keep secrets from people. The only leaders who keep secrets from their own kind are greedy, cruel little cowards who wish they were gods. I brought you here to show you this."

Beladorion bent forward and grabbed the end of an enormous sheet and pulled. Ashur looked as if he'd seen a ghost. He experienced fear for the first time in a long while. He took several steps back.

"What is that?"

"You know very well what it is," Beladorion said, completely calm.

"How did you get it?"

"The same way I get anything. Patience and power."

"It shouldn't be here. That should be in Leabharlann."

"No, commander. This isn't the one you knew before. This is the portal of House Erato, buried for centuries under the abandoned city of Raven Deep. The one you knew is still in your library in the mountain Brie."

"There's more than one?"

"There are eight. One in your university, this one, and six more, each hidden by one of the founding families. I had some of my Dead excavate the portal of House Thalia in New Carthage some months ago. It's now with the army marching on Arvall. They'll set it up somewhere before they reach Gordric's Pain."

"And they'll be able to walk right into the University," Ashur said, beginning to understand. "The University and the city won't know what hit them. I'm starting to believe you're as cunning as you keep saying you are."

"Indeed. I doubt if anyone knows these portals still exist. I don't even think the descendants have a clue. When the times is right you and I will lead our army here to Arvall as well. So now I've proven again how useful I can be. And what do you offer?"

"I have agents in the University and the city. It's amazing how easy it is to buy some people's loyalty. All it took was the promise of a few godhearts. Speaking of New Carthage, my men should be done stealing their precious stones by now."

"I see you're no stranger to intricate webs."

"Not at all. I also have politicians and diplomats in my pockets. Hundreds of them. We've worked hard to turn as many as we can in eastern and central Noelle. After you convinced the Chancellor to kill those eight hundred ambassadors and heads of state at the Winter Festival, there was a chaotic scramble to fill those seats. We got our people into most of them. Their loyalty, if you can call it that, is contingent on our winning this war. If we lose, they won't back us and they won't risk moving against the dragonborn on their own. But if we win we'll have their support, their resources, and their influence. If that's not enough for you, I've been in touch with the descendants of the founding family since I first started my training under the Chancellor. Their hatred for the dragonborn has never wavered. If we win Arvall, they can help us win and control everything. They've also already begun a plan to destroy the Church. And I mean literally destroy that massive eyesore. And who can forget the icons? Millions of people all over western Noelle have gone to the University in Arvall and all have been given an icon. I know the magic that can command those icons to kill their hosts. It will take the entire battalion and all the power we can muster, but imagine: millions dead in an instant if they challenge us."

Ashur relaxed against the trunk of a tree and grinned at Beladorion, completely satisfied with his work.

"So there it is," he said. "You offer me a dragon-free Arvall and I offer you all of Noelle. Is that enough for you?"

"Yes, commander. That will do just fine."

CHAPTER THIRTEEN

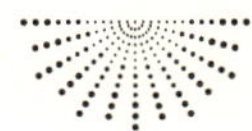

"We weren't prepared for this," said Raesh, pacing the floor of lecture room 594.

"We could never have been prepared for this," Sarinda said.

Lymir sat beside her, thinking, as he had been since the warrior showed up. He hadn't said much in the two days since, but seemed lost in his own shock and confusion.

"When Saeryn and Andie told me about the Beautiful Dead, they said nothing about what they were capable of," Raesh continued. "And now they're not even here to help. They're off on some secret mission. We don't even know if they're okay."

"But we do know that the dragonborn need help," Sarinda said. "We have to send somebody, anybody. I'll go. I'll lead a team across the—"

"Sarinda, even if I wanted to, I couldn't send you. The trip takes roughly a day and a half by dragon. Since none of us can even ride dragons and there's no transport in the city that can get us there fast enough, it makes no sense to go. We can't send more dragonborn because we need them here for the war and whatever these Dead have, it's strong enough to stop the dragon blood healing. It's been two days and Sven still hasn't completely healed from his wounds. I don't want to say this, but I have to: any dragonborn captured by the Dead are on their own until Andie and Saeryn get back and we win this war."

"And then I'll be on the fastest transport I can find to cut some Dead legs off."

"I'll be right behind you."

"Okay," she said, shifting in her seat. "If the Dead are capturing them instead of killing them, then they obviously have plans for them. They should be safe for now, at least until this mysterious spell is broken. I just radioed the ship before I came here and apparently Andie arranged for it to go out to the True Isles and bring something back."

"Bring what back?"

"You're not going to believe it, but... a portal. I guess history is wrong again. There was one buried in the jungle that Andie found. I'm guessing there are probably more and that's where Andie and Saeryn are. I want them here as badly as you do, but if they're out finding portals I have to say that's way more important than sitting on their thumbs all day and night."

"Yeah, and if Marcus can operate those portals as well as he said he can then we can get people in here that much faster. We need to get as many inside these walls as we can, as quickly as we can. They'll be safe here."

"We'll have him meet the captain at the harbor and

get people organized. But we also need to focus on getting people into the bunkers throughout the city. I think we're all safest here, but something just doesn't sit right with me about gathering everybody into one place. If by some chance the enemy *did* get into the University, the people of Arvall would be sitting ducks."

She stood and looked over at Lymir, waiting for him to speak. He returned her glance, then went back to staring into the middle distance. She turned back to Raesh.

"Well," she said. "Besides shelter I think we've got everything covered. We're as stocked as we can be with food and supplies, and the captain's also bringing the next loads of weapons and armor from the True Isles. I'll head back up to the summit and help with the training. It's just a waiting game now."

Sarinda left, touching Raesh on the shoulder as she went. Raesh stayed a while longer, hoping to get a conversation going with Lymir, but that effort bore no fruit. Soon enough he left, hoping sometime soon Lymir would be ready to return to his role. They might not have much time left.

Raesh went up to his apartment to pack a bag. When he was ready he took SKY1, then SKY 6, then the city shuttle train, then the crossland train, then the Sud, and then finally a cab, which dropped him off in front of the largest hospital in Taline. On the seventy-seventh floor, he had to go through a security checkpoint, an added measure to protect one of the most important people to him in the world. When he finally reached the room, Alecia was just finishing changing the drip.

"Raesh, hi," she said.

"Hey, Alecia. Any change today?"

"Well, for a moment earlier we thought so. There was a spike in brain activity and heart rate increased unusually, but she went back down. It was probably just a reaction to the drip. The doctor changed the medicine and dosing recently. Sorry, sweetheart."

"It's okay," he said, sitting in a chair beside the bed. "But I guess I have to ask: are you sure it was just a reaction?"

"Oh, I wish it were something more. You know, for a moment there I almost thought she was going to wake up. Her eyes. I could have sworn they were fluttering. Never mind. I'll leave you two alone. Goodnight."

"Goodnight."

Raesh settled in next to Carmen and changed her old flowers for the new ones he'd brought. He couldn't help thinking she looked so peaceful, so calm. It almost seemed like waking would be the real punishment. A part of him hoped that she wouldn't open her eyes for a while yet. He wanted her to wake to a new world, one where the war was over and everything that had been ruined had been rebuilt.

"Do you know what this is?" he asked her as he pulled a book from his bag. "This is one of my books. You've been begging me to let you read them forever. But I want you to know I didn't keep them from you because I didn't trust you. I just didn't think they were any good. But I'll let you decide for yourself. Before we get started, I don't know if you know this or not, but Andie and I are together. Together together. I know, it took us long enough. You can stop laughing now. She's not here tonight. She's off... being Andie. Sometimes I want to be mad her, but how can I? Her courage, her drive, her selflessness are all reasons why I love her. No, I haven't told her. Yes, I plan to as soon as I see her again. No one asked for your opinion, thank you very much.

"I love you, you know. And I miss you. You and your inappropriate, embarrassing jokes. We all miss you. But don't wake up yet. Not tonight. Wait a little while longer until Andie and I can fix this world for you, make it safe and beautiful for you again. You've been through so much, we all have. I just want to protect you. One more thing: we found more portals. Seriously. Yeah, I know... those things freak me out, too..."

Raesh began to read from his book. There were fifteen council fighters in the hall outside, but they didn't make a single sound, and, as he read, Raesh began to forget the world. For as long as he read it was just him and Carmen. He read until he couldn't keep his eyes open anymore. He closed the book and placed it back in his bag. He leaned forward and lay his head on top of his arms, right next to Carmen and fell asleep.

Sometime later, a hand moved through his hair. At first, he didn't respond.

"Raesh?"

The hand continued to move through his hair. Raesh began to stir.

"Raesh? Is that you?"

The voice and the hand combined finally brought him to the point of waking. Raesh yawned and looked around, blinking his eyes to bat away the blurriness. Finally, he looked at the face, the smile that was weak but familiar, the hand resting on his face. He couldn't believe it, even as he looked at her.

"Carmen?"

BACK IN THE UNIVERSITY, the portal was still open. Though Professor Iceubes now knew how to operate it, he'd been asked not to. No one wanted to do anything to it until Saeryn and Andie returned.

Just then the surface of the portal began to move, but the captain hadn't pulled into the dock yet and Marcus was still on SKY 6 on the mountainside. From the pretty, frictionless face of this device rose a man in robes. Five more followed him. In a perfect, slow-moving line the men walked forward from the Archives into the gargantuan space of Leabharlann.

They wandered, looking about them and examining books, but always moving steadily and deliberately toward the door. Without warning, those doors opened and all of the men stopped in their tracks. Two professors stood in the doorway, looking at the men in total bafflement. One of the robed men glided gracefully forward to just within a few feet of the professors. The professors took the stances they learned while training on the summit. But they were new recruits and had only had a couple classes. They came from money and privilege, and had never fought before. The robed man raised his hands beside him and held still. The professors were just about to attack when a great cloud of red sand bursts from his robe and engulfed the two professors. They didn't even have time to scream.

Once they were dead, the robed man, the priest, returned to his fellows, who gathered in the middle of the great library. They formed their line and moved just as slowly and deliberately back down to the portal. They leaned forward over the surface.

"It..."

"Seems..."

"The..."

"Way..."

"Is...

"Clear."

CHAPTER FOURTEEN

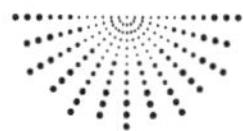

IT WAS THE NEXT MORNING WHEN ANDIE WOKE. SHE WAS lying in a room she didn't recognize. Outside the window, she saw they were still in New Carthage, though now they were on the other side of the city. She sat up slowly, her head was clear and at the same time heavy. She still didn't understand how dragonborn can be self-healing, but still faint.

"Be easy, princess. We're all safe."

At the sound of Saeryn's voice Andie turned to see her sitting on the next bed, smiling.

"I have to thank you for your fainting spell. If it hadn't been for that, I might never have had the experience of staying in a hotel. It's quite lovely.

"Was she real?"

"Yes. She is very real, Andie."

"Where is she?"

"You mean me?"

Just after her voice came around the corner, so did she. Andie needed a moment to make sure she wasn't dreaming and then she'd rush toward the girl she's missed so much. They threw their arms around each other.

"Yara," Andie whispered.

Andie hugged Yara as tight as Yara was hugging her. Saeryn watched from the bed.

"I thought you were dead," Andie said. "I saw you... I saw you..."

"You saw me carried away by a dragon. In its teeth, admittedly, but not dead. Although it did hurt. A lot."

"Wait, but then…" Andie paused, trying to remember her facts correctly. "When I learned the truth far later, Oren said he sent you through a time curse. Through the portal back to his time."

Yara smiled. "And he did, only it didn't work. He sent me back to a time somewhere between his own and ours, if I'm not mistaken. Only, something happened as soon as I arrived. The magic reversed and I was pulled back into our own world. I don't think anyone noticed, so I ran."

"I don't understand." Andie ran her hands through her hair, staring at her friend.

"Andie, it was the most beautiful place. And I suspect it might come in handy. I don't know how, or when. But just in case it helps…" Yara cast a strange and beautiful spell before the others, lifting her hands before her and chanting a short incantation. A shimmering image appeared before her and Andie and Saeryn both gasped in wonder. "This is what the spell in the portal looked like when Oren sent me through. If you can match this, we might be able to retrace my steps."

"Why would we ever do that?" Andie was incredulous, unable to take her eyes off the shimmering magic before her.

Yara dropped her hands and the image disappeared. "I don't know Andie, I hope we never will."

Andie sighed and rubbed her eyes. "Okay, that's something. But back to what's important, Yara. Everyone thought you were a traitor. I thought you were a traitor. They were going to execute you."

"And they probably would have. They'd only been on the mountain for a little while. They hadn't even built a real prison yet, so I just waited until I was alone. Then I ran. I ran for days, as far as I could go. I didn't stop until I reached the mine cities in the north. I collapsed next to a mountain of coal and I didn't think I'd ever wake up again. But a family found me there and took me in. They cleaned me up, fed me, nursed me, and let me stay with them as long as I wanted. I spent the next few days trying to figure out what I should do. I knew I couldn't go back to the Hot Salts or even to Arvall because all of you thought I was a traitor and the minute I showed my face I'd be dead."

"But why didn't you say something? When we were there on the beach and all of us accused you... when I accused you. You could've convinced us—"

"No, I couldn't have. The setup was pretty convincing and if I hadn't been in this body I would've thought I'd done it, too. And to be honest, I felt that I deserved punishment. I knew something was off about Marvo. You and Raesh had known him longer and had more of a connection with him, but you were blinded because you both loved him. I was working side by side with him those last few days and I knew, I *knew* something wasn't right, but I didn't say anything because I had no tangible proof and tensions were high enough as it was. I could see in your eyes every time you came around me you were growing more and more suspicious, and I wasn't exactly a ray of sunshine myself. I should've just knocked him out, hexed him, anything. I might've saved his life. All their lives. By the time we were standing there on that beach I was ready to die for having let things go on and turn the way they did."

"What changed your mind?"

"When they dropped me on the precipice, I started thinking. If the Chancellor had tapped into that kind of power, he had to be working with someone even more dangerous than he was. Myamar Mharú was cruel, but he was never that clever. But almost overnight he'd become a master manipulator and the leader of a vast battalion. It just didn't add up. I knew that you were focused on saving the dragonborn and taking down the University, and you didn't have the time or peace to notice that the Chancellor was a puppet master who had strings himself. That's when I knew I had to live.

"After the family got me on my feet again and I'd made up my mind to figure out who was behind the Chancellor's rise to power, I headed east. I tried to visit the village where I was born, but it was gone. Disease killed most of them, and the rest just left. It was totally abandoned. My journey also led me to the city I lived in when I ran away from home. It was a disaster, too, writhing with crime and corruption. A cesspool of evil. Finally, I ended up on the eastern coast of Noelle staring into the Divided Ocean. I had no leads, no allies, and no resources. So, I did the thing I swore I'd never do again. I stole. It's not something I'm proud of, but I still had the skillset and it save my life. Within two weeks I'd accumulated some considerable assets and disguised myself. Another week and I was having lunch with the affluent and leveraging the police. By the end of a month I achieved my goal and was invited."

"Invited to what?" Andie asked.

"To a ball given by House Polyhymnia," Saeryn said.

"How did you know?" asked Yara.

"When you were unpacking your bag, I saw a Braided Bangle, a common gift to those who get in close with the family. You must have quite the skillset, indeed."

"Admittedly. At the ball, I managed to ingratiate myself. It seems as long as you have money and a pretty face no one's interested in how you got where you are. Of course, the host family wasn't concerned with my past because they already assume they're better than everyone. I flattered, complimented, and lied. Before long I was sitting beside a group of the most recent generation of descendants. I plied them with champagne, no difficult task, and guided the conversation where I wanted it to go.

"It was incredibly disappointing at first. They were just complaining about how their family had fallen in stature and how they hoped the dragonborn would be hunted and killed before the year was out. I was about to leave when I decided to see what more they had to say on the dragonborn. That was the key. Soon they were telling me all about the horrors their family had committed against the dragonborn, bragging about it. They said the dragonborn were a cursed people even before the University began hunting them. They said their parents used to tell them stories about another group who were descended from the dragons and how that other group hated the dragonborn so much that they wanted to capture them and drink their blood. They said these other dragon descendants had helped the University in its hunt for dragonborn. I thought maybe they were just myths at first, but then one of them, Bonhaus, told me he'd been interested enough to do some digging around. He found out that the stories were more than just bedtime tales. They were actual history. That other group was known as—"

"The Beautiful Dead," Andie finished.

"So then it's true," Saeryn said. "We always suspected that they had a hand in helping the University destroy us. The University had never been anything but arrogant and incompetent. There was no possibility of them figuring out our weaknesses and being able to track us across the land on their own. It was the Dead helping them all along."

"So you've heard of them?" Yara asked.

"More than that," Andie said. "They're marching on Arvall and the University right now. They'll be there in less than two weeks. And Ash's battalion is coming, too."

"That doesn't surprise me. Bonhaus also told me his family and all the other founding families had recently been contacted by the battalion. He said that soldiers were stashed across Noelle and they were all coming together. The battalion wanted the support of the founding families and they got it. After that night, I started following the battalion."

"How did you catch their trail? We've been trying to find them for months."

"I didn't do it on my own. Bonhaus put me in touch with them. I followed them, picked a few of them off as I went, but I mostly just gathered information. I had enough money to afford a network of spies and there is hardly a police organization on the east coast of Noelle that can't be bought for the right price. It wasn't long before I realized the battalion were trying to contact the Dead. I knew that if they joined forces it would be catastrophic. I tried to stop it, but I could never figure out where the meeting was supposed to take place.

"But, like any sprawling and completely depraved organization, the Dead couldn't keep as lowkey and they wanted. There are only so many cookie jars a hand can reach into before people start asking questions and keeping track. I checked in with Bonhaus and he'd heard the same rumors. Someone was looking for something that belonged to his family, something House Polyhymnia wasn't supposed to have. Within a week there was a break-in at their mansion by a man and woman stronger and faster than was humanly possible. They tore the place apart, but didn't find what they were looking for. Because I already had it."

"What was it?

"A portal. The ancestors of House Polyhymnia hid one for themselves, right underneath their mansion. Bonhaus told me his grandfather had always filled them with stories about how they had a magical device more powerful than all the sorcerers of the world combined and that it was buried right under their feet. Assuming that story was as true as the others turned out to be, I got there first. It was too big for me to move by myself so I spelled it, just like I did Saeryn last night."

"So, it's still there," Andie said, impressed. "It's just invisible. The Dead must have been standing right on top of it and not even noticed."

"Exactly."

"Wait, I understand now. We were under the

impression that the families had forgotten about the portals and the secrets of their ancestors, but they haven't. At least not entirely. They keep the secrets and histories alive in oral tradition, telling the story to generation after generation, only they don't know the stories are real. I can't believe it... these people are sitting on the biggest secrets in all of Noelle and they don't even know it!"

"I figured the same thing. I used Bonhaus and his family to get in with House Erato, but by the time I finally fell into their secrets and tracked their portal to Raven Deep, the Dead had already beat me there. But that didn't stop me. There was only one more house within range of where I was. House Clio in east central Noelle. But even Bonhaus couldn't get me in with them. House Clio has become sequestered from the other founding families and won't have anything to do with them. I had to go there and try to charm them on my own, but that failed miserably. So, I broke in.

"After fighting side by side with you and the council fighters against the University, a little personal security was no problem for me. I made my way inside, but I had no way of knowing where the portal was or if it was even on the property. I snuck into the master bedroom and spelled the wife so that she wouldn't wake. Then I sound proofed the room. I'll spare you the distasteful details, but let's just say the husband and I had a very frank conversation that he didn't like very much. He told me all the stories he'd been told as a child, one in particular about a magic doorway that was supposedly buried on the family's forest estate two hundred kilometers north.

"I got there as fast as I could. The estate was just coming in sight when I started to see trees falling. As I got closer I could hardly believe my eyes: there was a man and woman there knocking the trees down with their bare hands, like the trunks with nothing but foam. I figured they were Dead. I was lucky enough to take the man out by catching him by surprise with a strong spell, but the woman wasn't so easy. I can hardly even begin to describe the way she moved. Strong, agile, so fast I couldn't even keep up with her. She nearly killed me. I kept trying to defend myself and she would dash by me in a flash and send me flying. Finally, I was able to trap her and then get her still long enough to get in close with my wind daggers. I'd don't like the idea of ever facing one of them again."

"Don't worry," Saeryn said. "When the time comes it will be the dragonborn who face them. This has been a long time coming."

"Fortunately, she and the other one had already done most of the work. Before I snuck up on them, I let them clear the way and dig up the ground. Less work for me. That time I was prepared. I'd paid some people I could trust to keep quiet to move the portal. Now it's beside the other one under the mansion of House Polyhymnia."

"Is that safe?" Andie asked. "If they figure out that the stories are true they'll search for their portal. And when they go under their house and find not one, but two portals, I don't think they're going to be too shy about using them. We have to go get them. Now."

"They're safe, Andie."

"How can you think that?"

"Because Bonhaus and I wiped the memories of all of his family."

"Bonhaus and you? You honestly think you can trust this guy? Yara..."

"He's in love with me. I kind of... manipulated him. I had no choice. I needed someone on the inside, someone I could trust."

Andie just hugged Yara. Yara cautiously put her arms around her, too. By the bed, Saeryn stood, looking at Yara intently. Saeryn walked around the end of the bed, never taking her eyes off Yara, who looked back at her over Andie's shoulder.

"Everything you've done," Andie said, still holding her friend. "It must have been hard."

"You have no idea," Yara said.

"Back and forth across Noelle, taking on the Dead, giving up everything for this cause. And then having to endure a son of a founding family. I'm so sorry."

"Andie, there's something you should know. In the interest of being totally honest."

"Yes, I thought so," said Saeryn.

As Andie released Yara, Saeryn came nearer and placed her hand on Yara's shoulder.

"I can see it on you," Saeryn said. "I wonder if the best thing might be to leave the subject as it is for now. I'm sure we'll have ample time to discuss it later. Perhaps now it is most prudent to leave the city and rejoin our party on the outskirts of New Carthage."

"Leave what subject?" Andie asked. "What aren't you telling me, Yara?"

"Bonhaus. We worked side by side for so long and I was so... alone. I was doing it all by myself and then something happened. Between us. And I fell in love with him, too."

Andie took several steps back, looking both disgusted and horrified. Saeryn moved to touch her, but

Andie shook her off. She advanced on Yara so menacingly that Yara took a step back in surprise.

"You fell in love with him?" Andie asked. "With a member of House Polyhymnia? One of the seven families who have been hunting and killing my people for centuries? Are you serious?"

"Andie, you don't know what it was like out there!" Yara countered. "I was all alone and I missed my friends, my city. I missed you! It was my own fault that I was out there, but when I needed someone Bonhaus was there. He gave me the information that helped me track the battalion and find both of the portals."

"He's one of *them*!"

"He went against his own family for me! For all of us! For you! He doesn't believe what they believe and he's never killed a dragonborn all his life. He's never even met one."

"He has the blood of killers and liars! It's in his blood, he's poisonous! They're all poisonous!"

"Andie, I would think you of all people would be the last one to judge someone because of what's in their blood."

"I don't care!"

"You act as if evil can be inherited like dragon blood. That's not the way it works, Andie, and I think you know that. I understand this is hard for you and I know that if I were in your shoes I'd be judging me, too, but I need you to hear me out. Yes, I was the one who stole, traveled, fought, infiltrated, manipulated, bought, bribed, and climbed my way to what I needed for you and for Arvall. But the information behind all of that comes from Bonhaus. He was the one who introduced me to important people and helped me get in places. He was the one who put countless hours into research over the last few months. He was the one who stitched me up after the Dead woman almost killed me. He kept me going. I know what he is and what he comes from, but that's not who he is or who he wants to be. You don't know him, I get it. Don't trust him, trust me."

Andie couldn't even bring herself to look at Yara. She spoke to the wall.

"Yara, I cant... I... I can't even begin to tell you how much I missed you. When we finally found out the truth, every one of us was devastated. I've cried myself to sleep thinking of you and not a day has gone by when letting you get taken by that dragon hasn't been the biggest regret of my life. But you need to understand that I'm not okay with this. I can't be okay with this. You're telling me that you fell in love with a man who is a son of the most evil syndicate of people to ever walk in Noelle, whose ancestors murdered thousands of my people, of Saeryn's people. His family has played a continuous part in the longest, most widespread, most malicious, most damning lie of all time. People in his family use to hunt dragonborn and rape them, rob them, skin them alive, eviscerate them, carry out all other kinds of atrocities against them. For centuries. Relentlessly for years and years and years. It's because of people like him that my mother is dead, my father, Marvo, my friends, *your* friends. How many millions of corpses can point to his family as the cause of their death? So I'm happy to see you, but there is nothing about your feelings that is okay."

"Andie... I love him."

"Then love someone else!"

The two girls stood face to face, not furious, but firm,

immovable. Saeryn stood nearby, unsure of what to do or if she should do anything at all. Andie slowly shook her head, trying to deny that this was happening or that she'd heard these words, still unbelieving. Yara stood with her arms held to her sides, overjoyed to be reunited with her friend and exonerated, but unwilling to abandon what she has gained in the meantime. Eventually, Andie reached for her bag and turned for the door.

"Saeryn's right," she said. "We need to get out of the city and regroup with the warriors outside."

She left without waiting for the others to get their things. Fortunately, it didn't take Saeryn and Yara long to catch up. The three women took the elevator down to the main floor and Andie poked out into the hall cautiously. She looked both ways and then checked for cameras, wishing they had been able to save the craiceanns. She saw one of the city police approaching and quickly leaned back inside the elevator, readying her hand to cast at him as soon as he was close enough.

"Andie, it's fine," Yara said. "You don't need to fight him."

"Me versus an overweight street cop? Not much of a fight."

"No, I mean I've taken care of it. No policeman in the city of New Carthage is going to give us any trouble."

Andie turned to face Yara, incredulous.

"And exactly how did you manage to do that?"

"When I first arrived in the city, I put on the craiceann I was wearing when you and I crossed paths, but while you were unconscious I just figured it would be easier if we didn't have to worry about sneaking around. I told you. Any police force can be bought for the right price."

"Well then."

Andie exited the elevator briskly and headed straight for the front of the hotel. As she passed the officer, he looked at her just long enough to register her face and then he turned deliberately away. So did the two guards standing at the entrance doors. Even the concierge conspicuously tucked his head into a book. They made it outside and just as they reached the street, a police car pulled up and stopped in front of them.

"I'm here to escort you to the outskirts of the city."

"What?" Andie asked, confused, looking behind and beside her to make sure the man was talking to her.

"You're the three, right? Andie, Saeryn, and Yara?"

"Yeah..."

"I'm your escort."

Andie looked over to Yara, who nodded in return. Saeryn needed no convincing and got in without hesitation, as if it were the most normal thing in the world. Andie was still looking at Yara.

"I can't believe you bought off the police. How much money do you have, anyway?"

"The real kicker is that I paid them in money I got from fencing the godhearts I stole from them."

The drive to the city wall was relatively long; the hotel was considerably further from the last place Andie was before she fainted. As the buildings passed her window, Andie reflected on how wonderful the city would be to visit under better circumstances, even if a large number of buildings were unfinished. As they rolled along, Andie counted at least seven major construction sites, and they went through several detours.

Andie didn't say anything the entire car ride, though Saeryn and Yara spoke in low tones beside her. Soon enough the car was dropping the three of them off outside of the gates. Saeryn led them over into the woods where the dragonborn were waiting anxiously. Saeryn's dragon came over to her and nuzzled her with its massive, enchanting face. Once the dragonborn warriors saw Yara, they looked shocked, and not a bit defensive.

"Apologies for the delay," said Saeryn. "But as you can see, we ran into a ghost. We'd best be going now."

The warriors mounted up and so did Saeryn.

"I'll see you all soon," Yara said, taking a few steps back.

"What do you mean?" Andie asked. "You're coming with us."

"I can't. I can't ride your dragons."

"But they can still carry you in their arms. It won't be the most comfortable, but—"

"I have another mission, Andie. And Bonhaus is waiting for me."

"Right."

The two girls watched each other, maybe waiting to see what the other would do. Andie was so furious and so confused that a part of her just wished the moment were over. But another part of her thought about Yara and how intelligent, brave, and strong she had to be to do everything she did on her own. She wanted to say something, anything, to let Yara know that she appreciated her. That she missed her.

"Did you tell the police who we are?" she asked. "If they know that we're not only dragonborn, but the Queen and princess, it'll be a diplomatic nightmare. They haven't chosen a side yet and there's still hope they could side with us."

"No, they don't know. I told them our first names, but they're not bright enough to figure it out. I don't know if anyone in this city has ever even seen a dragonborn before. As for them choosing sides, I don't know if they'll formally align with you, but I told them it was the battalion who stole from the godhearts, so I know they won't be siding with them. Speaking of, here."

Yara reached in her backpack and pulled out a smaller satchel. She opened it and Andie saw that it was full of godhearts. Gorgeous, priceless godhearts.

"I may have left out the part about my own pillaging. Take these with you. You'd be amazed how many doors open up to you when you tell people you have some."

"Thank you. When will we see you again?"

"Saeryn tells me you know how to operate the portals now. I'll go back to Bonhaus' mansion and wait there. When you get back to Arvall and you're ready for me just come through the portal. I'll be there."

"You and him."

"Me and Bonhaus."

Andie slide the satchel over her head and onto her shoulder. She turned from Yara.

"Take care of yourself," she said.

"You, too, Andie."

Andie got up on the dragon behind Saeryn and the party lifted off. Yara turned and headed on to her work.

CHAPTER FIFTEEN

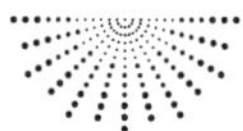

THREE DAYS LATER, ANDIE AND SAERYN STOOD AT THE entrance to the Black Grotto, on the southern coast of Noelle. It was the most sinister looking place Andie had ever seen. Every inch of the environment was blacker than any night sky she'd ever laid eyes on: the stone, the grass, even the water flowing through the grotto and the walls of the grotto itself. The air was thick and moved in acidic layers, the result of some dark incantation. They had not seen or heard a single life form within a hundred kilometers of the place and even the dragons, bravest of beasts, were unsteady here.

A day and a half before, Andie and the party landed just behind the suburban outskirts of Mastield, a wealthy southern city and the home of House Urania. The journal said the portal was hidden somewhere on the family's property, House Urania being rather paranoid and extremely suspicious. When they couldn't figure out how to proceed after an entire afternoon and morning of thought, Andie took a page from Yara's book and broke into the estate, finding the head of the family enjoying a brandy in the cigar room. He was the oldest son of Rasputraenir, whom the Chancellor had killed at the University. After a painful episode, he'd told Andie of a legend he remembered. The story ended with the family's most prized possession being stolen by an unknown group of infiltrators and taken away to the south. Andie and Saeryn searched the papers in the family's vault and discovered a watchlist of the family's enemies. Andie had heard of most of the groups and knew most of them didn't have the resources or foresight to know House Urania had a portal, let alone break in and take it. Saeryn was able to exclude a few more. Eventually, they were left with a list of five.

They spent the next day moving through Mastield and interrogating the groups on their list. Two of the groups had lost all their power and disbanded years ago. One had been completely forgotten when all of its members were slaughtered in a retaliation attack by a rival group. Another group was still together and still neck deep in dastardly deeds, but had absolutely nothing useful to say, even when Andie started breaking their bones. The final group on their list had split into organizations, one involved in corporate espionage and the other in the sale of black market goods. The latter sounded most promising, but Saeryn went to speak to the corporate group anyway. By the time they gathered that morning, Andie had gotten the location of the "large, round thing" the black-market group had stolen and Saeryn had turned the police onto the corporate espionage group.

Now they were there, at the Black Grotto, hesitant to go in, when they finally decided to enter, Saeryn instructed the warriors to follow them at a distance of one hundred meters. Just as a precaution.

"I've seen some shady places in my day," said Andie. "But this is the worst. By far."

"I can taste the dark magic in the very air," Saeryn said. "I fear terrible things characterize the history of this place."

"I'm more worried about terrible things happening today. It's getting harder to see."

The deeper they went into the grotto, the less they could discern about their environment. Eventually, the light was no more than a dot far behind them.

"*Solas*," Andie and Saeryn say in unison.

Light appeared as a ball in each of their hands, but it didn't shine very far. The magic of the grotto was strong. The dragonborn warriors behind them echoed the spell and still there was hardly any light at all. In fact, as each new light came into the dark, the power of the other lights dimmed considerably and by the time the final warrior cast her spell, the lights of all were almost completely extinguished. Andie noticed this.

"Wait," she said. "Myra, put your light out again."

The warrior extinguished her light and the rest grow brighter.

"Now you, Thydron."

The next warrior extinguished his light and again the rest grow brighter.

"Every further light brought to the darkness decreases the ones already lit," Saeryn said. "What manner of magic lies in these walls?"

"I don't know, but I'm liking it less by the second," Andie said, looking around her. "Okay, everyone put out your light. Saeryn will hold hers and we'll all have to stick close."

Andie put out her light and so did the rest. Saeryn's light grew much brighter, but it still showed no more than a couple meters ahead. Andie moved closer to Saeryn and put her hand on the Queen's shoulder. They move forward.

Deeper and deeper they went, surprised and dismayed by how deep the grotto ran. The only sound was that of the black water flowing back the way they came. Aside from that, it was eerily quiet. The black of the grotto was so pure and impenetrable that Andie began to believe she could taste it, feel the darkness coming over her skin. She's not afraid, but she grows more and more suspicious that they're following bad information. She can't see above them, but she can tell from the way the sound changed that the ceiling has opened, grown more cavernous.

"Saeryn, throw your light up," she said. "I want to see what we've gotten ourselves into."

Saeryn took the light and formed a hard ball. She threw it up and it just kept going higher until they lost sight of it. They waited. A few moments passed and then the tiny ball came into view again as it fell. Andie was not at all pleased with their circumstances; it reminded her too much of the months they spent hiding in the tunnels beneath the University. As the light came back down to find Saeryn's hand they all jumped back in terrible surprise and then the light went out. Just before the light was gone they got a glimpse of a man's torso, heavily muscled and shirtless, tall and fierce and standing not one meter from Saeryn's face.

"The Dead are here," is all Saeryn managed to say.

"We've been here for days," said the man in front of them, his voice moving through the darkness like floating death. "Waiting for you or the other one, the one who has already taken two of our portals. Perhaps you thought we would not find you or that we would not realize what you and your friends are plotting. But don't worry, our men will have caught up with her and her lover by now."

His voice made Andie's skin crawl. It was made all the more terrifying because the light had gone out and they were in absolute darkness. She began to hear movement on every side. It is the Dead, moving in the shadows, along the walls, even in the water. She realized she didn't hear them before because they didn't want her to.

"Perhaps you aren't familiar with the abilities of the Dead," said a different voice. "Our senses give us the advantage. I can see, smell, and hear you in here as well as if it were daylight. I can taste your sweat on the air. You're afraid. The darkness troubles you. Your training and your nerves are failing."

"You reek of despair," said yet another voice. "You cannot fathom the fate that awaits you. You come for a treasure you cannot contain and you seek safety beyond this war. But hope is not a thing you should aspire to. Embrace your death. Cede all control."

"Sorry to disappoint," Andie said. "But we're not really in a dying kind of mood."

With a single deft movement she exploded fire out from her body; the purple flames erupted in all directions eluminating the grotto with blinding flashes of colorful light.

"Child," said a voice in the dark. "The Dead do not

feel flames. You forget, that we, too, descend from the dragon."

"Oh, I wasn't trying to hurt you. I only wanted to see how many of you there are."

And she had. Andie knew that there were seven Dead in the grotto. Two in front. Three behind. One clinging to the wall beside her. One in the water. She tapped Saeryn their number and locations on her arm.

"Now!" Saeryn called.

In an instant, the grotto was alive with magic and power. Every other spell the dragonborn cast was fire, not to hurt but to illuminate. But the fight was quickly going against them; the Dead are quick, strong, and the darkness is nothing to them. Try as they might, the dragonborn were barely able to stay on their feet. Andie was no sooner up than she was knocked down again. She couldn't see anything at all and all she heard was the sound of the Dead flashing by and the dragonborn being beaten mercilessly. They would all be dead already if it weren't for the dragonborn healing. Then one of the Dead lifted her in their arms, holding her so tight she could feel her bones about to break.

"Fhealltóir Fola," the Dead said.

Andie struggled to work her hands up, to raise them across each other and place them on the forearms of the Dead. When she finally touched him, she cast a desiccation spell. The man cried out in pain and then his voice faded into a terrible croak before she heard a dull thud in the dark.

"One down!" she called.

She barely had the words out of her mouth before another Dead hit her. She felt herself flying up into the air and colliding with the wall. She dropped what must have been ten meters to collide back with the ground. She laid there for a moment, recovering.

"One down!" Saeryn called.

At the sound of the good news, Andie began to pick herself up. No sooner was she on her feet than the hand of a Dead wrapped around her throat from behind.

"Goodbye traitor," the woman whispered.

"Not today," Andie said. "*Spiorad.*"

Andie's body became incorporeal and she stepped backward, moving right through the Dead. The woman was totally baffled and by the time she turned around to look behind her, Andie was already blasting a bolt of lightning through her chest. The terrific light of the bolt illuminated the cave and Andie watched as the woman was blown far over to the other side of the grotto and collided with the wall, causing a small avalanche of stones to fall on her.

"One down!" Andie called.

There was a great sucking of air and stone for a moment and then it disappeared. Andie recognized the magic: a vortex spell she and Saeryn taught their people after finding it in an old grimoire.

"One do—"

The voice of the dragonborn warrior was cut short by a bloodcurdling slicing sound. Andie heard the body of the warrior thud against the grotto floor.

"One down!" Saeryn called.

Andie put her back against the wall, preparing herself for the next assault. Soon enough, she heard the sound of a Dead flashing by and felt a cold pain cut upward across her torso. She screamed and folded her arm over the wound, feeling the blood come thick and fast. What terrified her the most was that she wasn't healing. At all.

The wound hurt so badly she had to scream again. The Dead flashed by once more and sliced Andie's face. Then again to cut the back of her hand. Bleeding, in pain, and furious Andie forced herself to her feet and raised her good hand.

"*Eitilt mall comhlacht.*"

As Andie uttered the time curse the whole grotto froze. She began to feel her way forward. The first body was Saeryn; Andie could feel some blood on her, but she seemed fine. She moved over some more and nearly tripped over someone's corpse. She continued to feel around until her hand landed on the torso of a shirtless and heavily muscled warrior. She drew her sword and plunged it through the center of his chest. Moving on, she came across a dragonborn warrior in mid fall, badly injured, but possibly able to survive. It took her a few moments to locate the last Dead, who was in midair, frozen as she leapt to grab hold of the wall. Andie pushed her sword forward and felt it drive home with a grave slide.

"*Eitilt ar ais.*"

Time returned to normal. The Dead have been defeated, but Andie wondered at what cost.

"Any dragonborn still alive, identify yourself!" she called.

"I'm here," Saeryn said. "Multiple wounds, but nothing life-threatening."

"I'm here, too," Andie said. "I have a pretty bad cut on my chest, but I should be fine. Is there anyone else?"

There was only silence. Andie waited. Silence.

"Anyone? Please!"

"Still... here."

The voice sounded as if it was drowning in its own

blood. Andie turned to it and felt her way toward the voice. She heard Saeryn moving as well. She reached the fallen warrior and knelt in the dark.

"Myra, is that you?"

"Vernaylia... Vernaylia..."

"You're going to be fine," Saeryn said, reaching them. "As soon as we get you outside we'll take a look at you. Just hold on."

"I'm not... healing... my Queen... what did they... do to me?"

"They have evolved."

Andie stood, unsteadily, and tried to orient herself in the dark. She casts a ball of light.

"I'm going to look for the portal," she said. "Try to keep her conscious."

"No, Andie. We need to get Vernaylia help now. Help me lift her, as quick as you can."

"We came all this way, I'm not turning back now. We just lost our entire group."

"One is still alive and we might save her if we go now. You promised me, Andie! You promised to put your people first."

"That's what I'm doing."

Andie held the light out in front of her and hurried off deeper into the dark. She knew there was no time to waste and ran as fast as she could without running into the wall, all along clutching the horrible wound on her chest. Before long she heard the sound change again and knew the space was getting smaller, that she was reaching the end. She heard water ahead and slowed. As she drew near the sound, the light shone on a broken thing, round, ornate, and protruding out of the water. She leaned forward to see it better.

"No."

It was a piece of the portal and as she walked along the water's edge, she saw more pieces. It had been destroyed. She took a minute to register the result, the disappointment, then raced back to find Saeryn and Vernaylia. She and Saeryn helped the wounded warrior walk the long path back to the light and when they finally exited the Black Grotto, Andie had never been so happy to see sun. All three collapsed into the black grass. Andie looked over at Vernaylia and saw that she was bruised and cut on nearly every inch of her body. It wasn't until Andie saw that her eyes were glazed, her body still, that she realized the girl was dead. She probably died while they were carrying her.

Andie looked past Vernaylia to Saeryn, who had a deep cut on her back and appeared to have been pierced just inside of her shoulder. She also had a cut down her neck which only nearly missed her jugular artery. Andie looked down to assess her own wounds. She couldn't see the bruises, but she could feel them healing. She probably sustained at least one broken rib on each side, but those were healing, too. The cuts, however, were serious. The one on her face was not so bad and had already stopped bleeding, but she needed to bandage the one on the back of her hand quickly because it showed no signs of stopping. The cut on her chest was just beginning to clot, with the help of her clothes and armor, but it was deep and long. It would need stitches.

"Was it there?" Saeryn asked. "Did you find the portal?"

"It was there, but it's destroyed."

"Was it at the very back of the grotto?"

"Yes."

"And was there water there, a pond?"

"Yes. How did you know?"

"Legend tells of a cruel sorcerer who once lived in this place, performing all manner of evil and forbidden magic. They say the only person who could get close enough to kill him was his wife, who had lived as his slave and victim for years. As he was leaning over the pond to drink, his wife crept up behind him and slit his throat. She spilled all of his blood into the pond, but it was poisoned blood, full of magic so hateful it cannot even be uttered. The horrid power of his blood cursed this place, turned the air and the water sour. If the stories are to be believed, the pond at the back of the grotto can destroy anything that touches its surface."

"That portal is gone forever," Andie said, rolling on her back to rest. "Shame. I really wanted it. But this is better than it being used against us."

"Fine. Now let's tend to Vernaylia."

Saeryn rolled onto her side and crawled to Vernaylia. She tried to shake her awake.

"Vernaylia. Vernaylia."

When she realized the girl was dead, she went silent. Still. Nothing moved but her tears.

THE PORTAL STIRRED in the Archives at the bottom of Leabharlann. Two battalion soldiers emerged. They synchronized their watches and started their countdown. They rushed up from the Archives and through Leabharlann. They entered the hall and went separate directions. One of them went out through the front of the University, snapping the neck of the first person he ran into and hiding the body. He hurried along the front of the black marble, surveying the area and noting the position of the few guards. He saw that scores of people were getting off SKY 6 and passing through a checkpoint to go into the University. He turned on his camouflage and took up a position where he could observe.

The other soldier was still inside and had turned on his camouflage, too. He moved through the University, staying close to the walls to avoid detection. He reached the main hub and saw that it was filled with the citizens of Arvall who had fled to the University for protection. They were moving down into the tunnels and corridors, the bowels and deep caves of both modern usage and the ancient coin mint. Most of the city was here, with the exception of those who opted for the shelters in the city. He stayed long enough to gather some small intelligence. He checked his watch and headed back toward Leabharlann.

The soldiers reached the library at the same time. They hurried through the library, back into the Archives. But when they returned, the room was full of people. They were coming up from the portal at the dock in Arvall. The soldiers went unnoticed and stuck near the edge of the room. When that batch of citizens ended, the soldiers hurried to the portal and whispered the words they had been taught. The portal changed shades. The soldiers jumped in.

They came out in front of the army, high on the silver cliff that lines Gordric's Pain. The two soldiers walked over to the group of Beautiful Dead who had been placed in charge of the army

"I saw people getting off the train and going in," the first soldier said. "I overheard that Arvall City is completely empty. The train and the portal have been running nonstop. Everyone in the city is either in shelters under Arvall or in the University."

"They're vulnerable," said the second soldier. "They've tried to set up what security they can, but they don't have the numbers to protect an entire city. They can't even match our army. I heard their professors saying they only have a standing force of less than six thousand. They've been expecting more aid to come, but so far they haven't received any. They've heard about what Beladorion and the rest of the Dead did to the dragonborn in the Hot Salts and it has them all panicked. They're terrified. Most of their army is students and professors, and most of them come from privilege and peace. They'll never be able to stand against us. People were coming into the University through a portal and I would guess the other end is somewhere near the bottom of the mountain, in the city. Once we infiltrate the University, it will only take a handful of men to cover the entrances to the tunnels and corridors and hold them hostage in their own refuge."

"Such excellent news," the Dead general said. "I'm almost saddened to think the battle will be so easily won, though I trust there will be quite a satisfying amount of bloodshed before the door is shut on this war. What of the leaders?"

"Lymir, the head of the University, has apparently fallen into depression. They haven't been able to get him to say much the last few days. Raesh, the son of the council fighters' deceased leader, is running their defenses now. Capable enough and worth watching. Oren, their greatest dragonborn warrior and general, was killed in the Hot Salts. There are some other fighters of considerable strength who have a hand in the strategy as well. And I heard they have a professor, a Marcus, who knows how to operate the portals, which could work against us."

"I see. And what of the Queen of the blood traitors? What of their princess?"

"They're not there."

All the heads in the proximity turned to the soldier.

"What do you mean?" the Dead general asked.

"I mean they're not in the University or the city. They left days ago on a mission to cure the Maeludrax we spread in the True Isles. No one has heard from them since."

"Strange. The dragonborn do not contract disease, so they cannot have become sick. Assuming they've rediscovered the healing properties of their blood, they will have long since cured the Thabians and restarted the supply line. That would have taken mere hours. With an army marching on their city they wouldn't waste time there when their mission was complete, so where did they go? Of course. You mentioned a portal at the foot of the mountain. Before they only had one now they have two. It would appear they've gotten their hands on some very old and critical information. They found the portal in Thabes and had it shipped back to Arvall to help with the evacuation efforts. If they knew about one, then they would've known about the others as well, which means they went to find them. From the True Isles the closest destination is New Carthage, yet I know for a fact that Beladorion already has that portal and the one in Raven Deep. The portals of House Clio and House Polyhymnia are too far out of their reach and even if they risk some adventure, they wouldn't be willing to travel so far. That means that just now they're either at or near the Black Grotto and they won't be coming back from there. Beladorion will have figured out what they're up to and sent Dead to meet them. Strange news, but fortunate. We will attack now."

The general turned to give the order. The order was repeated all the way through the ranks, the columns, until it was spread through the entire army. They began to move forward. The battalion soldiers and the Beautiful Dead stood aside to let the rest go through first. Line after line of soldiers passed into the portal.

"We'll send two thousand men into the University," the general said. "Six thousand into the city. Two thousand will continue on foot and bring the portal. Three waves, three locations, one unstoppable assault."

CHAPTER SIXTEEN

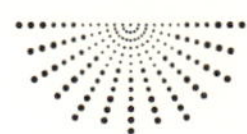

In the University, Raesh and Sarinda oversaw the sheltering of the citizens of Arvall. Reports came up from the foot of the mountain confirming that they had finally succeeded in evacuating the city. They smiled, happy to finally have that much off their minds. They walked to the center of the main hub, through which the final citizens were moving on their way to the tunnels.

"Who knew watching people walk could be so exhausting?" Sarinda asked, reclining.

"Well, when they number in the millions..."

"Right. How deep do these tunnels and corridors go anyway?"

"Deep. I don't think anyone's actually been all the way to the end in this cycle. I'm just going to lie here for a minute, rest, and then get back to the hospital."

"I'm coming with you. I can't believe Carmen's awake. How is she?"

"She's strong. Really strong," Raesh said, sitting up a little. "They still aren't sure what kind of magic caused it or what exactly it did to her. Whatever they were giving her in that drip before was helping to keep her under and they didn't know it. As soon as the doctor changed her medicine, she woke up. I'm so happy I can hardly think. She's already trying to walk."

"Andie's going to be so happy when she gets back. I know she's really missed her, we all have."

Just then they were startled by the sound of screaming. They leapt up and ran in the direction of the noise, but they were met by a phalanx of soldiers. Their instincts saved them. Raesh and Sarinda were casting before they even fully understood what was happening. The soldiers were strong and had been well trained by the Beautiful Dead, but they weren't trained for the hallways Sarinda and Raesh knew so well. The two fought back against the soldiers furiously and soon more professors came to their aid. What the professors lacked in fighting ability, they made up for in sheer knowledge. Raesh and his fellows fought admirably, but more and more soldiers were pouring from Leabharlann and marching down every hallway. Raesh knew it was only a matter of moments before they were surrounded.

"We've got to get back to the tunnels!" he called. "We can regroup and plan a defense, but we've got to move, now!"

They began to retreat, casting behind them and running as fast as they could amidst flying spells and flying debris from hexes exploding into the walls. As they reached the main hub, the citizens who had yet to enter the tunnels saw the coming army and began to panic. They flew to wherever they thought they were safest, leaving all their things behind. A few brave souls turned and tried to fight, but they were cut down instantly by the well-trained battalion. Raesh, Sarinda, and the professors held the battalion off just long enough to get the final stragglers into the tunnel, then they all entered. Once they crossed the barrier, Raesh touched the tunnel wall, which initiated the magic seal to keep the enemy out.

"I don't understand," Sarinda said, still gasping. "How did they get inside? How did they even get within ten kilometers of the city without us knowing?"

"I don't know," Raesh said, slumping to the floor. "This isn't right. They weren't supposed to be here for another week. We were supposed to have more time."

"Well, however they did it they're here now. What about this seal? Will it hold?"

"Yeah. We've been working on them for months, before we even knew an army was coming. Nobody gets through that we don't want to get through."

"Andie and Saeryn, wherever you two are, we need you now," Sarinda said, closing her eyes and trying to catch her breath. "There's no way we're going to win this without you."

Outside the seal, the soldiers set up a dense patrol to guard the tunnel entrances and commence trying to break in. The entrance to each tunnel was guarded by fifty soldiers, each armed to the teeth and dead-set on ending life in Arvall. The tunnels were full of screams, cries, and prayers. The people had been told about the terror and senselessness of war, but few of them had ever truly seen it. All of them were waiting for her to return, for Andie to cut the sky on the back of a dragon and save them.

Column after column of soldiers filed in through the Archives, up and out through Leabharlann, and then into the University. They went down every hall, tunnel, corridor, and passageway that hadn't been sealed off. They checked every room, lecture hall, closet, laboratory, and office. They found no innocents to terrorize, but they destroyed everything they touched, leaving trails of fire and debris all throughout the newly renovated university. They blew up whole sections of rooms, disintegrated critical loadbearing pillars. They filed out to the mountainside and begin ensuring that none would escape, blocking anything that even remotely resembled an entrance or exit. They stationed themselves across the mountainside and took up positions.

In Arvall City below, the next wave of the army swept into the city streets from the portal there. Professor Iceubes was still at the portal, attempting to perform a few final calibrations, when the second wave started. The soldier who killed him did not even give him a chance for his life, but merely ran him through with a spear of black bronze. The soldiers set about discovering the hidden shelters in the city. With the training they had received from the Dead, it wasn't as difficult as it should have been. However, the citizens were not completely helpless; knowing they would be ill equipped to physically take on the coming army, the citizens had set up traps over seventy-five percent of the city. Mines, darts, blades, tar, and other traps were soon going off as the army marched through the city. Even that was not enough because the army's sheer numbers guaranteed their progress. As some of the shelters were found, the soldiers commenced trying to break through the protective magic and barricades, hungry for death.

At last it was time for the battalion and the Dead to emerge from the portal. The battalion marched out in perfect ranks, strong, fierce, undeniable. Their sleek and powerful armor shone in the sun and their march shook the ground. They were bent on destruction. The Dead came through the portal too fast for the eye to track, racing through the city streets, effortlessly sensing and avoiding the traps. They leapt and climbed the buildings looking for vantage points and lives to end.

Raesh and Sarinda sat in the tunnel of the University, thinking how they might get out of this mess.

"THIS IS no time for one of your lectures, Saeryn."

"Then perhaps you'd like to schedule a later time for me to remind you of what damage the time spell can do? Do you truly need reminding of what it has done to your people, to you yourself not so long ago?"

"I did what I had to do," Andie said, turning from Saeryn to continue tending the wound across her chest.

"No, you did what you wanted to do. And you used a spell that is not only heinous, but dark. Tampering with time is no meager thing, princess, and if you had made even the slightest miscalculation or mispronunciation—"

"If this, if that. With you it's always about what could go wrong. You never miss an opportunity to second guess me. Can't you ever just be happy I've saved your life?"

"Being prudent does not preclude my ability to be grateful," Saeryn said, offended. "You act as if my berating you is a task I enjoy. You are not like other people, Andie. You're nothing like them at all. You cannot imagine the power in your blood. I know because it is the same blood that runs in my veins."

"Enough. I get it already. I'm special, I'm going to be Queen. You want me to put our people first, fine, but I'm going to do it my way. And I'll be glad when I'm Queen so I won't have to listen to these condescending tones anymore."

"You do not even see how far from the path you've strayed. Torturing people for information, putting your personal quests before your people, wasting precious time on missions you conjure up to soothe your own feeling of inadequacy, judging your friends—"

"What friends? Yara? She's in love with the enemy!"

"Do not tell me who the enemy is. I resisted and fought them as a child, and my friends and family were being slaughtered long before yours were ever born. Yara has traveled and worked on her own for months, winning priceless victories for our cause when we almost had her executed. I hardly think loving whom she loves should bar her from us. Unlike you, I trust her judgement."

"Why don't you just tell me what you're really upset about, Saeryn?"

"To put it bluntly, I worry that not only are you far from the girl I thought you were, but that you may never be fit to call yourself Queen."

Andie looked Saeryn squarely in the face, furious and hurt. She felt as if Saeryn had not only taken her birthright, but also threatened to cut her out from the dragonborn altogether, take away the last vestige of family she has.

"You would cut me out?" Andie asked, tears welling in her eyes.

"If I thought it was best for our people. I have told you time and time again that being a Queen is not easy, that it requires decisions that shake the very foundation of who you are. I love you, Andie. You have been a daughter and a friend and a partner to me. I would not cut you out willingly, but I cannot allow someone so caught up in their own pain to lead our people. And before you try to defend yourself, I must tell you what I know. I know you sneak down to the prisons and fight the Searchers and soldiers who have been imprisoned there. I know you've taken some of the grimoires from the collection. I know you've been studying dark magic. And I know that you found the Searcher who took your mother and I know what you've done to him. None of this makes you in any way fit to lead us or even join us. And if you think it brings me any pleasure to say this then you never knew me at all."

With that Saeryn turned from Andie and returned to tending her own wound. Andie turned, too, and lowered her head. She had no idea Saeryn had been watching her so closely. Now that she did know it dawned on her that Saeryn had spent every day hoping for her to change. Andie hadn't even realized how serious things had gotten. It started off so innocently. She fought in the prisons to train, test, strengthen herself. She took the grimoires, not to steal them, but to study the subjects she knew Saeryn wouldn't approve of and she only studied them because she knew they needed all the help they could get. But Saeryn was right. Andie had gone too far. She thought on this. And thought. And then she came to her decision, knowing it will shape the rest of her life.

"I don't care."

"What?" Saeryn asked, turning.

"I don't care. I don't care what you think of me or that you don't want me to be your Queen. I don't care that I'm reckless and selfish and that I'm willing to do anything to save the people you can't seem to protect yourself. I am bad. And angry. And hurting. And all those things have worked in me to get us here, alive. I pulled you from that portal. I tipped the scales in the Archives. I defeated the Chancellor and his battalion. I defeated Ashur. I saved those warriors from the Church. I found the portal in Thabes. I saved our lives in that grotto. What have you done? Walked around in all your dignity and integrity, judging me for getting my hands dirty when you knew you were too much of a coward to do those things yourself!"

"You forget your place, Andie," Saeryn said, rising. "I am your Queen and you will address me as such."

"As of right now, you're nothing but a means to an end. It's time to go. And when this is all over and I've saved the dragonborn and Arvall, then you can judge me while you sit back and enjoy the safe world I've handed to you."

Minutes later, they were in the air again, the other four dragons flying without riders behind them. By the next morning they should be back in Arvall. The search for the portals was at an end for the time being, the final portal the one belonging to House Melpomene, the Chancellor's family. Marcus' notes in the journal indicated that he believed the Chancellor had no idea that his family was in possession of a portal, but that he may have inadvertently had it sent to the Old World.

His research showed that the more power the Chancellor acquired, the more paranoid he grew. He was convinced the other families were plotting to steal his wealth; he arranged to have several barges of his most valuable assets sailed across the Spider Sea, including a wooden container described as being twenty-five meters long, thirteen wide, and ten deep, more than enough space to hold a portal among other family heirlooms. But those are thoughts for another day. Right then, Andie's mind was tuned to one thing and one thing only. Violence.

ON THE OUTSKIRTS OF ABHAINN, Lucas moved through the camp, ignoring both the dragonborn captives he passed and the crashing claps of thunder from the Hot Salts in the distance. They had finally moved out of that area the day before and had since already set up a portal that would take them straight to Arvall. Beladorion and the Dead appeared to know everything about the portals, every variation and fluctuation, yet Lucas had watched them very carefully as they manipulated it, just as he was directed to do. Now he made his way purposefully across the field to fulfill his mission. He entered the large black tent that sat at the head of the battalion forces.

Ashur was there, standing over a map that he read with great focus and intention. His burned and scarred face turned to look at Lucas when he entered. With a nod of his head, Lucas confirmed that his mission had been successful. Ashur nodded in return to express his gratitude. They began talking, making up a conversation that had nothing to do with what they wanted to talk about. They spoke of the weather, the war, the Hot Salts, any banal and common topic they could think of, because they knew that ears were listening.

By then they were fully aware of what the Dead were capable of and they knew that the only way to deceive them was to surprise them. An almost impossible task.

Part of every battalion member's training was learning to communicate in two different sign languages, for instances when silence was critical. Lucas and Ashur sat down at the table and never stopped talking, yet they had a completely different conversation with their hands.

"I think I've figured out how we can get our autonomy back," Lucas signed.

"Good," signed Ashur. "When we first got into bed with these people I had no idea they would take us over so quickly, without our even noticing. But the victory must be ours. I don't plan on sharing anything."

"I apologize, my leader. You warned us this was a dangerous move, and though it may pay off in the end by helping us destroy the dragonborn, it may also destroy us. But I have found the secret of controlling the portal."

"Excellent work, Lucas. You can recalibrate it to find and connect to other portals?"

"Yes, my leader, to any of the portals that are switched on."

"I'm not so sure they didn't let you learn how to control the portal as part of some master plan. We need to be careful now, more careful than we've ever been."

"I understand."

They laughed then, still having a completely different conversation by mouth than the very grave one they were having by hand. Lucas banged the table as if was the funniest thing he'd ever heard and Ashur gave a hearty laugh. Their hands told a different story.

"We need to kill these people," Ashur signed.

"Forgive me, leader, but we may not be able to."

"Have more faith in me, Lucas. I've had our engineers working on modifications for our suits since before we ever went groveling to the Dead. They tell me they're close to a solution. I believe that by the time we step through that portal it will be the Dead who are afraid."

"Excellent, my leader. Do you mean the engineers from Hessian's Bridge?"

"Yes. Our new recruits are proving indispensable. All we need to worry about now is making sure the Dead step through that portal as planned. As soon as they're all through we'll upgrade our suits and recalibrate the portal. By the time they figure out that we're no longer with them, we'll already be plunging our hands into their chests."

"I look forward to it. But—and forgive me if a I cross a line, my leader—but what about our forces who are already marching on Arvall. They won't know whose side to choose."

"They will either learn or die. We have no room for mercy now."

The night passed and the morning came. Lucas and Ashur did not so much as nod to each other when they came together with Beladorion. Ashur had guessed that Beladorion's bloodlust would outweigh his incredible intelligence, causing him to want to go through the portal first with his people. No sooner had the whole force gathered than the Dead began to go through the portal, dragging along the chained and captive dragonborn behind them. When all the captives have been taken through, the Dead flew the dragons through the portal. It seemed a kind of betrayal, that the dragons would allow the Dead to ride them, but no one quite understood how magic worked in the blood or how it passed things on from one species to the next hybrids. The dragons, after all, were only creatures. After some time, the Dead were finally all through, except Beladorion.

"We're not cannibals," he said, standing before the portal. "It's a common misconception. We don't like raw flesh and we don't eat human flesh at all. We don't care much for the taste of blood, though, to be fair, we don't mind it as much as others do. We will only have the blood of the traitors and only because it is the way to obtain their magic."

"And so you will," Ashur said. "When the time is right."

"The time is right when I say it is right," Beladorion said, rounding on Ashur. "I know you and your battalion are planning to cross us. I know that as soon as I step through this portal you'll have Lucas recalibrate so that you come out where you wish. Perhaps you thought you were actually fooling us. Perhaps you also thought we didn't know you were trying to enhance your suits."

"How could you know that?" asked Ashur.

"Because it's my business to know these things. Honestly, I haven't seen or heard anything to give you away, it was simply the logical thing to do. Think about it: you want the dragonborn destroyed, but you want to do it yourself because who would want to go through everything you've been through and not get the glory? Of course, you're going to try to go behind our backs because we're better than you and you can't confront us face to face, so you scheme and plot in the shadows. Not only that but we've practically taken all control from you and you want it back. And we've noticed your clumsy, dull-witted friend there lurking around. Your best and most logical course of action would be to let us go through the portal first, change it afterwards, come out in a different part of the city with enhanced suits and stab us through our backs when the fighting reaches its most intense. A perfectly reasonable plan except it's too reasonable, it's exactly what one should do in this situation. You lack creativity."

"But how did you know?"

"You're not very hard to figure out, commander. I wanted to know what you would do so I reasoned it out and now you've confirmed it. I would advise against this little coup of yours. We're willing to forgive you just this once. But I would advise this: if you do choose to cross us, don't miss."

Beladorion turned and stepped through the portal. Ashur stood still for a moment, looking into the portal and contemplating his next decision. Lucas and the entire battalion waited, anxious now that they know the Dead were onto them, but still undyingly loyal to their leader, Ashur. Finally, Ashur turned to Lucas.

"No one intimidates us. No one overshadows us. This is what we've trained for. A world with no more dragons or the abominations that came from them, and that includes the Dead. Let's end the war we started. Do it."

A cheer went through the battalion as Lucas set about his work of changing the destination. Ashur turned to his forces.

"Engineers! Engineers to my location, now!"

CHAPTER SEVENTEEN

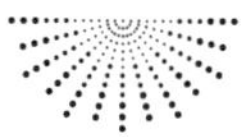

ANDIE AND SAERYN COULDN'T BELIEVE THEIR EYES. As they flew over the String Fields and Arvall came up across the horizon, they saw that the city was burning. The closer they went, the more damage they could see. Andie was shocked beyond words, having not expected the army to arrive for at least another week. She realized they were likely using the portals they had stolen to cover the distance. Tears came into her eyes as they flew lower and faster, desperate to reach the city to help.

As they finally breached the airspace over the city, Andie looked down into the streets and couldn't believe what she saw. No one was there. No one was mounting a defense or fighting back, aside from a few small skirmishes. She wondered where the professors and students were. Where Raesh was. She began to wonder if she had been gone too long, if she had lost everything and everyone because she gambled and lost. She didn't even know how long the army had been in the city.

Saeryn flew to where the army was thickest and then swooped the dragon straight down in a breathtaking nose dive, the other dragons following. The dragon slammed into the ground so hard the asphalt cracked. Saeryn and Andie dismounted and rushed to meet the army that was much too large for them to handle on their own. They were, above all, two of the bravest and most powerful women in Noelle, but still they were no match for what lay ahead.

Andie was the first into battle, casting furiously and swinging her blade with excruciating intensity. She cast an acid rain over a group of soldiers and parried the thrust of black and bronze spears. She opened the earth beneath them and then closed it over them. Her power had grown strong over the past year, and she held nothing back.

Saeryn came forward with as much grace as could be mustered when one was going into battle. She lifted a group of soldiers and then brought them crashing down onto the ground Andie had just sealed. She pulled glass from the windows of a nearby building and sent the glittering, razor-sharp cloud through the soldiers. The result was wave of crimson that painted the surrounding landscape in the colors of war. She drew her sword as well, though she swung it more cautiously than Andie.

They fought hard and long, staying at the edge of the army so that they wouldn't get surrounded or trapped. When they came across citizens in need, they helped as much as they could, half carrying them to safety, casting small healing spells in between offensive blasts of magic back toward the approaching enemies.

The army was well-trained in their short amount of time together, but they were still only a hodgepodge of men who had been soldiers for a few months. They could not match the power, skill, or intensity of the dragonborn women. Apart, Andie and Saeryn were a force to be reckoned with. Together, they were a formidable sight whose bravery would be carried down generation to generation through history books and bedtime stories. Both powerful dragonborn fueled each other's power, each drawing from the other and pushing everything they had into their magical attacks. Saeryn's magic was graceful, practiced. Andie's was more archaic, a ferocious mélange of sorcery and dragonborn magic.

The enemies fell one by one before Queen and princess. Andie was cautious of her surroundings, keeping a wary eye out for the Beautiful Dead, who she knew must already be there somewhere. They did come across some battalion soldiers, who posed a much graver threat than the simple soldiers. Andie took two down, as did Saeryn. They didn't go far before one of the soldiers regained his feet and, managing to surprise them, conjured a blade and sent it flying at Saeryn. The blade missed her organs, but cut a devastating gash in her side. Saeryn fell to her knees and Andie placed herself between the soldier and the Queen. She cast a spell that broke every bone in the soldier's body. She grabbed Saeryn and dragged her into a nearby building.

"You need to get over yourself," Andie said, kneeling to take Saeryn into her lap and held the wound until the dragon blood healed her. "This isn't a game."

"What are you talking about?"

"That soldier. If you had taken him out he never would have been able to do this to you."

"You mean if I'd killed him?"

"Yes, Saeryn. You need to kill. And I know you're not okay with that, but you need to get okay with it soon because if not, either you're going to die or you're going to get someone else killed."

"It may be easy for you, but I do not relish the thought of taking another's life."

"I don't like it either, Saeryn. It makes me sick inside. Sometimes I can't even sleep at night thinking about the things I've done, but I don't do them because they feel good. I don't do them because they're right. I do them because they're necessary. Thousands of trained and dangerous men have stormed our city and are roaming the streets killing innocent people. They can't be reasoned with or talked down. They've come thousands of miles to be here, to murder us. There's only one way this ends and that's with a pile of someone's bodies."

"But it never ends. The bloodshed never stops," Saeryn said, trying to control her emotion. "I have spent my entire life watching people die and it never gets easier. You think I don't realize the reality of war? That I don't understand our freedom isn't free? You forget I've killed before. So many I've killed. I thought that here, now, in a new time and a new place we could be different. I couldn't see how we could win this war if we fought the University with the very thing they used to destroy us—death."

"Saeryn the University didn't invent death, even if they perfected it. And everything they did was done in cruelty. I fight to survive, to protect our people and the people of Arvall who have risked their city and their lives so that we could have a home among them. Killing makes me sick, it makes me hate myself, it makes me hate war. I want what you want: peace, happiness, safety, a home. But all of that is in jeopardy now. We can't afford to spare the lives of thousands of evil soldiers. We don't have the prison space to hold them because the cells are already full of people we've spared. We have to let the world know that we won't continue to be bullied, to be ambushed. Do you understand?"

Saeryn was silent for a moment, healing there in Andie's arms. Andie held her close, wondering if the Queen of the dragonborn would do what was right or what was necessary. The two women had such differences and such love for one another.

"Perhaps I had forgotten," Saeryn said. "How it is to rule when the threat is imminent. My mother was the one who told me that being a Queen is about making difficult, but fair decisions. Later, when I led the rebellion, I learned that her wisdom was slightly incomplete. Being a Queen is about making difficult, but fair decisions and sometimes those decisions are about whether or not lives should be spared."

"And what will you do, Saeryn?"

"Protect my people."

"At all costs?"

"At all costs."

Fully healed from the wound, Saeryn began to raise herself. Andie helped her to her feet. They shared a look, but only for a moment. Then they return to the street. To the war.

One of the citizens they helped earlier had made his way back to his shelter. Once he had been seen to and treated, he moved through the crowded space to the back room, where all of the communications devices were. He was a radio operator, helping to relay information and keep the other shelters and the University tunnels informed of the progress. He had only stepped outside for a moment to get a better sense of what was happening. Now that he had returned, he re-took his seat and turned on his equipment. He took a deep breath and got to work.

"All stations, all stations, all stations. Critical update. Diamonds have been found in the streets, diamonds have been found in the streets. Two diamonds, two diamonds a little rough for wear, but still shining, still shining. Repeat: two diamonds have been found in the streets, still shining."

"...TWO DIAMONDS a little rough for wear, but still shining, still shining. Repeat: two diamonds have been found in the streets, still shining."

As the transmission came in over the radio, the professors and students who were familiar with the code began to rejoice. It was the only good news they'd had since the attack began the day before. They spread the word through the tunnels and corridors, and people began to cheer up for the first time since they left their homes.

When Raesh heared the news, his heart began to race. he hadn't said anything to anybody, but he had begun to seriously worry something had happened to Andie. There weren't words to describe how happy he was to hear that she and Saeryn were safe, were back, and were fighting. He jumped up to his feet and listened to broadcast again, just to be sure he heard correctly. Sarinda was on her feet as well, almost as relived as Raesh was. They embraced, thrilled to finally have some news in their favor.

"We have to go help them," Sarinda said. "Somehow, someway, we've got to fight through this army and get down to the city. Once they figure out Andie and Saeryn are back this army is going to rush down to the city to overwhelm them."

"I know, but first I need to get to my apartment. There's something Andie's going to need and I can't go down without it."

"I'll go with you. But first we have to organize our forces here. You and I fought these guys, so I know you saw what I saw."

"Trained, but still not soldiers."

"Exactly. Raesh, there were a lot of these guys, but I think we just might be able to take them or at least make them think twice about this assault. Now's the time. Everyone's getting excited about the return of the Queen and princess. We shouldn't wait any longer."

"Agreed. You try to find Lymir and I'll get on the radio."

Sarinda took off down into the tunnel and Raesh hurried over to the small station they had set up near the mouth of the tunnel.

"All stations, all stations, all stations," he began. "This is Raesh. I know we're supposed to be using code, but the enemy is already here and they don't care what we're saying. They just want to kill us. I want all of you to know that Andie and Saeryn have returned, they're back. I know some of you felt that they'd abandoned us, but they're down on the streets of the city right now, fighting alone against an army of thousands. I know you all have families and lives that you want to get back to, but I'm asking every able-bodied person with enough training and courage to stand with us.

"In just a few moments I'm going to lead a charge out of the tunnel. I know these are dark times and I know we're in an impossible position, but believe me when I say this fight is far from over. What I'm asking for now might turn out to be the ultimate sacrifice and maybe I'll go down, too, but what I won't do is sit back and watch while a cruel army destroys my city, my friends, my family, and my entire way of life. By coming here and declaring war on us they've challenged everything we believe in. I'm not going to allow that.

"I have power in my body and a girl I love who's fighting for us right now. We may not love her in the same way or for the same reasons, but I know you love her, too. I'm going now to fight the fight of my life and if I die I'll do it honorably and with the knowledge that as long as my heart beat I fought them with everything I had. If this is the end, let it be one they will never forget."

Raesh signed off and suddenly the University was alive with applause. All through the tunnels, passages, and corridors the people clapped, excited and inspired. All around him people were getting to their feet and preparing to go out and fight. Raesh himself felt a little more emboldened now. Soon Sarinda returned.

"Raesh, you're not going to believe this."

Lymir came in a few paces behind her, dragging a man through the dirt.

"What's going on?" Raesh asked.

"This is Murphy," Lymir said, throwing the man down at Raesh's feet. "Murphy is a spy, a mole for the battalion."

"What? Are you sure?"

"Positive. I've been unsteady for about a week now,

thinking that something wasn't right. It was that attack that Sarinda reported. I kept wondering how that advanced party could get all the way to the dock without being seen, and how they even knew to go there. I did some investigating and found some correspondence on the body of one of their soldiers. I knew then there was a mole. I had no idea who, though, so I had to be careful about what I said. That's why I've been so quiet when it came to discussing strategy. I managed to narrow down the suspect list by finding out who even had the clearance to know about Sarinda's mission. From there I knew it had to be someone in the communications department because they would have the ability and resources to contact the advanced party and track Sarinda's boat as soon as it was close enough to the city, because no one had heard from her in months. I was really struggling to narrow it down from there, but then I caught this little weasel trying to hijack a signal back there. and he told me where I can find the rest of Ash's spies. Investigation complete."

"It's great to have you back," Raesh said. "Don't dispose of him yet, though, he may prove useful. Sarinda and I are about to attack."

"Go," said Lymir, his foot on Murphy's neck. "I'll get on the radio and give the notice."

"What notice?"

"The notice for the secret groups of trained professors and council fighters I stashed around the city. You didn't think I was just sitting back enjoying the view the last week, did you?"

Raesh smiled and turned to Sarinda. She nodded to him and they both turned toward the tunnel. Outside the shield, the soldiers saw that something was about to happen. They stood, squared off, prepared their weapons for use or their hands for casting. Raesh touched the wall and the shield came down. Sarinda wasted no time and released a wave of magic that took the thirty nearest soldiers off their feet. As Raesh's seal came down, so did the others. The people had finally been roused to action. Raesh and Sarinda led the charge. They were magnificently brutal, showing no mercy to the men who had shown no mercy to them. Professors and students from all the tunnels came rushing out, and in no time the soldiers in the main hub were overwhelmed and calling for reinforcements.

Raesh and Sarinda made their way to SKY 1 and boarded it. The train took off. It climbed steeply at first, before making its customary journey out to the mountainside for the spiral ascent. Just as Raesh allowed himself to relax, a spell nearly took his head off. He cast back in retaliation, hitting the soldier right in the chest and knocking him off his feet. They hadn't even thought to check to make sure the train was safe. A mistake they would be sure never to make again.

CHAPTER EIGHTEEN

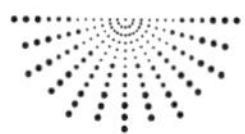

SOLDIERS CAME POURING INTO THE TRAIN CAR AT BOTH ends. Raesh and Sarinda fought back to back fending off spells, spears, and bullets. The train sustained serious damage, but continued its ascent. Raesh and Sarinda fought the soldiers all the way to the summit. The train stopped and the fight spilled out onto the platform.

Raesh and Sarinda hurried back into the mountain. Sarinda took up a position at the entrance to the apartments, allowing Raesh to rush to his and Andie's apartment for what he needed. It didn't take him long to find it. It had never been moved since they placed it there.

He came hurrying back out only to find that the danger was over and Sarinda had defeated the final soldier. They took the train back down, though it barely survived to get them back to the main hub. From there, they rejoined the fight, pushing forward to the front of the University.

Still, the sheer numbers of the army were overwhelming and they had their work cut out for them.

The army wasn't made of true soldiers any more than the professors were. Apart from Raesh, Sarinda, and the council fighters, the battle was evenly matched. Luckily, once they pushed forward far enough, Raesh and Sarinda made it to one of the hidden passages built for such an occasion. It was a dark, winding path that cut through the mountainside, but at least they had a break from the onslaught. Once they reached the end, they got an unwelcome surprise. The passage wasn't complete.

The exit was never made because the army arrived a whole week ahead of time.

"Great," Sarinda said. "Just what we need."

"I've got a spell for this," Raesh said, already raising his free hand.

"Yeah, I know, and I've got a couple. But we don't know what we're going to run into out there. If we just go blasting through the side of the mountain, we could end up right in the middle of them, surrounded."

"Well, we can't just stand here. So, either we go back and try to keep pushing to the front doors, which could take all night and I'm sure the front doors are even more heavily guarded, or you can help me blast through dirt and stone and we take our chances on the other side."

"Obviously, that's not much of a choice."

Raesh shrugged. "Here goes nothing."

The two raised their hands and began blasting their magic against the earth in front of them. They pushed and released with all they had, and fortunately they were not far from the end. But as soon as they found daylight, they also found themselves right in the middle of a dense crowd of soldiers.

Sarinda sighed. "Told you so."

Just quick enough to avoid a shotgun blast, Sarinda

whipped the wind around herself and Raesh, knocking all the soldiers far back. They took advantage of the opportunity to head down the mountain toward the train. Spells and bullets and projectiles flew, exploding into the ground at their feet and blowing huge chunks of earth into the air. Raesh and Sarinda ran so fast they almost tripped going down the slope, casting and ducking as they went. They finally reached level ground and headed for the train, only the commotion they caused seemed to have attracted the attention of virtually all the soldiers stationed outside of the University.

"I'm really doubting our plan now!" Sarinda called.

"We can make it!"

But before they could even get within a reasonable distance, more soldiers appeared and came together in front of them. Raesh and Sarinda paused, turning in every direction looking for an escape, but they were surrounded.

Raesh raised his hand and cast a spell. A massive byzantium purple ray of light shot up into the air, so powerful it made him stumble. The light shot up into the cloud, and Raesh maintained it for as long as he could before he had to go back to defending himself.

"Super pretty light," Sarinda said. "Want to tell me what it was for?"

"Just desperation."

"Can that thing you're carrying help us or is it just for Andie?"

"Just for Andie, I think."

"Come on, back to back."

Once again, they found themselves pressed upon and threatened. They parried and reflected, stringing out the inevitable end that awaited them. They were surrounded by more men than they could count, and each was doing his utmost to destroy them. When the bullets began to fly among the spells again, Sarinda clapped her hands above her head and a shield came down around them. She knew she couldn't hold it forever, not with so many attacking them at once.

But she only needed to hold it for a few seconds.

The first thing that happened was that a terrifying roar was heard. It was followed by four more. Within moments of the fantastic roars, five gargantuan dragons came soaring up over the precipice and swooped down over the soldiers there. The dragons opened their great jaws and spewed flames over the soldiers. The army scattered, every man running for his life, screaming as they abandoned the attack.

The dragons continued to spray fire until every man was cleared or burnt to a crisp. The creatures landed, and it was mere moments before Andie was in Raesh's arms. They both had never felt so relieved.

"So, you saw my distress signal," he said, still holding her.

"It was hard to miss."

She released him and then went to hug Sarinda.

"A few minutes later and we'd have been done for," Sarinda said.

"I was just waiting for a glorious entrance."

"Saeryn, it's good to see you back safe," said Raesh.

"It is good to be back. I'm only sorry we lost four of our own along the way. How have you fared here?"

"Well, we haven't really. The army got here a week ahead of schedule and we were completely caught off guard. We barely managed to get everyone to safety in time. But when we heard over the radio that you were back and that you were fighting, everybody found their courage. They're mounting an attack inside right now."

"No," Andie said. "They got into the University?"

"Yeah. We thought everyone would be safe in there and that it was impenetrable or at least would require a few days of siege, but one minute it was totally quiet and the next we were being overrun."

"The portal," Andie said, turning to Saeryn to confirm. "They're coming through the portal in Leabharlann. We were flying all over Noelle trying to track them down. But we know for a fact that the Dead have at least two. They must have set them up wherever they made camp and used them to cut the distance and get here earlier."

"And with the portal in Leabharlann they got to skip security and come right in."

"Is everybody safe? In the University or in a shelter?"

"Yeah. The city is completely empty."

"Good. Then we need to close that portal now."

"Come on. There's a secret entrance over here."

They hurried over to the exploded hole in the mountain where Raesh and Sarinda exited. They had to blast their way back in from where the opening collapsed. Raesh went down first, followed by Saeryn. Andie rushed up behind them and leapt into the hole.

She turned to look behind her and lost her breath.

A battalion soldier had snuck up on them and caught Sarinda by her throat. He held her in the air, as if her weight were nothing. With his free hand, he broke one of her arms and then held the other hand so she couldn't cast. Andie raised her hand to cast her spell, but just as her hand raised level with her face, the soldier flicked his wrist and Andie heard Sarinda's neck break.

For a moment, she was unable to think. Raesh sent a spell past her head and caught the soldier in his chest. It knocked him off his feet, but he rolled and got up again. But no sooner had he stood again than Andie raised her fist toward him and opened her fingers wide. He disintegrated on the spot. Andie's eyes grew wide as Raesh whistled in response. She didn't even know she was capable of such a thing.

Andie ran back out to Sarinda. She took her head in her hands and tried to wake her, but she was gone. There was no life left in her eyes.

"No," Andie said softly. "No."

Saeryn came back out and grabbed one side of Sarinda, indicating that Andie should grab the other. It took Andie a moment to focus, but then she lifted her ally, her friend, and they carried her into the mountainside. They both carried her along through the tunnel, Andie hardly able to see anything through the darkness and her tears. They arrived in the University and made their way to the main hub. They could still hear intense fighting going on in the distance, but the professors and council fighters had managed to push the army far back. Andie and Saeryn lay Sarinda down near the edge of the room. They and Raesh sat next to the body and mourned.

THE ENGINEERS HAD FINISHED their work on the battalion suits and Ashur was ready to lead his forces into battle. They did not have the natural ability of the Dead, but they were certainly not a force to be trifled with. They were one of the most formidable and dangerous armies to march those lands in living memory. No one truly knew the limits of their power. Lucas stood ready and alert, prepared to follow his commander into the most brutal and bloody wars of recent memory. All the soldiers shared that loyalty, that undying obsession to serve Ashur in any and every way possible. Such brainwashing was part of their training.

Ashur stood at the front of his battalion. He was only twenty-seven years old, but already he carried enough anger and hate in his veins to fill a hundred lifetimes. Large parts of his old armor merged with his flesh, and he wore a newer, stronger armor over that. His training was unimaginable, his desire unshakeable, his fury and his power undeniable. He had waited and waited for this day, his revenge on those who he felt had falsely taken up a residence in his world.

In his mind, there was only room for one leader, and it must be him. His face was terribly disfigured, half melted by the bolt from that despicable dragonborn Andie Rogers that nearly killed him. His body ached in constant pain. His mind twisted in part by insanity and part by the blinding need for revenge. But what he was capable of was both great and horrifying. Even Beladorion had underestimated him.

Without any pomp or circumstance, he gave the order and his men began to file toward the portal.

CHAPTER NINETEEN

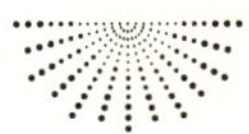

"NO. NO, WE'RE NOT GOING TO DO THIS. WE CAN'T afford to. Not now."

As she spoke, Andie got to her feet and pulled Raesh up with her. Saeryn stood, too, though all looked shaken and unsteady.

"Sarinda was brave and strong and she doesn't deserve this," Andie continued. "But we can mourn for her later. We have so much work to do, beginning with shutting down that portal."

Raesh nodded and all three hurried toward Leabharlann. They reached the library and rushed across the room to the Archives. Down and through they went until they reached the portal. Just as they entered the room, a battalion soldier emerged, followed by another, and another. Saeryn didn't even allow them the chance to raise their hand. She waved her arms in an inward sweep and the sand and dirt from the floor were brought up into a localized storm, picking the soldiers up and slamming them into the ground so hard Andie was sure they must have been pulverized. But, surprisingly, they stood. They marched forward again, and more were still coming.

"Upgrades," said Andie.

The three together began casting with ferocious speed and power. Raesh's pearlblood magic knocked the soldiers right back through the portal. Andie lifted the stone floor beneath the soldiers' feet and folded it over backwards, crushing them back into the portal. Saeryn's blade put down two soldiers. Once the room was clear, Andie rushed to the portal and recalibrated it. One soldier was caught half way between destinations and was promptly cut in two.

As the soldiers were thrown back through, barely alive, Ashur was surprised. One soldier looked through the portal and only the bottom half of him fell to the ground when it changed. Lucas, still standing beside the portal, looked completely baffled.

"My leader… I was sure… I thought…"

"Never mind, Lucas," Ashur said. "This is not your fault. It's the dragonborn. This is what they do. Maim and destroy. It doesn't matter. We'll just have to adapt our plans. Recalibrate it to follow the Dead. We'll land in Arvall and then attack."

Andie stepped back from the portal and breathed in relief. With the battalion's plans to enter through Leabharlann stopped, they had one less thing to worry about. Raesh stepped forward, looking down into the portal.

"I thought we were going to turn it off?" he asked. "At least it looks like there is no sign of the time curse. Doesn't stop the enemy from using it to transport across our own time, though."

"Yeah. Not just the enemy. But I almost forgot… Hang on."

And without warning, she jumped into the portal. Raesh rushed up and leaned over the surface of the device, so shocked he hadn't even calmed down enough to be afraid. Saeryn came up behind him and laid a hand on his shoulder, her face frozen in a look of shock as strong as Raesh's. Together, they waited and watched, but it was only a matter of moments before Andie resurfaced. And she was not alone.

With her came Yara and a handsome, intelligent-looking young man with blond hair and green eyes. Bonhaus. Raesh had a moment of absolute disbelief before he finally believed his eyes and embraced Yara.

"But you're dead!" he said.

"Not as dead as I could be. It's so good to see you," Yara said. She then turned to Andie and frowned. "I was starting to think maybe you weren't coming."

Andie shook her head and smiled. "I'm sorry. But you're here now."

Raesh was still frozen in shock. "I know we don't have the time right now, but someday soon you're going to have to tell me how it's possible for you to be here."

"I will, I promise. Everybody, this is Bonhaus."

"Hi," Bonhaus said, in a strong voice.

Yara paused for a moment and looked at Andie.

"Raesh," Yara started again. "You should know that Bonhaus is—"

"The man you love," Andie finished.

The two girls shared a look and then a smile. And just like that the bond was renewed.

Raesh scratched his head and turned to Andie. "But, how did you… Where did she… I don't…"

"Another time," Andie placed her hand on Raesh's shoulder and smiled. "I'm sure Yara has a lot to catch us up on her own adventures, but for now we must focus on our own."

"From the looks of you three I'd say we're already under attack," Yara said.

"They're here a week before we thought was possible. They're using the portals to travel faster. I'm shutting this one down now," Andie said, turning the portal off in some capacity, so that at least the enemy couldn't come through from the other side. "But they can still get in by the one down in the city. Our main concern now is to push the enemy out of the University and reclaim this as a safe haven."

"Let's go. Bonhaus and I are ready. We've been ready and waiting for a very long time. I'm just sorry more of us weren't around when you finally came through to find me, Andie. Does anybody know how Carmen's doing?"

Now Andie paused. She had forgotten that Yara hadn't seen her friend in months, not since that day in the Hot Salts of Mithraldia when the dragon carried her away.

"She's awake," Raesh said.

Both Andie and Saeryn turned their heads toward Raesh. Andie advanced on him.

"What?" she asked. "Since when?"

"Since a couple of days ago. I wanted to let you know, but I couldn't reach you. She's awake and she's strong and when this is all over you can both see her. She's in The Letter, in Taline."

A flood of relief and joy came over Andie as she stood there, her knees threatening to give out beneath her from shear elation. Before she knew what was happening, she and Yara were hugging again, rejoicing in the news they'd waited so long for.

"But as long as we're doing updates, there's more, and I'm afraid it's bad. Yara, you don't know, but we just lost Sarinda. And for all of you, we've lost Professor Iceubes and Oren."

"What?" Saeryn said, her hand moving up to her chest. "When? How?"

"The Dead attacked your home in the Hot Salts. They've captured all of your people who were there at the time, but they haven't killed them. They only killed Oren. He wouldn't stop defending your people. He took down his share of Dead before they got him."

Andie, Saeryn, and Yara were all heartbroken. It hurt that much worse when great news was followed by terrible. For the first time, Andie saw Saeryn's brave face falter. Tears threatened to spill from her lids, and it was no wonder. Oren had been one of her truest friends and strongest allies. Andie didn't know which made her feel guiltier. That Oren died because he had to defend their people alone, or that Professor Iceubes died performing a task she gave him. Ultimately, she knew it no longer mattered. She could pity them and herself later. They had to keep going. They had to save the city.

"Okay," she said. "Okay, okay. We've suffered some

losses. Heavy and early. But this war isn't over. It's only just getting stated. All of us need to get to the hallway now. We're the strongest fighters here and now is not the time to fall apart, no matter how weak we feel."

There were some halfhearted nods and the wiping of eyes. Everyone breathed. Bonhaus rubbed Yara's back for comfort. Andie took a breath and then turned to hurry back out to the hall.

When they reached the fighting, the professors rallied at the sight of them, parting to let them to the front. Armed with the heartache of their losses, the new group that Andie led cast spells more powerful and devastating than any that army had ever seen.

All through the hall, soldiers were falling or fleeing, terrified of the newcomers whose fury far outweighed their own. Andie, Saeryn, and Raesh worked as a perfect unit, casting and slicing their way toward the front of the University. Just left of them, Yara and Bonhaus were no mean feat, either. Despite his lithe form and handsome looks, Bonhaus fought like he was born to it, mixing casting and hand to hand combat in a seamless blend. He was stronger than he looked, smart, and lethal. Beside him, Yara was a force of nature, demonstrating all the things she learned from Andie and the new tricks she'd picked up on the eastern shores of Noelle. Andie also noticed a new strange flare to her magic, one she must have picked up from wherever and whenever she had ended up on the other side of the portal when Oren sent her through. She would have to ask more about that place when they had more time. Andie was just fortunate she was able to use the portal to their own advantage while they still had it, and that the time curse didn't somehow send her back in time when she jumped to get Yara and Bonhaus.

The army tried to maintain some sense of dignity, but the close space and the fury of Andie and her team unnerved them to the point where they could no longer take it. One of the soldiers called for a retreat and suddenly the whole mass fled. Andie had half a mind to shoot spells into their backs, but she was heavy with the thought of what had already been lost. She let them run for their lives.

She continued forward until she came out of the University's front doors. The mercy she showed had only spared a few, for no sooner were the men outside than the dragons began to spray fire again. Saeryn called to the dragons to calm them, her soft song carrying in the wind. The mountain side was alive with scrambling soldiers racing down the slopes. It would take them all night and part of the morning to finally reach the bottom.

A cheer went up through the professors and students. They had finally reclaimed the University, but Andie knew the battle was far from won. The men would regroup at the base of the mountain and join the rest of the army. The battalion would launch its attack. The Dead, who were hiding somewhere among the buildings, would seek their revenge. Blood would be shed, and much of it.

Amidst the celebrations, the dragons began to call out. It almost sounded as if they were hurt. Andie and Saeryn rushed to them and tried to calm them, but they were inconsolable. The celebrations dwindled as all heads turned to the dragons, who were growing more and more agitated.

"What's wrong with them?" Andie asked.

"I've only ever seen them react this way once," Saeryn said, taking a nearby dragon's head in her hands. "It is how they react when one of their own is suffering."

"But I don't understand, there aren't any dragons up here. I know they can sense each other, but wouldn't they need to at least be within a few kilometers of each other?"

"The city," Saeryn said. "If the Dead are here they surely brought our people as their captives. And they're dragons, too. They would want them near to make sure they could not escape and to have ready access to their blood once the spell is broken. We must go now."

Saeryn leapt up onto the dragon and Andie climbed up behind her.

"What can we do?" Yara asked.

"Nothing," Andie said. "The only way to get there fast enough is to fly down on the dragons. We'll be back as soon as we can."

The dragons lifted off and plunged down the mountainside, as fast as Andie had ever seen them fly. In mere seconds, they passed the soldiers who fled from the University. Down and down the dragons flew in a slanting dive, racing to their brothers' and sister' aid. They flew so fast and purposefully that Andie had to hold on tight or risk being lost. After a very brief time, the dragons reached the bottom and leveled out, shooting into the city and down the streets like enormous, breathing bullets. The force of the wind rushing past was so strong and loud that Andie couldn't even hear the dragons' wings beating.

Finally, Andie saw the dragonborn prisoners ahead. She could hardly believe when the dragons found a way to go even faster. Andie could see roughly a dozen Dead standing guard. She hoped the dragons would aid them in taking out the Dead, but instead the dragons simply landed and sat, their enormous forms frozen in place somehow.

Andie couldn't believe it. Saeryn didn't seem surprised. They both dismounted and drew their swords. The Dead began to circle in that flashing way of theirs and Andie wasted no time. She targeted the locks of the cages with her magic and closed her hands. At least a hundred cages were instantly opened and the dead were outnumbered. The Dead grouped together and stared at the dragonborn, contemplating their next move. They grimaced, unhappy to be taken by surprise. Andie targeted more locks and crushed them, too. And all the free dragonborn raced to free their people and their dragons. The Dead knew better than to fight now. They turned and ran.

Andie and Saeryn joined the others and continued taking the locks off the cages. Their people laughed and cried to have their freedom again. As soon as they were all free, Saeryn urged them to mount their dragons and fly up to the University. The streets vibrated with the sound and force of so many wings beating up into the sky. Andie and Saeryn were last, making sure they had freed every last one of their people.

Andie couldn't help trying to delude herself that Oren might still be there, waiting for them to save him. She and Saeryn mounted up and took off. But they were only in the air for a few moments before Andie saw something. Saeryn must have seen it, too, because she turned the dragon in the very direction Andie stared. A large group were coming toward the city from the direction of the String Fields.

Andie was still too far away to see clearly, but they weren't moving in any formation she had seen before, not of the battalion or the army. They moved at a moderate pace, so they were not of the Dead either. The dragon landed just in front of them. They'd already stopped moving when they saw the creature flying toward them. Andie observed them before getting down. They wore dark clothes, heavy boots, bags and crates marked "Explosive," not to mention a smell of extreme cleanliness, their scent pungent in the crisp air.

"You're from the mine cities in the north," Andie said.

"Yes, ma'am," one of the men said. "Are you Princess Andryne or Queen Saeryn?"

"I'm Andie. This is Saeryn. What are you doing so far from home?"

"Well, if you'll pardon the intrusion, a few months back me and my wife found a young girl in pretty bad shape. We took her in got her back on her feet and she stayed with us a while until she figured out what she wanted. Then she left. Well, truth be told, she made quite an impression on me and my wife and we told her she could call on us for anything, any time. Then a few days ago, we get a call telling us she's part of a revolution and they need as many hands as they can get as fast as they can get. She explained everything to us.

"I don't know how much you know about the cities in the north, but we never liked the University. They've been stealing from us and keeping us poor for too many cycles to count. And we never hated you or your people. You've never done anything to us. But more than all of that, when Yara called and said she needed our help, we came directly down and we brought our explosives, too."

The mining cities in the north were famous for their explosives and combustible mixtures. They were also noted builders and refiners, and a people tougher than the steel they used to excavate.

"We spread the word through the towns and everyone came when they could. We've been gathering in your neighbor city and when everyone got here, we came the rest of the way on foot. We're ready. Put us to work."

CHAPTER TWENTY

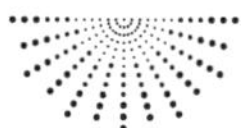

THE MINERS CAME IN A GROUP OF JUST OVER ONE thousand, a number that could go a long way in changing the outcome of the war. They had also brought enough powerful explosives to blow up Arvall three times over. Andie and Saeryn talked with them and made a plan for a coordinated attack. Andie warned them to stay out of the city until nightfall to protect themselves from the Dead, and then she gave them the locations of shelters that still had available space. They set a plan for the next day before Andie and Saeryn left for the University.

Once they reached the school again and were inside, the first person Andie ran into was Lymir. He threw his arms around her as she approached.

"Aye, we've missed you around here, girl," he said.

"You, too, Lymir."

Raesh and Yara came running up, their expressions ecstatic.

"We've got news," Raesh said. "The Thabians radioed us from their ships. They're on their way to Arvall. They're coming to help us and they'll be here by morning. They asked us to call them back with our attack plan."

"We've got news, too," said Andie. "We ran into some people from the mining cities in the north. Friends of yours, I believe," she said, looking at Yara. "There's about a thousand of them and they brought all the explosives we'll ever need. I've spread them throughout the city."

"This war might finally be looking up for us."

"Well, don't stop enjoying the good news yet," said Lymir. "As long as surprise forces are coming to our aid, I might as well tell you that the forces I've stashed all over the city will be ready tomorrow, too. No one's been able to get an accurate count yet, but I'd say we have a fighting chance now."

"My only concern are the Dead," said Saeryn. "They will not go quietly. They have been waiting centuries for the chance to obtain our power. It will be the defining battle of our people. I ask that, if at all possible, the rest of you avoid confronting the Dead. They will hunt my people out on the battlefield and my people are best equipped to handle them."

"What shape are they in? Will they be able to fight?"

"With a little food and rest, they'll be ready by morning."

"The dragonborn can all ride their dragons down to the city, but what about the rest of us?" Yara asked. "How are we supposed to get our forces down to Arvall in time to launch a coordinated attack?"

"We'll use the portal," Raesh said. "By now everyone who's coming through to the city is here. It should be safe to use."

"We need to get everyone together," Andy said. "The

Thabians and the miners are going to be waiting for our signal in the morning and we need to have our plan down. I think for this the Grand Mirror Hall will do. Let's spread the word."

They all turned and began heading for the largest of the mirror rooms, the Grand Mirror Hall of Terpsichore. Everybody went ahead except Lymir, who stopped in the hall and placed his hand on the intercom system that was usually used for the siren's call. Using his magic, he connected his voice to the intercom and urged every person who planned to fight with them in the morning to make their way to the Grand Mirror Hall. Aside from the main hub, it was the only room in the University that could hold so many people at once. Lymir asked that everybody who was not going to fight look after the wounded and try to clear the halls and tunnels of any blockage.

In the Grand Mirror Hall, the people poured in. The room was completely empty and, in fact, hadn't been used since Chancellor Mharú killed the diplomats the night the dragonborn arrived in their world. But now the people rushed in, filling all the available space. They seemed much better now, more excited and hopeful. Winning the small victory in the University had done more for their morale and determination than any speech could have.

Andie, Raesh, Yara, Bonhaus, Saeryn, and Lymir all stood on a bare platform Saeryn had conjured. When the room held as many people as it could, the spectators began to quiet down as they looked up to their leaders. Andie and the others on the platform looked back and forth among each other, trying to decide who would speak. Somehow, the silent consensus gave the honor to Andie. She took a last look at Lymir, head of the University, and Saeryn, Queen of the dragonborn, to make sure it was not overstepping her bounds. When they all bowed their head to her, she stepped forward.

"I want to thank each and every one of you for what you've done today. I know it was only a small victory, but you fought hard and showed the enemy that if they want this city they need to be willing to die for it. Because we are. And to the dragonborn, I'm so happy to have you back here, safe and among friends. I only wish we had found you sooner. We took a big step in getting back our courage today and I'm proud.

"But this war has only begun. We've flown over some of the enemy strongholds down in the city and it looks as if they're prepared for a full siege. It could last days. Our enemies are many. There is the army made up of hundreds of different factions from all over Noelle, but also more dangerous foes. The Church of Stone and Sea has weaponized the red sand, combined with its other abilities, and they've marched against us. The battalion has returned, stronger, more full of hate, and lead by Ashur—trained by the Chancellor himself—and they march against us. A very old, very powerful enemy has risen from the shadows. The Beautiful Dead, descendants of the dragons and sworn enemy of myself and my people. Their physical abilities are astounding and incredibly dangerous, and they march against us. The enemy outnumbers us and they have some pretty terrifying abilities.

"But we have not been abandoned. Lymir has been training a force in secret and they're ready to fight with us tomorrow. The Thabians are sailing to us from the True Isles with their incredible weapons, and the miners have come down from the north with more explosives than we could use in a lifetime. And the dragonborn have been rescued, and when they're rested they and their dragons will fight as well. And everyone you see here onstage will be down in the city giving the battle everything we have.

"Tomorrow, at dawn, we're going down to war. Lymir and I will coordinate our allies and forces throughout the city. The dragonborn will fly down the mountain on their dragons and lead the attack. The rest of you will go down on EARTH 1. Let me explain. I went to the city transport department after we defeated the Chancellor and asked them to begin constructing an underground train from the city to here in case of emergencies. That giant dome at the foot of the mountain that everybody thinks is a fertilizer plant is actually the construction site. They finished building about a month ago. I didn't tell anyone except Lymir and Saeryn. I wanted to play it close to the vest. EARTH 1 is faster than SKY 6 and can get you to the base of the mountain in half the time. It can also hold more people. I think two trips should be enough to get everybody down. The best part is no one will be expecting it and that's exactly what's going to win us this war. The element of surprise. The enemy has no idea that we have allies coming, that we have men stashed throughout the city, or that we have EARTH 1. And they certainly won't be expecting what I have planned for SKY 6. None of us will be riding that.

"Right now, I want you all to eat and get some rest because beginning at dawn we're going to be at war in earnest."

Andie took a step back and watched the people as they filed out of the room. It took a while because there were so many, but the people were in a rush to get themselves ready and to rest. Lymir left, too, to get on the radio with his secret forces. The dragonborn were the last to leave, taking a few last moments to look on their Queen and princess. Andie tried to hold on just a little longer. Finally, she saw him. Gordenson, chief physician of the dragonborn. She motioned for him and he came smiling, as happy to be safe and among friends as Andie was to have him. He came to a stop just in front of her and she gestured for him to wait. When the last person left the room, Andie let herself go. She fell backward, but Raesh was there to catch her. Yara, Bonhaus, and Saeryn crowded around her. Gordenson knelt beside her.

"Princess," he said. "What's happened?"

"The Dead," she said. "We ran into them in southern Noelle. The Black Grotto. Saeryn and I were the only ones who escaped, but we didn't get out unscathed. The Dead have special daggers. Wherever they cut us, our bodies refuse to heal."

"Wrothsaield," said Bonhaus. "It's the name of their blades. Yara and I came across it in our research. The blades are made of cursed metal, no one is sure exactly what kind. Part of the curse was to infuse the blades with the blood of the first Dead who wielded them. Those daggers can cut through anything, even dragon hide if they wanted to."

"One more thing to worry about," said Andie.

"The blades were cursed because they were made for a special purpose. To break the spell and allow the Dead to take on the magic of the dragonborn. All they need to do is plunge the blades into the hearts of all the living descendants of the man who paced the spell on them."

"So that's it," Saeryn said. "That's how they'll do it."

"Yeah, that's not happening," said Raesh.

"I hate war," Andie said. "How does it look Gordenson?"

The physician tore the top of Andie's shirt to examine the cut.

"It's starting to become infected, but I can clean it for you. The one on your cheek isn't too bad, but the one on the back of your hand is all the way to the bone. Thank goodness you did such a job wrapping it or you would have bled out hours ago. I can treat the wounds and stitch them. Your dragon blood won't heal these, but your body will, at a normal rate. I haven't seen wounds like these since the old days."

"Well, as soon as you're done with me, see to the Queen, too. These cuts hurt like you wouldn't believe."

"You'll tear your stitches fighting tomorrow," Raesh said.

"No, she won't," said Gordenson. "I'll spell the stitches to move as she moves. It'll still hurt, but it won't interfere with the healing process."

"Okay. Thank you," Andie said. "Since I'm going to be here for a while, Yara I need you and Bonhaus to get on the radio and coordinate the miners. They should have reached the shelters by now. Make sure everyone is eating and resting. You rest, too."

"I want to stay with you," Yara said.

"I not quite sick of you either," Andie said with a smile. "But there are very few people I trust to lead this fight. You're one of them. By extension, you, too, Bonhaus. So, please, help me out here."

Yara huffed a bit, but bent down to take Andie's hand for a moment, then she and Bonhaus hurried out. Gordenson went to get his bag and then he saw to Andie while Raesh held her. He also treated Saeryn's wounds. He gave them both something for the pain, something tailored especially for their dragon blood. Within moments, they felt better, though there was too much pain to be rid of it completely.

Andie and Saeryn got to their feet and they all made their way out of the mirror hall. They moved toward the main hub and there they found everybody eating and resting. They walked into the room and first there were smiles. But then there were gasps. Andie turned around, moving Gordenson to the side with her arm so she could cast. There were six battalion soldiers standing in the hall. Four in the front and two behind.

"You must be on a suicide mission," Andie said.

"No exactly," one soldier said. "We were already in the Archives when you stopped the others. And now we're going to kill you."

"Now I know you're delusional."

"Let's see who laughing in ten seconds. Boys, camouflage."

The four soldiers in front tapped something on their wrists. But nothing happened. They tapped it again. Nothing happened. Now they began to panic. Andie was seconds from casting, but before she could send even one spell, the two soldiers in the back raised their hands and broke the backs of the four soldiers in front. The whole room went still. No one knew what is happening. Andie looked at the two soldiers, her hand still raised.

"Who are you?"

"Old friends," one of the soldiers said.

The soldiers took their helmets off. It was Kent and Lilja.

An hour later, Andie, Raesh, Saeryn, Lymir, Yara, Bonhaus, Kent and Lilja were rested and fed, as was everyone else. The forces were spread out through the University, sleeping, or not sleeping if they were praying or talking with their families. It was the first real moment of peace they'd had since they first got the news that the army was marching on the city. A peace before the calm. Kent and Lilja were broken when they heard about Sarinda, especially Lilja, who hadn't seen her since the day they split up in the Hot Salts of Mithraldia. Now she'd never be able to know if Sarinda forgave her or not.

Lilja and Kent had travelled to the Old World, the continent on the other side of the vast reach of the Spider Sea. They had been following a lead for Andie, based on information she'd gotten from Saeryn. During the first war with the University in Saeryn's time, many dragonborn families fled to the Old World to escape persecution. The University's power couldn't reach that far, and the dragonborn were safe there.

Weeks before she was pulled through the portal, Saeryn made a journey across the sea to convince her people to come home. Many of them did return, but a lot stayed behind, preferring to stay safe rather than to fight. Andie had charged Kent and Lilja months before with finding any dragonborn descendants on that side of the sea. Saeryn was sure none would have survived the curse that threatened to wipe her people out back in her original time—the curse she had called to Andie in the future to save them from—but she allowed them the chance to go investigate in case. To everyone's surprise, they had found some, but they were even less willing to fight than their ancestors.

Kent and Lilja journeyed all the way across the Old World and returned to Noelle from the east. From there, they began tracking the battalion, taking out as many as they could before finally disguising themselves and joining the ranks. The two climbed their way up. They'd both had engineer training and so they put their skills to use, working on the suits for the battalion and connecting them all to the same network. The enhancements for the suit were real, but Kent and Lilja installed new programming that allowed them to disable the suits remotely, just as they'd done to the four soldiers who tried to turn on their camouflage. They hadn't brought back the dragonborn reinforcements, but they had come home able to shut down the battalion's suits, leaving Ashur and his men with nothing but some very expensive pieces of clothing. The only catch was they didn't have the clearance to get access to a level of the network high enough to have a trickledown effect. They would need to capture either Lucas or Ashur and plug into their suit.

"Looks like we've got a few secret weapons after all," Raesh said, holding Andie.

By then, everyone else was asleep and Andie and Raesh curled up in a corner of the main hub, exhausted.

"It's still going to be a longshot," she said. "We have to coordinate all these groups perfectly."

"And fight. Are you ready?"

"I never have been. Never will be."

"Me neither."

"So… we don't need to have one of those emotional and uncomfortable conversations about our feelings, do we?"

"Nope. I know how you feel about me."

"Good. I know how you feel about me, too."

CHAPTER TWENTY-ONE

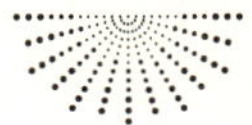

THE NEXT MORNING, RAESH FINALLY GAVE ANDIE THE thing he brought from their apartment. It was her armor. They were outside, in front of the University, surrounded by all the professors, students, and citizens who chose to fight with them. The dragonborn were there, too, beside their dragons, their hands on the hilts of their swords. Saeryn, Gordenson, Lymir, Yara, Bonhaus, Kent, Lilja, and even Murakami were there. Andie had never put the armor on before. She has been afraid of it and of the terrible things she might do inside of it. But a look from Raesh and Saeryn reassured her. She nodded and Raesh and Saeryn helped her put it on.

The armor fit perfectly. The smooth contours of the scaled metal fit her muscles and curves as if it were cut from her very own body. It felt incredible. In her head, Andie couldn't think of any way to describe it other than that it felt like home. The dragon scales glistened and changed color in the sun, and there must have been some powerful, beautiful magic flowing through it because she felt stronger, braver. Or maybe it was simply being surrounded by so many friends and allies in that short, rare moment of peace.

She tried to hold back the tears, but gave up and let them fall. She knew they were good, not tears of shame or weakness, but tears of joy and pride. She looked around her at all the hopeful faces that looked back. She knew how much they were depending on her. She was just shy of twenty-four years old and never completed even one year of higher magical academic training, yet she and the Queen of her people were about to lead a force into war.

The people around her were hoping, praying she could save them, and she understood just then what Saeryn had been trying to tell her since the day they met. Being a Queen was sometimes about making difficult choices and sometimes about playing executioner, but it was always about protecting your people, no matter the sacrifice to yourself. Andie felt the burden take hold of her as she witnessed every emotion passing over the faces of the crowd around her. She was surrounded by everyone and everything living in the world that mattered to her. And it was time to protect it.

A path cleared for her to a dragon. Andie gasped when she recognized the beautiful creature. It was Ronen, Oren's dragon. Ronen met her gaze as she gazed into the stunning emerald depths of the dragon's eyes. A single tear formed in the dragon's eye, and Andie stepped forward to gently wipe it away. She placed her hand on Ronen's neck, and the creature craned her head to press against Andie's side.

Saeryn went first and mounted up. Andie turned to face her people, more determined than ever, and the people reached out to touch her as they crowded around.

Something happened to her as she stood there, looking out over her people and the beautiful dragon who had lost her life-long companion. Something changed. She realized, for the first time with any true gravity, that she may never return. She thought to herself that that was okay, so long as the city and everyone in it were safe. She reached the dragon and turned to Raesh. She kissed him as if the war were over and they were staring into the face of a lifetime of peace.

"You still good on that conversation?" he asked.

"Yeah. You?"

"Still good." He smiled.

Andie levitated up into the air to see the crowd. She had never been prouder.

"I have only one thing to say to you," she called out. "So long as you can, fight."

With that, she settled onto Oren's beautiful green dragon, and all of the dragonborn rose into the air as one. Andie watched as Raesh, Yara, Lymir, and all her friends disappeared beneath them. Then with a ferocious roar, Saeryn's new fierce green companion began its dive down the mountainside, with all the other dragons following. Their descent was strong, straight, true. The city rose before their eyes as the dragons dashed for the foot of the mountain. As they neared the bottom, Andie could see the train station was crawling with soldiers who were guarding the portal that Marcus set up. This was what she'd hoped for. She sent a byzantium ray of light into the air as a signal to Raesh up on the mountain. He'd know what to do.

The dragons reached the bottom of the mountain and leveled out, heading into the city. They sprayed fire down on the soldiers, and, even at their incredible speed,

Andie could still hear them screaming. The dragons wove through the streets, throwing their full weight into the enemy army's makeshift bunkers and wrapping their great powerful jaws around the posts supporting the army's watchtowers. As they came around for another pass, some of the dragonborn dismounted and ran ahead to fight on foot, allowing their dragons to target the enemy as they please. Saeryn brought Ronen around for another pass through the streets, this time targeting the supplies the enemy has stockpiled along the streets for easy access.

After wiping out nearly all the visible supplies in the area, Saeryn brought the dragon high above the city to get a view of their surroundings. Andie could see the Thabians and the Thabian ships pulling into the city docks, hundreds of them racing into the city to attack the enemy from the western edge. She turned and saw a series of explosions going off in a very tight, precise pattern from the opposite side of the battle. The miners. The explosions made her think of the trap she had set the night prior.

When she met with the miner yesterday, they gave her some explosives to take with her. It was a small amount, but the man said they were the most powerful in Noelle. Perhaps even in all of Shaeyara. Andie and her friends loaded those explosives onto the train last night and cut the breaks. Her purple light in the sky was the go-ahead for Raesh to release SKY 6. Just as she turned to look, the train came barreling into the station unable to stop. It jumped the tracks, plowed through the crowd of soldiers, and collided with the train station.

The explosion was both magnificent and terrifying. The combustion blew the windows out along twenty blocks of the city. The smoke and flames rushed into the air and reached even higher than the tallest skyscraper. The sound of it was something no one would ever forget. The train station was irrevocably obliterated and all that was left of where the massive crowd of soldiers stood was a monumental crater. Andie did not relish that such violence and death were the result of her planning, but she knew she had to defend her people. What made her feel better was the sight of their forces rushing out of the white dome, having just gotten off EARTH 1.

Saeryn brought them down again and they took a survey of the city. Their secret forces and the miners had come up from the shelters to fight, and the enemy army looked unpleasantly surprised. The miners had explosions going off all along the eastern edge of the city, and, though it was hard to tell from where she was, she thought the Thabians had made quite an entrance on the other side. She and Saeryn did a last pass to burn up some more of the enemy's supplies and then they dismounted to fight on foot. They touched down just in front of some battalion soldiers and got to work.

The war had begun.

THE FIGHTING RAGED all day and night. From the moment they soared down over the precipice of the mountain, the dragonborn hardly had a chance to rest. The professors and students, too, had proven themselves beyond valorous, fighting until they thought they couldn't, and then fighting some more. The fighting covered the entire city, from the foot of the mountain to the northern edge of the city, and from the Spider Sea all the way across to the String Fields. The dragons swooped in to catch an enemy in their claws or teeth, and sprayed their fire when they could, but they had sat the fight out for the most part so as not to hurt the good fighters who were battling in such close quarters with the enemy.

The two armies went after each other with everything they had. The streets rang with the deafening sound of gunfire and screaming. The air was thick and brilliant from endless spells and hexes being hurled through space and glass. Colors and collisions of all kind flashed in the air and against buildings as the armies cast simultaneously. Buildings were shaken and some even collapsed as the expression of magic filled nearly every street of Arvall. The sun rose in the east beyond the fields and set in the west against the horizon made by the shimmering sea, and still the fighting raged on without stop, without mercy.

Many were wounded, some gravely so. Many were dead. Those who were wounded were dragged far enough out of the fray to safety, until they could rest and recover and then take to the streets again. In some parts of the city the fighting slowed as the armies cast across boulevards from their hiding places. In other places, the stench of death was overpowering as soldiers from both sides collided in a close, furious brawl for the city and its soul. There was even fighting inside the buildings as soldiers chased their enemy inside and upstairs. The destruction and hatred knew no bounds, no limits.

Andie and Saeryn fought side by side, so elegant and powerful that they were almost never hit, not even by the battalion. On the rare occurrence they were hit, it was only a momentary wound, for the dragon blood healed them quickly—though the wounds they sustained from the Beautiful Dead in the Black Grotto still pained them. To conserve the magic in their blood, they did as much fighting as they could with their swords, though it was truly a magnificent sight to see them effortlessly cast a spell that could take out a dozen men. Andie went from casting spells, to using her sword, to hand to hand combat, and back again. Andie's arm ached from swinging the sword so much, so wildly. A part of her conscious just wanted the fighting, the inevitable death, to be done with, and she knew Saeryn felt the same way. She also knew what she was doing was right. She continued protecting her people.

Raesh, Yara, and Bonhaus fought in close quarters all day. Raesh's pearlblood magic was as wild as ever, and during the battle it served him well. Most of the enemy had never even heard of pearlblood magic, let alone seen it in action. Bonhaus was at his best, mixing his superb combat skills with his precise casting abilities. Yara's capabilities had grown remarkably since the last time she faced the battalion. She brought with her now all kinds of spells and hexes she picked up during her self-imposed exile, but her most lethal method was fighting with her wind daggers, which cut and flew back simultaneously. She was fantastic and undeniable. She, Bonhaus, and Raesh could be found wherever the fighting was thickest.

The Thabians and the miners managed to keep the battle contained on both sides. Some soldiers tried to flee across the sea, but they couldn't break the line of the Thabians who, for all their disdain for modern technology, were such skilled fighters that not even the battalion could break their formation. Their weapons, crafted in their beautiful secluded isles, were strong, true, and deadly. Soldiers laughed to see their bow and arrows, but their laughter did not lasted long. The miners, though lacking training and even rudimentary military skills, proved themselves a great help. They spent the night laying out mines along the border of the String Fields, horrifying traps for any enemy so bold as to try to escape that way. They had weapons that created both far-reaching jets of flame and multiple combustions. They were also incredibly skilled at localizing fire and manipulating it to their will.

Kent and Lilja spent the day seeking out battalion soldiers. They knew they didn't have the strength, even combined, to take down Ashur, but if they could find and defeat Lucas, they'd be able to hack his suit and send a command through the battalion network to make all of the suits useless. They hunted down battalion members wherever they could. They could still shut down the suits of any battalion soldiers in their immediate vicinity, and their work went a long way in helping to even the playing field. Many had forgotten just how powerful the battalion suits were. Kent and Lilja had to give the battalion the impression that they were helping them, so the enhancements were real, initially, but they were programmed to return to normal function the minute they came through the portal.

Even functioning at a normal level, however, the battalion was still incredibly dangerous. They were already combat specialists months ago, but their time among the Dead made them even more lethal. Their suits amplified what they could do naturally, which essentially meant they didn't need to stop and rest, a considerable advantage in a battle that lasted days.

Though Ashur was not yet fighting, Lucas had been on the streets of Arvall since before even Andie. His training was impeccable, precise, deadly. He was molded by Ashur, the commander himself, and thus he felt no remorse or pity, only a thorough hatred for the dragonborn and anyone who sided with them. Many died by his hands.

Lymir and Murakami fought long and hard, despite their age. They moved from shelter to shelter, helping to protect those who could not protect themselves. They also got on the radio and called out positions and patterns, giving their forces the best possible chances. Between fighting in the streets and their broadcasts, Murakami and Lymir made sure the supplies of all the shelters were still good, and they organized scavenging missions for their forces to steal supplies from the enemy.

The council fighters were as strong as ever, fighting in formations and varying the patterns so the enemy couldn't learn them. Despite their high numbers, they fought as a single unit, one well-trained and powerful body. They, like everyone else, fought thinking of all they had lost because of motions the University set into play centuries ago. They fought thinking of all they knew they would have to sacrifice before this war was over. With magic, fists, and guns they moved through the city, giving the battle everything they had.

CHAPTER TWENTY-TWO

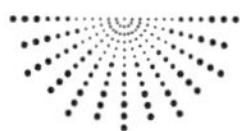

THE WAR RAGED ON. THE DEAD STILL HADN'T SHOWN their faces, but Andie knew they were simply waiting for the most opportune moment. Morning became day, day became night, and in the darkness the fighting continued. The city was lit by the deranged flight of a thousand perilous spells.

"YOU..."

"Seem.. ."

"To..."

"Have..."

"Lost..."

"Heart."

"WILL..."

"You..."

"Simply..."

"Watch..."

"From..."

"Safety?"

Beladorion turned slowly to the priests and looked down at them, so much smaller and less intimidating than himself. But he knew better than to compromise the plan.

"It almost sounds as if you question my courage," he said. "One might even think you question my ability. I would advise against that. I have not underestimated you and I would suggest you not underestimate me. I know exactly what this looks like, as if I fear the blood traitors and only want to face them when they're weakest. That is half true. My people and I have no interest in fighting, at least not for very long. I've realized we can take no glory from this battle whether the traitors are fresh or exhausted. All we want is to kill the Queen and princess and drink of them. It will not hurt our pride if we have to take them at their lowest. Our aim is to evolve. Still, fear not. These blood traitors are strong and when the sun comes out again in the morning it will rejuvenate them. The morning will also be the day that we have waited for. And then we will descend upon them."

"We... "

"Shall..."

"Go..."

"Down..."

"At..."

"Midnight."

"Six priests in robes against this army? You're either extremely brave or much more naïve that even I believed. I suppose I understand why this is personal for you. The traitor princess is the first person to ever escape from your clutches. It is a total embarrassment. Have your fun priests. I will watch from here."

"Just..."

"Watch..."

"For..."

"The..."

"Red..."

"Sand."

THE NIGHT WORE on and the hours fell away. The war shifted its way around the city, winding through the streets, its fronts changing. The thickest fighting breaking apart, the thinnest converging, the city fell to pieces everywhere. Whole buildings collapsed and fires raged too big and too numerous to be extinguished. There had been heavy losses on both sides and some streets were impassable because of the bodies, but neither side wavered in its resolve.

As the night wound to its close, to the point where it became yet again morning, Andie came to a shelter for water and a moment's rest. She was also listening to the radio for news of Raesh and her other friends on the other side of the city. As midnight struck, a kind of wave passed through her. She felt awkward for a moment, but the feeling passed. Having heard neither good nor bad news about Raesh, Andie cleared her head and rushed back outside. On the street, she found Saeryn, who seemed a bit woozy.

"Are you okay?" Andie asked.

"Yes. I believe so. It just felt as if something passed through me."

"Yeah, I felt it, too. I have no idea what it was. Maybe the De—"

Andie couldn't finish her sentence because she saw something coming in their direction. It must have been thirty blocks away, but it closed the distance fast. It was massive, wild, blasting the glass from the windows and sweeping cars along as it came. The closer it got, the more Andie could see its color. Red. It didn't take her long to realize that it was the red sand of the Church of Stone and Sea. They had finally joined the war in the streets.

"Oh, yes," Andie said. "I've been waiting for you. Saeryn, our friends from the church here look a little sad. Let's brighten them up."

"With pleasure."

Saeryn put her hands to her mouth and made a very distinct call. She and Andie then waited, watching the looming threat draw near. The massive cloud of red sand continued to come toward them, sweeping everything in the street along and causing terrible damage. It was almost upon them, fierce, sprawling, morphing before their eyes, a huge cloud of magical and deadly grains. Just as it bore down on them, fire and black smoke billowed into its face. Ronen and the other dragons had heard her call.

The dragons flew above the cloud and sprayed down some of its heaviest and hottest flame yet, the entire surrounding city was cast in a red glow. The cloud became a giant mass of red glass and fell, shattering across the street. Among the shards and chunks were six priests, badly burned yet still strong enough to regain their feet. They clearly weren't expecting such a welcome. Just like in the Church weeks prior, they began to come together to merge as one. Very calmly, Andie drew her sword and held the blade in the opposite hand. She whispered an incantation over the blade, her eyes closed and her mind focused. The six priests became one.

"Little princess," the multi-voice said. "We now give you the choice to—"

Andie threw her blade right into the middle of the face and it stuck between its eyes. The spell began to spill out from the sword and the face started to melt, turning into a dripping, steaming jelly before dissolving completely. Andie held out her hand and the sword returned to her. Simple, quick, effective. She and Saeryn turned and walk away.

IN TALINE, across Noelle from Arvall City, the third wave of the army arrived. There were far too many of them to arrive on the train, and so they descended on the city from above, parachuting down from the silver cliffs. When the citizens of Taline looked up and see two thousand men descending on them, they panicked. But Stefan was calm. He surmised that an army marching on Arvall from the north might detach a faction to march on his city as well, and he had been prepared for this moment for days. He had organized the city's small force and even reformed the council.

The army rushed through the streets of Taline, hungry for bloodshed and pillaging. It was true that Taline had not been back on its feet long and still has a long way to go before reclaiming its former glory, but the one thing they did have was Stefan. Stefan the

Unkillable, he was called in the old days. He was very old and very powerful, and he loved one thing above all others. His precious Taline City. It was a shame the soldiers didn't know this.

Taline's standing army was very small, and Stefan sent half of them to fight alongside their allies in Arvall city. But what the forces of Taline lacked in numbers, they made up for in training. They were originally trained to hunt and capture the terrorists who plagued the city years before. Because of the frequent attacks, there was little order and much chaos, and these men hardened themselves fighting some of the worst and most ruthless criminals in western Noelle. They were a force to be reckoned with, and Stefan had organized them flawlessly. No sooner did the men touch down than the forces of Taline ambushed them and delivered an attack worthy of record in every history book.

Stefan himself was also in the streets fighting like a young man, despite his more than two hundred years. His spellwork was the product of more than two centuries of rigorous training and discipline. Not one of the soldiers could even get close to him without being vaporized. Stefan was a kind man, but he showed no mercy to those who wished to destroy his city. His magic was great and terrible. And beside him, fighting as if she had never been hurt, was Carmen.

She was as beautiful and deadly as ever, moving quickly and dexterously through the invading army, cutting them down with ease. She and Stefan forced the soldiers back toward Bane, a two-thousand-foot-tall, sun-fueled, living structure capable of defending itself. As the enemy was pushed within its reach, Bane's loveglass windows lashed out and snatched the soldiers from the streets, delivering them to an agony that made them glad for the death it eventually delivered.

Stefan and Carmen fought viciously, alongside the other council members, defending the city and ensuring more soldiers didn't arrive in Arvall.

CHAPTER TWENTY-THREE

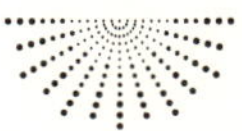

SAERYN STUMBLED FIRST, THEN FELL. ANDIE KNELT TO help her, though she didn't feel very strong herself.

"What was that?" Saeryn asked, her eyes scanning their surroundings wildly.

"I felt it, too," Andie said. Her body was consumed by a great weakness, as if her very magical essence had been torn from her body.

"What is happening?" Both women looked panicked, their bodies weakening by the second. They could not track the source of the attack, but both felt their magic and physical strength slowly extinguish like a dampening flame.

Before Andie could answer, she was knocked twenty feet back and into a concrete column. She had to lay there for a moment to catch her breath, but before she could, a bolt of lightning struck her, knocking her backward through the pillar. She could hardly open her eyes as she waited for the dragon blood to heal her.

"That one's mine," Ashur said, pointing to Andie. "You're more than welcome to the Queen."

Andie saw him now and she saw his accomplice: Beladorion. She guessed from his dress and suffocating arrogance that he was the leader of the Dead. Ashur made his way over to her and lifted her with one hand. He held her in front of him, giving her a long look at the irrevocable damage she'd done to his face.

"It's not a pretty sight, is it?" he asked.

He punched her with all his force and then cast an acid spell right in her face. The pain was blinding and Andie dropped to the ground in agony. She put her hand to her face and only managed to have her palm eaten away, too. Ashur came in for his next strike, and, as he leaned forward, Andie cast an explosion right into his chest. She was thrown, skidding across the concrete and Ashur was blasted up through the steel and concrete overhang of the building.

Across the street, Beladorion was beating Saeryn to within an inch of her life.

"You know, I never understood you traitors," he laughed. "All we want is to have what you have. It's not as if we need to drink all your blood, though of course now we'll bleed you dry simply out of spite. Generations upon generations of both our people could have been spared if you had only shared your birthright."

"If you were to obtain our power, you would destroy everything," Saeryn said, crawling away to give herself time to heal. "By denying you we have protected the world."

"You've only put off the inevitable," he said, kicking her across the intersection. "You've only angered us."

Saeryn looked to her left, her right, and down the street in front of her. Everywhere she looked the Dead were beating the life out of her people. The dragonborn fought bravely, but the Dead's natural and physical attributes were formidable. Andie saw the carnage as well. She looked over to Saeryn, wondering how they would survive.

IN OTHER PARTS of the city the tides were turning against the defenders of Arvall. Murakami and a large number of council fighters were killed in a magical bombing by the battalion. Lymir had been missing for hours. Yara and Bonhaus collapsed from exhaustion and had to be carried off for rest and water. Raesh was still fighting valiantly, but he was being cornered by a phalanx of fifty battalion soldiers. The miners had been pushed out of the east side of the city and some of them had even run across their own traps. The line of the Thabians had finally been broken.

The Beautiful Dead were gaining the upper hand on the dragonborn, who were simultaneously suffering from the same odd weakness that was affecting Andie and Saeryn. The battalion had strong-armed its way into a position of advantage. The defenders of Arvall lacked the numbers and they were beginning to lack the will. Andie and Saeryn were taking a terrible beating at the hands of Ashur and Beladorion, and it seemed the spell was only moments from being broken.

But all hope was not lost. Kent and Lilja had searched all day and night for him and now they had finally hunted him down. Lucas. He was standing behind the phalanx of battalion soldiers. They finally had him. They wasted no time, stealthily running up to him from behind. Lilja jumped up and landed a knee to the back of his head, a perfect blow that dazed him and brought him down. Kent fended off the soldiers as they rounded on him.

Lilja worked quickly, getting out her equipment and hacking into the suit. It didn't take long to work, but Lucas came around for a few seconds, just long enough to blast a hole through Kent's back. Lilja screamed; she drew her knife and plunged it into Lucas's chest, repeatedly. The battalion soldiers all looked confused as their power dwindled, leaving them with nothing but their own meager ability. Sensing the change, Raesh gathered his magic in a wild, unstable ball in his hands.

"Lilja, get down!" he screamed.

He released the magic, the energy, and blew the soldiers away. The shutting down of the battalion suits was a turning point. Without their advanced suits, the battalion soldiers lost both their power and their arrogance. However, they were still skilled sorcerers. The defenders of Arvall sensed the opportunity and drew their will for one last try.

ASHUR FINALLY REGAINED consciousness and slammed back into the street. Andie had recovered enough to regain her feet. She saw him and moved in his direction. He pulled a whip from his back and it began to glow green with some kind of magic Andie knew must be dangerous. She drew her sword.

Ashur snapped the whip, but Andie was quicker. She cut it off, only to find that it grew back. She began casting as she defended against the flying whip. Ashur cast, too, though he was less precise than Andie.

They traded spells as if they were born to do only

that. Ashur performed through rage and hate, Andie through necessity. The whip caught Andie's leg across her shin and snapped her bone. He snapped it again across her face. When the whip came around again, Andie dove to the side, replacing her original form with a magical ghosted shadow, allowing the whip to pass through. She walked right up to Ashur and swung her fist just as he realized his whip had gone through empty air and landed her punch. Ashur spun on his feet and Andie landed more blows. But soon he was squared again and they engaged in hand to hand. They were both skilled fighters, catching each other with incredible blows, but Ashur's armor made him stronger, faster. He slapped Andie and she went spinning through the air.

But she was tougher than he could have imagined. She was right back on her feet, throwing her sword with such force and accuracy that it went right through his thigh. As he screamed in pain, Andie got a running start and jumped, coming down with a spell that crushed Ashur into the ground. She turned her fist to stone and began to pound him mercilessly. But his new armor and the old that was melded to his skin had made him strong.

He opened his mouth and screamed, amplifying it with a spell so that the sound came out in percussive rings. Andie was blown back. She cast a spell at Ashur that caused him to bleed inside. She didn't notice until the final two seconds were ticking away that he'd placed a grenade on her. She wasn't concerned, since fire couldn't hurt her, but this was no regular grenade. As it exploded, it sent a wave through her that completely drained her. She dropped.

SAERYN RALLIED AGAINST BELADORION. She felt herself weakening every moment, but still she pressed on. She had drawn her sword and dueled against him and his Wrothsaield blades. Her footwork and form were excellent and she cast a spell to make her faster, leveling the playing field.

"Very good, traitor," Beladorion said. "For a moment, I worried I was fighting a common rat."

"You forget your place, boy," said Saeryn. "You descend on us when we are weakest and think you have cause to be proud. What a shame to find the great Dead are merely frightened children."

Beladorion lunged, and, although Saeryn blocked his blade, he moved to throw his shoulder into her and knocked her across the street. She recovered just in time to stab the arm that reached for her throat. He screamed. Saeryn launched an assault, slicing him so fast and expertly that even Beladorion had trouble tracking her. He was able to protect his main arteries, but Saeryn had free reign with everything else. She cast a spell that snatched a pillar from its support position and slammed it into Beladorion, knocking him two blocks away. Two more Dead arrived to help their leader, but Saeryn beheaded them both on her way to Beladorion.

But he was waiting for her and as she neared him. He regained his feet and aimed a kick at her chest in a mere second, sending her flipping over backwards and colliding with the ground. In a flash, he was on top of her, digging his blade into her hand.

MEANWHILE, a group of battalion soldiers had found

Andie. Ashur was still in the crater she had beaten him in, recovering. The grenade that went off on Andie was designed to instantly shrivel the adrenal glands, instantaneously ridding the body of adrenaline. Andie was too weak to even move a finger. Adrenaline played a large role in dragonborn healing, so it was taking her a while to get back on her feet. The ten soldiers held her up and took turns beating her, like only cowards would do. But every punch they landed only made her stronger. She was healing. Slowly, she felt herself coming back.

Soon Ashur was on his feet and he cast a spell at one of the soldiers that completely froze him. He kicked the boy over and his body shattered.

"What do you think you're doing?" he shouted. "She's mine! Mine!"

Andie spat a mouthful of blood on the ground. "Aw, that's so sweet. I didn't know you wanted me that badly, but if you insist..."

Ashur launched himself away just in time. Magic rushed from Andie's body in an explosion of fire and lava. She was filled with such rage and such fury, she felt a renewed energy flood her veins, and she used it to its full potential. The other nine soldiers were burned away instantly. Ashur managed to escape, but his leg was badly burned. He struggled to his feet, but Andie pushed the wind between them with such force that he was thrown up at an angle, smashing through to the twelfth floor of a building and landing inside. Andie levitated up to the floor. Ashur was insensible on the floor and Andie kicked the arm he was trying to push up on, breaking it. He screamed in pain.

"I can't believe you were dumb enough to come

back," she said. "You barely escaped with your life last time. Why would you test me?"

"And who are you supposed to be? An orphan? A prey? A lovesick imposter, pretending these people will ever actually love you? You disgust me."

Andie turned her hand and broke all his ribs. He screamed in agony.

"Trust me," she said. "The feeling is mutual."

But Ashur's scream of pain morphed into a deranged laughter. Andie grew uncomfortable. She began to cast again, but in the space of a second his armor pulsed blue and then exploded in a wave of energy that sucked the solar radiation right out of Andie. She collapsed. Ashur got to his feet. He didn't say a word, just walked up to her and kicked her so hard she went flying out of the window. She collided with the glass of the other building across the street, then fell.

BELADORION SWUNG his quick and powerful fist at Saeryn, but instead of connecting with her flesh, he hit metal. Saeryn had transformed her body to steel as best she could, though her memory of the spell in the grimoire grew faint in her battered head. She swung a punch of her own and sent Beladorion flipping and tumbling across three blocks. The blow was so hard the other Dead along the street stopped to look. The dragonborn, though still weak, had begun to rally. They started pulling out the best and strongest spells they knew, and wielded their swords as if they would never have the chance to wield them again.

By the time Beladorion got to his feet, Saeryn was

upon him, beating him senseless with her steel fists. She weakened, but still she had her magic. The Beautiful Dead were strong, but they did not have the dragonborn healing. Beladorion's blood began to flow and he knew terror for the first time in his long life. He got a few good shots in, but Saeryn was a supremely skilled warrior and she mixed her hits with spells. She broke his wrist. Then his arm. She touched his chest and he began to cough up sand, but a stealthy and vicious backhand sent Saeryn reeling. Beladorion drew his blades and he and Saeryn returned to dueling. But he was, after all, physically superior and he began to move just too fast for Saeryn to follow. He cut the main artery of her leg and she fell. Were it not for her dragon blood, she would have died that very moment. Beladorion kicked her over and over again, smiling the whole time.

ASHUR HIT Andie again and by this point, she was hardly breathing. Being the highest member of the battalion, his suit wasn't affected like the others. Andie looked for Saeryn, who may have been dead already, but she couldn't see her. Her people had begun to rally against the Dead, but the weakness that had come on them all was beginning to win. By the way she witnessed her people around them slow, she knew they were affected by more than just the weariness of battle. Something was happening to them, but she didn't understand what. Some strange and powerful spell seemed to be targeting just the dragonborn, but Andie couldn't think of any such spell that could do such a thing. Her people were hardly able to stand and the Dead began to take advantage of it. They were losing.

"You're all cowards," Andie shouted, though even that proved difficult through her newfound weakness. "You wouldn't fight us when we were strong. You sneak in at the end of war, when we're tired and beginning to fade."

"I'll admit, it's not my proudest moment, but I don't care. I just want you dead, Andie. I think I always wanted you dead. I hated having to pretend I cared for you, to work with you, to be with you. Kissing you used to turn my stomach."

"Well, in hindsight, I'm not too thrilled about your face on mine either."

Ashur held his hand over her and it began to glow. Pain spread throughout Andie's body as frostbite overcame her in seconds, turning most of her body black. Ashur lowered the hand and the pain went.

"I've been practicing that one," he said. "You like? Cold seems to be sore point for your kind."

"Were you always this evil?" Andie asked, shivering.

"No. I used to be weak. Now I'm strong. Don't try to reason with me, Andie. I'm beyond your reach and your words. As a matter of fact, I'm about to take your head from your shoulders."

"Do you have any idea why you can't beat us?" she asked.

"It looks like I already have."

"No. It looks like sun."

As she said the words, the sun rose over the String Fields, high enough that its light broke into the city. As the rays hit her, Andie found her strength. She knew she couldn't lose. Not here. Not today. Ashur came in again and she drew her sword so quickly that he didn't even see it until after she'd cut him.

He cast at her and she dodged. He cast again and she countered. He drew a dagger and threw it at her, but she stopped it in midair. She still felt strangely weak, but she had figured out why. She and Ashur traded spells, but his anger was no match for her power. Her body became a humanoid flame, right down to her very core, and she became so bright he could hardly stand to look at her. She weaved around him with her blade, cutting him so fast and deep he could not keep up with her. She grabbed his arm with her flaming hand and he screamed form the pain as his flesh melted away.

"You can't beat us because you're nothing. We are the past and the future. You were never a match for me, Ashur. Or should I say *Tarven.* When we fought before I wasn't trying to kill you. I was trying to spare you. I won't make that mistake today."

"I am the commander of the—"

"You are the leader of murderers and you waited until I was weakest to face me again because somewhere, deep inside, you know you can't beat me. You were never going to win. You are a coward and a weak man. There exists no victory for people like you. You have terrified us, hunted us, and murdered us. I tried caring for you. I tried saving you. But no more. No mercy, Tarven."

She brought her other hand forward slowly, making sure it burned as hot as possible. She began to slowly push it into his chest, letting him feel every second of the pain and heat. It had been a long time coming and he has had a hand in so many atrocities, but now she was bringing him to justice, even though he could never suffer as much as he deserved. She took pleasure in the fact that he was suffering now. The shock of her white-hot hand penetrating his chest was written across his disfigured face and the last expression he wore before she turned him to a pile of smoldering Ash was one of utter confusion.

Several blocks away, Beladorion had completely overcome Saeryn. He had beaten her, cut her, and thrown her like a toy. Only some of her wounds healed. All around her, her people were being overwhelmed. The Dead had come upon them when they were at their absolute weakest.

"Do you know what's happening to you?" he said. "I do."

"The sun," Saeryn whispered. She gazed up at the red glow in the horizon as the sun rose and brought with it a new strength. Only, she didn't feel strengthened. Not fully. She felt confused, betrayed by her own blood. Why wasn't the sun strengthening her?

Beladorion laughed. "You're fading away, stupid Queen. You see, coming through the portal erased you from history, thus you never existed. And if you didn't exist then, you can't exist now. When I heard you and your people had returned, I began my calculations and I'm so happy to see that they were accurate to the very hour. First, you'll grow weak, then you'll simply fade away. Look to your people. It's happening now."

Saeryn rolled over and turned her head and gasped. It was true. Her people were falling. Some were even fading out of existence right before her eyes. She could hardly believe it. Beladorion took his Wrothsaield blade and plunged it into Saeryn's stomach, not a wound that would kill her instantly, but one she would not survive. She was surprised by how little it hurt. She just felt cold. But this is what it had come to. And now she knew, now she realized that there was only one way this would end. Just like Andie said.

"So, this is how we end," she said. "Fading away in the devastated streets of Arvall. I suppose that's fine with me. What's not fine is you."

She raised her broken arm toward Beladorion and froze him. Even he wasn't expecting this. Before his eyes, she snapped the bone back in place and it healed. All her wounds that weren't caused by Beladorion's blades healed. She rose, holding her bleeding stomach. She turned her wrist slowly and rose the temperature of his blood. She spread her fingers and weakened his bones.

"I have never understood one thing about your kind," she said, spitting up blood, but standing straight. "What makes you think you are a match for us? Yes, you're physically magnificent, but unless you're sneaking up on us in the forest, surprising us in a dark grotto, or descending on us when we are the weakest and most exhausted we've ever been, what makes you think any of your gifts can compare with magic?"

"You filthy traitor. I am Beladorion, leader of the—"

"The Dead? A rather appropriate name, I think. You see, all my life I've feared you, and it wasn't until today, when you and your kind snuck up on us like cowards, that I realized something. You pose no threat. You bring no danger. You are a disgrace to the dragons that gave birth to you. You are the true blood traitors."

"I will... drink... of your blood."

"You will do nothing but be what your name implies. Dead. *Eitilt mall comhlacht*."

As she cast the time curse, the entire city froze except for the dragonborn. Saeryn limped over to Beladorion. She stared into his face.

"What is it you're so fond of saying? Oh, yes. Fhealltóir Fola."

With that she drew her sword and plunged it through his chest. She had used most of her strength and went down to her knees. She turned to address her people.

"Put them to the sword!"

The dragonborn heeded the command of their Queen and within moments the Dead were no more. Andie came rushing up to Saeryn and kneeled beside her.

"I see you took a leaf out of my book," Andie said.

"Well, they cheated. I figured we should as well." As she spoke, her people cheered. A sound so glorious yet so haunted that echoes between the crumbling structures around them. The enemy was retreating, what was left of them, and those who remained slowly perished by the hands of the fading dragonborn.

"We have to get you and our people back through the portal, Saeryn. You're fading because you've removed yourselves from the timeline. And if you all never existed, neither can I. Oh, no. What did he do to you? Oh, no, no, no..."

"We can heal me later, Andie. Let us lead our people back together."

"Some victory," Andie said.

Saeryn nodded grimly, a small smile spread across her shivering lips. "Yes. Some victory, indeed."

Saeryn called for her dragon, as did the other dragonborn. Soon they were all up and soaring through the city toward the mountain, the echoes of the songs of victory rising up in the air from the city below as the rest of the dragonborn made their way back to the University. The songs were mixed with laments of mourning, the sound eerie and haunting as they flew away from those who celebrated and wept, the rest of the city still frozen in place, unaware of the departure of their people and the dragons.

As they flew, some of the dragonborn were disappearing right from the air, their dragons, too. As they neared the foot of the mountain and began their ascent, Saeryn nearly slid from the dragon, but Andie caught her and held her tightly, trying to will her to live. They were running out of time.

They reached the University and rather than try to fit through the front doors, Andie focused her magic in one massive blast: it exploded into the mountainside, sending debris and dirt hundreds of feet in every direction. The dragonborn disappeared into the cloud.

They flew down through the clouds of dust, the exploded dirt, and entered the archives above the portal, just as the dragons and the dragonborn had first came into her time. Andie steered Ronen aside, and she kneeled down to allow her riders safely off.

Andie leapt off and inspected the portal. The portal was empty. Her heart willed with sorrow. She had to try. Andie squeezed her eyes shut and imagined the conjured image Yara had showed her in the hotel. She began whispering an incantation, almost a song, as she fought with every ounce of her being to restore the magic that Yara had shared. When she opened her eyes, she caught a trace of a glimmer. Raising her voice, Andie shouted the incantation louder, her voice echoing across the vast room. The dragonborn watched in silence as she worked her magic. Not a moment later, the portal blasted to life again, the magic within the same as she had witnessed from Yara. She smiled.

From what Yara had said, the portal was set to a time somewhere between Saeryn's and her own. Sometime after the deadly spell Saeryn's original enemy had cast to destroy all the dragonborn, and before this horrendous battle where they nearly lost to their new enemy. This was exactly what they needed.

"Oren must have found a way to calibrate the portal to this specific time when he sent Yara back," Andie whispered to herself in awe. "Yara…" Andie couldn't help but laugh. That girl had proven herself time and time again. Without her, they would have nowhere to do. She truly was a remarkable ally.

Andie grasped the smooth stone carving around the perimeter of the portal, peering into its depths. She could almost see the lush forests and waterfalls on the other side. It was a time of peace, and Oren must have somehow known it would prove useful by sending her there. Andie's heart ached at the thought of him being gone forever. She steeled herself and turned back toward her people in the room.

If she could just get the dragonborn and their dragons back to this in between time, to rejuvenate the dragon population and establish their race back into their timeline, then perhaps, just perhaps, it would stop them from fading in their current time. All they had to do was establish themselves in history, populate their people, ensure they survived until present time. Time was a dangerous thing, but it was their only hope.

"Everybody in, now!" she commanded.

There was a pause, a long moment where all the dragonborn stared at their princess. But with a slight nod from their Queen, they moved with ferocious speed. For even the dragons began to fade, and their time was running out. The dragonborn all dove directly into the portal, some only just avoiding fading into nothing. As they were all entering, Andie hurried to Saeryn.

"Saeryn, come on, we have to get you into the portal."

"No, Andie. I'm to stay here."

"Don't be ridiculous. If you stay here, you'll die. Our people need you to lead them back to their own time and reestablish our lineage."

"No, they don't need me. They need you. You're ready, Andie. I've been grooming you since you pulled us out of the portal. I know I said I doubted you, but you have proven yourself. You have even managed to teach me."

"Saeryn no, no, no. Please don't do this. I can't go, I belong here."

"In a way you do, and in a way you never have. You're the Queen the dragonborn deserve, Andryne Rogers. You're strong, intelligent, courageous, fearless, and selfless. No one will do more or go farther for our people than you. You are the perfect Queen. Let me stay here, in the world where I finally found a bit of the peace I have searched for."

The portal began to shake and pull Andie out across the surface. The last dragonborn entered, but the portal looked as if it was collapsing in on itself.

"It has been used too much," Saeryn said, weakly, barely able to hold her head. "It is unstable. You must go now."

"What about you?"

"I die knowing I played my part in the salvation of my people. It is as proud an accomplishment as any Queen can hope for."

"I can't lose you, Saeryn. You're the only family I have in the world. I'm begging you to live."

"This wound has ended me. And it's okay. It's perfectly okay."

Andie thought of Raesh and of all the things she'd never get to say to him. She thought of the life they would never have and the memories that she had now, but that will never be enough. She loved him. She loved Carmen and Yara. She wanted to stay and to be with her friends and enjoy the world they've fought so hard for. But that was not her destiny and she knew that.

With tears streaming down her face and the room shaking to pieces around her, Andie pulled Saeryn into her arms and held her, hoping her arms and this embrace could convey how truly thankful she was for all that Saeryn had done for her. The pain in Andie's heart was unimaginable.

A soft song rose in the room just then. A lament so sweet and so beautiful, it brought a tear to Andie's eye. The sound came from the portal, and both dragonborn royalty turned their heads toward the haunting melody.

"They're calling to you," Saeryn smiled.

"Who are?"

"The dragons."

Andie turned down to look at her Queen. She couldn't hold back the tears. "You have been my mother, my sister, my friend, my inspiration."

"And you have been my whole world, Andie. I love you, princess."

"I love you, too, my Queen." The melody grew louder, their call more desperate as the magic of the portal wavered once more.

Andie pressed her lips to Saeryn's forehead and laid her down gently. She rose and levitated up and over the portal. She wished beyond anything that she could say goodbye to her friends, to make sure they were okay, to say goodbye to Raesh. To give him one last kiss. But they were out there somewhere, frozen in the time curse. She would have to live the rest of her days hoping that they survived. With one last look to her Queen and then up to the sky, she allowed herself to fall into the unstable surface of the portal, called by the song of the dragons.

The portal imploded just as she cleared it.

Saeryn laid on the ground, her hands and feet numb and fading, her dragon already vanished. She was not in pain nor was she scared. She thought of Andie's face, the faces of her people, the face of her mother from so long ago. She smiled, knowing she had done her duty.

"*Eitilt ar ais.*"

EPILOGUE

WHEN SAERYN LIFTED THE TIME CURSE, THERE WAS confusion and chaos, but the defenders of Arvall won the war and it wasn't long before reports came in from Taline that the third wave had been defeated and the portal they brought recovered. The city began the work of putting itself back together.

The Thabians and miners were sent home with commendations and the promise of aid whenever and however they should need it. The Beautiful Dead had all been killed by the dragonborn, except for Olthrion and a few others who were captured, with effort, and executed before the week was out. The Church of Stone and Sea was formally investigated, its priests imprisoned or executed as sentenced, and the Church itself demolished. The battalion was completely over; one soldier had tried to activate the icons and kill millions in a last desperate move, but Andie had deprogrammed the system months before. The politicians Ashur had bribed were rooted out and sentenced, too.

Stefan was finally able to begin rebuilding Taline in

earnest. With the old University, the battalion, and the army gone, the city began to enjoy its longest peace in nearly twenty years. Yara and Bonhaus rested after the war. Some weeks later they were married and settled in Arvall. Yara and Carmen were reunited, at last. Carmen took over Marvo's restaurant, splitting her time between there and teaching at the rebuilt university, though she could never bring herself to eat the chocolate Andie brought. Lilja was never the same after losing Sarinda and Kent; she threw herself into working for the council fighters and became one of their best and most efficient.

Lymir was found unconscious, but alive beneath some rubble. When he came to some days later, he was the one who put together what happened to the dragonborn. With what he had predicted all along and the eyewitness reports of citizens who had seen the dragonborn disappear, he was able to figure out the tragic events. The news devastated millions across Noelle who had hoped the dragonborn would find peace. Lymir was broken to his core at their loss, but he put on a brave face and lead the University to the beacon of light and secured it as it always should have been.

But there was no one more broken than Raesh.

At first, Raesh couldn't bear to be around the University, so he decided to lead the council fighters in his father's stead. They went on long missions across Noelle, and even to the Old World across Shaeyara, outside the boundaries of Noelle, hunting down the last of Arvall's enemies and helping to create the safe world they deserved. When that was done, he moved to Michaelson, to Andie's old home, and commuted into Arvall every day. Lymir eventually convinced him to return to teaching and he did, becoming one of the sharpest and most beloved instructors. He never spoke of Andie, though Lymir always seemed to want to say something to him about her, as if he could somehow comfort him. Eventually, he finally submitted his books in the publishing district, only twenty blocks from his old home, and they were well received. And, after some time had passed, he finally opened his father's briefcase and joined Carmen at the restaurant.

But there was always a hole in him.

SIX YEARS PASS.

RAESH STOOD IN VICTORY GARDEN, looking out over the mountain Brie and down into Arvall City. It had almost finished its reconstruction, the scars from that awful war finally gone. Many things were a distant memory for him, but not those four days of horrific carnage. As he stood there, he was as content as he could be, proud to have had a hand in bringing peace to the city. It all seemed so surreal, to have finally achieved lasting peace. But it still didn't fill the void he felt in his heart. He sighed and looked up in the crimson evening sky.

There was something there. Something small and moving through the clouds. He blinked, but the thing was still there. It was moving, flying, diving toward earth, toward the mountain. He watched it descend, and, as it finally came lower, he saw what it was.

A dragon.

A dragon whose scales shone the same Byzantium hue as his beloved Andie's eyes.

Made in the USA
Columbia, SC
15 December 2019

84977850R20452